Marx, Women, and Capitalist Social Reproduction

Historical Materialism Book Series

The Historical Materialism Book Series is a major publishing initiative of the radical left. The capitalist crisis of the twenty-first century has been met by a resurgence of interest in critical Marxist theory. At the same time, the publishing institutions committed to Marxism have contracted markedly since the high point of the 1970s. The Historical Materialism Book Series is dedicated to addressing this situation by making available important works of Marxist theory. The aim of the series is to publish important theoretical contributions as the basis for vigorous intellectual debate and exchange on the left.

The peer-reviewed series publishes original monographs, translated texts, and reprints of classics across the bounds of academic disciplinary agendas and across the divisions of the left. The series is particularly concerned to encourage the internationalization of Marxist debate and aims to translate significant studies from beyond the English-speaking world.

For a full list of titles in the Historical Materialism Book Series
available in paperback from Haymarket Books, visit:
https://www.haymarketbooks.org/series_collections/1-historical-materialism

Marx, Women, and Capitalist Social Reproduction

Marxist Feminist Essays

Martha E. Gimenez

Haymarket Books
Chicago, IL

First published in 2018 by Brill Academic Publishers, The Netherlands
© 2018 Koninklijke Brill NV, Leiden, The Netherlands

Published in paperback in 2019 by
Haymarket Books
P.O. Box 180165
Chicago, IL 60618
773-583-7884
www.haymarketbooks.org

ISBN: 978-1-64259-047-0

Distributed to the trade in the US through Consortium Book Sales and
Distribution (www.cbsd.com) and internationally through Ingram
Publisher Services International (www.ingramcontent.com).

This book was published with the generous support of Lannan
Foundation and Wallace Action Fund.

Special discounts are available for bulk purchases by organizations and
institutions. Please call 773-583-7884 or email info@haymarketbooks.org
for more information.

Cover design by Jamie Kerry and Ragina Johnson.

Printed in the United States.

10 9 8 7 6 5 4 3 2 1

Library of Congress Cataloging-in-Publication data is available.

In loving memory of my parents,
Angelica E. Ribo and Pablo R. Gimenez Rossi,
and my grandmother, Mamina,
who taught me to read at a very early age.

∵

Contents

Acknowledgements

Through the years, as I wrote the chapters of this book, I have benefitted from helpful comments and advice from many friends, colleagues and students. First and foremost, I want to thank my former professors and thesis advisors, John Horton, who introduced me to the complexities of Marx's work, and Georges Sabagh; they both supported my choice of theory, particularly Marxist theory, as the centre of my intellectual development and professional specialisation.

I am grateful for the useful suggestions and criticisms from Margaret Anderson, Anatole Anton, Sandra Bartky, Johanna Brenner, Renate Bridenthal, Val Burris, Paul Cammack, Norma Chinchilla, Jane Collins, Joel C. Edelstein, David Elliott, Carmen Diana Deere, Nancy Folbre, Jan Demarest, Christine DiStefano, Hester Einsenstein, Terry Fee, The Frontiers Editorial Collective, Benjamin Hadis, Suzanne Helburn, Suzanne Hudson, The Insurgent Sociologist Collective, Thomas Mayer, Betsy Moen, Suzanne and Michael Neuschatz, John Newton, Shirley Nuss, Deborah Palmieri, Francine Rainone, William Regensburger, Richard Rogers, Janet Sayers, Robert Slenes, Lise Vogel, and Vicky Welch.

Renate Bridenthal, Barbara Engel, Suzanne Hudson, Irene Majerfeld, Marki LeComte, and Suzanne Helburn were generous with their time, listened to my questions and gave me emotional support when I needed it, in addition to sharing their expert knowledge and wisdom.

I thank Susan Ferguson for her useful comments about the introduction, and the anonymous reviewer for their thoughtful reading of the manuscript and valuable suggestions.

I wish to thank Rosanna Woensdregt and Danny Hayward, at Brill, for their patience with my questions and helpful assistance in the process of preparing the manuscript. And I am most grateful to my editor, Sebastian Budgen, for insisting that this book was possible.

I owe a special debt to Don Roper, whose love and support allowed me to dedicate most of my time to the preparation of this book.

Notes on Essays

With the exception of Chapters 4 and 13, the chapters in this book were originally published elsewhere; they are reprinted here – some of them updated, combined, abridged or modified – with permission from the publishers.

Chapter 1: 'Marxism and Feminism', *Frontiers: A Journal of Women Studies*, Vol. 1, No. 1 (Fall 1975): 61–80.

Chapter 2: 'Structuralist Marxism on The Oppression of Women'. This chapter combines, with permission of the publishers, 'Structuralist Marxism on "The Woman Question"', *Science & Society*, Vol. XLII, No. 3 (Fall 1978): 301–23, and 'The Oppression of Women: A Structuralist Marxist View', in *Structural Sociology*, edited by Ino Rossi, New York: Columbia University Press, 1982, pp. 292–324.

Chapter 3: 'Marxism, and Class, Gender and Race: Rethinking the Trilogy', *Race, Gender and Class*, Vol. 8, No. 2 (2001): 23–33.

Chapter 4: 'Reflections on Intersectionality'.

Chapter 5: 'What's Material about Materialist Feminism? A Marxist Feminist Critique', *Radical Philosophy*, 101 (May–June 2000): 19–28.

Chapter 6: 'Population and Capitalism', in *Latin American Perspectives*, Vol. IV, No. 4, (Fall 1977): 5–40.

Chapter 7: 'Feminism, Pronatalism and Motherhood', in *International Journal of Women Studies*, Vol. 3, No. 3 (Summer 1980): 215–40.
    I have exercised due diligence in attempting to identify the rights holder for this article published in the *International Journal of Women Studies*. I believe both the Journal and Eden Press Women's Publications (the Journal's publishers) no longer exist. In case of an oversight, I welcome correspondence from anyone associated with the Journal or Eden Press Women's Publications.

Chapter 8: 'Reproduction and Procreation under Capitalism: A Marxist Feminist Analysis'.
    Portions of this chapter have been published in *Das Argument*, 242, Jahrgang Heft 4/5 (2001): 657–70 and *Gender & Society*, Vol. 5, No. 3 (September 1991): 334–50; they are included in this chapter with permission from the publishers.

Chapter 9: 'The Feminization of Poverty: Myth or Reality?', *The Insurgent Sociologist*, Vol. 14, No. 1 (Fall 1987): 5–30.

Chapter 10: 'The Dialectics of Waged and Unwaged Work: Waged Work, Domestic Labor, and Household Survival in the United States', in *Work without Wages: Domestic Labor and Self-Employment under Capitalism*, edited by Jane C. Collins and Martha E. Gimenez, New York: SUNY Press, 1990, pp. 35–48.

Chapter 11: 'Loving Alienation: The Contradictions of Domestic Work', in *The Evolution of Alienation: Trauma, Promise and the Millennium*, edited by Lauren Langman and Devorah Kalekin-Fishman, London: Rowman & Littlefield, Inc., 2006, pp. 269–82.

Chapter 12: 'Self-Sourcing; How Corporations Get Us To Work Without Pay', *Monthly Review*, Vol. 59, No. 7 (December 2007): 37–41.

Chapter 13, 'From Social Reproduction to Capitalist Social Reproduction'.

Chapter 14: 'Connecting Marx and Feminism in the Era of Globalization: A Preliminary Investigation', *Socialism and Democracy*, Vol. 18, No. 1 (January–June 2004): 85–106.

Chapter 15: 'Global Capitalism and Women: From Feminist Politics to Working Class Women's Politics', in *Globalization and Third World Women: Exploitation, Coping and Resistance*, edited by Ligaya Lindio-McGovern and Isidor Walliman, Farnham: Ashgate, 2009, pp. 35–48.

Chapter 16: 'Capitalism and the Oppression of Women: Marx Revisited', *Science & Society*, Vol. 69, No. 1 (January 2005): 11–32.

Introduction

This collection of essays is a contribution to the literature on the relationship between Marxism and Feminism, and the significance of Marxist theory for the understanding of current processes of economic, political and social change. It is intended to illustrate the relevance of historical materialism for the study of some important academic and political questions: the oppression of women,[1] social reproduction, identity politics, the relationship between paid and unpaid work, and the key and often unacknowledged importance of class for deepening our knowledge of these and other aspects of capitalist social formations. More importantly, these essays show, in different contexts, my contribution to the development of Marxist-Feminist theory and, in retrospect,[2] to Capitalist Social Reproduction theory.

My approach to theorising about the topics listed above is informed by my professional training as a sociologist, my theoretical and political commitments to Marxism and Feminism, and my biography. Though I was born and grew up in Argentina, I have lived in the United States for more than half of my adult life. My yearly trips to Argentina to visit my parents kept alive the experiential knowledge of a very different social and political context, thus enriching the outlook I bring to my work. In the late 1950s I studied Law at the University of Cordoba, in Cordoba, Argentina. With the support of a scholarship from the Institute of International Education, I studied for two years at Montana State University, in Missoula, Montana, where in 1962 I received a BA in Political Science and History. After my return to Argentina, I switched from Law to Sociology and joined the first cohort of students admitted to a new masters-level programme that opened at the brand new Institute of Sociology at the University of Cordoba. The programme offered standard American Sociology,

---

1   In my work I have focused on the class determinants of the social and economic oppression of women. Rape, domestic violence, forced sterilisation, lack of control over reproductive capacity, sex trafficking, and other dimensions of oppression, though irreducible to class, are nevertheless interrelated with the effects of class and other dimensions of inequality such as race, ethnicity, and citizenship status. For example, contraception's costs and legal restrictions on the availability of abortion affect primarily working-class women, particularly those near to or below the poverty level.

2   Some of my work could be considered a contribution to a theory of *capitalist* social reproduction because, like all social phenomena, social reproduction is affected by its historical context, i.e. by the mode of production; capitalism is the dominant mode of production today and, as I argue later in this introduction and other chapters, particularly Chapter 13, – under capitalism production *determines* reproduction.

with large doses of Max Weber, who was the programme director's favourite theoretician. He considered Marx's work unworthy of consideration, because of Marx's alleged economic determinism and class reductionism.[3]

Some of my more knowledgeable fellow students questioned the director's exclusion of Marx's work and Marxist literature from our assigned readings, pointing out flaws and absences in the sociology we were taught. Soon enough, even those of us, including myself, who had never read that literature, had to question a social science that excluded or minimised the aspects of Argentine and Latin American social reality which were familiar to us, part of our history, culture, and experience. For us, classes, class struggles, class interests, oligarchy, exploitation, imperialism, colonialism, and revolution were not just sociological categories of debatable social science validity and relevance, but ordinary concepts, elements of ordinary political discourse and of a common sense understanding of social reality. Having lived through the 1955 revolution that ousted Argentina's President, General Peron,[4] and being accustomed to the presence in our lives of military mobilisations and coups, and students' and workers' political activism and general strikes, we found the view of society American sociology offered, a perspective that stressed order and consensus, unrealistic and incomplete.[5]

After I finished the sociology programme in Cordoba, I returned to the United States where, in the late 1960s, I entered the graduate programme in Sociology at UCLA and discovered Marx and Marxism in a seminar on classical sociological theory. Reading Marx was an entirely new experience; his work was dense, complex and utterly compelling because it illuminated the role of capitalism in the history of Latin America and the foundations of contemporary social reality in ways that offered a deeper understanding of the more obvious, superficial aspects that sociologists limited themselves to studying. His work, as well as the work of Marxist scholars, negated the economic determinism and other misleading labels used to dismiss such work in the average textbook.

---

3   This attitude toward Marx's work was peculiar to this Sociology programme, unlike the Department of Sociology in the University of Buenos Aires, for example, where Marx and Marxist scholarship had a strong presence.

4   General Juan Domingo Peron, three-time president of Argentina, was an important and controversial political figure. He served his first term from 1946 to 1952; elected again in 1952, he was ousted by a military coup in 1955. He lived in exile, in Spain, until his return in 1973, when he was elected president again. He died in 1974.

5   That perspective was questioned in the US in the 1960s; functionalism and structural functionalism were challenged first by conflict theories and then by the resurgence of interest in Marx and Marxist scholarship in the late 1960s. See, for example, Dahrendorf 1959; Horton 1966; Demerath and Peterson 1967.

In graduate school, I also became acquainted with the women's movement and the emergent critical thinking about women's place in society. One of the first formulations of this issue, 'women as a minority group', puzzled me – as women were numerically the majority – until I read the comparison between the way members of racial minorities and women were treated. An important slogan of the movement was 'sisterhood is powerful' which, given my awareness of class differences among women, I considered unrealistic and misleading. I also found it very difficult to understand the notion, prevalent in the emergent feminist literature, that women were oppressed 'as women'.

However, as I read feminist manifestoes, essays, and the fledgling feminist social science literature, it became increasingly clear to me that the US, supposedly the most 'developed' country in the world, was rather backward with respect to women. I grew up in a context where I took for granted women's participation in politics and what in the US were considered, at the time, 'male' professions such as medicine, dentistry, engineering, and law. It would have never occurred to me to refer to a professional woman using her gender as a qualifier (e.g. as a 'woman dentist'). I myself had studied law. It was not an unusual career choice among Argentine middle-class women in the late 1950s, but my goal at the time was to be a lawyer, not a 'woman lawyer'. Nevertheless, leaving aside the issue of women's educational and occupational opportunities in the US, the feminist idea that women could be oppressed 'as women' remained puzzling. From my perspective, being male or female was only one aspect of a person's being in the world and far less important than social class and social status, the key sources of individuals' cultural and economic resources.[6] It took some time until I learned that in the US women faced discrimination in the workplace, unequal pay, and social stereotypes about their intelligence and capabilities that affected their occupational and educational opportunities. I finally understood what the women's movement was about and why women organised themselves as women. However, having grown up in a context where, unlike in the US, class was the dominant social identifier, I remained critical of feminist thinking that ignored or minimised class and other divisions among women.

Also in graduate school I learned about the struggles of Mexican Americans and about the differences between Mexican-American students, and foreign students from Latin America, like myself. A Mexican-American student reacted

---

6 Later on, I argued that 'early feminists examined the oppression of women without taking fully into account the historical specificity of feminism itself (that is, the conditions under which people would self-identify primarily in terms of gender rather than class)' (Gimenez 1995, p. 178).

negatively to the possibility that I might participate in a research project as a Spanish-speaking interviewer. I was understandably upset, because I naively believed that among Spanish-speaking people differences of national origin did not matter. Discussing this situation with other graduate students I came to realise how ignorant I was about US racial and ethnic relations, about the oppression of Blacks, Mexican-Americans, and other 'non-white' populations, and about the meaning of minority status.

These brief reflections about my encounter with the women's movement and with the racial and ethnic divisions in the US may seem small, unimportant observations, typical of the experience of foreign students as they struggle to decipher their new environment. In retrospect, however, as can be seen throughout my work, they were a source of important insights, and most helpful in my intellectual development and scholarly work.

My reading of Marx and Marxist scholarship in graduate school and beyond was, as I now realise, rather idiosyncratic and intended to help me identify the elements of historical materialism suitable for the study of specific topics. I was particularly interested in learning how to transcend what I understood to be the limits of mainstream sociological and feminist theory and research, by bringing in the theoretical and methodological insights I could glean from reading Marx, Engels, and the Marxist scholars I 'discovered' while in graduate school, including Althusser,[7] Godelier,[8] Lukács,[9] and the Frankfurt School.[10] At the same time, I did not fully discard feminist and social science theories and research findings. Rather, in line with Marx's observation that 'science would be superfluous if the outward appearance and the essence of things directly coincided',[11] I looked upon them as sources of insights and knowledge about the 'outward appearance' of social reality. Following Godelier's reformulation, 'a structure is part of social reality but not of visible relationships',[12] I sought in Marx's work and the work of Marxist scholars the theoretical and methodological tools useful for identifying the elements of the capitalist mode of production underlying the sphere of 'appearance' and 'visible relationships'.

The premise underlying the approach I eventually developed to theorising and research was that the contributions to knowledge from historical materialism and the social sciences could be critically and fruitfully integrated because

7   Althusser and Balibar 1970; Althusser 1971 and 1976.
8   Godelier 1970 and 1972.
9   Lukács 1971.
10   For example, Marcuse 1962, 1964, and 1971; Horkheimer 1969.
11   Marx 1968, p. 817.
12   Godelier 1970, p. 347.

the social sciences yielded useful – albeit incomplete – knowledge about social phenomena. The social sciences studying capitalist societies have each chosen as their subject an aspect of social reality (e.g. the state, society, the economy, or culture), leaving outside their purview the key historical phenomenon that underlies it and gives it meaning and context as part of a historical totality, namely, the capitalist mode of production. The social sciences thus sever the connections between capitalism and their object of study. By ignoring the links between capitalism and social phenomena, the social sciences universalise the historical causes of social phenomena, and reify them into natural laws, functional prerequisites and/or the result of human nature. In contrast, historical materialism is the science of the capitalist mode of production as a whole, of the relationship between the level of the production of commodities, its structure, relations and contradictions, and their corresponding ideological and political integument. It is also the science of social formations, the historically specific contexts within which the mode of production operates. It is by using the theoretical and methodological tools of historical materialism that it is possible to establish the historically specific foundations or conditions of possibility of the social phenomena studied by the social sciences. I applied the same criteria to feminist theories and research because, to the extent they rejected Marx and Marxist scholarship, and postulated systems of patriarchal or unequal relations between men and women independent from, though interacting with, modes of production, they did not fully grasp the historically specific determinants of women's lives.

My reading of Marx, Engels, and Marxist scholars was not primarily aimed at finding everything they might have written about a specific topic such as women, the family, or population, for example. Learning from them and finding appropriate citations was only an aspect of the reading process. And, while aware that some of Marx's and Engels's views might be considered objectionable in the context of contemporary sensibilities, I did not think that such views detracted from the importance of their work, nor were these sufficient grounds to discard their work as the product of 'dead white European males'. I focused primarily on theory and methodology, on learning how to think about the topics that mattered to me through the lens of Marx's and Engels's theories and methodological insights, as articulated in their work, and as further developed and explained in the secondary literature. Whether or not I succeeded in my intellectual project is something readers must decide.

The chapters included in this volume were published between 1975 and 2009. Political commitment is perhaps more evident in the articles published in the 1970s, written at a time when I was politically active and in the process of developing my intellectual skills and theoretical allegiances through lively

debate with colleagues and friends. In the late 1960s and early 1970s I participated in the Sociology Liberation Movement within the American Sociological
Association, and the Radical Caucus that followed it. To be part of this movement,[13] which in 1975 led to the creation of the ASA Section on Marxist Sociology, was very important for my intellectual development; it gave legitimacy
to my work and a community of peers that compensated for my relative intellectual isolation at my place of work. Invited by several undergraduates, I joined
the students and faculty who worked together and eventually succeeded in the
creation of a Women Studies Program at the University of Colorado (where I
taught, at the Department of Sociology, between 1973 and 2007). During my
first years at the University of Colorado, I belonged to an interdisciplinary faculty Marxist reading and discussion group that lasted until the late 1970s.

Feminist theories have changed throughout the years. At the time I became
a feminist and started to write and teach about feminist issues, it was taken for
granted that women were oppressed 'as women'; as Gunnarsson asks, 'is it not
the very point of departure of feminist theorising that women are oppressed/
exploited/discriminated/excluded *by virtue of their being women?*'[14] While the
affirmative answer to this question would seem obvious, such a reply would not
be unanimously accepted today, because 'the stigmatization of the category
"women" has become such a taken-for-granted element in feminist discussions'.[15] Readers should know, then, that throughout this volume I have continued to use the categories 'women' and 'men' because, at the level of analysis at
which I use them, they denote structural positions within the gender structure
underlying gender relations. The categories women and men do not assume an
essential identity common to everyone, nor common experiences that ignore
the complex locations of people in the various social structures and power relations that shape their lives. At the level of analysis of concrete individuals, it is
impossible for them, and for observers, to partition their experiences and sense
of self into gender, race, ethnicity, national origin, and other dimensions; at the
same time, 'the structures of race, gender and class have distinct existences in
so far as they exercise their causal force on [people's] lives in ways relatively
independent from each other',[16] which, I add, may or may not influence how
individuals identify themselves.[17] Most of my work is about feminist theory

---

13   Oppenheimer et al. 1991.
14   Gunnarsson 2011, p. 24.
15   Ibid.
16   Gunnarsson 2011, p. 32.
17   Identity is both an individual choice and a relational phenomenon; individuals do not
      control how others might identify them or how imputed identities might affect them. This

and feminist politics; 'without some sense in which "woman" is in the name of a social collective, there is nothing specific about feminist politics'[18] though, as the years went by, I came to the conclusion that feminist politics cannot be separate from class politics.

One's politics become more obvious when writing in the context of political engagement and theoretical debate, but scholarly social science writing is always political: under the veneer of objectivity there is always a dialogue with those whose work academics approve and disapprove of, plus one can find telling omissions, silences, and euphemisms. To acknowledge the political dimension of one's work, however, does not necessarily make the work tendentious or misleading, just as the pursuit of scientific objectivity does not eliminate the political implications inherent in social science scholarly work. Therefore, as I show how I appropriated elements of historical materialism in the process of criticising feminist and social science theories and developing theoretical alternatives, I will also describe the political and personal contexts which led me to become interested in the topics examined in this volume.

Marxist-Feminist Theory

The first two chapters in this section were written between the mid- and late 1970s, when I was involved in a feminist consciousness-raising group and in the Women Studies Program. As I worked to build a Marxist theoretical alternative to the liberal, radical and socialist feminist perspectives emerging at the time, I combined my reading of Marx, Engels, Althusser and Godelier to develop what, at first, I called a 'Structuralist Marxist' theoretical perspective, the basis for my version of Marxist-Feminist theory.

Most of the colleagues, students and friends with whom I exchanged ideas about feminism adhered to views that could be broadly categorised as liberal feminism, i.e. they assumed that there was a civil rights solution to the problems affecting women, or radical feminism, i.e. they assumed that the source of women's problems was patriarchy. Socialist feminism, which combined a critique of capitalism with a critique of patriarchy, did not yet have followers among the feminists I knew at that time. Feminists shared similar concerns for the manifold problems affecting women's lives in the United States, but disagreed about their causes and potential solutions. Women interested both in

---

is why racial profiling, for example, is so pernicious. See Chapters 3 and 4 for a discussion of these issues.

18   Young 1994, p. 714 cited in Gunnarsson 2011, p. 24.

feminism and Marxism were rare in the small city where I worked and lived, but abundant on the East and West Coasts of the United States. In New York, they formed study groups focused on the study and criticism of Marx's and Engels's works, as they evaluated their potential relevance for feminist theory and research. In time, they produced conference papers, journals, books, a prolific and important literature shaped by their professional training (as sociologists, economists, historians, or anthropologists) and by their interpretations and criticisms of Marx's and Engels's works. In contrast to this milieu, I worked alone, outside the main feminist social and intellectual networks, developing my ideas through lively debates in the context of the Women Studies Advisory Board and fruitful discussions with some graduate students, but mostly through critical engagement with the dominant feminist literature. My work was not published in the main feminist journals or cited in the 1980s feminist literature. Though disappointing at the time, this lack of recognition is not, in retrospect, unsurprising: my work was critical of the dominant views in feminist theory, and offered a theoretical alternative outside the mainstream.

The first two chapters are interrelated: Chapter 1, 'Marxism and Feminism', presents an overview of the place of women within capitalism and an examination of the scientific and political importance of Marxism for feminism; Chapter 2, 'Structuralist Marxism on The Oppression of Women', makes explicit the principles of Structuralist Marxism underlying the previous chapter and discusses in some detail the mode of capitalist reproduction and its effects on sexual inequality;[19] it offers a theoretical introduction to Structuralist Marxism, and offers a critique of feminist theories of the 1970s followed by the application of Structuralist Marxism to the elucidation of the capitalist determinants of sexual inequality. These two chapters show how I proceeded to develop a Marxist-feminist theoretical approach to sexual inequality, eschewing theories of patriarchy and other abstract, ahistorical explanations.[20]

According to the premises of historical materialism, the biology of sexuality, human procreation, and physical reproduction is a transhistorical material condition of all modes of production. The social organisation of the production of the necessities of life presupposes the social organisation of the production and reproduction of human beings (e.g. kinship networks), and the production

---

19   I am using the concepts current at the time; i.e. sexual inequality, sexism, sex struggles, sex differentiation, sex stratification, sexual division of labour, etc.

20   I have found Structuralist Marxist theoretical insights helpful but it is more accurate to refer to my perspective as Marxist feminist, because of my reliance on Marx's work and Marxist theory in general and rejection of dual systems approaches and patriarchy theories.

and reproduction of social relations and forms of consciousness. The production of things to satisfy needs, the development of new needs, and the production and reproduction of human beings and social institutions and relations are not to be interpreted as different historical stages; dialectically, they are aspects or moments of complex processes which function simultaneously today as they did at the dawn of human history.[21] According to Marx and Engels, 'The production of life, of one's own life in labour and of another in procreation, now appears as a *double relationship*: on the one hand as a *natural relationship*, on the other as a *social* one'.[22] The activities necessary to sustain human life are 'natural' in that they stem from the very physical and biological requirements of the human species and, at the same time, they are 'social' because they entail cooperation among the producers of things as well as the producers/reproducers of life. Just as there are historical modes of production, so, I argue, there are historical modes of producing human beings; *every mode of production implies a mode of sexual reproduction*.[23]

But just as the material necessity to produce the means of production and subsistence does not determine the historically specific social relations in which they are produced, the biology of procreation does not determine the *mode of reproduction*, i.e. social relations in which children are born and raised, although it imposes limits on their variations. This statement would seem to be easily contradicted by the apparently timeless and universal nuclear family unit of parents and children. Murdock, for example, argued that the nuclear family is universal because it fulfils four functions essential for the survival of human societies: sexual relations, procreation, socialisation, and economic cooperation.[24] At the level of observable social relations, this family form is prevalent in capitalist societies; it is not, however, universal because those functions can be fulfilled within a variety of social arrangements.[25]

---

21   This does not mean that production and reproduction occur outside history; on the contrary, they are rendered historically specific in each mode of production. There is a unity between the particular and the universal and historical materialism differentiates between the two 'in order not to overlook the essential differences existing despite the unity that follows from the very fact that the subject, mankind, and the object, nature, are the same' (Marx 1970, p. 190); see also Marx and Engels 1994, pp. 107–8; 115–16. Engels 1972, p. 71.

22   Marx and Engels 1994, p. 116.

23   Gimenez 1973b, p. 148.

24   Murdock 1949, cited in Reiss 1965, p. 443.

25   Basing his conclusion on cross-cultural evidence, studies of nonhuman primates, and studies of mother separation in human societies, Reiss argues that, while the four functions of the nuclear family are indeed functional prerequisites of human society, they can be fulfilled by other social arrangements besides the nuclear family. There is, however, a

Given that women are responsible for childcare and most of the household labour, it would seem obvious that the source of women's oppression is to be found in their biological role in reproduction and in the ensuing sexual division of labour and domestic activities which curtail their educational and occupational opportunities. I agree that women's role in procreation and household labour contribute to the strengthening of sexual inequality. However, framing the issue in abstract and universal terms, as if the limits nature imposes on social relations[26] determine the historical specificity of those relations, exonerates the capitalist mode of production from its role in producing and reproducing male dominance. *To examine this issue historically, in the context of the capitalist mode of production, one must identify the capitalist processes that place men and women in unequal relationships; i.e. the relationship between the capitalist modes of production and reproduction.* 'Men' and 'women', however, are abstractions,[27] for people are 'an ensemble of social relations'[28] and the key relations determining people's options – and often their fate – under capitalism are class relations. The prevalence and apparent sameness of the nuclear family hides the qualitative differences between working-class and capitalist families, the different social relations of reproduction within the working class and, consequently, the differences in the sources of male power and in the forms or kinds of oppressions shaping the lives of capitalist and working-class women.

The family is a useful concept and I use it descriptively in my work; it is, however, ideologically charged with expectations about what families and family roles should and should not be. On the basis of Althusser's analysis of the mode of production and its elements,[29] I constructed a theoretical concept,

---

universal functional prerequisite of human society which needs to be fulfilled for human society to survive: the nurturant socialisation of the newborn. Newly born humans require nurturant care to survive, but this biological requirement does not determine the social relations within which that care is optimally or sub-optimally provided; e.g. nuclear families, large extended families, single parent families, care provided by biological mothers, older siblings, adoptive parents, nannies, wet nurses, orphanages, and so on. On this basis, Reiss defines the family institution as a 'small kinship structured group with the key function of nurturant socialization of the newborn' (Reiss 1965, p. 449).

26   For the importance of acknowledging the constraining, material effects of nature on individual and social relations see, for example, Timpanaro 1975; for a feminist defence of the materiality of nature see Gunnarsson 2013.

27   However, 'although the category "women" does not reflect the whole reality of concrete and particular women, it nevertheless refers to something real, namely the structural position as woman'. Gunnarsson 2011, p. 23.

28   Marx 1976, pp. 41–8.

29   'The elements of any mode of production are the labourer, the means of production (the object of labour and the means of labour), the non-labourer, a property connection and a real or material appropriation connexion'. Althusser and Balibar 1970, pp. 214–15.

'*mode of sexual reproduction*',[30] which I eventually modified, expanded and called '*mode of physical and social reproduction*',[31] though generally I refer to it in abbreviated form, as '*mode of reproduction*'. Readers might wonder whether it is necessary to replace a known concept, 'family', with the elaborate notion of 'mode of reproduction'. The concept mode of reproduction calls attention to the material conditions, economic and biological,[32] that shape activities and mediate relations within the family which are glossed over by the dominant ideologies about marriage and family roles.[33] Like the mode of production, the mode of reproduction is constituted by the combination of its elements – means of biological, physical and social reproduction, labour and objects of labour – in the context of relations between the agents of reproduction mediated by their relationship to those elements. For example, in households where men are the only breadwinners, and women are full-time domestic workers – the stereotypical nuclear family – their relationship is mediated, shaped, by their different relationship to the means of exchange – which men tend to control and is the basis for their power, exceptions notwithstanding. Men and women 'own' part of the biological means of reproduction and sexual relations eventually result in procreation.[34] Unlike family, a concept that presupposes marriage and heterosexuality as its 'normal' form and tacitly relegates single parent, gay and lesbian families and other arrangements to 'deviant' or exceptional status, 'mode of reproduction' is a concept that calls attention to the biological, political and economic basis of its contradictory relations, and allows for the exploration of the relations of reproduction among other kinds of agents (e.g. cohabiting couples, couples and hired domestic workers, foster parents, orphanages, workers' hostels, etc.) in different contexts, within different classes and social strata.

---

30   I developed this concept in the context of exploring, in my doctoral dissertation, the relationship between changes in the capitalist economy, and the material and social context of reproductive behaviour; Gimenez 1973a, pp. 148–71.

31   I describe the elements of this concept in Chapter 2, and discuss it in varying degrees of depth in several other chapters. The notion of 'mode of reproduction' developed among feminists who explored the relevance of Marx's work for illuminating the determinants of the oppression of women; see, for example, Mitchell 1969; 1971; Bridenthal 1976.

32   Seccombe refers to fertility as 'the infrastructure' of the generational reproduction of labour power' (Seccombe 1983, p. 29).

33   While teaching a course on Family and Society, I used a cartoon that clearly made this point. While two little girls play with dolls, one says to the other, 'My mother told me all about love, it leads to housework!'

34   See Chapter 8 for an examination of the effects of assisted reproductive technologies on the relations of reproduction.

In the context of the capitalist mode of production, the functioning of the mode of production determines the mode of reproduction.[35] The premises of my argument are the following: Family formation and stability in the working class depends on the employment of at least one of its adult members; the interaction between sex differentiation and sex stratification results in women's over-representation in low paid, low skilled jobs. Competition for scarce jobs in a context that rules out full employment, at a living wage, for all male and female workers, turns family formation, for working-class women, into an alternative to employment in the public sector, thus placing them in a subordinate position, dependent on a gainfully employed husband or partner, and reinforcing working-class women's subordinate place in the occupational structure and inside the home. This, I argue, is the material basis for the oppression of working-class women. Given that the vast majority of the population in capitalist social formations is propertyless,[36] depending on wages or salaries for economic survival,[37] the observable manifestations of the oppression of working-class or propertyless women appear as the oppression of women in general.

The capitalist processes that place working-class men and women in unequal economic locations within the occupational structure and unequal relationships inside and outside the household are the processes of capital accu-

---

35   I learned about the existence and rising profile of social reproduction theory at the time I finished writing the introduction to this volume. Because I often use the concepts 'reproduction' and, sometimes, social reproduction in my work, readers should know that – except when reproduction refers clearly to biological human reproduction – I use those concepts as shorthand for the ways in which workers' needs are met in the context of capitalism, through a combination of the use values produced by domestic labour and wages. I examine some social reproduction theories and present my own views about social reproduction in Chapter 13, 'From Social Reproduction to Capitalist Social Reproduction'.

36   I use propertyless and working class interchangeably to refer to the vast majority of the population in capitalist social formations which does not own means of production and must sell labour to survive. At the level of analysis of the mode of production, this population comprises the working class – but at the level of analysis of social formations, this population is fragmented by occupation, income and education into a variety of socioeconomic strata, some considered part of the 'traditional' blue-collar, working class, while others are placed into various status categories; e.g. lower middle class, middle class, upper middle class, etc. Regardless of the differences in socio-economic status, all these layers are vulnerable, perhaps to differing degrees, to the vagaries of capital accumulation and economic change.

37   In social formations where capitalism has not fully proletarianised the population and large sectors live in semi-proletarianised households, the specific patterns of capital accumulation and their effects on male and female employment, earnings, and the mode of reproduction will vary from one country to another.

mulation that continuously revolutionise the forces of production and the locations of investments, thus continuously changing the quantity, quality and
location of the demand for labour and therefore continuously changing the size
and composition of the employed layers of the labour force as well as the size
and composition of the reserve army of labour. In this situation of permanent
job scarcity and relentless competition and change, the family becomes a site of
oppression as well as a survival strategy for the working class, particularly for
working-class women.[38] While the inequality between men and women pre-
cedes capitalism, what matters is not its chronological origins but its 'organic
connections'[39] or 'ideal genesis'[40] within capitalism, established in the relationship between the capitalist modes of production and reproduction[41] and
observable in its effects, the division between the public production of commodities and the private reproduction of labourers and labour power.

I give causal weight, as the material basis of the oppression of working-class
women under capitalism, to the effects of the struggle for survival into which
capital's pursuit of profits, at any cost, forces the working class.[42] I argue that
because capitalism produces and reproduces unemployment and insecurity in
a context of universalised commodity production, where working-class consumption depends on the prior sale of labour power, the family form of the
mode of reproduction emerges as an alternative source of economic survival
for working-class people. Women's unpaid domestic labour stretches wages
and salaries, thus enhancing the quality of life for the men whose earnings
support them and ensuring their own and their children's well-being in the pro-

---

38 See Humphries 1977.
39 Marx 1972, pp. 41–2.
40 Godelier 1970, p. 352.
41 See in Chapter 2 the discussion of the second principle of Structuralism: '... the study of
    the internal functioning of a structure must precede and will throw light on the study of
    its coming to being and subsequent evolution'.
42 At the abstract level of analysis of the capitalist mode of production as a closed system,
    and in light of the premises of historical materialism discussed above, the reproduction
    of labour power and the reproduction of capital are moments in the dialectical reproduc-
    tion of the system as a whole: 'The maintenance and reproduction of the working class
    is, and must ever be, a necessary condition to the reproduction of capital' (Marx 1974,
    p. 572). However, as Marx went on to say, 'the capitalist may safely leave its fulfilment to
    the labourer's instincts of self-preservation and of propagation' (Marx 1974, p. 572). This is
    so because, at the historical level of analysis, in the context of specific social formations,
    capital is indifferent to the conditions in which labour power is reproduced unless these
    might threaten capital accumulation. As documented by the ever-present inverse correl-
    ation between socio-economic status and mortality rates, 'Capital cares nothing for the
    length of life of labour power' (Marx 1974, p. 265).

cess. But this alternative has a price: economic and social inequality outside the home, and economic dependence and oppression within the home.

Chapter 3, 'Marxism, and Class, Gender, and Race: Rethinking the Trilogy', is a critique of the race, gender and class mantra that emerged as a critique of feminism's political subject, which generalised from the experience of white, mainly middle-class women, and as an alternative to Marxism's alleged class determinism. The trilogy minimises the importance of class, insofar as it reduces it to 'classism', i.e. another form of oppression equal in its significance to race and gender, or to class in the social stratification sense, i.e. socio-economic status. From the standpoint of trilogy supporters, everyone has a class, gender and racial identity because everyone is located at the intersection of those structures. That presupposes the same kind of determinism or reductionism attributed to Marxism with respect to class. But if race and gender reductionisms are rejected, then individuals' identities cannot be taken for granted in any instance, except when an identity is attributed to them by an observer. This attribution of identity is particularly important when the observer is someone in a position of power, e.g. the police, doctors, teachers, employers. The a-theoretical nature of the trilogy is thus exposed; it is a set of two categories – three, if class is included in the sociological, descriptive sense – which can be used to classify people, but these are floating categories, with no theoretical context identifying the system or structure within which they may make sense. This is why the efforts to connect class, gender, and race through a plethora of metaphors (intersectionality, interconnection, interplay, for example) are unsuccessful. As the trilogy is supposed to identify the intersection of three systems of oppression, thus entailing power relations, while at the same time class is considered no more causally significant than gender and race, an abstract notion of power relations is invoked as the more basic structure of inequality underlying the trilogy. I have argued that the abstract structure of power and privilege that is invoked to account for the effects of oppression and exploitation is no other than the unmentionable capitalist class structure and relations, unmentionable because the limits of political discourse allow the expression of grievances, particularly work-related grievances, only or primarily through the lens of identity politics.

In Chapter 4, 'Reflections on Intersectionality', I argue that the same criticisms presented in the previous chapter apply to the expanded trilogy, i.e. intersectionality. Other 'axes of oppression' (e.g. age, disability, citizenship status, ethnicity, sexual preference) were eventually added to the original three, and intersectionality, one of the metaphors used to connect them, eventually became the dominant perspective within feminist theory. I examine in this chapter intersectionality's theoretical shortcomings, its ambiguous scope –

does it apply only to women or to men also? Does everyone have a complex identity or only the disadvantaged? Is it a feminist perspective or a perspective on social inequality? – and its problematic relationship to identity politics.

In Chapter 5, 'What's Material about Materialist Feminism? A Marxist Feminist Critique', I seek to ascertain the meaning of Materialist Feminism, a trend in feminist thought I initially misinterpreted as a return of Marxist-Feminism. I discovered that there is a Materialist Feminism open to consider all sorts of things as material such as discourse, the body, ideology, culture and language, while rejecting as economism the materiality of the mode of production. However, closer to Marxist-Feminism is the Materialist Feminism theorised by Hennessy[43] and Hennessy and Ingraham,[44] a subtle blend of Marxism, structuralism, feminism and postmodern theories of the subject that does not avoid acknowledging the importance of historical materialism as a source of emancipatory knowledge, and the need to relate the discursive to the materiality of the non-discursive, the globalised mode of production or 'global analytic', in Hennessy's terms. The coexistence of these two very different kinds of feminist theories under the same label, Materialist Feminism, is bound to be confusing and obscures the need for a return to Marxist-Feminism, as the effects of global capitalism on working women intensify the latter's exploitation and oppression.

Capitalist Social Reproduction

In this section, I brought together chapters in which reproduction – biological, physical, social, daily and generational – figure more prominently than in others. *Social reproduction* is a complex concept which, in contemporary societies, involves market level relationships among various institutions (e.g. the family, the state, educational institutions, healthcare systems, elder care, childcare) which, together with the input of domestic labour, enter into the processes of maintaining and reproducing, on a daily and generational basis, labour power and the labouring population.[45] However, most of this volume can be viewed as a contribution to *capitalist social reproduction*. Abstractly considered, social reproduction is a functional requirement in all societies; it is about the social relations and institutions surrounding the reproduction of the population and

---

43   Hennessy 1993.
44   Hennessy and Ingraham 1997.
45   See, for example, Dickinson and Russell 1986, p. 3; Bezanson and Luxton 2006, pp. 3–7.

the social groups, classes, strata within classes and any other divisions characterising the population in a given society. *Capitalist social reproduction* involves
similar phenomena but posits that, under capitalist conditions, reproduction
takes place under historically specific conditions in which production *determines* reproduction.

I became interested in the area of population studies while studying demographic methods. At the time, in the late 1960s and early 1970s, overpopulation
in the Third World,[46] population control, and family planning seemed to be the
primary concern of public and private funding agencies and the main focus of
demographic research. Ehrlich's *The Population Bomb*[47] had recently been published with extraordinary academic and public success. Most social scientists,
journalists and the average person believed that excessive population growth
was the major threat facing the world, that Third World poverty, social and
environmental problems and underdevelopment were largely caused by overpopulation, and that population control would benefit poor nations as much as
the use of birth control would benefit the poor everywhere. Those Malthusian
and neo-Malthusian beliefs[48] were taken for granted, at that time, as unquestionable truths. The literature about Latin America's poverty and underdevelopment emphasised cultural determinants of high fertility (e.g. Catholic values
against abortion and birth control, and men's need to prove their masculinity
by fathering many children). Such cultural explanations ignored the effects of
the capitalist exploitation of people and natural resources upon the relations
between the sexes, family formation, access to education, healthcare, and so on.
It was this critical stance that led me to consider the possibility of developing
a Marxist theoretical analysis of the determinants of population phenomena.

My main thesis advisor was a demographer, not a Marxist scholar; nevertheless, he listened sympathetically to my critiques of Malthusian and neo-
Malthusian explanations of poverty and underdevelopment and, to my sur-
prise, encouraged me to explore the usefulness of Marxist theory for the study
of population. I wrote an essay[49] comparing Marx's and Malthus's principles

---

46   This is how poor countries were described at the time. Today's terms, the Global North
      and Global South, are just as unsatisfactory.

47   Ehrlich 1968.

48   Unlike Malthus, who equated birth control with 'vice', neo-Malthusians thought that if
      workers used birth control and reduced their family size, they could reduce the supply
      of labour and bargain for higher wages. This strategy cannot work because rather than
      lowering profits by paying higher wages, capitalists use technology to displace labour or
      increase the labour supply through immigration.

49   Gimenez 1973a.

of population[50] and, eventually, a theoretical dissertation in which I presented a critique of the theories about fertility, migration and mortality dominant at the time in population studies and developed the concept 'capitalist mode of sexual reproduction', examining its superstructural and structural basis and its contribution to the oppression of women. I also developed a Marxist theoretical framework for the study of population, the basis for Chapter 6, 'Population and Capitalism'.[51]

The core of the theoretical framework is the law of capital accumulation which affects fertility, mortality and migration through changes in the demand for labour, quantitative and qualitative, which, in turn, alter the social and economic contexts within which people make decisions, and engage in behaviours ultimately affecting macro demographic processes. Changes in capital accumulation, in turn, are never purely 'economic'; they take place in the context of capitalist social formations and are affected by their historically specific characteristics, e.g. political, legal, and ideological structures and processes. Figure 1 is an attempt to depict the framework in a way that unavoidably simplifies a very complex and dialectical network of relationships.

Economists and demographers use the demand for labour as an independent variable to predict short- and long-term changes in fertility and the labour supply.[52] The framework I developed is intended to identify the capitalist historical and political context underlying changes in the demand for labour. It is not intended to predict specific outcomes such as changes in fertility rates reflected, in time, in changes in the supply of some types of labour, but rather aims to make explicit the socio-economic and political context within which men and women work, live and act in ways largely determined by their class location and place in the socio-economic stratification within classes which, in turn, influences access to their conditions of reproduction, result-

---

50   Malthus explains poverty and unemployment in terms of natural laws; i.e. population has a natural tendency to grow beyond the means of subsistence because it grows geometrically, while the latter grow only arithmetically. These natural laws create an insurmountable barrier to abolishing poverty and creating a more egalitarian society (Malthus 1933, pp. 5–11). Marx rejected Malthus's laws and considered all explanations based on natural laws as nothing more than ideological justifications of the capitalist status quo; he explained periodic unemployment increases and poverty as effects of the law of capital accumulation, which result in the creation of an ever-present surplus population or reserve army of labour. For a collection of Marx and Engels's critique of Malthus and Malthusian thought, see Meek 1971.

51   Gimenez 1973b.

52   See, for example, Coontz's 'theoretical framework for the long-run analysis of population changes which is consistent with the short-run analysis based on geographical and cyclical changes in the demand for labour' (Coontz 1979, p. 166).

ing in changes affecting family formation, family size, migration, and so on. The theoretical framework outlines some of the links between production and reproduction; it can be read as a road map intended to make explicit some of the complex processes that open up and close down possibilities for the working classes (who are the majority of the population in capitalist social formations, and whose ability to have access to their conditions of reproduction is affected by processes that sustain or undermine communities), that create imbalances in the age and sex composition of the working population thereby affecting marriage and family formation, that compel some to migrate within or across national boundaries, and so on. The framework sheds light on the many variables through which the changing social and economic terrain within which the working classes struggle for economic survival affect their bodies, their ability to reproduce, their health, life expectancy, opportunities, the relations between the men and women, and the extent to which they can build lives rooted in one place or find themselves compelled to uproot themselves in search of employment. Underlying the market level relationships among the variety of institutions (e.g. households, the market, the state, educational institutions, healthcare systems, and so on) which, together with the input of domestic labour, enter into the processes of maintaining and reproducing labour power and the labouring population, there is the complex network of processes flowing from changes in capital accumulation, within the historically specific conditions characterising different capitalist social formations. The full understanding of the determinants of the social reproduction of the social classes, the working class in particular, and the reproduction of the environmental conditions of production and reproduction needs to bring together these levels of analysis; mode of production and social formations.[53]

In Chapter 7, 'Feminism, Pronatalism, and Motherhood', I examine Blake's[54] arguments for the importance of demographically relevant determinants of sexual inequality, i.e. pronatalist institutional and ideological pressures toward compulsory parenthood, making parental roles indispensable for the fulfilment of masculinity and femininity. In Blake's view, pressures supporting par-

---

53   This chapter was originally a journal article published in 1977, two years after 'Marxism and Feminism', the first chapter in this volume (Gimenez 1977). Given the main objectives of the article, and the journal's page limits, it was not possible to include an in-depth discussion of the relationship between generational reproduction and the oppression of women. I do point out, however, and in the language of those days, that the material basis of 'sexism' under capitalism was to be found in women's responsibility for the reproduction of the relations of production, daily and generational, physical and social.

54   Blake 1974.

ental roles, rather than male supremacy, are the source of the problems women face when making educational and occupational choices in conflict with family demands. Blake also argued – and this is what caught my attention and prompted me to write this chapter – that the Women's Liberation Movement, in supporting only or primarily women's right to do both, i.e. to have families and to work, including having a career,[55] at the same time supported the pronatalist policy engrained in dominant sex role expectations.

With the exception of Firestone,[56] who was exceedingly critical of compulsory motherhood, my examination of the literature showed that Blake was correct; women's option not to procreate was not mentioned in the discussion of reproductive rights.[57]

The 1960s and the 1970s were years of important struggles for women's and gay rights, which emerged at a time when most people in the US lived under very strict social controls over sexuality; homosexuality was shunned, and single people, particularly men, were under suspicion so that many bought respectability through heterosexual marriage. Eventually, not only heterosexuals (especially women), but also gays and lesbians rebelled against those ideological constraints; today, those constraints have been weakened and no longer signify for a substantial proportion of the population. Today there are more women with professional and business careers than 50 years ago, the marriage rate has fallen drastically while cohabitation is now more socially acceptable; gays and lesbians live more openly and many claim the right to marry and have children. This right, already granted in several states at the time I wrote the first draft of this introduction, has become the law of the land because of a landmark Supreme Court decision.[58] Despite these changes, struggles

---

55   I realised, as I was reading Chapter 7, that I had originally described 'the right to do both' as the right to have families and careers, thus unwittingly focusing on the options open to more privileged women. The conflict between the demands of family and work affect all working women; it is more severe for working-class women because they are less likely to be able to afford childcare and take days off without pay to care for a sick child. Careers are likely to be more time-consuming than a 9 to 5 job, but they pay more and allow women the option to hire nannies, house cleaners, and/or place their child or children in paid day care centers.

56   Firestone 1971.

57   The editors of *Pronatalism: The Myth of Mom and Apple Pie* suggest that pronatalism is embedded in the vocabulary and propose the term 'childfree', instead of 'childless', which has negative connotations. See Peck and Senderowitz 1974, p. 7.

58   According to this decision, issued 26 June 2015, 'The right to marry is a fundamental right inherent in the liberty of the person, and under the Due Process and Equal Protection Clauses of the Fourteenth Amendment, couples of the same sex may not be deprived of that right and liberty'. Editorial Board, 'A Profound Ruling Delivers Justice on

for sexual and reproductive freedom and women's struggles for equal opportunities continue. Ideologies supporting sexual inequality have fewer vocal adherents today than 50 years ago but have not been entirely undermined. In the US, pronatalist ideologies and policies supporting parenthood for all continue, ensconced in right-wing battles and policies against legalised abortion, broad availability of contraception for women, and gay and lesbian marriage and adoptions. Right-wing policies, ostensibly designed to protect marriage (defined as the union of a man and woman), the integrity of the family and life itself, have the effect of narrowing women's reproductive choices and the direction they would like their life to take. And that gay, lesbian and heterosexual couples and individuals seek to have children, through adoption or with the use of reproductive technologies, attests to the strength and persistence of prescriptive parenthood despite fertility problems, marital status, and sexual orientation.

To be critical of pronatalism is not equivalent to condemning parenthood; it is to shed light on its prescriptive nature and propose that it would be socially and ecologically desirable that parenthood cease to be considered as a natural instinct and/or a religious or a social duty. The 'biological clock' that some women claim to hear ticking is also a 'social clock' reminding them that whatever else may be going on in their lives, motherhood is their destiny, the road to social acceptance and integration. It is because parenthood is not a natural instinct, but socially and prescriptively imposed, that many people unsuited for family formation bear or adopt children; domestic violence and child abuse result from the often deadly interaction between sexual inequality and pronatalism. Today, pronatalist ideologies and social pressures continue to curtail women's opportunities and ability to shape their future, and place them in a disadvantaged position relative to men, thus sustaining the inequality between men and women despite considerable gains in sexual liberation, civil rights, and economic opportunities for women.

In Chapter 8, 'Reproduction and Procreation under Capitalism: A Marxist Feminist Analysis', I present different feminists' views about reproductive technologies, and explore the impact of these technologies on women, and on the mode of reproduction. I argue that these technologies, as they fragment the biological process of reproduction, separating sexuality from procreation and

---

Gay Marriage', http://www.nytimes.com/2015/06/27/opinion/a-profound-ruling-delivers -justice-on-gay-marriage.html?action=click&pgtype=Homepage&module=opinion-c -col-left-region&region=opinion-c-col-left-region&WT.nav=opinion-c-col-left-region&_ r=0.

creating the material conditions for the emergence of a market in eggs, sperm and wombs, have become the basis for the structural and functional differentiation of the mode of reproduction into a *mode of social reproduction* and a *mode of procreation*. In the context of the mode of social reproduction, individuals or couples raise children who may or may not be genetically related to both or one of them; within the mode of procreation, individuals or couples buy eggs and/or sperm, and lease or rent a woman's womb in order to obtain a child or children who may or may not be genetically related to them. Furthermore, the globalisation of the market in the elements of biological reproduction is contributing to the oppression of women in both wealthy and less developed countries. The rise of the mode of procreation has opened up another terrain where working-class and poor women are oppressed, and it has deepened class divisions among women.

The poverty of women is an issue that gained notoriety in the late 1970s and early 1980s; I examine it in Chapter 9, 'The Feminisation of Poverty: Myth or Reality?', where I identify and criticise some problems stemming from the use of the categories of identity politics,[59] such as gender, in accounting for women's higher poverty rates compared to those of men.

At the time I wrote it, in the mid-1980s, households headed by women were the fastest growing type of family structure in the United States. The poverty rate among these households was high; suddenly, the increasing poverty of women and children became very visible and the phrase 'feminisation of poverty' acquired prominence in the feminist literature and in public discourse. Given the disproportionate poverty rate among racial and ethnic minorities, a large proportion of poor single mothers were non-white. Though acknowledging the importance of racism, the functioning of the economy, and the place of women in the occupational structure as contributing factors to the feminisation of poverty, feminists argued that gender was the main cause, because women's poverty had causes specific to women such as family responsibilities, low-paying jobs and dependency on men's economic support. Most women were just a man away from poverty.

Is it correct to state that most women are just a man away from poverty? Yes, it is, but only as long as it is acknowledged that most women are propertyless, members of the working class, many of them depending, for economic

---

59   Identity politics is a mode of organising and theorising – eventually generating a body of
     political and academic literature – that takes as its starting point the sense that groups of
     people are oppressed on the basis of their identity such as gender, age, ethnicity, race or
     sexual preference. See http://plato.stanford.edu/entries/identity-politics/.

survival, on a relationship with a male willing to share his income. To disregard class location, to consider it 'redundant to say that class causes poverty'[60] and focus only on gender as the cause of women's poverty is to isolate women not only from their class but also from history. There are no abstract women, whose lives are shaped only or primarily by their gender; in the real world, women have a place in the class, socio-economic, racial and ethnic structures within capitalist social formations.

In the Addendum that follows Chapter 9, I update some of the poverty data and discuss recent research findings that point to the relationship between changes in the economy, declining economic prospects for working-class men, and the rise of cohabiting relationships and out of wedlock births which often place women at the risk of becoming single mothers, thus jeopardising their ability to work full-time and improve their economic prospects.

The next three chapters have their origins in insights gathered from personal experiences, critically examined through the lens of Marxist theory. Having grown up in a context where paid domestic workers were taken for granted as a feature of most households except those of the very poor, it became clear to me that among the structural determinants of the development of the Women's Liberation Movement in the US, and the importance given in feminist theory to the effects of the unequal division of labour in the home, was the fact that most women in the United States, except the wealthy and the few with very good incomes, were entirely responsible for domestic labour whether or not they also worked outside their homes. This situation created a real and important source of conflict between men and women within the home and imposed material constraints upon women's opportunities. Reflecting on the political and economic significance of domestic labour, I eventually wrote the first two chapters included in this section.

In Chapter 10, 'The Dialectics of Waged and Unwaged Work: Waged Work, Domestic Labour and Household Survival in the United States', I examine the relationship between proletarianisation, the rise of wage-dependent households, the variable relationship between income levels and the ability of people to use various kinds of domestic labour to improve their quality of life, and the impact of these phenomena on the oppression of women. In the US, where most people depend on wages or salaries for economic survival, the lack of income entails the impossibility (exceptions notwithstanding) of relying on domestic labour as a potential source of income, and the erosion of people's ability to use domestic labour on their own behalf, for the ordinary tasks of

---

60   Ehrenreich 1987, p. 12.

reproduction. The domination of production over reproduction is manifested in the subordination of unwaged labour to waged labour, of useful labour to abstract labour in ways that vary by class and strata within classes.

Domestic work is inherently contradictory; it can be a source of oppression for women who are full-time domestic workers for themselves and their families; it is a source of oppression for women who are paid to do other women's domestic chores. Sometimes domestic workers are doubly oppressed, by the woman who pays for their services and by the company through which they are hired. However, as I also argue in Chapter 11, 'Loving Alienation: The Contradictions of Domestic Work', some areas of domestic work (childcare and cooking, for example) can be creative and enjoyable, the material basis for non-market, non-utilitarian, caring forms of social relations, consciousness and experiences. As people undertake to do things together, with family and friends, cooking, sharing meals and homemade preserves, gardening and sharing their crops, practicing or teaching each other crafts, playing musical instruments, etc., they do so in a free, self-actualising manner, in a space free from market relations and calculations where people can envision and practice what it is like to relate to each other outside the competitive exchange mentality fostered by the experience of working and living in a context where everything has a price. Individuals on their own also appreciate the contrast between the experience of alienated labour in their place of work, and the free exercise of their skills at home, be it in the kitchen, baking bread, in their gardens, workshops, tinkering and fixing things. Granted, domestic work has its tedious, routine, 'never done' dimensions, but it also has its creative aspects, as a set of practices that have the potential to create an alienation-free space, a space for the experience of non-market relations, where bonds of friendship and cooperation can flourish. This space is being eroded by the commodification of domestic labour, and of the material conditions of reproduction, processes that will continue unabated as long as the pursuit of profit, rather than social reproduction and the satisfaction of human needs, is the central aim of economic activity.

Chapter 12, 'Self-Sourcing: How Capitalism Gets Us to Work Without Pay', originated from my encountering computers for the first time in the mid-1980s, and reflecting on their implications for the organisation of work. Since then, the amount of unpaid labour that enters into paid work, and into consumption processes, has increased extraordinarily with the development of the Internet and the online economy. Corporations reap enormous profits by intensifying the amount of unpaid labour done by consumers. Jobs are lost because people, particularly but not exclusively women, are increasingly doing more unpaid work, both online and offline, at work and at home. This form of unpaid labour is not gender specific; it is done by women and by men. It is not just women who can now complain of being oppressed by being forced to do unpaid labour.

Chapter 13, 'From Social Reproduction to Capitalist Social Reproduction', is the result of exploring the extent to which my work might be considered a contribution to the literature on Social Reproduction Theory. After a brief and critical examination of the literature, I concluded that my approach is different. Social reproduction theories emphasise the integrated nature of the processes of production and reproduction and stress the dependence of production on the reproduction of labour power. At the highest level of abstraction, production presupposes reproduction, and vice versa; societal survival presupposes the production and reproduction of the means of production, the means of subsistence, and the population in an integrated system. Historically, however, at the level of analysis of the capitalist mode of production, in capitalist social formations, production determines reproduction. The social reproduction of the capitalist class and intermediate, economically secure, classes is assured. However, the social reproduction, i.e. the economic survival of the working classes, their access to their conditions of reproduction, is subordinate to changes in capital accumulation that constantly create a surplus population or reserve army of labour. Given that the economic survival of the vast majority of the population in capitalist social formations is dependent on wages or salaries, their social reproduction is subordinate to the ups and downs of the capitalist economy.

Whither Feminism?

The chapters included in this section also deal with matters pertaining to social reproduction; I placed them in this section because they also pose the question, from different angles, of the political relevance of feminism today, or, to put it otherwise, of the future direction of feminism. Implicit in my answers is the idea that as the effects of globalisation increase the polarisation of income and wealth ownership everywhere, and capital's efforts to reduce labour costs even further result in declines in the demand for male labour, a feminism focused exclusively on the oppression of women, or on women's rights, is not likely to find followers at this time of crisis, when the employment of women is often accompanied by the unemployment of their fathers, sons, husbands or life companions. At the very least, feminism needs to change focus, expanding its reach by narrowing its constituency to focus on working-class women and on the problems afflicting the working class as a whole. Underlying racial, ethnic and other antagonisms, workers share – in the last instance – common interests whereas racial and ethnic minorities are themselves divided by class; what benefits members of minority populations with higher incomes and in the capitalist class does not necessarily benefit the working-class majority.

In Chapters 14 and 15, 'Connecting Marx and Feminism in the Era of Globalisation: A Preliminary Investigation', and 'Global Capitalism and Women', I examine the effects of globalisation on working women and on growing inequality. Global capitalism is in the process of eroding the advantages the working classes in the advanced capitalist countries enjoyed in comparison to the rest of the world. In the US, the levelling process is harsher because of the inadequate safety net for the poor, near poor, and the unemployed. I also explore the relationship between the worldwide deepening of inequality caused by globalisation, declines in the demand for male labour, increases in women's participation in the labour force, and changes in the relations of reproduction in poor and wealthy countries. As working-class poverty increases and male employment opportunities decline in poor countries, women are forced to migrate, looking for employment in advanced capitalist countries. Millions of women have become migrant workers, and new phrases have entered the literature: 'feminisation of migration', 'feminisation of the proletariat', and 'feminisation of the labour force'. These phenomena indicate that global capitalism is changing the relationships between men and women, and among women both in Western and non-Western countries; in the process, it is creating a very complex terrain for feminist politics, a terrain favourable to the resurgence of Marxist-Feminism.

Chapter 16, 'Capitalism and the Oppression of Women: Marx Revisited', offers a systematic account of the Marxist-feminist theory that underlies my writing about women. I revisit not only Marx but also myself, having achieved greater clarity in the presentation of the key elements of the Marxist theory of the oppression of women I have sought to develop over the years. I argue that the relevance of Marx for understanding the capitalist basis of the oppression of women is to be found in his methodology. This guided my thinking in identifying the material base for the oppression of working-class/propertyless women in the articulation between production and reproduction, which subordinates the latter to the former. I also argued that, in light of Marx's analysis of the limitations of civil rights and liberties, the oppression of propertyless women would continue as long as capitalism continued to be the dominant mode of production.

Looking Back

More than forty years have passed since the publication of my first article, 'Marxism and Feminism'.[61] Looking back at the chapters in this volume, I can see how their subject matter is related to the historical context in which they were originally written. In the mid-1980s there is a shift in my work, from theory building to the critical examination of specific issues affecting women. And, as the discourse on inequality became subtly changed into a discourse about cultural differences, diversity and identity, I also wrote about the ways in which an exclusive focus on identities – be it gender, race, or ethnicity – is theoretically, methodologically, and politically counterproductive. In the last three chapters I revisit and sum up my contribution to Marxist-feminist theory and, inevitably, I look into the effects of globalisation on women's lives. Is the theoretical analysis I developed in my earlier work still relevant? I believe so, because capitalism remains the dominant mode of production. The empirical effects of global capitalism, however, have altered the material conditions in which we live today, changing the organisation of reproduction in some sectors of the working class.[62]

The last few decades have seen vast ideological and economic changes. In the realm of ideology, strict social controls over sexuality gave way to the increased social acceptability of sex and childbearing outside marriage, same-sex relationships and marriage, and cohabitation among couples of all ages. The availability of contraception and the legalisation of abortion in 1973, the cultural and political revolt in the 1960s against the Vietnam War and the strictures of the 1950s middle-class morality, and the ideologies of the social movements for civil rights, women's and gay rights converged to result in dramatic changes in the sphere of personal life.[63] These changes were and continue to be met by a conservative reaction that seeks to set back civil rights (especially voting rights), repeal the legalisation of abortion, and curtail as much as possible women's ability to control their childbearing capacity.[64]

In the economic sphere, de-industrialisation, downsizing, automation and outsourcing in the United States accelerated after the fall of the Soviet Union, as global capitalism engulfed the world. Income and wealth inequality deepened

---

61   See Chapter 1 in this volume.
62   I describe and discuss the significance of those changes in this section of the Introduction, in the Addendum to Chapter 9; also relevant to this issue is Chapter 13.
63   For a discussion of cultural changes affecting family formation, see Cherlin 2014, pp. 15–23.
64   See, for example, Sreenivas 2013, pp. vii–viii; also Robles 2015.

everywhere.[65] In the US, the most unequal among all advanced capitalist countries,[66] the result of these economic changes, which a politically defeated working class has been unable to restrain, has been the rise of the 'hour glass' economy, or 'polarised' labour market.[67] Relative to the demand for labour at the top and bottom of the occupational structure, there is 'a declining demand for labour in the middle of the labour market, [which] has been hit the hardest by changes that have occurred in the American economy since 1970'.[68] These changes have affected male and female workers differently. The material conditions that placed most working-class men in a position of economic and social superiority over women are no longer widespread. Some men and women continue to pool incomes but on different terms.[69] Young working-class women and men without a college education are less likely to marry; women are likely to earn more than men and prefer to remain single or to enter into a cohabiting relationship when they become pregnant, sharing the economic costs of reproduction with men who are not financially responsible, in the last instance, for the household economic survival. Most cases in which children are born to unmarried mothers happen to women in a cohabiting relationship, and 'in 2013, as it was during the last six consecutive years, 41 percent of all births were to unmarried women'.[70] Unmarried low income men are also more likely to become single fathers and, if they have children with more than one woman, they are unlikely to develop a stable relationship with all of their children or to provide much economic support.[71]

---

65   See, for example, Stiglitz 2013.

66   According to researchers from the Federal Reserve, 'The wealth share of America's top 3 percent rose from 44.8 percent of the nation's wealth in 1989 … to 54.4 percent in 2013. The top 3 percent now holds over double the wealth of America's poorer 90 percent of families' (which hold 25 percent), http://inequality.org/wealth-inequality/.

67   These notions refer to changes in the demand for labour reflecting the decline in manufacturing jobs. There are employment opportunities for college graduates, especially for those with degrees higher than a BA, and for high school graduates (or less educational attainment) willing to enter poorly paid, mostly low skill but necessary service and manual jobs, jobs that cannot be outsourced. Jobs in the middle – e.g. manufacturing jobs, jobs requiring computer skills, jobs in state and local government, health industry, shipping and delivery – have not completely disappeared but they do not grow as fast as jobs at the top and the bottom of the occupational structure. Cherlin 2014a, p. 14, pp. 124–5.

68   Cherlin 2014a, pp. 124–5.

69   'Mothers are the main or sole breadwinner in 40 percent of households with children under age 18; 5.1 million (37%) of these mothers are married and earn more than their husbands, and 8.6 million (63%) are single mothers'; see Wang, Parker and Taylor 2013.

70   Births to Unmarried Women, http://www.childtrends.org/?indicators=births-to-unmarried-women.

71   Carlson and England 2011, pp. 5–6.

Marriage requires a solid economic foundation;[72] to the extent that working-class men's economic opportunities decline, the proportion of families headed by young women as well as the proportion of cohabiting couples raising children rises, while the marriage rate declines.[73] Census data show that, in 2013, married couples with children – no information is given about whether one or both adults work – comprised only 19 percent of all households, down from 40 percent in 1970.[74] In the country as a whole, marriage has become out of reach for most Americans, except for college educated workers who hold stable and well paid jobs.[75] College educated women are far less likely to become single mothers and, when they marry, they will form 'dual-career' families if they marry men with similar or greater earning potential and job stability.[76] This is why the rise in non-marital childbearing has intensified socio-economic status differences among women.[77]

It is unlikely that inequality and the education gap between working-class men and women will diminish in the near future, so the trend toward an inverse correlation between marriage and income is likely to intensify. As the earning potential of working-class men decreases, and more employment opportunities open up for women with and without a college education, women will enter and remain in the labour force even if their children are very young.[78]

Families in which men are the sole or main breadwinners have not disappeared, but they are now most likely in the minority within the set of different reproductive contexts: i.e. families headed by single mothers below the poverty

---

72   See, for example, Cherlin 2014b.

73   Cherlin 2014a, pp. 134–40; Sawhill 2014, pp. 16–38.

74   Babay 2013.

75   The economic advantages of a college education, however, might not last forever unless it involves an advanced degree; 'Since 2000, college graduates between the ages of twenty-five and thirty four without advanced degrees ... saw their income fall 9.6 percent. A four-year college education may no longer be the ticket to financial security' (Carbone and Cahn 2014, pp. 80–1).

76   Cherlin 2014a, pp. 126–7, 135–9.

77   'The median total family income of married mothers who earn more than their husbands [women who tend to be older, mostly white and college educated] was nearly $80,000 in 2011, well above the national median for all families with children and nearly four times the $23,000 median income for families led by a single mother [women who are younger, likely to be non-white and less educated]', in Wang, Parker and Taylor 2013.

78   'In 2013, 57.2 percent of women were in the labour force; the rate of labour force participation for married women was 58.9 percent. The rate for women with children 6 to 17 years old was 74.8 percent; the rate for those with children under 6 years old was 64.7 percent and for those with children under 3 years old was 62.1 percent'. In Bureau of Labor Statistics Report 2014, pp. 1–2.

level; single mothers who are the sole breadwinner and live in relative poverty, above the poverty level; single employed mothers involved in one or more cohabiting unions;[79] married mothers who are also the main breadwinners; dual pay-check couples wherein the husband is the sole or main breadwinner; and dual career families, which are the most affluent and least likely to experience conflicts between work and family demands.

In the context of these different forms that the mode of reproduction can take, working-class women's divergent experiences of oppression unfold and labour power is reproduced.

In light of these changes, I will address the question that I posed at the start of this section: is the theoretical analysis I developed in my earlier work still relevant? I argue that it is. These changes support the historical materialist premise underlying my work: under capitalism, changes at the level of production alter the mode of reproduction, i.e. the kinds of social relations within which the processes of physical and social maintenance and reproduction of labour power and of the social classes occur are largely dependent on the resources that the functioning of capitalism and the state of the class struggle eventually make available to the different classes. As far as the working class is concerned, reproduction is left largely to the workers themselves,[80] who manage as best they can under conditions they do not entirely control. The survival strategies open to female and male workers with different levels of training, skills, and resources, strategies reflected in the different types of relations of reproduction found in a given social formation, result from changes in capital accumulation, the opening and closing of opportunities for different sectors of the labour force, the state of the class struggle, and dominant ideologies about sex, procreation, gender, and so on.

The family supported by a male breadwinner represented less than 50 percent of all families even during the economic boom of postwar years, and its decline in the last 40 years accelerated after the 2008 recession. Married couples with children made up 42.9 percent of all family households in 1940, but only 20.2 percent in 2010.[81] Most women do not live with or raise children

79   In 2014, there were 3.1 million (1.2 million in 1996) cohabiting couples with children under 18 and 7.9 million (2.8 million in 1996) with or without children. http://www.childtrends .org/?indicators=family-structure.

80   'The maintenance and reproduction of the working class is, and must ever be, a necessary condition to the reproduction of capital. But the capitalist may safely leave its fulfilment to the labourer's instincts of self-preservation and of propagation'. Marx 1974, p. 572.

81   Altogether, family households were 66.4 percent in 2010 (down from 90 percent in 1940); 28.2 percent were married couples without children; 9.2 percent were single parents with children, and other family households were 8.5 percent. Nonfamily households in 2010

today with a man who is also the sole or principal breadwinner. *Just as it became important, theoretically and politically, to take into account class, race and ethnic differences among women, so it is important to consider how different relations of reproduction affect the oppression of women.* Furthermore, *these different family arrangements suggest that the oppression of working-class women cannot be fully understood in isolation from the economic exploitation and oppression of working-class men.* Men's lack of economic resources or earnings lower than those of the women with whom they become involved do not keep them from forming attachments and eventually bringing children into the world, but will keep men and women from forming stable relationships within or outside marriage.[82] What I wrote about the feminisation of poverty in 1987 applies today to cohabiting families as well: their increase '... is a real, important, albeit partial dimension, of a vast process of social transformation resulting in a drastic decline in the overall level of wages and the standard of living of the US working class'.[83] Since then, the prospects for the working class have worsened. From the standpoint of Marxist-feminist theory, then, an exclusive focus on the oppression of women in general, or solely on the oppression of working-class women, would neglect the relational nature of women's and men's lives and the extent to which their interests and that of their children, if any, are tied together.[84] Marxist-Feminism can be of more than academic interest to the extent that it directs its theoretical and political analysis toward the oppression of the working class, keeping in mind that more than half of the working class is female, that the most disadvantaged members of the working class are women of racial and ethnic minorities, and that what is at stake, at this time in history, is not only a better life for women but the maintenance and reproduction of the working class as a whole.

Reflecting on the relevance of my work for understanding the oppression of women in today's context has led me to realise that my arguments tend

---

were 33.6 percent of which 26.7 percent were one person living alone. http://www.prb
.org/pdf12/us-household-change-2012.pdf.

82   See, for example, Cherlin 2011, pp. 68–84; Edin, Nelson and Reed 2011, pp. 85–107; and
      McLanahan 2011, pp. 108–33; Carbone and Cahn 2014, Sections I and II.

83   See ending of Chapter 9.

84   I am aware that often it is not the lack of resources, but divorce, separation, domestic
      violence and other problems that result in women becoming single mothers. My ana-
      lysis does not imply that all would be well if only all workers earned enough to afford
      the expenses associated with marriage: e.g. home ownership, health insurance, childcare,
      educational expenses, and so on. Under capitalist conditions, however, in the absence of
      a well-remunerated job or a supportive kinship or family network, life is very difficult for
      single mothers.

to coalesce around the analysis of the oppression of working-class women, a tendency that culminates in the final chapters and is clearly expressed in the subtitle of Chapter 15: 'From Feminist Politics to Working-Class Women's Politics'. In this light, I argue that, from the standpoint of Marxist-feminist theory, current changes in women's education, labour force participation, earning capacity, marriage patterns and childbearing decisions, such that now many prefer to remain single mothers despite the hardship that such a choice entails, show that the socio-economic oppression of many working-class women stems from capitalist macro-level economic and political determinants. At the level of analysis of interpersonal relations it is appropriate to consider the role of individual men in affecting the well-being, health and peace of mind of individual women and their children. At the macro-level of analysis, however, changing economic and political processes can place working men and women in unequal locations, placing some working-class men in a position to establish relations of economic cooperation while often exerting economic power over the women they live with, married or unmarried. This possibility is withheld from others and in proportions that vary with the nature of the sectoral changes in the economy.[85]

In this context, the proportion of households headed by single mothers, alone or in cohabiting relationships, above and below the poverty level, is likely to continue to grow, thus increasing income inequality among working-class women and increasing the growth, through natural increase, of a surplus population of a relatively unemployable, poorly educated sector of the working class.

Given that the ability of married, college educated women to bear children, pursue their careers, and enjoy the standard of living of dual career families is made possible, mainly but not exclusively, by the labour of working-class women, often immigrants or members of racial or ethnic minorities, what are the theoretical and political implications of the fact that it is not only men who oppress women?

What are the long-term implications, for working-class women, of declining job and earning prospects for working-class men? How can we, as Marxist-Feminists, keep our focus on the issues that affect women and, at the same time, place those issues in the context of the relentless impoverishment of the working class?

---

85   Employment in manufacturing has been declining for over 30 years; in absolute numbers, jobs declined by 30 percent since 2000; 'in 1960 manufacturing accounted for 28.4 percent of nonfarm employment in the US economy. By 2013 the share had fallen to 8.8 percent', in Moran and Oldenski 2014.

In light of the variety of relations of reproduction within which working-class women bear children and engage in domestic labour – with and without a male partner, above or below the poverty level, in a secure or a fragile economic situation – it is clear that current processes of economic change have complicated, at the level of the social formation, the material conditions within which women experience oppression, at home and at work.

These and other questions call for Marxist-feminist answers. A short time ago I might have doubted that such answers might be forthcoming, because I believed Marxist-Feminism had lost ground to other feminist perspectives. There are, however, reasons to expect a resurgence of Marxist-feminist theory, research and activism.

Looking Forward

I am not sure when I noticed – perhaps after the mid-1980s – that everyone seemed to have been suddenly swept away by the postmodern/poststructuralist turn.[86] Socialist, Radical and Marxist feminisms receded into the intellectual practice and political activism of a small number of aging scholars, whose publications I stopped seeing in the book catalogues that publishers routinely sent to university professors. Although my work continued to be published, I believed that interest in Marxist-feminist theory was limited to specialised venues and a tiny readership. I retired in 2007; since then, until the last couple of years, I turned my attention to non-academic pursuits. The publication, in 2010, of Einsenstein's *Feminism Seduced: How Global Elites Use Women's Labour and Ideas to Exploit the World*,[87] reminded me that there were still scholars for whom it was not a contradiction to be both Marxist and feminist.

When several years ago Sebastian Budgen, the editor responsible for this volume, first asked me to edit a collection of my published work, I refused; I said that I was retired and did not think anyone would be interested in Marxist-Feminist work. He replied that, on the contrary, there was a lot of interest in Marxism and feminism, something I did not quite believe. Eventually, I agreed to edit this book, because of his persistence and because the publication of Brown's *Marx on Gender and the Family: A Critical Study*[88] and the reissue of Vogel's important Marxist-feminist theoretical analysis, *Marxism and the*

---

86   For a critical perspective see Epstein 1995; Eagleton 1995; Ebert 1995 and 1996.
87   Einsenstein 2010.
88   Brown 2013.

Oppression of Women: Toward a Unitary Theory[89] convinced me that there was still some interest in Marxism and feminism. That the interest is real and more widespread than I had imagined was recently confirmed. In 2014 I was invited to attend and participate in an International Congress: *The Strength of Critique: Trajectories of Marxism-Feminism*.[90] It turned out to be a very exciting and successful event that brought together a large number of feminists who, in one way or another, combined Marxism and feminism in their work. More importantly, it was most encouraging to see a fairly large number of scholars and students, many of them very young, intensely involved, who asked thoughtful questions and for whom the ideas the participants presented seemed to matter a great deal. The purpose of the Congress was to bring feminists together to identify pressing issues of feminist concern, build on our energies and creativity, and establish new theoretical and political agendas. The topics presented and discussed ranged widely, from the 'classic' feminist concerns with domestic labour and patriarchy, to identity politics and intersectionality, racism, colonialism, and the effects of neoliberalism and austerity politics in Europe and elsewhere; from critical assessments of the limits of liberal feminism, co-opted by capitalism, to a call to bring back into feminism the recognition of the importance of class. There were, perhaps, as many perspectives about the relationship between Marxism and feminism as there were participants; some appeared to give more emphasis to elements of Marxist theory, others to feminist theories, thus illustrating the possible self-identifications discussed at the very start of the Congress by one of the organisers: Am I a Marxist-Feminist? Am I a Feminist Marxist? The goal of one of the Congress's organisers, the formation of a global union of Marxist-Feminists, might be considered utopian; but the principle that would cement this union – 'Under no circumstances may the questions of life be subordinated to the drive for profit'[91] – expresses, in a general, perhaps cryptic way, the Marxist and feminist critique of the many ways in which access to the material conditions for social reproduction – i.e. employment, food, housing, education, job training, healthcare, and so forth – is subordinate, under capitalism, to the pursuit of profits. What matters most at this time of deepening inequality and exploitation, when the success of a minority of

---

89   Vogel 2014.

90   That the Congress was organised and convened in Europe, in Berlin, is perhaps a good indicator of the state of Marxist feminism in the United States. http://www.rosalux.de/documentation/52209/the-strength-of-critique-trajectories-of-marxism-feminism-marxfem.html

       A follow up conference met in Vienna, 6–9 October 2016 and there are plans for a third conference, in Sweden, in 2018.

91   Haug 2014, p. 42.

upwardly mobile women stands in stark contrast to the difficult lives of most women, is the development of Marxist-feminist perspectives that shed light on the material conditions that oppress women as the most oppressed members of the working classes, and as members of families or kin-like groups; i.e. as embedded in a network of relationships with children, parents, partners, and friends who need their care and support.

I left the Congress no longer feeling intellectually isolated and, more importantly, knowing that this book will be a contribution to what I hope will be the coming together of Marxism and Feminism in new theoretical and political trajectories that reflect the vision of the younger generations in conjunction with the demands posed by the effects of global capitalism.

If there is one message in this book, besides its potential significance as an instance of Marxist-Feminist theorising, it is the political need to surmount the theoretical and political problems posed by the fragmentation of the political subject, an effect of the 'retreat from class'[92] and the rise of identity politics. The key theoretical and political question is not, therefore, how class (in the Marxist sense) 'intersects' with the various identities where individuals are presumably located, but how to differentiate between the effects of capitalist class power upon large and heterogeneous (in terms of identity) sectors of the working class, and the effects of identity-based interactions and conflicts within those sectors. In the absence of this distinction between levels of analysis, the effects of class tend to be perceived as the effects of identity. Wood, for example, argues that an important ideological effect of identity politics is to camouflage capitalism's tendency to create underclasses: 'When the least privileged sectors of the working class coincide with extra-economic identities like gender or race, as they so often do, it may appear that the blame for the existence of these sectors lies with causes other than the necessary logic of the capitalist system'.[93] And that coincidence stems from the ease with which capitalism '... integrates and employs pre-capitalist power relations to create hierarchies of exploited and oppressed, digging trenches and raising barriers'.[94] I started to explore these issues in some of the chapters of this book; hopefully, others will continue the theoretical investigation and empirical research needed to elucidate the terrain where workers can unite across gender, race, ethnicity and other differences.[95] This should not be too difficult because, after all, most of

---

92   Wood 1986.
93   Wood 1995, p. 267.
94   Arruza 2013, p. 126.
95   I am aware that these arguments leave me open to the charge of being a class reductionist, economic determinist or a utopian dreamer who ignores the realities of identity and

the problems or demands that, if solved or attained, would make women's and members of racial/ethnic minorities' lives easier, are working-class problems exacerbated, these days, by stagnant wages and intensified exploitation, for despite large increases in productivity, most of the gains have gone to capital.[96]

This book reflects my own intellectual trajectory from abstract theory building about the oppression of women to using theory to illuminate specific manifestations of oppression, a process that led to the realisation that *the focus of feminism itself had to change, in a dialectical understanding that many working-class women's problems are also the problems of the working class as a whole.* Stepping back from my own work, I can see how, in the process of writing this introduction, my views about what I wrote have begun to change and I have developed new understandings, looking back and examining my arguments and conclusions in light of the changes that have occurred in the last four decades. Looking forward, I hope this book contributes, together with the works of other academics and activists in the US and abroad, to the development of a new generation of feminists, Marxist-Feminists who are not afraid of the subtle political control inherent in the strictures against 'economic determinism' and 'class reductionism', and are willing to fully acknowledge the implications of the fact that – paraphrasing Marx – we make history but not under conditions chosen by ourselves.[97]

---

socio-economic divisions within the US working classes and elsewhere. However, we live in times that call for utopian thinking and for a return to class in our academic theorising and political analysis. For a critique of 'the retreat' from class within the left, see Wood 1986.

96   See, for example, Krugman 2012; Greenhouse 2013.

97   Marx 1969, p. 15.

PART 1

Marxist-Feminist Theory

∵

Marxism and Feminism

'Marxism and Feminism', in *Frontiers, A Journal of Women Studies*, Vol. 1, No. 1 (Fall 1975): 61–80.[1]

Feminism is the struggle against sexism, or discriminatory social practices and ideologies that result in male supremacy and female oppression. Sexism as a form of social oppression is not a modern phenomenon. Paraphrasing Marx and Engels,[2] it can be stated that the history of all hitherto existing society is the history of class struggles and sex struggles because the existence of classes presupposes private ownership of the means of production, monogamy, and therefore sexism.[3] The presence of sexism throughout history accounts for the ease with which it has been taken for granted as a universal feature of all societies or as the product of innate differences between the sexes. This also explains why women today search for its historical origins in an effort to understand its present manifestations. Within the social sciences, the conceptualisation of sexism depends upon the basic assumptions about human nature, society, and their relationship which underlie current theories about society and social behaviour; theories vary in the emphasis given to either human nature or society. If priority is given to human nature, persons are considered to have inherent traits such as selfishness, competitiveness, and utilitarianism. Social relations and institutions are viewed, consequently, as products of those individual traits. In this context, men and women are considered to have innate traits that make them different from each other. For example, while males are aggressive, strong, instrumental, etc., females are weak, submissive, affective, nurturant, etc. Sex differences in power and in social participation are conceptualised as consequences of these inherent differences between the sexes. When the emphasis is placed upon society, persons are viewed as empty slates, the product of the socialisation process which integrates them into a powerful and coercive social reality. Sexism emerges, within this context, as a product of social organisation; men and women are different and have different powers and social participation because they are socialised differently. Socialisation

---

1 Gimenez 1975; abridged with permission from the publishers.
2 Marx and Engels 1994, p. 158.
3 Engels 1972.

patterns are then explained in terms of social needs and/or processes of functional differentiation and division of labour.[4]

From a Marxist standpoint, the social sciences present competing idealist and materialist explanations of sexism which do not preclude their combination in explanations which take into account both individual and social factors. Marxism transcends the dichotomy between innate and acquired traits and posits, instead, the notion that 'man is the ensemble of social relations'.[5]

This notion is the basis of the Marxist theory of human nature, which negates the notion of an isolated human nature and affirms the inextricable unity between persons and their natural and social environments. Marxism postulates that neither persons nor their natural and social environment can be viewed in isolation, as things in themselves which 'interact' with one another or which are the 'cause' or the 'effect' of the other. The theoretical focus shifts from the abstractions of 'persons' and 'environment' (natural and social) to the processes through which persons, nature, and society acquire definite objective forms. These processes are historically specific and can be identified for the purposes of scientific analysis. In this context, the key to understanding sexism rests upon the exploration of its historically specific forms within concrete modes of production. The understanding and conceptualisation of sexism today presupposes, therefore, an understanding of its place within the capitalist mode of production.[6]

---

4   The notion of functional differentiation refers to social processes which result in the loss of functions by a given institution and the emergence of new institutions that take care of those tasks. For example, education and job training used to take place in a family context. The concept of division of labour refers to the social distribution of tasks, who does what and where.

5   Marx and Engels 1976, p. 7.

6   Within social science terminology and everyday language, social reality is perceived through a very general and abstract concept: *society*. Societies are classified in several types: industrial, developed, developing, traditional, underdeveloped, etc. This way of looking at social reality emphasises continuity. Although societies change, it is assumed that they will always present certain characteristics such as social inequality, families, sexism, and institutions of social control. Those characteristics will remain in the context of changes in the division of labour and functional differentiation which increase the complexity of society without changing its basic nature. While Marx acknowledges the existence of elements common to all social epochs, he argues that: a) there are other elements which are not common to all epochs (e.g. social inequality, wage labour, private property); and b) it is necessary to distinguish those definitions that apply to all societies in general 'in order not to overlook the essential differences existing despite the unity that follows from the very fact that the subject, mankind, and the object, nature, are the same' (Marx 1970a, p. 190). All social reality stems from the interplay between man and nature in production; the concept of *society* emphasises the continuity that emerges from that fact while the concept of *mode of production* grasps the qualitatively

This chapter is a contribution to the development of a Marxist analysis of the capitalist roots of sexism and the implications for changes in the present and future status of women which such analysis suggests.

Capitalist Development and Its Effects on Women

As Marx and Engels repeatedly stated throughout their work, capitalism is both a progressive and a regressive force because it contains contradictions.[7] The two fundamental contradictions are: a) the contradiction between the capitalist class and the working class, which is manifested through the class struggle; and b) the contradiction between the development of the productive forces (or productive capacity of the capitalist mode of production) and the private ownership of the means of production; this contradiction is expressed through chronic unemployment and periodic economic crises.

The development of the productive forces means the development of science, technology, and efficient forms of productive organisation which are reflected in the growth of the productivity of labour and the capacity to produce an ever-greater amount of goods at lower prices. This progressive aspect of capitalism is counteracted by the private ownership of the means of production. This means that the productive capacity will be harnessed to the interests of the capitalist classes and that it will be maintained within limits that do not threaten the maintenance of the class structure. Investments are therefore made only when profitable, and monopolies and other forms of capitalist power establish price controls so that high prices are artificially maintained. This contradiction is intuitively grasped by people when they ponder, for example, how it is that the United States can send a man to the moon

---

different ways in which the process of production takes place throughout a given historical period. From a Marxist standpoint, social inequality stems from the private ownership of the means of production, a characteristic common to all modes of production based upon private property: slavery, feudalism, and the various forms of production found in Asian countries. Capitalism is a mode of production in which one class – the capitalist class – owns the means of production while the majority of the people own nothing except their labour power and are socially, politically, and economically subordinate to the other class who controls their means of livelihood.

7   It is important to differentiate between conflict and contradiction. Conflict refers to antagonisms at the level of conscious relations while contradiction refers to the level of the social structure. What is essential to the notion of contradiction is that it indicates the existence of incompatible processes which disrupt and eventually destroy the system. One can speak meaningfully of conflict resolution but not of contradiction resolution.

while healthcare, housing, education, and transportation remain as seemingly unsolvable problems. In addition, this contradiction has consequences that affect women both within and outside the household and set the basis for the maintenance of sexism as an inherent feature of capitalist social reality.

Growth in the productivity of labour is reflected in the changes in the number of workers needed in the production process. The greater the technological development and, therefore, the greater the productive capacity, the smaller the number of workers needed. This process, which under different relations of production would result in the growth of free time for human development, results in unemployment and poverty under capitalism. This is why automation, which has the potential of liberating humankind from the realm of necessity and of opening the doors to the realm of freedom, is viewed with dread by the working class; for it signifies, within capitalist countries, the growth of unemployment and the spread of poverty and increasing competition among workers for the scarce jobs available.[8]

How does this process affect women? On the one hand, it has relegated women to a subsidiary component of the labour force. While at the beginning of the process of capitalist development the whole family was included in the ranks of the labour force, as the forces of production developed and fewer workers were needed, children and women were slowly phased out of the labour force and were kept as a reserve army of labour ready to be used when needed; e.g. as strikebreakers, as sources of cheap labour in those sectors of production where the ratio of workers to machines is high (e.g. the clothing industry), and to do men's work, during World War II. On the other hand, this process of excluding women from the labour force was reflected in the consolidation of the family as a separate realm where domestic labour became the exclusive domain of women. There are, therefore, two consequences of the built-in tendency of capitalism to generate unemployment: 1) the relative exclusion of women from the labour force, and relegation to lower status, poorly paid jobs; and 2) the separation of domestic production from the sphere of socially-recognised productive activities and its transformation into the sphere of private interpersonal relationships

It is not argued that women do not generally work outside the home. On the contrary, the participation of women in the labour force has been increasing in advanced capitalist countries and it tends to rise in times of economic crises. But the overall effect of the fluctuating demand for women's labour and relegation to the lower levels of the occupational structure contributes to: a)

---

8   See Marx 1974, Ch. XXV, for the complete development of this argument.

keeping women in their home as much as possible; b) using them sporadically when needed; c) devaluing the full-time participation of women in the labour force and lowering their wage levels (it is presumed that women are part of a household headed by a male and as such their wages need not be sufficient to support a family independent from a man); d) obfuscating the economic nature of domestic labour and its economic value to the capitalist class; e) obfuscating the socially necessary nature of domestic labour and its importance for the country as a whole; and f) maintaining the subordination of women to men, because they control the means of production (capitalist males) and exchange (wage earners and salary earners).

These processes operate at the level of the mode of production, the level of unobservable structures and social relations; i.e. the level of capitalist relations of production, class relations, and capitalist contradictions resulting in a dynamic and changing organisation of production that splits the productive process between a public or industrial sector and a private or household sector, and gives men control over the means of production and exchange. The observable effects of the functioning of the mode of production at the level of sex stratification and sex differentiation[9] (within the occupational structure and within the household) vary from one country to another, as well as among areas of a given country. Those variations are linked to the stage of capitalist development characterising a given country, the dominant or subordinate place which a given country has within the worldwide network of imperialism, and the extent of uneven development within the country.

Both Marxist and non-Marxist social scientists would agree about the significance of the manifestations of sexism as depicted at the levels of sex differentiation and stratification. While Marxists would explain those processes as the effects of specifically capitalist contradictions, structures, and processes, social scientists explain them either in terms of social requirements, social processes of functional differentiation, division of labour, or according to inherent differences between the sexes. Such general explanations overlook the capitalist roots of sexism and cannot provide feminists with guidelines for an effective struggle. On the other hand, the social sciences provide excellent documentation of the consequences of capitalist processes from which Marxists and Marxist-Feminists have a great deal to learn. There is, however, an inherent weakness in an analysis of sexism limited to the levels of sex stratification and

---

9   Sex stratification refers to the differential power and prestige associated with male and female roles. Sex differentiation refers to the division of labour by sex within and outside the family. See Holter 1973, pp. 9–53.

differentiation. At those levels, it appears as if all men were equally powerful and all women were equally subject to oppression. On the contrary, men
and women who belong to the capitalist class have more economic and social
power than working-class men and women, although these specific power differentials are obscured by the focus upon sex-linked differences that characterise all analyses of sexism if undertaken in isolation from an analysis of class
structure.

This discussion of the position of women within capitalism and the capitalist basis of sexism cannot end without a brief discussion of some of the main
contradictions and antagonisms affecting and dividing women:

1. The primary contradictions affecting women are the two main capitalist
   contradictions, both in their national and in their international manifestations. This means that the effect of imperialism upon the capitalist
   structures, processes and contradictions within a given country cannot
   be overlooked in the study of the oppression of women.
2. Sexism: Male dominance cuts across class lines and stems from male control over the means of production, exchange, and the conditions of physical and social reproduction.
3. Contradiction between capitalist women and working-class women: their
   different relationship to the means of production creates contradictory
   interests between working-class and capitalist women which are stronger
   than the common interests that the struggle against sexism may generate.
   The utopian notion of 'sisterhood' arises precisely in abstraction of irre-
   concilable class-based differences among women.
4. Antagonism between working-class men and working-class women:
   chronic unemployment generates a constant antagonism between
   working-class men and women. Because of the sex segregated nature of
   the labour market, the competition for jobs is more acute among women
   than between men and women. Nevertheless, as women are a reserve
   army of cheap labour that can be used to displace male workers, this antagonism is an ever-present feature of capitalism. It tends to remain latent
   in times of economic growth, but is likely to become exacerbated in times
   of economic crises. Politically, it supports sexism and the capitalist social
   order for it blocks the development of class solidarity within the working
   class as a whole.
5. Antagonism between 'middle-class' and working-class women: there are
   wide income, educational, occupational, and lifestyle differences among
   women that are readily perceived at the level of social stratification and
   which are mistakenly conceptualised as 'class' differences. Differences in
   socio-economic status are found among women who, structurally, belong

to the working class because they and/or their husbands make their living mainly or exclusively from the sale of their labour power. The material problems confronted by women from the 'middle class' are different from those of working-class women only in their outward manifestations. Manual workers, white-collar workers, professional and career women face different struggles in the context of their work. Also, many 'middle-class' women are able to pursue their interests because of paid domestic labour and the labour of low-paid administrative and clerical workers. The common structural situation shared by all women workers is obscured by this antagonism that stands in the way of the development of working-class solidarity among women workers.

The complex relationship between capitalist contradictions, sexism, and the split in the productive process which determines the position of women, and the specific contradictions and antagonisms affecting women, are the same in all capitalist countries. Their observable manifestations, however, vary from country to country. There is no capitalist country where the working class is not only fragmented along sexual lines but also along occupational, racial, and ethnic lines. This produces a struggle for survival that pits men against women, status groups against status groups, dominant ethnic groups against ethnic minorities, and the latter against each other and against women, and so on.

Sexism, together with racism and status distinctions, is thus one of the ways in which men and women are oppressed within capitalist countries and become conscious of the class struggle and fight it. This means that awareness of class antagonisms tends to be obscured by the more immediate awareness of interpersonal and intergroup conflicts which thus contribute to maintaining unchanged the structural source of those conflicts. This statement does not deny the reality or the pain associated with those forms of social oppression; it simply indicates that they all have a common source which must be taken into consideration at some point if those forms of oppression are to be effectively overcome.

The Scientific and Political Relevance of Marxism for Feminism

The analysis of the position of women presented above, although incomplete, illustrates the importance of the theoretical contribution of Marxism to the understanding of sexism within capitalism, and suggests important avenues of theoretical and empirical inquiry. Perhaps the most important point of the discussion, at this level, is the identification of the common grounds for Marxist and sociological concerns and of the basis for the critical integration of the sociological analysis of sex differentiation and sex stratification with the Marxist analysis of the specifically capitalist structural and superstructural supports for those processes. The basis for that integration is given by the Marxist argument that the capitalist contradictions and the interests of the capitalist class impose limitations to empirical variations in sex differentiation and sex stratification within capitalist countries. Theoretical and empirical investigation of their historically possible range of variability within a given country at a given time would not only increase the scientific understanding of capitalist processes but would also provide feminists with a realistic basis for the evaluation of their short- and long-run political objectives.

The relevance of the Marxist analysis of sexism is not only scientific but also political. Marxist theory provides feminists with guidelines for acquiring knowledge of the structured limitations and possibilities available to women at a given stage in the development of the capitalist mode of production. It increases the value of that knowledge as a basis for sound political practice because it stresses the relevance of determining both the historically specific influences exerted upon those possibilities by the superstructure and by national and international circumstances which affect each country in which such analyses are formulated. It provides knowledge of the concrete links between sexism and capitalism, its contradictions, structures, and processes; and it elucidates the inherent limitations of feminism if, as a movement, it remains isolated from the class struggle.

From a Marxist perspective, feminists have two options:

1. To remain focused purely on improvements in the status of women and carry on an economic, political, and ideological struggle for the rights of women to economic self-sufficiency, full social and political participation, and self-definition in terms of personal achievement. On the basis of the analysis presented above, it can be argued that such a struggle may succeed in achieving changes in the following areas: a) sex differentiation or division of labour (within and outside the household); b) sex stratification or power differences between the sexes (within and outside the household). Such changes would be concretely manifested in a more egalitarian division of labour within the home, increased participation of women in the labour force in the most challenging and best paid positions, and an increased ability to control their lives actively and effectively.

A mere listing of those possibilities indicates that such changes support the interests of the capitalist class. Given that changes at the level market and social relations leave untouched the basic structures of the capitalist mode of production – including sexism – such gains do not imply a change in the position of women as a whole but, on the contrary, the advancement of some women while the majority remain at the bottom of the job and pay scales. Although improvements in the status of women are important and the increase in the number of professional and career women may be viewed as a good sign that better times are coming for women, it must not be forgotten that improvements that affect individual women can take place without changes which may improve the position of all women. This means that so long as feminists struggle only for those goals, the advancement of 'middle-class' women will continue to be predicated on the continued exploitation of the majority of women who, through their labour in factories, offices, and other women's homes, provide the structural support for their sisters' privileged 'liberated' status. Furthermore, given the constraints which the contradictions of the capitalist mode of production exert upon the size and composition of the labour force, whatever gains 'middle-class' and working-class women may achieve will be inherently unstable and will be dependent on the fluctuations of the business cycles and on the immediate political interests of the capitalist class.

It is therefore of key importance for feminists to keep in mind Marx's warning:

> Men [and women] make their own history, but they do not make it just as they please; they do not make it under circumstances chosen by themselves, but under circumstances directly encountered, given, and transmitted from the past. The traditions of all the dead generations weigh like a nightmare on the brain of the living. And just when they seem engaged in revolutionizing themselves and things, in creating something that has never yet existed, precisely in such periods of revolutionary crisis they anxiously conjure up the spirits of the past to their service and borrow from them names, battle cries and costumes ...[10]

To the extent that feminists turn to the past for guidance, and search for goddesses and matriarchies; to the extent that feminists seek to play again the struggles for civil, political, and economic rights and raise the banner of equality; to that extent women will simply gain entrance to the deceptive life of the political community in which their social, political and economic equality implies also their full membership in capitalist society. They will be active as private individuals, they will use others as means to their own ends, and reduce themselves to the role of playthings of powers outside themselves. To

---

10   Marx 1969, p. 15.

the abolition of privileges associated with birth, property, status, religion, and race, feminism would add the suppression of privileges based on male supremacy. As the abolition of the privileges associated with property does not abolish property, as the black experience shows that the abolition of the privileges associated with white supremacy does not abolish racism, women will learn through long and arduous struggle that the abolition of the privileges associated with male supremacy does not abolish sexism.[11]

2. The second option is to link the feminist struggle to the struggle of the working class: Theoretically, it means that the problems and goals of women should not be analysed in isolation from the contradictions, structures, and processes of the capitalist mode of production. Practically, it means using the theoretical insights and research findings of Marxism as tools to further the understanding of sexism. Feminists must rethink, in the light of Marxist theory, the many problems, setbacks, and successes which arise in the course of women's individual and collective struggle for existence, selfhood and self-determination. It is in this context that the crucial problem of the relationship between professional and nonprofessional women arises. While professional women and 'middle-class' women in general run the risk of becoming isolated from the needs, concerns, and consciousness of working-class and nonprofessional women, the latter run the risk of falling into an anti-intellectualism that contributes to their oppression because it stands in the way of their attaining a clear analysis of their situation. Pursuing endless theoretical refinements that are never translated into dialogue and practical action is as ineffective as engaging in endless talks about personal problems and feelings without ever looking at them as social problems. These problems are social, not only in the sense of being shared by many women, but more importantly because they are socially determined and are the product of concrete and historically specific class, legal, and political relations and forms of consciousness.

Consciousness-raising should mean, therefore, moving from the personal level where women's position in capitalist society is analysed in terms of individual, social, economic, political, and sexual problems associated with femaleness, to class consciousness where those specific, painful, concrete forms of personal oppression are linked to their roots in the common fate of women who, like male wage and salary earners, own nothing but their labour power and depend on its sale in order to support themselves and their families.

---

11   This argument relies heavily on Marx's analysis of the limitations of civil liberties within capitalism. See Marx 1994, pp. 2–21.

Feminist consciousness is, therefore, a double-edged weapon. In itself, isolated from the analysis of the broader capitalist forces that buttress sexism, it can only formulate limited goals and guide struggles likely to attain reforms of limited impact upon the liberation of all women. On the other hand, if linked to the analysis of capitalism, it can provide a key step in the process of the development of working-class consciousness and the struggle for the liberation of both men and women.

Because this work has been focused upon women's problems, interests, and goals, nothing has been said about men except that, structurally, they are more powerful than women. It is nevertheless obvious that women cannot achieve liberation independently from men. This means that the position of women in the mode of production cannot be radically changed without concomitant and equally radical changes in the position of men. As long as 'liberation' is narrowly defined in terms of socio-economic equality with men within the present conditions, such 'liberation' does not preclude the continued struggle against sexism within and outside the household, and it is nothing but an illusion that ensures the continued social oppression and economic exploitation of both men and women. Because sexism cuts across classes, it obscures the real powerlessness of working-class men and misleads working women into believing that all men are the enemy and that all women are potential allies. Under capitalist conditions, both men and women work under conditions of alienated labour. This means that workers develop their talents and skills because of their market value rather than as an expression of creativity; they have no control over the labour process and its product; and they are placed in constant competition with each other. An important way in which alienated labour is made bearable is through sexism and sexist ideologies that give men the illusion of power and superiority over women and which give women the dubious 'power of sexual surrender'. (There are other forces for divisiveness, such as religion, bigotry, racism, and consumerism). The power sexism confers upon working-class men, although real and concrete in its painful consequences for women and in the material advantages it may bring to men, is also – like all 'powers' that capitalism bestows upon the oppressed – an illusion that lasts as long as the system can profitably provide men with the economic means to control women. To overlook the fact that sexism dehumanises and contributes to the exploitation of both men and women leads to the isolation of the feminist struggle from the class struggle and the adoption of limited goals which may lead to the 'liberation' of some women in the short run and which may further the oppression of all in the long run.

Conclusion

The two options discussed above are historical ones whose significance can best be understood in the context of the development of feminist consciousness and feminist struggle within a given country at a given time. The development of feminist consciousness through the analysis of visible relationships and the possibility of changing those relations is an important step in the development of class consciousness. The limitations of that reformist approach can be learned in the course of struggling for those goals and the assessment, at the same time, of the present struggles in terms of both theory and of the lessons from the past. This activity presupposes the full development of the scientific contribution of Marxism and also requires going beyond the widespread antagonism towards rigorous intellectual practice on the grounds of its 'male' nature. Scientific analysis is necessary because, as members of capitalist society, women do become aware of their subordinate position in terms of experience and observable relationships; who does what within the home, who learns what at school, what kinds of work they can obtain and how much they are paid, how their status depends on the status of their fathers and husbands, how men have more power to initiate and terminate relationships, how they find themselves always apologising, temporising, smoothing situations, smiling away their powerlessness.

The conceptualisation of phenomena 'everyone knows' and has experienced in terms of sex stratification and sex differentiation, as well as the specification of their links to the capitalist mode of production, is more than an academic game. It is necessary to help women differentiate between those levels of social reality which they know because they consciously and painfully live through them, and those levels which, although perceived with the help of scientific analysis, are nevertheless as real as the others. A realisation of the differences between those levels as well as their interconnections leads to an understanding of the reason why, even though changes in the division of labour within and outside the home may take place, women find through their daily experience that sexism remains unchanged. Sexism, in other words, persists despite changes in occupations, division of labour in the home, salary improvements, and access to managerial positions. To be aware of capitalist contradictions, structures, and processes as aspects of social reality that remain indifferent to such changes is, therefore, important not only scientifically but also at the level of personal and collective awareness. It thus becomes possible for women to understand why, although they may follow what appear to be the rules of the game to 'liberate' themselves, the struggle is nonetheless permanent, a ceaseless combat against sexism within and outside themselves.

In the absence of a rigorous analysis of the social forces and relations that remain unchanged despite changes in women's education, employment, and income, it is easy to turn inward and return to self-recrimination and blame. Feminism, isolated from theoretical and practical links to the class struggle, eventually will lead 'middle-class' women back to the psychiatrist's couch or to some form of collective therapy. More importantly, it will unwittingly contribute to division and political paralysis within the working-class movement and will further the maintenance of the oppression and economic exploitation of working-class women.

The move from a purely feminist consciousness to class consciousness is a long and complex process likely to vary from country to country according to its historically specific circumstances and to its place within the world capitalist network. This process does not imply the replacement of feminist consciousness by class consciousness, but the transcendence of that dichotomy into a class consciousness that embraces not only awareness of economic exploitation but also sexual oppression and the other forms of social oppression which may be prevalent in a given country. It is a class consciousness which views concern with sexual, ethnic, cultural, and racial oppression not as a manifestation of 'false consciousness' but as a first step in understanding the many faces of exploitation and as the formulation of concrete goals without which the notion of liberation loses meaning. From a Marxist standpoint, the feminist struggle for women's equality should be linked to the working-class struggle for liberation which is the struggle for the material conditions that will render possible the actual practice of equality.

CHAPTER 2

Structuralist Marxism on the Oppression of Women

'The Oppression of Women: A Structuralist Marxist View', in *Structural Sociology*, edited by Ino Rossi, New York: Columbia University Press, 1982, pp. 292–324.[1]

'Structuralist Marxism on "The Woman Question"', in *Science and Society*, Vol. XLII, No. 3 (Fall 1978): 301–23.

Modern feminism has led to the emergence of an ever-growing body of literature seeking to ascertain, using social science and Marxist theories, the origin of the oppression of women, the reasons for its perpetuation throughout history, its functions in contemporary society, and the conditions that would lead to its demise. The heterogeneous class, racial and ethnic composition of the women's movement as well as the differences in the academic training of individual writers are reflected in the political splits within the movement and in the theoretical and methodological heterogeneity of these writings. More importantly, as intellectual productions rooted in a historically specific political and ideological conjuncture, these writings have been affected by the hegemony of idealist and empiricist assumptions underlying current common sense views of the world, social science paradigms, and dominant interpretations of Marxism. Indeed, idealist (i.e. Hegelian, phenomenological, humanistic, existentialist, psychological, voluntaristic) versions of Marxism seem to be more acceptable and respectable within feminist, Marxist, and non-Marxist academic and non-academic circles in the US. On the other hand, theoretical developments that claim to maintain the dialectical materialist outlook of classical Marxism and stress the non-subjective dimension of social processes are generally ignored or criticised and dismissed on the grounds of their alleged determinism, economism, or functionalism.

An interesting case in point that highlights the nature of the parameters governing intellectual production in the US today is the absence of Structuralist Marxism from American feminist theory. Neither non-Marxist social scientists

---

1 This chapter combines a previously published article (Gimenez 1978) and a chapter (Gimenez 1982).

seeking new ideas for theory construction nor feminists sympathetic to Marxism seem to have found Structuralist Marxism compelling enough to warrant some consideration.

An investigation of the complex historical determinants of this theoretical conjuncture is beyond the scope of this chapter, which is intended, primarily, as an exploration of the potential relevance of Structuralist Marxism for the development of a Marxist theory of women's oppression under capital. The noted feminist Juliet Mitchell once made a suggestion which has been taken with approval by most other feminists attempting to develop a Marxist analysis of the oppression of women: 'We should ask feminist questions, but try to come up with some Marxist answers'.[2] In my view, the only way to come up with Marxist answers is to begin by asking Marxist questions. For that purpose, Structuralist Marxism offers important conceptual tools conducive to the formulation of Marxist questions and the elaboration of Marxist analyses of concrete issues: analyses that go beyond the use of Marxist categories in isolation from the logic of Marxist theory and methodology.

In the first section of this chapter, I shall offer a summary version of important Structuralist Marxist theoretical and methodological contributions. In the second section, I shall critically examine some sociological and feminist theoretical statements, and in the third section, I shall present theoretical and methodological insights obtained by approaching the question of the oppression of women in the light of Structuralist Marxism. While Structuralist Marxism is not exempt from problems, it is my contention that a judicious incorporation of its major insights into the analysis of the oppression of women cannot but further our understanding of its structural supports and the conditions necessary to overcome them.

Structuralist Marxism: Theoretical and Methodological Issues

Structuralist Marxism is not a fully developed theory; it is a descriptive label, which, although rejected by those to whom it is applied, is currently used to indicate the heterogeneous production of Marxists who have introduced structuralist terminology into their writings and have acknowledged some degree of overlap between structuralist and Marxist principles. The most important representatives are Louis Althusser and Maurice Godelier and it is with their work that this chapter will be primarily concerned.

---

2 Mitchell 1971, p. 99.

The reason why Structuralist Marxism has had a deep impact on the development of Marxist scholarship is because it articulates fundamental methodological principles and theoretical constructs which were largely tacit in classical Marxist works. Godelier convincingly argues that the two main principles of structuralism were discovered by Marx, who can thus be considered as 'a forerunner of the modern structuralist movement'.[3]

The first principle is that '*a structure is part of social reality but not of visible relationships*'.[4] This principle has the following implications:

A.   *There are two levels of social reality:* The level of visible social relationships and the level of invisible structures whose laws of functioning and transformation account for changes at the observable level.

B.   *The aim of scientific study is to discover those hidden structures.* Marx's scientific project was precisely that of the discovery of the structure and laws of motion of the capitalist mode of production concealed by the visible reality created by its functioning.

C.   *The systematic study of appearances cannot provide a scientific knowledge of social reality.*

D.   *This failure to attain knowledge taking appearances as a starting point is not a cognitive failure.* The concealment of the structure by appearance is inherent in the nature of the structure itself. Structures are made up of social relations that cannot be directly apprehended, for they vanish behind forms of physical or social objectification. For example, capital appears as machines, money, etc.

E.   *To each structure corresponds a form of appearance.* And scientific study must take into account both, explaining the appearance in terms of the structure.

F.   *To each structure corresponds a form of consciousness or spontaneous representations held by individuals whose activities reproduce the structure.* The systematic study of those representations, far from disclosing the underlying logic of the structure, can only reproduce, at the level of theory, the mystifications created by the very functioning of the structure.

The second principle of structuralism is that '*the study of the internal functioning of a structure must precede and will throw light on the study of its coming to being and subsequent evolution*'.[5] The historical analysis of the emergence of the constituent elements of a structure and their interrelations presupposes a

---

3   Godelier 1970, p. 343.
4   Godelier 1970, p. 347.
5   Godelier 1970, p. 347.

prior knowledge of the structure and its processes. Thus, Marx presents his brief historical discussion of the genesis of primitive accumulation *after* the basic structure, processes, and contradictions of capitalism have been identified.[6] After the structural level of social reality has been discovered, the next step is that of establishing the articulation between that structure and its observable manifestations which can now be defined according to their 'real function in the system and their internal compatibility with the essential structures already studied'. This process amounts to the description of 'the ideal birth of the various elements of a system on the basis of its internal laws of composition'.[7] This 'ideal birth' or 'ideal genesis' of categories cannot be confused with their historical or real genesis. Godelier argues that Marx's stress on the priority of structural over historical analysis 'is total and anticipates by more than half a century the radical rethinking in linguistics and sociology which led de Saussure and Lowie to reject the evolutionist approach of the 19th century'.[8] Marx is very specific in this respect:

> It would be impractical and wrong to arrange the economic categories in the order in which they were the determining factors in the course of history. Their order of sequence is rather determined by the relation which they bear to one another in modern bourgeois society, and which is the exact opposite of what seems to be their natural order or the order of their historical development ... [W]e are interested in their organic connections within modern bourgeois society.[9]

This is an important principle which establishes the difference between Marxist historical analysis and history as chronology or as the study of arbitrary periodisations based, for example, on the dominance of specific ideas or of 'great men'. It indicates the methodological priority of the theoretical investigation of the mode of production as a whole over the historical investigation of the real (i.e. chronological) origin of its isolated elements.

The two main methodological principles of Structuralist Marxism have been presented. It is now necessary to examine the Structuralist Marxist contribution to the analysis of historical phenomena: the concepts of mode of production and social formation. Mode of production is a theoretical construct

---

6   Godelier 1970, pp. 348–50.
7   Godelier 1970, p. 352.
8   Godelier 1970, p. 353.
9   Marx 1972, pp. 41–2.

that denotes the historically specific combination of the elements of the production process (labourers, non-labourers, and means of production) in the content of structurally compatible political, legal, and ideological structures. These elements are combined in two kinds of relations: relations of 'real or material appropriation' or technical relations of production (e.g. cooperation, manufacturing, modern industry, automation); and 'property connections' or social relations of production which are the relationships between labourers and non-labourers mediated through their property relations to the means of production. In the capitalist mode of production, these are the relations between capitalists and wage workers.[10] The forces of production, which cannot be considered as things or techniques taken in themselves, are all the factors of production in their historically specific combination within the process of production, considered from the standpoint of their actual and potential productivity.[11] Modes of production differ qualitatively from one another in the way in which unpaid surplus labour is extracted from the direct producers. The mode of surplus extraction corresponds to the level of development of the productive forces and the nature of the relations of production and constitutes the unifying principle of the mode of production as a whole.[12]

The concept mode of production is an abstract one that captures the fundamental features that constitute the organising principle of the economic, legal, political, and ideological structures that characterise different historical epochs. Empirically, in a given social formation, modes of production are always found in varied combinations with other modes of production. In the structuralist reading of Marx, the alternative to the abstract notion of society is the concept of social formation, a 'complex structured whole where the mode of production is determinant "in the last instance" and the superstructure (legal, political, and ideological structures) is relatively autonomous'.[13] In all social formations it is possible to identify the following: a complex economic base formed by the historically specific articulation of several modes of production one of which is always dominant; and a complex superstructure whose elements have forms and functions the origins of which can be traced to the different modes of production that make up the economic base.[14] Scientific analysis must be aimed at establishing first the nature of the hierarchical articulation of modes of production (i.e. the specific ways in which

---

10   Althusser and Balibar 1970, p. 215.
11   Althusser and Balibar 1970, pp. 233–41.
12   Marx 1968, pp. 791–2.
13   Althusser 1970, p. 111.
14   Godelier 1978, p. 63.

the dominant mode of production subjects the others to its own requirements and transforms them into conditions of its own reproduction) and, second, the nature of the hierarchical articulation among the elements of the super-structure which is also constituted as a set of conditions for the reproduction of the dominant mode of production.[15] The structure of the superstructure reflects the articulation of the economic base; it overdetermines the base as it reproduces it in historically specific ways – ways peculiar to the characteristics of the social formation being considered. On the other hand, the economic base determines the superstructure 'in the last instance', through a system of internal constraints which has its origins in the material conditions of production and expresses the conditions of reproduction for the dominant mode of production. The structural compatibility between the form and content of the elements of the superstructure and the system of constraints is itself a structural effect of the system of constraints which ensures the reproduction of the mode of production. It is, consequently, through the structural effects of the system of constraints, which simultaneously affect all the elements of the social formation, that the mode of production determines, in the last instance, the overall structure of the social formation as well as the form and function of its instances.[16] The category of determination 'in the last instance' has a twofold theoretical importance: it reaffirms the materialist philosophical standpoint of Marxism (it is the base that determines the superstructure, not vice versa) and, at the same time, it stresses the dialectical nature of the Marxist concept of determination by making explicit the relative autonomy and causal efficacy of the other instances of the social formation which, in turn, 'overdetermine' the base.[17]

Modes of production based on the private ownership of the means of production are inherently contradictory and subject to qualitative changes brought about by the operation of those contradictions. Given that the mode of production is the locus of the two main contradictions of capitalism (the contradiction between capital and labour and the contradiction between the forces and the relations of production), the fact that the mode of production is 'overdetermined by the superstructure means that those contradictions are never found "active in the pure state but, on the contrary," overdetermined ... always specified by the historically concrete forms and circumstances in which it is exercised'.[18] This process of specification operates from the different ele-

---

15   Godelier 1978, p. 63.
16   Godelier 1978, pp. 52–3.
17   Althusser 1976, p. 177; see also Althusser 1970, pp. 89–128.
18   Althusser 1970, p. 106.

ments of the social formation and includes the national and international circumstances affecting the social formation at a given time. Whatever the nature of those processes, 'in the last instance' it is in the internal and contradictory properties of the mode of production that the crucial source of change is to be found. Godelier makes this point as follows:

> whether the causes ... [of change] are external or internal they only have an effect because they bring into play (and are made to act as final causes) the structural properties of systems ... these properties are always, in the final count, immanent in this system, explaining the unintentional role of its functioning.[19]

Althusser makes a similar point:

> For Marxism the explanation of any phenomenon is in the last instance *internal*: it is the *internal* 'contradiction' which is the 'motor.' The external circumstances are active: but 'through' the internal contradiction which they over-determine.[20]

Within class-based modes of production, structures are thus both complementary and contradictory; the relationship of complementarity through which the mode of production is reproduced throughout time is, at the same time, unstable and operates within limits beyond which contradictions assert themselves. Within capitalism, the contradiction between the forces and the relations of production emerges as the unintentional product of the objective property of various structures and their interrelationship, including the class struggle; it is not a consciously willed result. Quoting Marx's concise statement of this key point, 'the real barrier of capitalist accumulation is capital itself',[21] Godelier stresses the non-teleological nature of the processes leading to the demise of capitalism and the creation of the material conditions for the rise of socialism. It is not 'the revolt of the "true essence" of man against the "dehumanized existence" imposed on the workers by the bourgeoisie',[22] but the social processes generated by the objective properties of the forces and the relations of production that necessitates the emergence of socialism.

---

19   Godelier 1878, p. 37.
20   Althusser 1976, p. 80, emphasis in the text.
21   Godelier 1970, p. 353.
22   Godelier 1970, p. 355.

Through his emphasis upon the analysis of structures, their hierarchical articulation, objective properties, and conditions of emergence, reproduction, and change, Godelier makes a methodological point similar to that expressed by Althusser's dictum: 'History is a process without a Subject or Goals'.[23] While individuals act *in* history within the parameters set by modes of production, they are not, Althusser argues, the *subjects of* history in a philosophical sense. It is Althusser's aim to establish a clear-cut difference between idealistic inter-pretations of history based upon the identification of a Subject (Man, God, the Human Race, the transcendental ego, etc.) as the Origin, Cause, and Goal of History, and the Marxist historical and dialectical materialist view of history as the history of modes of production unfolding in terms of the class struggle: while history lacks a Subject, it does have a *motor*: the class struggle.[24]

Althusser's theoretical anti-humanism is thus akin to Godelier's anti-teleo-logical standpoint. Both are rooted in their appraisal of the scientific import-ance of the theoretical and methodological discoveries of the mature Marx. In their view, Marx's analysis of the processes whereby capitalist development creates the material conditions for its own end and for the rise of a new mode of production does not rest upon a philosophical anthropology or upon a theory of the human essence; it rests, on the contrary, on the scientific investigation of the material conditions surrounding the emergence, development, and dis-appearance of historically specific modes of production. Both are concerned with delimiting the boundaries between Marxism as a science, and Marxism as an idealistic, humanistic ideology; they do so by stressing the anti-humanistic, anti-historicist, anti-psychologistic nature of the Marxist method. It is precisely this methodological standpoint which makes it possible to formulate specific-ally Marxist questions and come up with Marxist answers.

I have outlined and discussed some of Althusser's and Godelier's most sig-nificant insights. Given the specific objective of this chapter, I have neither explored the full range of their contributions to Marxist theory nor the extent of their political and theoretical differences. The question of the relative import-ance of structuralism in their reading of Marx is, however, pertinent to this work and I shall examine it briefly.

Althusser argues that the rationalistic, mechanistic, and formalistic tend-encies of structuralism are antithetical to Marxism; he pleads guilty to 'a very ambiguous flirtation with structuralist terminology'[25] and emphatically denies

---

23   Althusser 1976, p. 94.
24   Althusser 1976, pp. 94–9, emphasis and capitalised words in the text.
25   Althusser 1978, p. 128.

any commitment to structuralism. On the other hand, Althusser identifies an area of overlap between Marxism and structuralism: both reject historicist, psychologistic explanations of social phenomena. It was precisely in the effort to formulate his Marxist thesis of theoretical anti-humanism that Althusser found it necessary to borrow structuralist terminology without, at the same time, adopting structuralism in its entirety.[26] Althusser, for whom the class struggle is the motor of history, cannot be appropriately described as a structuralist. Godelier, on the contrary, finds a greater convergence between Marxism and structuralism. He considers Marx as a forerunner of modern structuralism and, more importantly, he seems to have incorporated, in his analysis of social change, the mechanistic tendencies of structuralism. To my knowledge, the class struggle is absent from Godelier's work, where modes of production succeed one another purely through the mechanistic operation of the objective properties of their structures. While Althusser might agree with Godelier's rejection of purely idealistic, humanistic justifications of the necessity of socialism, he would most certainly disagree with Godelier's assumption about the automatic nature of the process. This theoretical and political difference does not, in my view, invalidate Godelier's methodological contributions. After all, a crucial feature of Marxist 'theoretical practice' (and the works of Marx, Engels, and Lenin are an object lesson on this point) is the critical dialogue with one's theoretical opponents. In the sections that follow I hope to show, through my own 'theoretical practice', the significance of Althusser's and Godelier's insights for the analysis of the oppression of women.[27]

A Critical Look at Current Perspectives on Sexual Inequality

Empirically, at the level of 'visible relationships' and personal, immediate experience, women's disadvantages appear and are experienced as men's advantages. Social scientists have produced abundant historical and cross-cultural

---

26   Ibid.

27   In the Althusserian framework, the notion of practice refers to 'any process of *transformation* of a determinate given raw material into a determinate *product*, a transformation effected by a determinant human labour, using determinate means (of "production")' (Althusser 1970, p. 106, original emphasis). Theory is a 'specific form of practice' in which intellectual labour transforms existing concepts (raw materials) – themselves the products of previous practices – into knowledges (products) through the use of theoretical tools. Theoretical practice must be understood in a materialist way (i.e. in the historical conjuncture that makes it possible) to avoid failing into a theoreticist error. (For further elaboration of this point, see Althusser 1976, pp. 119–25).

evidence documenting the different rewards, power, and prestige allocated to men and women by past and present societies. This has shaped the questions that have been raised about the origins of the oppression of women and the conditions that reproduce it through time. Questions about the oppression of *women* unavoidably become questions about the power of *men*, and about the differences between the sexes that may account for the ubiquity of sexual inequality. This 'men vs. women' problematic has been reinforced by the dominant empiricist approach to the question of socialism and its impact on the status of women. Socialism is a transitional stage between two modes of production, capitalism and communism; it is characterised by a contradictory combination of features pertaining to both modes and, consequently, by heightened class struggles. Like the transition from feudalism to capitalism, the socialist transition is a complex and protracted process whose impact upon people's lives should be assessed taking into consideration the lessons from the past as well as the unique characteristics of each socialist social formation and its place in the international political conjuncture. The dominant view, however, suggests that socialism has already happened and has not fulfilled its promises, particularly with respect to women. Accepting this view means judging the socialist experience ahistorically, from the standpoint of an ideal model of what socialism should be. Taken thus outside its historical context, the persistence of sexual inequality in the socialist countries is unwarrantedly perceived as 'proof' that changes in the mode of production will not liberate women. This, together with the obvious fact that sexism predates capitalism, has lent support to the conceptualisation of sexism independently from modes of production and to the search for its origins (in the chronological sense) and mechanisms of support elsewhere. Given this formulation of the problem, what kinds of theoretical insights have been produced?

Sociologically, an early and influential explanation for sexual inequality was found in the interaction between sex differentiation and sex stratification. Sex differentiation refers to the division of labour by sex within and outside the family. In contemporary society, occupational roles are the core of the male role cluster, while family roles are at the core of the female role cluster. Sex stratification refers to the different power and prestige attached to the male and female roles. Differential power and prestige stem from individuals' differential access to socially valued scarce resources. Sex differentiation, in confining women to household tasks, childbearing, and childrearing, has impaired their opportunity to secure wealth and power in comparison to men. Functional sex differentiation or sexual division of labour would appear as the source of sex stratification as well as the condition for its maintenance: 'sex stratification, like other functional differentiations, entail a *"rank ordering"* of the position of men and women. It is noted that this tendency towards *rank differentiation* has a feedback effect that contributes to the support of the underlying functional differentiation.[28]

Current patterns of sex differentiation or sexual division of labour which assign public roles to men while relegating women primarily to domesticity became the core of feminist theorising about the determinants of women's oppression. Collapsing the two levels of analysis, differentiation or division of labour and stratification or differences in status and power, the notion of hierarchical sexual division of labour was developed to denote the power differences between the sexes linked to the sexual division of labour reflected in the public/private split. Projected into the past, the hierarchical sexual division of labour served as the basis for a theory of patriarchy, a social system in which men oppress women, as the earliest form of social organisation.

Firestone argues that sex class (male dominance) stems from men's and women's unequal biological roles in procreation.[29] The fact that women bear children and care for them during the lengthy period of dependency required by human infants to develop has placed them, from the beginning, in a situation in which their physical survival as well as that of their children was dependent on their relationship to men. Inequality, in her view, is thus inherent in the biological family, structurally and psychologically. The type of psychosexual development determined by biological inequality generates a need for power as a crucial dimension of male personality, which eventually results in the development of class societies. Class differences have their root, therefore, in sex class which, in turn, rises from the biological inequality between the sexes linked to procreation.

Firestone's biological determinism has found few supporters. More recent theories about the origins of male dominance give, like Firestone, a determinant role to the family, to sexual and reproductive relations, and to the type of psychosexual development generated within the family. Representative of the major trends in American Feminist theory today are the works of Rubin,[30] Chodorow,[31] and Eisenstein[32] whose contributions I shall briefly outline.

Rubin's two major contributions to feminist theory are the following:

---

28   Holter 1973, p. 53, emphasis added.
29   Firestone 1970.
30   Rubin 1975.
31   Chdorow 1978.
32   Einsenstein 1979.

1.   The notion of sex/gender system, a societal universal that denotes the existence, in all societies, of 'a set of social arrangements by which the biological raw material of human sex and procreation is shaped by human intervention'.[33]

2.   A theory of the oppression of women based on Lévi-Strauss's theory of kinship, and on the psychoanalytic theory of gender formation. The origin of human society, for Lévi-Strauss, is the incest taboo which ensures the exchange of women between kinship groups. Marriage is not a relationship between individuals but an exchange relation between kinship groups that reinforces a sexual division of labour that makes the interdependence between the sexes essential for their survival. Rubin carries Lévi-Strauss's analysis further by arguing that because men exchange women (whereas women can neither exchange women nor exchange themselves), the sexual division of labour thus created is inherently oppressive. The exchange of women generates enforced heterosexuality, the social repression of female sexuality, and the creation of gender identity in ways that repress the natural similarities between the sexes. The stages of psychosexual development articulated by Freud are, on the other hand, the processes through which male dominance and female oppression are perpetuated. In Rubin's view, there is a 'striking fit' between Lévi-Strauss and Freud, which implies that the sex/gender system today 'is still organized by the principles outlined by Lévi-Strauss'.[34]

For Rubin, the value of Lévi-Strauss's and Freud's works lies not only in the importance of the questions they raise, but also in the fact that their theories are conducive to the development of an analysis of sex and gender in isolation from the mode of production.[35] She does point out, on the other hand, that as sex, politics, and economics are interrelated, a complete analysis of women should take 'everything' into account.

At the highest level of abstraction the concept of sex/gender system denotes a social science truism; i.e. the fact that the personality structure associated with gender, sex roles, sex stratification, and kinship relations is socially determined. To say that every society has a sex/gender system is as enlightening as to acknowledge that every society has an economic system; both are 'sensible abstractions' that follow from the fact that at all times, 'the subject, mankind, and the object, nature, are the same'.[36] However, as Marx points out,

---

33   Rubin 1975, p. 165.
34   Rubin 1975, p. 198.
35   Rubin 1975, p. 203.
36   Marx 1970a, p. 190.

'even the most abstract categories, despite their validity in all epochs ... are equally a product of historical conditions even in the specific form of abstractions, and they retain their full validity only for and within the framework of these conditions'.[37] From the standpoint of Marxist theory, a major problem with the use of ahistorical categories like sex/gender system is that questions about the historical conditions determining their full validity – i.e. questions about their historically specific origins and underlying conditions of reproduction – are displaced by questions about their historical and cross-cultural variations. Such categories are mere empty vessels to be 'filled' with empirical 'content'; theory is replaced with description and taxonomy, and the discovery of empirical correlations pre-empts the task of theoretical investigation as a prerequisite for significant empirical research. Studies about the historical and cross-cultural variations of the sex/gender system could provide useful descriptions and predictions about, for example, the kinds of institutional factors likely to be correlated with a given kind of sex/gender system; those findings, however, would not provide an explanation, because questions about the underlying, hidden, historically specific structures, processes, and contradictions that produce those empirically observable phenomena remain outside the purview of such approaches to the study of social reality. But there are other considerations that limit the usefulness of this concept. It can be used descriptively, as a shorthand way to refer to several levels of analysis: gender identity, sexual and reproductive behaviour, sex differentiation, sex stratification; or it can be synonymous with kinship system. Theoretically, on the other hand, the concept offers no clue as to the nature of the system to which it presumably refers; it does not specify the nature of the interrelationship between its elements except, of course, at the meta-theoretical level established on the basis of Lévi-Strauss's and Freud's works. Given its ahistorical origins and conditions of reproduction (the exchange of women, the Oedipal struggle), questions about the historically specific determinants of each level, the historically specific way they might be interrelated and their 'mutual interdependence' with 'politics' and 'economics' are ultimately irrelevant. Sexual inequality, given that the social organisation of sex and gender rests upon gender identity as constructed through the Oedipal struggle, will only be abolished through qualitative changes in psychosexual development leading to the emergence of an androgynous, 'genderless' world.[38] The call for the abolition of differences as a sufficient condition for the abolition of inequality cannot but follow from an

---

37   Marx 1970a, p. 210.
38   Rubin 1975, p. 204.

analysis that postulates the identity between the two. This is also Chodorow's standpoint: historically and cross-culturally, it is impossible to separate the sexual division of labour from sexual inequality.[39]

Chodorow's[40] theory of the origins of male dominance and the conditions that reproduce it combine feminist theoretical insights with those of Parsons's sociology, psychoanalytic object relations theory, and the Frankfurt School's (particularly Horkheimer's) analysis of changes in the personality structure brought about by the impact of capitalism upon the family. For Chodorow, the root of male dominance is the universal fact that women mother; mothering and the reproduction of mothering have psychological and social consequences which create and perpetuate sexual inequality. Mothering is the unintentional effect – at the level of the personality structure – of the asymmetrical organisation of parenting. Women are the primary parent for both sexes, and that creates crucial differences in children's relational experiences, which determine qualitative differences in masculine and feminine personality. Women's sense of gender identity develops through the process of identification with their mothers in a context of primary relationships between them. The female role-learning process is thus characterised by diffuseness, affectivity, and particularism; and these features shape women's personality and women's roles inside and outside the family. Men, on the other hand, develop their gender identity and relational capacities through the denial of their first identification with their mothers and the development of secondary relations with their father in a content of affective neutrality. The male role-learning process is characterised by specificity, affective neutrality, and universalism and – because it rests upon the rejection of the mother and the devaluation of the feminine – it results in the development of a psychology and ideology of male dominance. Furthermore, the sex roles and occupational roles men and women find outside the family partake of similar characteristics: women's roles are essentially 'particularistic' and centred around the family and 'primary' interpersonal relations, while male roles are 'universalistic' and centred around the requirements of the organisation of production.

This is indeed an astonishing account. The 'fit' between Parsons's sociology and the discoveries resulting from the use of psychoanalytic object relations theory is as striking as the previously mentioned 'fit' between Lévi-Strauss and Freud. The private/public split mirrors the traditional/modern society dichotomy and Ortner's[41] (1974) question, 'Is Female to Male as Nature is to Cul-

---

39   Chodorow 1978, p. 214.
40   Chodorow 1978.
41   Ortner 1974, pp. 68–87.

ture?' could now be restated as 'Is Female to Male as Traditional Society is to Modern Society?' without increasing our comprehension of these issues. It is, undoubtedly, important to investigate the structural effects of the asymmetrical organisation of parenting to determine the extent to which the 'message' (if there is one) that is meta-communicated by the structure has its sources in the structure itself or in the historical context of which the structure is a part. Chodorow's analysis, in my view, only succeeds in legitimating Parsons's categories of analysis by endowing them with a veneer of universality and a-temporality grounded in the ahistorical fact of mothering.

Looking at the reproduction of mothering under capitalism, Chodorow points out that women's mothering in the isolated nuclear family 'reproduces both the ideology and the psychodynamic of male superiority and the submission to the requirements of production'.[42] Women's mothering during the transition to capitalism produced capitalists endowed with 'inner direction, rational planning and organization', and workers endowed with 'a willingness to come to work at certain hours and work steadily, whether or not they needed money that day'.[43] Today women's mothering produces a malleable 'other directed' personality characterised by a 'generalised achievement orientation' among the middle and upper middle classes (Parsons's argument, which emphasises the intense mother-child relationship that emerges in isolated nuclear families where fathers are relatively absent), and an 'authoritarian personality' among the working classes (the Frankfurt School argument that stresses the decline in the 'real' authority of the father brought about by the growth of wage labour and the concomitant vulnerability of workers to the market). Given the primacy given to mothering in determining sexual inequality and sex roles, it is not clear why it should produce such different effects. It would seem, rather, that inner direction and other direction as personality types have their origins outside the family and that mothers simply convey socially determined personality structures, sex roles, etc. Chodorow's efforts to introduce history into her analysis are not very successful because history remains external to the core of her theory: the universal fact of mothering. Her answers to critics who point out the basically ahistorical nature of her account[44] do not clarify the nature of the relationship between mothering, modes of production, personality structure, sexual differentiation, and sexual stratification.

42   Chodorow 1978, p. 181.
43   Chodorow 1978, p. 186.
44   See, for example, Chodorow 1978, pp. 215–16.

Einsenstein[45] develops her theory through a critique of Marx, Marxism in general, and radical feminism. Marx and Marxist theorists are guilty of 'breaking the real connections of everyday life' and of 'oversimplification of political reality', because they posit class exploitation as the primary contradiction.[46] Radical feminists are guilty of similar sins because they posit sexual oppression based on biological inequality as primary.[47] Marxists have an 'economic theory of power', while radical feminists have a 'sexual theory of power'. The alternative Eisenstein proposes is socialist feminism, an approach that seeks to integrate Marxism and radical feminism in a theory of capitalist patriarchy according to which capitalism and patriarchy are mutually interdependent.[48]

Patriarchy is defined as male power through sexual roles or relations of reproduction based on male control over reproduction. The basis for patriarchy is the 'sexual division of labour and society' which has 'material form (sex roles themselves) and ideological reality (the stereotypes, myths and ideas that define those roles)'.[49] The sexual division of labour and society has its origins in 'ideological and political interpretations of biological difference ... [M]en have chosen to interpret and politically use the fact that women are the reproducers of humanity'.[50] Patriarchy seems to be synonymous not only with sex roles and relations of reproduction but also with the family. Patriarchy and capitalism (i.e. family and economy) cannot be treated as separate systems because they are interrelated by the sexual division of labour and society which cuts across them and is 'at the base of them; because it divides men and women into their respective hierarchical sex roles and structures their related duties in the family domain and within the economy'.[51] Both systems are analytically irreducible to one another; they are functionally interdependent and responsive to each other's needs for self-perpetuation although their relationship is becoming increasingly 'uneasy' because the growth in women's participation in the labour force tends to undermine some aspects of patriarchal control.[52] Because of her reliance on Ollman's[53] interpretation of Marx's philosophy as a philosophy of internal relations, Eisenstein cannot avoid the pitfalls of multiple causality. This is reflected in the stress given to the mutual interdependence

---

45   Einsenstein 1979.
46   Einsenstein 1979, p. 21.
47   Einsenstein 1979, p. 18.
48   Einsenstein1979, p. 22.
49   Einsenstein 1979, pp. 24–5.
50   Einsenstein 1979, p. 25.
51   Einsenstein 1979, p. 27.
52   Einsenstein 1979, pp. 28–9.
53   Ollman 1971.

between capitalism and patriarchy throughout her work, which, however, does not yield very useful conclusions: capitalism uses patriarchy and patriarchy uses capitalism and both 'operate within the division of labour and society',[54] a rather confusing concept that seems to denote a reality that predates both capitalism and patriarchy.

Underlying these otherwise different perspectives is a theoretical analysis of sexism in isolation from modes of production, a standpoint that has serious theoretical and methodological drawbacks because it unerringly leads to the search for the chronological origins of the oppression of women while neglecting the historically specific context that surrounds concrete instances of sexual inequality.[55] This is tantamount to separating men and women from their historical conditions of existence; instead, they are thrown into the limbo of the genesis of human society where, isolated from concrete relations of production, they mate in a context that seems to unavoidably generate sexual inequality either because of biological 'inequality' in procreation (Firestone); because men exchange women (Rubin); because men 'choose' to control reproduction in order to oppress women (Eisenstein); because women mother (Chodorow); or because of functional, adaptive sex role differentiation based on women's role in procreation and childcare (Sociology). These are universal, ahistorical explanations that lead to the elaboration of universal, formal categories of analysis (e.g. sex class, sex/gender system, patriarchy, mothering, sexual division of labour and society, sexual differentiation, sexual stratification) themselves produced and perpetuated by unchanging and universal sexual, reproductive, and family relations. The content of those categories may vary through time because of their 'interrelationship' or 'mutual interdependence' with social institutions. Nevertheless, they persist in spite of qualitative changes in modes of social organisation because their origins as well as the conditions for their continuity and change have been postulated independently from modes of production, as if the forces of historical change were impotent to substantially change the nature of sexual, procreative, and parental relations and their impact on individuals' psychosexual development.

---

54   Einsenstein 1979, p. 27.
55   For a trenchant non-Marxist critique of this perspective, see Rosaldo 1980.

The Structuralist Marxist Alternative

From the standpoint of Structural Marxism, the key to developing an adequate explanation of sexual inequality is to be found not in individual biology or psychology, in the organisation of parenting, in ahistorical accounts about the origins of human society, or in abstract processes of functional adaptation and structural differentiation. Instead, regardless of its pervasiveness, sexual inequality should be investigated, in each instance, as a historically specific phenomenon with historically specific roots located in the invisible levels of social reality; namely, in structures concealed by those visible processes which are, in fact, the effects through which the existence of those structures manifests itself.[56] This concept of structure corresponds to social relations which evolve in the process through which people produce their material and social existence and which are independent from individuals' will.[57] Production has a twofold nature: 'on the one side, the production of the means of existence ... on the other side, the production of human beings themselves'.[58] The variety of visible, institutionalised ways that 'men oppress women' are effects, at the levels of 'society' and 'market relations', of the articulation between the two aspects of the mode of production which determine relations between men and women that are independent of their will: i.e. relations determined not by what individuals think, believe, want or need – consciously or unconsciously – or by whatever social constraints the 'market' or 'society' imposes on them; instead, they are relations mediated by the historically specific relation of men and women to the material conditions of production and of physical and social reproduction.[59] The general methodological principle is that the material basis of sexual inequality is to be sought in the articulation between class relations or relations of production and the relations of physical and social reproduction valid within a historically specific mode of production. I shall limit my analysis to the capitalist mode of production in an effort to delineate, following the second structuralist methodological principle, the capitalist basis of sexual inequality.

To clearly distinguish between the various forms assumed by female oppression under capitalism, it is necessary first to analyse the structure of the household as a mode of reproduction. By mode of physical and social reproduction

---

56   For a critical perspective on the arguments that follow, see Arruza 2016, p. 26.
57   Marx 1970a, p. 20.
58   Engels 1972, p. 71.
59   Althusser 1976, pp. 200–7.

I mean the historically specific combination of labour and means of reproduction (the material basis for the performance of reproductive tasks: the tools, goods, utensils, raw materials, foodstuffs, etc.) with relations between men and women.

1   *The Elements of the Mode of Physical and Social Reproduction*[60]
a) *Labour:* household labour reproduces labour power (i.e. the capacity to work) both physically and socially, and on a daily and generational basis.[61]

	Daily reproduction	Generational reproduction
Physical reproduction	Housework (e.g. shopping, cleaning, cooking). Expressive and nurturant tasks.	Pregnancy/childbirth. Childcare and housework. Expressive and nurturant tasks.
Social reproduction	Sexual relations. Maintenance of 'emotional input-output balance' of wage earner.	Socialisation. Reproduction of relations of production (tasks shared with schools and other institutions).

b) *Means of Reproduction:* these include the subject of labour and the instruments of labour. Daily and generational levels must be distinguished.

---

60   For the conceptualisation of some of the elements of the capitalist mode of physical and social reproduction (e.g. visible and invisible labour, daily and generational reproduction), I am indebted to the growing body of feminist and Marxist literature on the social and economic significance of household labour in the capitalist mode of production. See, for example, Benston 1969; Larguia and Dumoulin 1972, pp. 3–20; Mitchell 1971; Seccombe 1974, pp. 3–24. I have elaborated some of these ideas in my PhD dissertation, 'Population Structure and Processes in the Capitalist Mode of Production' (UCLA, 1973), pp. 148–71.
61   Larguia and Dumoulin 1972, pp. 4–6; Gimenez 1973b, pp. 159–69; Seccombe 1974.

	Daily reproduction	Generational reproduction
Subject of labour	The wage earner (actual number varies between households; typically there is only one, i.e. the male).	The child (future member of the capitalist class or the working class).

	Broadly defined	Narrowly defined
Instruments of labour	The household infrastructure (i.e. home appliances, tools, vehicles, goods, etc.), which provides the material basis for the performance of housework and childcare (instruments of daily and generational relevance).	The specific set of appliances and/or goods that enter into the performance of specific tasks.

2   *The Relations of Physical and Social Reproduction*[62]

Within the mode of physical and social reproduction, the relations between the agents of reproduction (men and women) becomes more complex because they are *doubly* mediated. Both men and women 'own' part of the *natural conditions* for physical reproduction at the generational level of analysis,[63] which are themselves useless unless brought together through the technical and social relations of reproduction. On the other hand, men and women relate differently to the *material conditions* of physical and social reproduction (i.e. instruments of household labour, household infrastructure, and so on), because of their different roles in the technical relations of reproduction. This is in turn determined by their class position or relationship to the means of production.

---

62   In the realm of the production of material goods, the relations of production are the relations between the agents of production (labourers and non-labourers) mediated through their relationship to the means of production; they have a technical (i.e. visible, expressed through the technical and social division of labour), and a social (i.e. invisible, expressed through the power differences rooted in their relationship to the means of production) dimension.

63   See footnote 60 above.

The combination of these elements through the relations between men and women, or relations of reproduction, reproduces the present and future members of social classes by procreation, physical care (cleaning, food preparation, etc.) and nurturant and supportive services (sexual relations, socialisation of children, cooperation, etc.). The dominant visible forms taken by modes of physical and social reproduction throughout history have been family and kinship structures as well as kinship structured groups (groups in which adults and children are not related by blood). In capitalist social formations, the nuclear family emerges as the dominant but not exclusive context in which social classes are reproduced; empirical variations documenting not only the existence of other forms (e.g. single-parent households) but also the conditions under which nuclear families remain to a greater or lesser extent embedded in broader kinship networks must be understood in terms of underlying relations of physical and social reproduction which are determined, for each class, by the capitalist organisation of production, distribution, and consumption.

Capitalist families live off profits from capital and are surrounded by extensive kinship networks which are also economic networks through which wealth is preserved, increased, and circulated. Men and women own the means of production and are free from the necessity of selling their labour to survive; they are the 'bearers' or 'supports' of the capitalist class[64] and reproduce it under legal and ideological conditions that ensure the preservation of property and its transmission to legitimate heirs, the future bearers of the class. Given the different biological role of men and women in procreation, these superstructural conditions involve control over women's sexuality and reproductive capacity; the pre-capitalist relationship between private ownership of the means of production and class control over women as producers of the future members of the class is preserved and reproduced under capitalism through superstructural conditions (legal, ethical, religious, ideological, etc.) that universalise it for all classes, obscuring the qualitative differences between classes in the process of defining everyone as a legal, political, ethical subject.[65] These superstructural conditions (the legal apparatus surrounding marriage, divorce, and inheritance; bourgeois morality; ideologies about abortion, contraception, etc.) contribute to create the circumstances in which the control exerted by the capitalist class over the conditions for the reproduction of all classes, including itself, appears, at the level of visible relations, as control exerted by men over women. Class control over the means of production and over the condi-

64   Althusser 1976, p. 206.
65   Althusser 1971, pp. 162–86.

tions for its own reproduction as a class places capitalist men and women into social relations independent of their will. They are unequal relations in which, at the level of 'society', men appear in control of capital, female sexuality, and reproductive capacity. On the other hand, within capitalist households, labour and means of reproduction are brought together through a division of labour or technical relations of reproduction that ensure women's complete freedom from the routine and menial dimensions of reproduction as well as partial freedom from social reproduction. Paid domestic workers (most of whom are likely to be women) do housework, childcare, and some aspects of child socialisation under the direct or indirect supervision of capitalist women who often delegate the managing tasks to workers hired for that purpose. The existence of a primarily female strata of domestic servants is, therefore, the basic underpinning of the almost exclusive dedication of capitalist women to social reproduction on a daily and generational basis (child socialisation, social activities that enhance and complement their husbands' public roles, etc.), and of the unique characteristics of domestic relations between men and women in the capitalist household; a context in which contemporary discussions about the desirability of childcare by persons other than the biological parents, or about the need to change the division of labour between men and women to increase men's domestic activities in order to liberate women for greater social involvement and self-fulfilment, have no meaning.[66]

Working-class families live off the sale of the labour power of their adult members and rely on the domestic labour of women for the daily and generational reproduction of labour power. The dominant pattern is one in which men are the only or most important wage earners and wives are the primary domestic workers, whether or not they are also employed. The mutually reinforcing relationship between women's domestic responsibilities and their social and economic oppression has been discussed and documented at great lengths and need not be re-examined here. Also, I am not going to dwell on the debate about the nature of domestic labour: whether it is paid or unpaid labour and whether or not it produces surplus value.[67] What is relevant here

---

66   The use of domestic servants is not restricted to the capitalist class; at certain levels of income, 'middle class' and 'upper middle class' women do purchase domestic labour. The qualitative differences between the capitalist use of servants and the practice of hiring household 'help' with varying degrees of regularity is a matter that cannot be fully explored at this time. It is important to point out, however, that the existence of differences in class and socio-economic status that allow some women to purchase their full or partial freedom from the 'drudgery of housework' contributes to the maintenance of class relations and of sexual inequality within the working class.

67   See, for example, Seccombe 1974; Coulson et al. 1975; Gardiner 1975.

is that domestic labour is a form of socially necessary labour that expands the goods and services available to the working class beyond what it would be possible to purchase with wages. Domestic labour is thus an important component of the standard of living of the working class and a source of use values which enter in the process through which labour power is produced and reproduced on a daily and generational basis. On the other hand, domestic labour benefits the capitalist class because its presence lowers the overall level of wages, thus increasing the amount of surplus that can be extorted from the direct producers. But neither the division of labour within the home and its impact on the status of women, nor the relationship between domestic labour and the level of wages, can explain in themselves the existence of sexual inequality within the working class. To find the specifically capitalist material basis of sexual inequality it is necessary to examine the material conditions leading to family formation within the working class.

Capitalism, as a historically specific mode of production, rests upon a class structure based on the private ownership of the means of production and the concomitant expropriation of the direct producers who, as free labourers owning nothing but their labour power, must sell it to the owners of capital to get access to the means of subsistence necessary for themselves and their children. Hence, there is inherent in capitalism a tendency toward the universalisation of commodity production generated by the separation of the direct producers from the conditions of production and reproduction which affects not only capital goods and consumer goods but also an ever growing variety of services. An important exception to this trend is labour power, a crucial commodity which is not produced on a capitalist basis although its daily and generational reproduction requires a constant flow of market goods and services and is, consequently, shaped by the requirements of capitalist production. Within the working-class household, goods and services purchased with the means of exchange obtained through the sale of labour power are combined with domestic labour in the context of relations of reproduction that presuppose the employment, as a wage labourer, of at least one member of the household. Domestic labour produces use values for the consumption of *all* the members of the family;[68] this is 'consumptive production' because persons produce their own body, and I may add their own physical and intellectual capacities, through the consumption of goods and services.[69] The consumption of the use values produced at home is thus, simultaneously, the production and reproduction of

68   Benston 1969.
69   Marx 1970a, p. 195.

the present and future members of the working class. The capitalist mode of producing material goods *produces* consumption, i.e. consumptive production 'by providing the material of consumption ... by creating in the consumer a need for the objects which it first presents as products and *by determining the mode of consumption*'.[70] Crucial for the understanding of sexual inequality in the working class is the determination exerted by the mode of production upon the mode of consumption or, which is the same, the mode of consumptive production or physical and social reproduction.

Under capitalist conditions, the production of surplus and its extraction from the direct producers is concealed by the appearances of the market and social relations; this is the sphere of Freedom, Equality, Property, and Bentham.[71] At this level, individuals meet and engage in equitable exchanges that result in the distribution of the product: rent, profits, interest, and wages are allocated to different individuals on the basis of their function in the production process. This level is an intermediate phase between production and distribution.[72] It is both a structural effect of the underlying relation of production and a crucial condition for the reproduction – over time – of the capitalist mode of production as a whole. It mystifies the nature of the production process by hiding class rule and its effects under the guise of unmanageable laws (e.g. supply and demand, the Malthusian population principle) and other 'social facts'.

The relations of structural compatibility between these phases or moments of the mode of production as a whole – i.e. production, exchange, and distribution – set structural limitations to the possible forms in which labour power can be reproduced. The mode of consumption or consumptive production cannot itself be isomorphic with the mode of production: the reproduction of labour power on a capitalist basis would destroy the material basis for the production of free individuals, autonomous and responsible for their own success or failure, which constitute the cornerstone of capitalist social and market relations. On the other hand, the lack of isomorphism between the mode of production and the mode of reproduction of labour power is not the product of design but the complex structural effect of the relations of production, exchange, and distribution, overdetermined by the superstructure and mediated by the biological level and by the class struggle.

At the level of production, the creation of a propertyless class, bound to capital for its survival in a context of chronic unemployment and periodic eco-

---

70   Marx 1970a, p. 197.
71   Marx 1970b, p. 196.
72   Marx 1970b, p. 204.

nomic crises, has created an objective situation of job scarcity and fierce competition among the members of the working class. This situation is exacerbated by the tendency toward the universalisation of commodity production and the concomitant transformation of all social relations into market relations.

At the level of exchange, this objectively competitive situation is ideologically understood and experienced in terms of visible and 'obvious' cleavages based on sex, age, racial, or ethnic differences or differences in national origins, religion, and so forth. It is in the interest of capital to have a divided labour force, and sexual antagonism is one among the many divisions that capital uses and reinforces to its advantage. While segregated labour markets may reduce the amount of competition, they never obliterate its objective existence, which tends to reassert itself in times of economic crises, shifts in the organic composition of capital, and drastic reorganisation of the labour force.

These objective conditions place men and women in antagonistic and competitive relations. At the biological level, on the other hand, men and women are placed in complementary sexual and procreative roles; this is the material basis for the fact that, at the levels of distribution, exchange, and visible social relations, they also confront each other as potential sexual partners and potential parents – i.e. as potential agents of reproduction. While other cleavages within the working class can be overcome through unionisation and other forms of collective organisation, the family – the major site where labour power is reproduced – emerges as the most important institution bringing the sexes and generations together. At this level of analysis, men and women freely meet and enter into apparently free relationships; this is the sphere not only of Freedom, Equality, Property, and Bentham but also of Love, Motherhood, ideologies about femininity and masculinity, and other forms of legitimation. These 'freely' entered family relations create bonds of interdependence between men and women and between families; kinship relations become an important source of economic support for unemployed workers as well as for those unable to work because of age, illness, or other circumstances.[73]

But the interdependence between families and between men and women rests upon underlying relations of personal economic dependence. The relations of production, exchange, and distribution place those who earn wages in a position to gain access to the material conditions of reproduction and, consequently, in a position of power over those with little or no access to those conditions. Kinship relations legitimate the claims of the latter upon the former while the absence of such bonds place people in an objective situation

---

73   Humphreys 1977.

of dependence leading to the emergence of forms of political control (e.g. wel-fare) and personal dependence. Sexual inequality is one among the many forms of inequality thus generated by the mode of production within the working class. The overall effect of the capitalist relations of production, exchange, and distribution is to recruit men and women for the positions of agents of repro-duction within the mode of physical and social reproduction in a context that places those agents of reproduction who are also wage earners in a position of power over those who are only domestic workers and that turns the position of domestic worker into a structural alternative to that of wage worker. These conditions are outside the control of individuals whatever their sex may be and express the rule of the capitalist class – mediated by the anarchy of the market and the relations of dependence thereby generated at the level of distribution. Under such conditions, domestic labour becomes an unavoidable economic 'option' for women which places them in a dependent position with respect to men which is independent of their will.

It may be argued that this account does not explain why women, rather than men, are expected to become domestic workers and that an answer to that question would have to rely on arguments such as those discussed in the previ-ous section which seek the origins of sexual inequality outside the mode of pro-duction (in biological or psychological differences between men and women or in pre-capitalist 'patriarchal' ideologies, division of labour, power relations, etc.). My answer to those arguments is that pre-existing structural and super-structural instances do indeed overdetermine the relations between the sexes within and outside the family. Pre-existing ideologies and practices set the parameters for the way men and women – at the level of visible relations – have perceived their options and the nature of their relationships from the very beginning of capitalism. But one must 'distinguish between the material transformation of the conditions of production ... and the legal, political, philo-sophical ... ideological forms in which men become conscious of this conflict and fight it out'.[74] It is the transformation of the conditions of production and reproduction (the mode of producing and distributing goods and its impact upon the reproduction of life) which places working-class men and women in different locations which imply unequal access to the conditions of reproduc-tion. This unequal access, which is the basis for their asymmetrical relations at the level of visible relations, stems from their relationship to the conditions of production, as propertyless workers, and to the conditions of procreation and reproduction, as agents involved in the daily and generational reproduction of

---

74   Marx 1970a, p. 21.

labour power. Pre-capitalist sexist patterns can persist, new ones can develop, and all of them can overdetermine the relationship between the sexes because the material conditions that place men and women in an unequal relationship determine, in the last instance, the efficacy of those patterns. These material conditions are the outcome of the combined effects of the relations of production, exchange, and distribution *mediated* by the biological level of sexuality and procreation and by the class struggle and *overdetermined* by pre-capitalist and capitalist superstructures.

Mediation is a mode of determination according to which a given social process or a given set of material conditions shape the consequences of other processes.[75] To acknowledge biology as an important mediating condition is neither 'vulgar materialism' nor biological determinism; it simply means to take into account the effect of the biological level *in itself*, which cannot be reduced to its social construction or production, nor can it be reduced to a moment in the subject-nature dialectic.[76] Biology shapes the consequences of capitalist relations of production, exchange, and distribution which place all individual workers in competition for scarce jobs by establishing the material conditions for the development of relations of cooperation between male and female workers based on sexuality and procreation. The class struggle, in turn, modifies the impact of the capitalist organisation of production by reinforcing the working-class family as a locus of resistance. Humphries[77] has convincingly argued that the persistence of the working-class family as well as its changing fortunes cannot be purely explained in terms of the sexism of male workers or the needs of capital accumulation, as an institution passively reflecting such needs while fulfilling ideological functions supporting the hegemony of the capitalist class. An adequate explanation should also take into account the state of the class struggle and its relative success in securing a family wage and other benefits.

The mode of production sets structural limitations to the possible modes of reproducing labour power that could be structurally compatible with capitalism and to the possible survival strategies that working-class people could develop to overcome their fragmentation and vulnerability to the vagaries of the labour market and to changing forms of surplus extraction. The class struggle, on the other hand, modifies and challenges those limitations in manifold ways. Through the combined mediation of the biological level and the class struggle, the working-class family emerges as the dominant survival strategy

---

75   Wright 1976, p. 25.
76   Timpanaro 1975, p. 34.
77   Humphries 1977.

open to male and female workers. It should then be clear that it is not the power of working-class men (or women's reproductive roles) that keeps women as the primary agents of reproduction within working-class households nor is it the power of men that creates segregated labour markets and other barriers to equality between the sexes. It is the power of capital which establishes structural limitations to the possible ways in which the propertyless class can have access to the conditions necessary for its daily and generational reproduction and it is the relative powerlessness of working-class men and women as *individuals* struggling for survival that forces them into these relations of reproduction which are both relations of cooperation and unequal relations of personal economic dependence. The contradiction between capital and labour, between production and reproduction, and the protracted class struggle thereby generated are the determinants of the contradictory nature of the relations between working-class men and women. The mode of reproducing labour power can thus be accurately understood as a unity of opposites, where bonds of cooperation and solidarity are also bonds of dependency grounded in the set of structural possibilities open to male and female members of the working class under capitalist conditions.

Conclusion

Capitalist and working-class relations of physical and social reproduction are subject to similar structural constraints in all capitalist social formations. On the other hand, their empirically observable manifestations will reflect the unique characteristics of each social formation such as, for example, the specific form in which capitalist and pre-capitalist modes of production are articulated; the characteristics of the superstructure which reflect the complexity of the base and overdetermine it; and the internal characteristics of the social formation itself as well as its location in the international structure.

The essence of my argument is that, in capitalist social formations, the observable forms of sexual inequality are determined, in the last instance, by the historically specific way in which the mode of production (conceived as a complex structured whole in which the capitalist mode of production is dominant) affects the access of the labouring and non-labouring members of the subordinate classes (wage and salaried workers, peasants, agricultural workers, the unemployed, etc.) to the material conditions necessary for their daily and generational reproduction. While the actual effects of the mode of production upon the mode of physical and social reproduction among those classes is always modified or overdetermined by the class struggle and other mediations, the maintenance of capitalist relations of production sets structural limits to such modifications, and may even reverse them on occasion, depending on the nature of the crises affecting the social formation at a given time. Moreover, in any social formation the level of social stratification reflects the complexity of the base; consequently the empirical study of sexual inequality must rest upon the previous theoretical work of developing propositions about the underlying relations of production and reproduction determining the observable relations between men and women within classes, fractions of classes, and 'contradict- ory class locations'.[78]

It should be clear, then, that from the standpoint of Structuralist Marxism, the issue of whether 'class' or 'sex' is primary, or what forms their 'mutual inter- dependence' may take, are oversimplifications of very complex matters that cannot be resolved by a priori political commitments or by automatically react- ing against the ghost of the 'economism' of 'orthodox Marxism', which seems to haunt the American intellectual scene. A straightforward analysis of the capitalist mode of production in all its moments (production, exchange, distri- bution, and consumption) clearly shows that the mode of production determ- ines the mode of consumptive production or physical and social reproduction. The control exerted by the capitalist class over its own conditions of reproduc- tion and over the conditions necessary for the reproduction of the labouring classes determines, in the last instance, the nature of the relations between the sexes and the relative significance of the family within social classes. The major theoretical task becomes, therefore, that of unravelling the specific paramet- ers within which the reproduction of different classes and fractions of classes takes place under capitalism and, in so doing, mapping out the historically possible relations between the sexes that those parameters regulate. From this standpoint, all explanations of the observable forms of sexual inequality within capitalist social formations based on various analyses of the biological, psycho- logical, or social differences between the sexes, or an analysis of the mode of reproduction in isolation from but interacting with the mode of production, are overlooking the historically specific determinants of the phenomena they attempt to explain. On the other hand, sociological analyses of sex differen- tiation and sex stratification and feminist analyses of sexuality, reproductive oppression, psychological oppression, etc. could be *critically* – not eclectically – integrated with the Structuralist Marxist analysis of their specifically capitalist structural and superstructural determinants. The main theoretical assumption underlying such critical integration is the following: the capitalist relations

---

78   See Wright 1976 for a definition of that concept.

of production and the relations of physical and social reproduction (which are relations into which men and women enter independently of their will) impose historically specific structural limits to the range of empirical variations in sexual inequality in capitalist social formations which feminist scholarship has abundantly documented. Theoretical and empirical investigation of the specific articulation between the visible forms of sexual inequality and their underlying structural determinants would presuppose the investigation of the most important mediating and overdetermining instances. This would not only heighten the scientific understanding of sexual inequality, but would also give feminists a sound basis for the evaluation of both short- and long-term political and economic objectives.

The analysis of sexual inequality developed in this chapter is a preliminary contribution to the work of others similarly engaged in the task of elaborating a Marxist theory of the oppression of women, asking Marxist questions, and developing Marxist answers.[79] Structuralist Marxism is not indispensable for this project, but greatly facilitates it; Structuralist Marxism formulates import- ant methodological considerations and key analytical distinctions which are not clearly and systematically stated in the works of the classics. Given the nature of the present historical conjuncture, Structuralist Marxism is not likely to have a noticeable impact in the development of American feminist theory. But what is at stake is more than an academic debate about the explanatory power of different theories. Theories inform policies and political struggles and the success of the struggle against sexual inequality depends on the extent to which the factors that produce it and reproduce it through time are correctly identified. From the standpoint of Structuralist Marxism, the development of theories that acknowledge the determinant role of the mode of production are more likely to succeed in identifying those determinants and in generating effective political strategies.

---

79   See, for example, Vogel 1979; Chinchilla 1980; Dixon 1979.

CHAPTER 3

Marxism and Class, Gender and Race: Rethinking the Trilogy

'Marxism, and Class, Gender and Race: Rethinking the Trilogy', in *Race, Gender & Class*, Vol. 8, No. 2 (2001): 23–33.

Introduction

Most social science publications today, especially those about inequality, take for granted the ritual critique of Marx and Marxism in the process of introducing theoretical alternatives intended to remedy its alleged 'failures'. This practice became popular in early feminist literature: Marx and Marxists were criticised for not developing an in-depth analysis of the oppression of women, their 'economism', 'class reductionism', and 'sex blind' categories of analysis. Soon after, it became commonplace to assert that Marxism was also at fault for neglecting race, demography, ethnicity, the environment, and practically everything that mattered to the 'new social movements' in the West. As the movements died, scholarship informed by those political concerns flourished; the energy that might have been spent in the public arena found expression in academic programmes (e.g. women's studies, racial/ethnic studies) and efforts to increase 'diversity' in the curriculum and the population of educational institutions.

Publication of the journal *Race, Sex & Class* (changed afterwards to *Race, Gender & Class*), in 1993, signalled the convergence of those political and intellectual interests into a new social science perspective that soon acquired enormous visibility, as demonstrated by the proliferation of journal articles and books with race, gender and class in their titles. This perspective, put forth primarily but not exclusively by social scientists of colour, emerged as a reaction to feminist theories which neglected racial/ethnic and class differences among women, theories of racial/ethnic inequality which neglected sexism among men of colour and, predictably, as a corrective to Marxism's alleged shortcomings. For example, Jean Belkhir, editor and founder of *Race, Sex & Class*, prefaces an article on this topic as follows: 'The "Failure" of Marxism to Develop Adequate Tools and a Comprehensive Theory of Ethnicity, Gender and Class Issues is Undisputable'.[1] The list of putative failures could be as long as we wanted it to be but what would that prove, beyond the fact that Marx's and Engels's political and theoretical priorities differed from those of contemporary social scientists? Less biased, albeit debatable, is the conclusion that Marxism, although offering 'crucial and unparalleled insights' into the operation of capitalism, 'needs to develop the analytical tools to investigate the study of racism, sexism and classism'.[2] To refer to class as 'classism' is, from the standpoint of Marxist theory, 'a deeply misleading formulation'[3] because class is not simply another ideology legitimating oppression; it denotes exploitative relations between people mediated by their relations to the means of production. Nevertheless, it is the case that neither Marx nor Engels devoted the intensity of effort to the investigation of gender and race (and other issues) that would have satisfied today's critics. It is (and any literature review would support this point) far easier to emphasise their 'sins' of omission and – in light of current political sensibilities – commission than to use their theoretical and methodological contributions to theorise and investigate those aspects of capitalist social formations that today concern us. Notable exceptions are Berberoglu,[4] who has examined the underlying class forces leading to gender and racial divisions in the US working class, linking gender and racial oppression to capital accumulation, and Kandal,[5] who has forcefully argued for the need to avoid the racialisation and feminisation of social conflicts while minimising or overlooking the significance of class.

In this essay, I intend to argue that Marxism does contain the analytical tools necessary to theorise and deepen our understanding of class, gender and race. I intend critically to examine, from the standpoint of Marxist theory, the arguments for race, gender and class studies offered by some of their main proponents, assessing their strengths and limitations and demonstrating, in the process, that Marxism is theoretically and politically necessary if the study of class, gender and race is to achieve more than the endless documentation of variations in their relative salience and combined effects in very specific contexts and experiences.

---

1   Belkhir 1994, p. 79.
2   Ibid.
3   Eagleton 1996, p. 57; see also Kandal 1995, p. 143.
4   Berberoglu 1994.
5   Kandal 1995.

Race, Gender and Class as a Social Science Perspective

Long before the popularisation of the *Race, Gender & Class* (RGC) perspective, I suspect that most Marxist sociologists teaching social stratification were
already adept practitioners. For many years, for example, the Section on Marxist sociology of the American Sociological Association included in its annual
programme a session on Class, Gender and Race. I certainly called my students' attention, in 29 years of teaching social stratification and other subjects
in which inequality matters, to the fact that everybody's lives are affected by
class, gender and race/ethnic structures (in addition to age and other sources
of inequality). We are, in Marx's terms, 'an ensemble of social relations',[6] and
we live our lives at the intersection of a number of unequal social relations
based on hierarchically interrelated structures which, together, define the historical specificity of the capitalist modes of production and reproduction and
underlie their observable manifestations. I also routinely called students' attention to the problems inherent in the widespread practice of assuming the
existence of common interests, ideologies, politics, and experiences based on
gender, race and ethnicity because class location and socio-economic status
differences within classes divide those population aggregates into classes and
strata with contradictory and conflicting interests. In turn, aggregates sharing the same class location, or similar socio-economic characteristics within
a class, are themselves divided by gender, race and ethnicity so that it is problematic to assume that they might spontaneously coalesce into class or status
self-conscious, organised groups. This is why, in the late 1960s and early '70s, I
was critical of feminist theories which ignored class, racial and ethnic divisions
among women and men, and theories of patriarchy that ignored how most
men under capitalism are relatively powerless.[7] Later on, I published a critical
assessment of the 'feminisation of poverty' thesis because it was not sensitive to the effects of class, socio-economic status, racial and ethnic divisions
among men and women; it neglected the connections between the poverty of
women and the poverty of men and overlooked the significance of this thesis
as a powerful indicator of the immiseration of the lower strata within the US
working class.[8]

I am aware, however, that most sociologists do not take Marxism seriously
and that theorists of gender and racial oppression have been, on the whole,
hostile to Marxism's alleged reductionisms. More importantly, this is a coun-

---

6   Marx 1976 [1845], p. 7.
7   Gimenez 1975.
8   Gimenez 1990.

try where class is not part of the common sense understanding of the world and remains conspicuously absent from the vocabulary of politicians and most mass media pundits. This is why, despite the US history of labour struggles, today people are more likely to understand their social and economic grievances in gender, racial and ethnic terms, rather than in class terms, despite the fact that class is an ineradicable dimension of everybody's lives. I am not arguing that racial and gender based grievances are less important, nor that they are a form of 'false consciousness'; in the present historical conjuncture in the US, it has become increasingly difficult, exceptions notwithstanding, to articulate class grievances separately from gender and racial/ethnic grievances. The ideological and political struggles against 'class reductionism' have succeeded too well, as Kandal pointed out, resulting in what amounts to gender and race/ethnic reductionisms. This situation does not indicate the demise of class as a fundamental determinant of people's lives, but that the relationship between structural changes, class formations and political consciousness is more complex than what simplistic versions of Marxism would suggest. It is an important principle of historical materialism that it is necessary to differentiate between material or objective processes of economic change and the ideological (e.g. legal, political, philosophical, etc.) ways in which people become conscious of these processes of transformations and conflicts and fight them out.[9] This is why I welcomed the emergence of the RGC perspective because, I thought, it would contribute to raising awareness about the reality and the importance of class and the extent to which neither racial nor gender oppression can be understood in isolation from the realities of class exploitation. My expectations, however, were misplaced: the location of class in the RGC trilogy, at the end, replicates its relative significance within this approach; class is 'the weak link in the chain'.[10] But altering the place of class in the trilogy would not matter, for the RGC perspective erases the qualitative differences between class and other sources of inequality and oppression, an erasure grounded in its essentially a-theoretical nature.

What is RGC's object of study? Essentially, it is the 'intersections of race, gender and class'.[11] Authors vary in the metaphors they use to describe the nature of these intersections: e.g. triple oppression, interplay, interrelation, cumulative effects, interconnections;[12] interactive, triadic relation, overlap-

---

9   Marx 1970, p. 21.
10   Kandal 1995, p. 143.
11   Collins 1997, p. 74.
12   Belkhir 1994.

ping, interactive systems;[13] multiple jeopardy, meaning 'not only *several, simultaneous* oppressions but also the *multiplicative* relations among them';[14] multiplicative, simultaneous, interconnected systems of a whole.[15] Collins, however, appears to disagree with mathematical interpretations of these relationships, for she states that they (meaning race, gender and class) cannot be 'added together to produce one so-called grand oppression';[16] it follows they cannot be multiplied either. Collins's views are the most helpful for identifying the main elements of this approach:

1.   Race, gender and class are 'distinctive yet interlocking structures of oppression'.[17]

2.   'The notion of interlocking refers to the macro-level connections linking systems of oppression such as race, class and gender'.[18]

3.   'The notion of intersectionality describes micro-level processes – namely, how each individual and group occupies a social position within interlocking structures of oppression described by the metaphor of intersectionality'.[19]

4.   'Everyone has a race/gender/class specific identity'.[20]

5.   Every individual is, simultaneously, 'being oppressed and oppressor'.[21]

6.   Oppressions should not be ranked nor should we struggle about which oppression is more fundamental: to theorise these connections it is necessary 'to support a working hypothesis of equivalency between oppressions'.[22]

7.   This perspective requires that we ask new questions such as 'How are relationships of domination and subordination structured and maintained in the American political economy? How do race, class and gender function as parallel and interlocking systems that shape this basic relationship of domination and subordination?'[23]

As Collins acknowledges (and this is something evident in the preceding sample of metaphors attempting to deal with this issue), 'the area of race, class

---

13   Belkhir 1993, p. 4.
14   King, cited in Barnett et al. 1999, p. 14, emphasis in the text.
15   Barnett et al. 1999, p. 15.
16   Collins, cited in Barnett et al. 1999, p. 15.
17   Collins 1993, p. 23.
18   Collins 1997, p. 74.
19   Ibid.
20   Collins 1993, p. 28.
21   Ibid.
22   Collins 1997, p. 74.
23   Collins 1993, p. 29.

and gender studies struggles with the complex question of how to think about intersections of systems of oppression'.[24] One solution, based on the assumption that gender, race and class are simultaneously experienced, is to consider them as 'situated accomplishments'; they are not only individual attributes but 'something which is accomplished in interaction with others' who, in turn, render these accomplishments accountable within institutional settings.[25] From this ethno-methodological stance, people simultaneously 'do' difference (i.e. gender, race and class) in the process of interacting with others and, through their 'doings', contribute to the reproduction of those structures. As Collins rightly points out, this postmodern, social constructionist analysis, which reduces oppressive structures to 'difference', leaves out 'the power relations and material inequalities that constitute oppression'.[26] The ethno-methodological solution is unsatisfactory for other reasons as well, which follow from its basic RGC assumptions; i.e. that everyone has a race, gender, class identity, and that the effects of all social interactions are simultaneously 'gendered', 'raced', and 'classed'.[27]

To postulate an isomorphic relation between structural location – whether location is conceptualised singly or intersectionally makes no difference – and identity or identities entails a structural determinism similar to that imputed to 'orthodox Marxism'. While it is true, as it could not be otherwise, that all members of a given society are simultaneously located in a number of structures which, together, shape their experiences and opportunity structures, structural location does not necessarily entail awareness of being thus located or the automatic development of identities corresponding to those locations. It cannot be assumed, then, that everyone has a race/gender/class identity, as Collins argues, though it is true that everyone, by definition, is located at the intersection of class, gender, and racial/ethnic structures. That most individuals in this country are more likely to adopt and self-consciously display gender and racial/ethnic rather than class identities is not an automatic reflection of their structural locations, but the combined effect of many factors such as the heritage of slavery, the presence of colonised minorities, the composition of past and current immigration flows, McCarthyism, the balance of power between classes and characteristics of the class struggle and, last but not least, the effects of the 1960s social movements and dominant ideologies defining the limits of political discourse. RGC thinking conflates objective location in the intersec-

24   Collins 1997, p. 73.
25   West and Fenstermaker 1997, p. 64.
26   Collins 1997, p. 75.
27   West and Fenstermaker 1997, p. 60.

tion of structures of inequality and oppression with identities; i.e. individuals' subjective understanding of who they really are, and this conflation opens the way to the ethno-methodological solution to 'intersectionality', which assumes that everyone deploys those identities in the course of social interaction, so that all social exchanges are 'raced', 'gendered', and 'classed' (and the list could go on; 'aged', 'ethnicised', etc.).

As most institutional settings are characterised by hierarchical structures which distribute people in locations associated with different statuses, power, privilege, etc. it is likely that, whatever individuals' conception of who they really are might be, their behaviour is routinely interpreted in different terms by their peers and by those who are located higher in the hierarchical structure, in positions that give them the power to make decisions affecting other people's lives. Identities are a contested terrain, both a product of individuals' spontaneous, common sense self-understanding and political choices that help them make sense of their existence, and a product of labelling from above (e.g. by employers and by the state) or by their peers; i.e. the effects of acts of power. It is important, therefore, to differentiate between 'legitimating identities', which are the product of dominant institutions and groups, and 'resistance identities', which emerge from the grassroots.[28] How 'intersectionality' is experienced, then, is itself a thoroughly political process that raises questions about the possibility that what once were 'resistance identities', when linked to social movements, might in time become 'legitimating identities', when harnessed by the state to narrow legal and political boundaries that rule out other forms of political self-understanding.

How are we to understand, at the macro-level of analysis, the racialisation, genderisation and the placement of people in given class and/or socioeconomic status locations? Are these and other structures of inequality reproduced simply by 'doing difference?' While empirical research on these matters is important to document the persistence and pervasiveness of gender, class, and race prejudice and stereotypes that permeate ordinary, day to day interactions, it demonstrates at the same time the limited, descriptive, nonexplanatory nature of 'intersectionality'. In the context of Marxist theory, the argument that people are 'an ensemble of social relations', meaning everyone is located at the intersection of numerous social structures, counteracts onesided, abstract, ahistorical notions of human nature. As an RGC insight, it is also useful to criticise dominant stereotypes which associate poverty, race, and ethnicity with women and with 'minority' (i.e. 'non-white') status, as if 'whites',

---

28   Castells 1997.

besides having 'culture' (ethnicity being the culture of the relatively power-less) were mostly rich and male. But this insight, captured in the metaphor of 'intersectionality' and having as a referent the multiple locations of individu-als in the structures that make up the social formation as a whole, allows us only to: a) map the distribution of the population in these manifold locations where most individuals occupy 'contradictory' locations; i.e. locations where dominant and subordinate relations intersect;[29] and b) investigate empirically the extent to which locations and identities coincide or not, and the patterns of recognition and misrecognition that ensue. A graphic depiction of several of these intersections, placing individuals and couples in the intersection of wealth ownership, income levels, occupations, gender, race, ethnicity, age and employment status is the well-known 'American Profile Poster' accompanying Rose's periodic description of US social stratification.[30] A description, however, no matter how thorough, has meaning only within a specific theoretical con-text. Intersectionality in itself, as an account of the multiplicity of locations affecting individuals' experiences, or as a study of the patterned variations in the identities individuals claim for themselves regardless of those locations, cannot explain either the sources of inequalities or their reproduction over time; intersectionality must be placed in the 'institutional bases of power shap-ing race, class and gender'.[31] What are these institutional bases of power? How do we identify them? How do we link intersectionality to its macro-level con-ditions of possibility, those 'interlocking' structures of oppression? It is here that the RGC perspective runs into a theoretical dead end which the abund-ance of metaphors (e.g. interlocking, intersecting, etc.) can neither hide nor overcome. Collins postulates the existence of a 'basic relationship of dom-ination and subordination' within the American political economy, which is 'shaped' by the 'race, class and gender interlocking system'.[32] RGC studies, as Andersen and Collins point out, require the 'analysis and criticism of exist-ing systems of power and privilege'.[33] While they postulate the existence of a more fundamental or 'basic' structure of unequal power relations and privilege which underlies race, gender and class, no macro-level theoretical perspective is offered to identify this basic, fundamental structure. It is at this point that the formal nature of the RGC perspective becomes clear: race, gender and class have become, for all practical purposes, taken for granted categories of analysis

---

29   Wright 1978.
30   Rose 1992.
31   Collins 1997, p. 74.
32   Collins 1993, p. 29.
33   Andersen and Collins 1995, p. xiii.

whose meaning apparently remains invariant in all theoretical frameworks and contexts. There are many competing theories of race, gender, class, American society, political economy, power, etc. but no specific theory is invoked to define how the terms race, gender and class are used, or to identify how they are related to the rest of the social system. To some extent, race, gender and class and their intersections and interlockings have become a mantra to be invoked in any and all theoretical contexts, for a tacit agreement about their pervasiveness and meaning seems to have developed among RGC studies advocates, so that all that remains to be done is empirically to document their intersections everywhere, for everything that happens is, by definition, raced, classed, and gendered. This pragmatic acceptance of race, gender and class as givens results in the downplaying of theory, and the resort to experience as the source of knowledge. The emphasis on experience in the construction of knowledge is intended as a corrective to theories that, presumably, reflect only the experience of the powerful. RGC seems to offer a subjectivist understanding of theory as simply a reflection of the experience and consciousness of the individual theorist, rather than as a body of propositions which is collectively and systematically produced under historically specific conditions of possibility which grant them historical validity for as long as those conditions prevail. Instead, knowledge and theory are pragmatically conceived as the products or reflection of experience and, as such, unavoidably partial, so that greater accuracy and relative completeness can be approximated only through gathering the experiential accounts of all groups. Such is the importance given to the role of experience in the production of knowledge that in the eight-page introduction to the first section of an RGC anthology, the word 'experience' is repeated 36 times.[34]

I agree with the importance of learning from the experience of all groups, especially those who have been silenced by oppression and exclusion and by the effects of ideologies that mystify their actual conditions of existence. To learn how people describe their understanding of their lives is very illuminating, for 'ideas are the conscious expression – real or illusory – of (our) actual relations and activities',[35] because 'social existence determines consciousness'.[36] Given that our existence is shaped by the capitalist mode of production, experience, to be fully understood in its broader social and political implications, has to be situated in the context of the capitalist forces and relations that produce it. Experience in itself, however, is suspect because, dialect-

---

34   Andersen and Collins 1995, pp. 1–9.
35   Marx 1994, p. 111.
36   Marx 1970, p. 21.

ically, it is a unity of opposites; it is unique, personal, insightful and revealing, and, at the same time, thoroughly social, partial, mystifying, itself the product of historical forces about which individuals may know little or nothing about.[37] Given the emancipatory goals of the RGC perspective, it is through the analytical tools of Marxist theory that it can move forward, beyond the impasse revealed by the constant reiteration of variations on the 'interlocking' metaphor. However, this would require a) a rethinking and modification of the postulated relationships between race, class and gender, and b) a reconsideration of the notion that because everyone is located at the intersection of these structures, all social relations and interactions are 'raced', 'classed', and 'gendered'.

In the RGC perspective, race, gender and class are presented as equivalent systems of oppression with extremely negative consequences for the oppressed. It is also asserted that the theorisation of the connections between these systems requires 'a working hypothesis of equivalency'.[38] Whether or not it is possible to view class as just another system of oppression depends on the theoretical framework within which class is defined. If defined within the traditional sociology of stratification perspective, in terms of a gradation perspective, class refers simply to strata or population aggregates ranked on the basis of standard SES indicators (income, occupation, and education).[39] Class in this non-relational, descriptive sense has no claims to being more fundamental than gender or racial oppression; it simply refers to the set of individual attributes that place individuals within an aggregate or strata arbitrarily defined by the researcher (i.e. depending on their data and research purposes, anywhere from three or four to 12 'classes' can be identified).

From the standpoint of Marxist theory, however, class is qualitatively different from gender and race and cannot be considered just another system of oppression. As Eagleton points out, whereas racism and sexism are unremittingly bad, class is not entirely a 'bad thing' even though socialists would like to abolish it. The bourgeoisie in its revolutionary stage was instrumental in ushering in a new era in historical development, one that liberated the average person from the oppressions of feudalism and put forth the ideals of liberty, equality and fraternity. Today, however, class has an unquestionably negative

---

37   For a critical assessment of experience as a source of knowledge, see Sherry Gorelick, 'Contradictions of Feminist Methodology', in Chow, Wilkinson and Baca Zinn 1996; applicable to the role of experience in contemporary RGC and feminist research is Jacoby's 1973 critique of the 1960s politics of subjectivity.

38   Collins 1997, p. 74.

39   For an excellent discussion of the difference between gradational and relational concepts of class, see Ossowski 1963.

role to play as it expands and deepens the rule of capital over the entire globe. The working class, on the other hand, is pivotally located to wage the final struggle against capital and, consequently, it is 'an excellent thing'.[40] While racism and sexism have no redeeming feature, class relations are, dialectically, a unity of opposites; both a site of exploitation and, objectively, a site where the potential agents of social change are forged. To argue that the working class is the fundamental agent of change does not mean that it is the only agent of change. The working class is, of course, composed of women and men who belong to different races, ethnicities, national origins, cultures, and so forth, so that gender and racial/ethnic struggles have the potential of class struggles because, given the patterns of wealth ownership and income distribution in all capitalist countries, those who raise the banners of gender and racial struggles are overwhelmingly propertyless workers, technically members of the working class, people who need to work for economic survival whether it is for a wage or a salary, for whom racism, sexism and class exploitation matter. But this vision of a mobilised working class where gender and racial struggles are not subsumed but are nevertheless related requires a class-conscious effort to link RGC studies to the Marxist analysis of historical change. Insofar as 'class' in RGC remains a neutral concept, open to any and all theoretical meanings, just one oppression among others, intersectionality will not realise its revolutionary potential.

Nevertheless, I want to argue against the notion that class should be considered equivalent to gender and race. I find the grounds for my argument not only on the crucial role class struggles play in processes of epochal change but also in the very assumptions of RGC studies and the ethno-methodological insights put forth by West and Fenstermaker. The assumption of the simultaneity of experience (i.e. all interactions are raced, classed, gendered) together with the ambiguity inherent in the interactions themselves, so that while one person might think he or she is 'doing gender', another might interpret those 'doings' in terms of 'doing class', highlight the basic issue that Collins accurately identifies when she argues that ethnomethodology ignores power relations. Power relations underlie all processes of social interaction and this is why social facts are constraining upon people. But the pervasiveness of power ought not obfuscate the fact that some power relations are more important and consequential than others. For example, the power that physical attractiveness might confer on a woman in her interactions with her less attractive female supervisor or employer does not match the economic power of the latter over

---

40   Eagleton 1996, p. 57.

the former. In my view, the flattening or erasure of the qualitative difference between class, race and gender in the RGC perspective is the foundation for the recognition that it is important to deal with 'basic relations of domination and subordination' which now appear disembodied, outside class relations. In the effort to reject 'class reductionism', by postulating the equivalence between class and other forms of oppression, the RGC perspective both negates the fundamental importance of class but it is forced to acknowledge its importance by postulating some other 'basic' structures of domination. Class relations – whether we are referring to the relations between capitalist and wage workers, or to the relations between workers (salaried and waged) and their managers and supervisors, those who are placed in 'contradictory class locations'[41] – are of paramount importance, for most people's economic survival is determined by them. Those in dominant class positions do exert power over their employees and subordinates and a crucial way in which that power is used is through their choosing the identity they impute to their workers. Whatever identity workers might claim or 'do', employers can, in turn, disregard their claims and 'read' their 'doings' differently as 'raced' or 'gendered' or both, rather than as 'classed', thus downplaying their class location and the class nature of their grievances. To argue, then, that class is fundamental is not to 'reduce' gender or racial oppression to class, but to acknowledge that the underlying basic and 'nameless' power at the root of what happens in social interactions grounded in 'intersectionality' is class power.

Conclusion

As long as the RGC perspective reduces class to just another form of oppression, and remains theoretically eclectic, so that intersectionality and interlockings are, in a way, 'up for grabs', meaning open to any and all theoretical interpretations, the nature of those metaphors of division and connection will remain ambiguous and open to conflicting and even contradictory interpretations. Marxism is not the only macro-level theory that the RGC perspective could connect with in order to explore the 'basic structures of domination', but it is, I would argue, the most suitable for RGC's emancipatory political objectives.

---

41   Wright 1978.

CHAPTER 4

Reflections on Intersectionality

Introduction

The emergence of the race, gender and class (RGC) perspective and the creation, in colleges and universities, of programmes such as Women's Studies and Race and Ethnic Studies anticipated the rise and hegemony of intersectionality in the US, Canada, Western Europe and beyond. At the time I wrote the preceding chapter,[1] I understood 'intersection' and 'interlocking' only as metaphors used to indicate how race, gender and class came together, in some fashion (e.g. interacting, interplaying, intersecting, overlapping, and so forth), to affect women's experiences and identity. More recently, other categories of difference and identity (e.g. nationality, citizenship status, ability, sexual preference) have been added to the original three, and the analytical framework taking into account several of them at the same time, has become known as intersectionality.[2]

The literature is vast and complex, reflecting writers' professional specialisations, theoretical commitments and countries of residence.[3] I have concluded that there are no substantive differences between the basic analytical framework today known as intersectionality and the original race, gender and class approach: my critique still stands because intersectionality is the trilogy writ large. The literature also indicates that intersectionality has developed in two different directions,[4] first as a practical intervention in social policies and legal changes intended to fight discrimination (a topic I will not be examining at this time),[5] and second, as a framework, widely used across the humanities and

---

1   The chapter was probably written in 2000; it was published in 2001.
2   For accounts of the history of Intersectionality and its global dispersion, see, for example, Collins and Bilge 2016, Chapters 3 and 4; Lutz et al. 2011, pp. 1–4; Carbin and Edenheim 2013, pp. 234–5.
3   There are important differences in the way feminists approach intersectionality in English-speaking countries and European countries and, within Europe, in Northern and Southern European countries (Lutz et al. 2011, Chapter 1).
4   In practice, of course, inquiry and intervention go together but I wanted to indicate that there is, nevertheless, a difference; not all academics are political activists.
5   Intersectionality has been incorporated into the international and European discourses on human rights, equal rights and anti-discrimination laws and social policies. See, for example, Lutz et al. 2011, pp. 6–7; and Crenshaw 2014, pp. 17–22, in Grzanka 2014.

the social sciences, and regarded as 'one of the more important interventions in feminist theory',[6] 'essential to feminist theory'.[7] In this chapter, I will examine intersectionality in the context of feminist theory, focusing on theoretical questions, and some complex issues raised by its concept of identity and relationship to identity politics.

Theoretical Limitations

The term 'intersectionality' refers to the confluence of oppressions resulting in complex identities and unique experiences. Feminist accounts of its origins trace it to the experience of US black women and other women of colour, and to black feminist thought, particularly the Combahee River Collective Statement: 'We believe that sexual politics under patriarchy is as pervasive in Black women's lives as are the politics of class and race. We also find it difficult to separate race from class from sex oppression because in our lives they are most often experienced simultaneously'.[8] It is also an extrapolation from a metaphor used by a legal scholar, Kimberlé Crenshaw (credited with coining the term) to depict the situation of black women workers, who could not sue their employer for discrimination as black women because the courts recognised discrimination based either on sex or on race, but not on both. Crenshaw argued that neither gender nor race alone could account for their experience of oppression because they were at the 'intersection' of gender and race.[9]

That the fundamentals of intersectionality have not changed since the publication of the preceding chapter is evident from recent definitions: 'When it comes to social inequality, people's lives and the organization of power in a given society are ... shaped not by a single axis of social division, be it race or gender or class, but by many axes that work together and influence each other. Intersectionality as an analytical tool gives people better access to the complexity of the world and of themselves';[10] 'Intersectionality ... refutes the compartmentalization and hierarchization of the great axes of social differentiation through categories of gender/sex, class, race, ethnicity, disability and sexual orientation ... [it] postulates their interplay in the production and repro-

---

6   Carbin and Edenheim 2013, pp. 233–4.
7   Davis 2011, p. 43.
8   Combahee River Collective, cited in Lutz et al. 2011, p. 3.
9   Crenshaw 2011, pp. 25–8, in Lutz et al. 2011.
10   Collins and Bilge 2016, p. 2.

duction of social inequalities';[11] '[Intersectionality] is the study of how these dimensions of inequality [race, gender, class, sexuality and other dimensions of identity] co-construct one another'.[12]

Despite its privileged status as 'the most important theoretical contribution to date of feminism',[13] there is, to my knowledge, no specific and widely accepted intersectional theory. There is agreement about intersectionality's key ideas – as identified above and in the preceding chapter – but feminists differ in how they conceptualise the relationships between axes of inequality at the macro-level of analysis, and the ways in which they shape individuals' identities and experiences. The meaning of terms such as 'interlocking',[14] 'interplay', 'co-construct', 'co-constitute', 'mutual constitution', and so on, is not self-evident.[15] At what levels of analysis are these postulated relationships relevant? Do class, gender, race, ability, and so on 'mutually constitute' or 'co-construct' at the macro, micro, or individual levels of analysis? If so, concretely, how does that work out? Are complex identities primarily the effects of individuals knowingly participating in the presumably intersecting 'axes of oppression', the effects of discourse or an interaction between the two? And what does it mean to say that the axes of inequality intersect? Do the axes intersect and individuals end up in the intersections, or is intersection just a metaphor for the fact that in any society everyone partakes of certain characteristics, such as gender and age, that we all participate in various social institutions – thus playing multiple and differently valued social and occupational roles – and are situated somewhere in the ranking order dividing the main axes of inequality? If so, in what ways is intersectionality not ultimately based on a sociological truism? How do identities differ from social roles?

Intersectionality lacks explanatory power; it cannot, *in itself*, answer such questions and account for the existence of the 'axes of inequality', the nature of the processes that bring them together, the processes leading to identity formation, and the resulting complex, rather than unitary, nature of identity it postulates. As Wallis asks, '... is there a structure that links the oppressions together in some historically discernible way? ... [If so,] what is the nature of

11   Bilge 2010, p. 58.
12   Grzanka 2014, p. xiii.
13   Bilge 2010, p. 58.
14   Collins (see the preceding chapter) reserves the term 'interlocking' for describing the macro-level relationship between the systems of inequality, and 'intersectionality' as a metaphor for describing how individuals and groups occupy a place in the systems of oppression.
15   See Bilge 2010, pp. 63–5 for an illuminating discussion of these issues.

the links and how did they come to acquire their present form'?[16] Social reality is constantly in flux, constantly changing in minor and major ways, but there is no inherent social dynamic in the 'axes of inequality'; that has to be brought from the outside also, i.e. they have to be placed in some theoretical context within which the present and the past are understood and potential sources of social change can be identified.

Feminists have proposed various ways to compensate for those limitations, some of which Bilge identifies as she explores the literature in search of answers to her question: 'how can the theoretical reach of intersectionality be broadened?'[17] Some suggest increasing the complexity of intersectional analysis, while others advocate intersectionality's integration with other theoretical frameworks such as critical social theories, systems theory improved by complexities theory, and constructivist and poststructuralist theories. Ferguson, for example, proposes integrating intersectionality and social reproduction feminism, arguing that social reproduction theory can provide intersectionality the theory of the totality it lacks.[18] Yuval-Davis argues that intersectionality '[should] be accepted as the most valid contemporary sociological theoretical approach to stratification'.[19] Marxists, and sociologists who remain unconvinced by intersectionality, would undoubtedly disagree about such an approach being 'the most valid'. But given intersectionality's focus on multiple sources of inequality, it is reasonable to see it as an approach to social stratification that looks into its macro-level features and their potential effects – complex identities – at the micro-level of analysis. The main theories of stratification derive from Marx and Weber; Yuval-Davis prefers Bourdieu's more 'fluid' approach which 'identifies inequalities as the result of interplay between embodied practices and institutional processes, which together generate far-reaching inequalities of various kinds'.[20] Her choice makes sense in light of her commitment to intersectionality: individuals, given their economic, social and cultural capital and their complex identities, can presumably construct a variety of social distinctions. Intersectionality, as is clear from the preceding observations, has to be linked to other theories if it is to be more than an analytical tool or conceptual framework guiding empirical research, investigating intersectional complexity within or between categories (e.g. gender, race, ability,

---

16   Wallis 2015, p. 605.
17   Bilge 2010, p. 65.
18   Ferguson 2016; see Chapter 13 for a discussion of Ferguson's arguments.
19   Yuval-Davis 2011, p. 156.
20   Yuval-Davis 2011, p. 163.

sexuality) or deconstructing them.[21] Collins focuses on power and the domains where intersectionality should investigate it;[22] furthermore, the categories of analysis identifying the axes of oppression and social divisions (i.e. gender, race, class, age, and so on) 'gain meaning from power relations of racism, sexism, heterosexism, and class exploitation'.[23]

When placed in this context, it is legitimate to wonder about the reasons for intersectionality being acclaimed as *the* feminist theory[24] at this time. Carbin and Edenheim present an intriguing explanation; intersectionality owes its success to having become a 'consensus-creating-signifier' that glosses over important political and theoretical differences and conflicts among feminists: white middle-class feminists produced theories based on the experiences of white middle-class women for whom, given their class and race privilege, gender inequality was the main source of oppression, thus overlooking other power relations and sources of oppression based on race, ethnicity, immigrant status, and so on.[25] They were challenged, in the US and Europe, by the critiques developed by Marxist-Feminists, black feminists, women of colour, lesbians and postcolonial feminists. From their standpoint, feminist theory did not address their experiences of oppression and questioned the primacy of gender in feminist theory. Intersectionality 'arrived "just in time" to preserve both a unifying history and guarantee for a recognizable future ... Intersectionality could save an otherwise disappearing field of gender studies and at the same time, provide the field with a progressive way of doing feminist analysis. Thus, gender could be saved as the most important category for feminist research, despite or because of listings such as "gender, race and class"'.[26] Those struggles have not ended; feminists are divided between a political intersectionality oriented, as a 'critical praxis', toward 'social justice oriented change', and an academic intersectionality enmeshed in meta-theoretical debates, engaged in 'whitening intersectionality' by altering its genealogy, downplaying its origins

---

21   McCall 2005, cited in Grzanka 2014, pp. 302–3.
22   These domains are 'the *structural* (laws and institutions), the *disciplinary* (administrative and bureaucratic management), the *hegemonic* (cultural, ideological naturalization of relationships of domination) and the *inter-personal* (everyday interactions influenced by various hierarchies)' (Collins 2000, pp. 277–90, cited in Bilge 2016, p. 65).
23   Collins and Bilge 2016, p. 7.
24   Carbin and Edenheim 2013, p. 345.
25   Gunnarson 2011, p. 25; she suggests, however, that intersectionality's arguments have been built against a stereotyped or 'caricature-like representations of "earlier", "Western" or "hegemonic" feminist theories' (Gunnarsson 2011, p. 26).
26   Carbin and Edenheim 2013, pp. 344–5.

in Black feminist thought and changing its objectives from challenging oppression to fitting within the neoliberal agenda of diversity.[27]

These developments are unsurprising; a framework unattached to a specific theoretical foundation, no matter how important its political roots, is open to co-optation, transformation and multiple interpretations, thus becoming a 'common ground for all feminisms' despite important differences among feminists.[28] That intersectionality is like an empty slate in which all feminists can write has been viewed as a reason for its spectacular rise to becoming *the* hegemonic feminist perspective today, thus accounting for its puzzling success and vulnerability to criticisms as well; e.g. 'in feminist circles, the term "intersectionality" has come to stand virtually as a synonym for the way in which the "litany" of oppressions ... inflect and inform one another – to the extent that common usage makes it acceptable for one to use the term "intersectionality" without specifying what, in particular, is intersecting or how'.[29] Intersectionality is a 'floating signifier' which feminists – depending on their professional training, and political and theoretical commitments – understand in different ways, e.g. as a metaphor, theory, methodology, discourse, paradigm, analytical tool, empirical framework, even as a 'way of thinking' or an 'analytic sensibility', such that an analysis can be intersectional even if the term 'intersectionality' is not used; what makes it so is '... *its adoption of an intersectional way of thinking about the problem of sameness and difference and its relation to power'.*[30] Indeed, as I argued at the end of the previous chapter, because intersectionality is open to any and all theoretical interpretations, it will remain ambiguous and open to conflicting and even contradictory interpretations.

Marxism and Intersectionality

Denial of the fundamental role of class relations and struggles in the production of oppression and inequality defines intersectionality's macro-level assumptions about the relationship among its key elements. Regardless of the politicised vocabulary, i.e. references in the intersectionality literature to imperialism, capitalism, neoliberalism, class, and so on, intersectionality – like the RGC perspective that preceded it – is an abstract analytical framework which, like sociology, approaches the study of social phenomena ahistorically,

---

27   See Bilge 2013 for a comprehensive, thought-provoking examination of these issues.
28   Bilge 2010, pp. 65–8; Carbin and Edenheim, pp. 3–5.
29   Carasthatis 2008, p. 24.
30   Cho, Crenshaw and McCall 2013, p. 794, cited in Grzanka 204, p. 303, emphasis in the text.

i.e. in abstraction from their capitalist conditions of possibility.[31] Skeggs makes the point as follows: 'when people say that we need the intersectional gesture to include race, class, gender, and everything else, what it usually means is to think about these things which exclude understandings of the relationship to the capitalist system',[32] and, I add, of the Marxist historical and theoretical analysis of capitalism.

From a Marxist standpoint, it is important to differentiate between the abstract level of analysis of the theory of the capitalist mode of production, and the concrete, historical level of analysis of social formations, i.e. the level of analysis of a country or region where capitalism is the dominant mode of production. While intersectionality seems to take for granted its 'axes of inequality', as elements present in all societies, Marxists insist on the importance of taking into account their historicity, i.e. their capitalist foundations and the specific ways in which their place in the functioning of the social formation and in the consciousness of the different classes has been affected by the history and institutions of a given social formation (e.g. the state, ideologies, the legal system, culture, and so on). At the level of analysis of the capitalist mode of production, class is identity blind. The logic of class relations, exploitation and capital accumulation is indifferent to the identity of capitalists and workers. At the level of capitalist social formations, the aggregates of individuals sharing the same class location are divided in terms of identity and placement in the socio-economic (based on income, occupation and education, for example) and gender, racial, ethnic, and so on, stratification. To each of these groups corresponds an ideology that reifies it, endowing it with a reality that transcends history even though they might have roots in the history of the social formation or be newly created in the context of political struggles, the effects of immigration, and the aftermath of qualitative economic change. For example, at what level of capitalist development, and under what historically specific conditions, is it possible to argue that women are oppressed 'as women?' What is the relationship between capitalist accumulation, slavery, the rise of racial ideologies and the notion of race? In this context, capitalists – whatever their identity or nationality might be – act within the identity blind constraints imposed by the logic of the mode of production and, at the same time, they can and do

---

31   From the standpoint of Marx's methodology, historical analysis is not about the chronology of events, or the origins of social phenomena, but about the relationships between categories of analysis within a historically specific mode of production; see 'The Method of Political Economy', in Marx 1970, pp. 205–13.

32   Skeggs 2008, p. 41, cited in Carbin and Edenheim 2013, pp. 242–3; see also Aguilar 2015, pp. 211–13.

use the identity and status divisions within the working class to manipulate the level of wages and pit workers against each other, thus undermining the potential power inherent in a united working class.[33] This critique does not entail reducing social oppressions to class exploitation; as Aguilar observes, 'it is the capitalist mode of production and the social relations underlying it which provide the key to understanding why gender, race and other identity markers evolve into oppressions ... identity categories are activated as mechanisms to facilitate exploitation'.[34] And it must be kept in mind that 'the working class is a majority not only within the total population, but also within the particular populations of the various "non-class" categories'.[35] Although intersectionality may deny the fundamental importance of class, the phenomena that concerns it, gender, racial, ethnic and other forms of oppression and inequality, have capitalist causes and call for a Marxist theoretical analysis; excluding the relationship between class, socio-economic inequality and gender, race and other sources of discrimination and oppression exonerates capitalism from responsibility and strengthens the ideological ways people spontaneously understand the causes of their problems. They do so, and it could not be otherwise in the US, through identity categories.[36] On the other hand, intersectionality is not necessary for the Marxist analysis of class, inequality and oppression.

Intersectionality, Identity, and Identity Politics

Intersectionality is hailed as a *feminist* 'theory'; i.e. a theory focused on the oppression of women. To some extent, it is: its focus seems to be the oppression of women with intersectional or complex identities, i.e. the 'hyper-oppressed subject'.[37] Crenshaw, however, refers to the 'intersectional vulnerabilities of marginalized women and *occasionally marginalized men* as well'.[38]

If *narrowly understood*, intersectionality is applicable to women only. However, besides gender, race and other oppressions, the terms 'hyper-oppressed', 'marginalised', and so on, imply economic disadvantage; i.e. poverty, near pov-

---

33   Capitalists, whatever their gender, race, ethnicity, nationality etc. may be, must do what the logic of capitalist accumulation requires – i.e. the 'rational' pursuit of the most efficient ways to increase the production of surplus value – or risk the failure of their enterprises.

34   Aguilar 2015, pp. 211–12.

35   Wallis 2015, p. 618.

36   I have made this argument in the preceding chapter.

37   I borrow the expression from Carasthatis 2008, p. 25.

38   Crenshaw 2014, in Grzanka 2014, p. 18, emphasis added.

erty, low wages, reliance on social assistance and welfare provisions. Consequently, within the logic of intersectional thinking, only women at the bottom in all the axes of oppression have complex, intersectional identities. If so, is intersectionality a new label for the 'feminisation of poverty'? Should it be called 'feminist' without qualifications, as if it were applicable to all women, even though it excludes privileged women of all races?[39] It would appear that the 'intersectional' female subject is as particular, exclusionary and problematic as the prior white, presumably middle-class, unitary female subject underlying the earlier focus of feminist theory on the oppression of 'women as women'.

Broadly understood, intersectionality applies to everyone, male and female and of all races and ethnicities. After all, if the vulnerabilities of 'occasionally marginalised men' matter as well as those of marginalised women,[40] it follows that intersectionality is a gender and race 'blind' analytical framework according to which everyone, *including white males*, is placed at the intersection of axes of oppression. And, if that is the case, intersectionality could be more accurately portrayed as an analytical framework for the study of social inequality, rather than as a feminist theory. Indeed, as Yuval-Davis and her colleague Anthias 'strongly' argue, 'intersectional analysis should encompass all members of society and thus intersectionality should be seen as the right theoretical framework for analysing social stratification'.[41]

The source of these ambiguities can be partially traced to the context in which race and gender, as categories of analysis, are understood and used. Within intersectional thinking, as it is in the world of everyday life and within the boundaries of media and political discourse, the categories of analysis are coded; as Carasthatis observes, race and gender are understood in a social context where race is gendered (thinking Black entails thinking male) and gender is racialised (thinking woman entails thinking white); this is why Carasthatis is critical of the intersectional model of identity: '[I]n construing race and gender as analytically separable and relegating Black women to their intersection, it implicitly perpetuates the racialization of gender and the gendering of race'.[42] And, against the logical inference, from the way the key elements of intersectionality are posited, that everyone has intersectional identities,

---

39   McCall argues that 'in its emphasis on black women's experiences of subjectivity and
       oppression, intersectional theory has obscured the question whether all identities are
       intersectional or whether only mutually marginalized subjects have an intersectional
       identity' (McCall 2005, p. 1774, cited in Yuval-Davis 2011, p. 159).
40   Crenshaw 2014, p. 18, in Grzanka 2014, p. 18.
41   Anthias and Yuval-Davis 1983, 1992, and 2006a, cited in Yuval-Davis 2011, p. 159.
42   Carasthatis 2008, p. 31.

Carasthatis points out that white males have 'unified' identities because 'whiteness is implicitly rendered masculine' while 'maleness/masculinity is implicitly racialized white'; therefore, not everyone has intersectional identities: '*only hyper-oppressed subjects do*'.[43]

These opposite claims, i.e. *everyone has intersectional identities* and *only the disadvantaged or the hyper-oppressed do*, capture the tensions between universalism and particularism inherent in intersectionality and the problems that ensue from the ideological and political context that code the categories of analysis used to identify the axes of oppression and complex identities. Collins sums up this context when she observes that '... current assumptions see African Americans as having race,[44] White women as having gender, Black women as experiencing both race and gender, and White men as experiencing neither'.[45]

In the US context, the ways in which gender and race are coded affect how intersectional identity is conceptualised and, consequently, the forms taken by intersectional politics. Complex identities are the subject of intersectionality research and politics, for intersectionality has a political dimension; it is both a form of 'critical inquiry' and of 'critical praxis' in the pursuit of social justice. Critical means 'criticizing, rejecting, and/or trying to fix the social problems that emerge in situations of social injustice' including 'global economic inequality and social inequalities'; this notion of critical 'is drawn from twentieth-century social movements for equity, freedom, and social justice'.[46]

From a Marxist standpoint, the concepts of justice, injustice, freedom and equity, when isolated from the class struggle, serve all interests, progressive and regressive. Just as intersectionality's theoretical vagueness renders it 'up for grabs', open to all theoretical interpretations, so its politics are open to all individuals and groups that experience oppression, including those for whom justice, equity and freedom entail injustice, inequality and un-freedom for other groups. For example, Collins and Bilge observe that 'Surprisingly, some projects invoke intersectional rhetoric in defense of an unjust status quo, using intersectional frameworks to criticize democratic inclusion ... and *justify* social inequality'.[47] White supremacist literature 'identifies the connections among

---

43   Carasthatis 2008, p. 33, emphasis added.
44   Carasthatis points out that Collins is affected by those assumptions as well, because in her statement, implicitly, African Americans seem to be male. Carasthatis 2008, p. 32.
45   Collins 1998, p. 79, cited in Carasthatis 2008, p. 32. I should add, however, that there is a field of masculinities studies and scholars who apply intersectionality to the study of intersections among men; see, for example, Hearn 2011.
46   Collins and Bilge 2016, pp. 39–40.
47   Collins and Bilge 2016, p. 40, emphasis in the text.

women, blacks, Jews, "mud people," lesbians and various forms of mixing as the root cause of the declining fortunes of white men'.[48] This is not surprising at all; according to Lilla, writing about the failure of 'identity liberalism' after the 2016 US elections, 'the first identity movement in American politics was the Ku Klux Klan, which still exists in the US'.[49] The racial and gender coding of oppressions and the effects of economic exploitation shape identity politics and open up the issue of the relationship between intersectionality and identity politics.

Arguably, some of intersectionality's roots can be found in the identity politics movements of the late 1960s, as black feminists and women of colour articulated their critique of feminist theories generalising from the experience of white middle-class women. Collins and Bilge defend identity politics as 'a starting point for intersectional inquiry and praxis and not an end in itself'.[50] Disadvantaged groups can use 'strategically essential' identities which enable people to organise and form coalitions despite their differences: 'identity is central to building a collective we'.[51] But it is important to establish whether these identities emerge from the grassroots, from the state, or from politicians who favour the status quo.[52] This is why I tend to agree with Carasthatis when she argues that individuals become intersectional subjects through a political discourse that 'assigns them to that location', even though they are, objectively, thus placed.[53] Intersectionality is such a discourse; for example, Crenshaw states that the purpose of a series of models or 'topologies' describing, in different contexts, how intersectionality may affect the lives of vulnerable women, is '*to introduce a language for people to attach to their own experience*'.[54] As intersectionality takes the status quo for granted, it can teach people to understand

---

48   Daniels 1997, cited in Collins and Bilge 2016, p. 40.

49   Lilla 2016, p. 5.

50   Collins and Bilge 2016, p. 132.

51   Collins and Bilge 2016, pp. 134–5.

52   Group and individual identity formation is a complex topic that I will not fully examine in this addendum. See the previous chapter for some critical observations about the relationship between intersectional location and individual identity.

53   Individuals may or may not resist state imposed identities; for example, Latin American immigrants, depending on their social class and political leanings, might choose to self-identify as Latinos (a grassroots identity), Hispanics (a Census imposed identity) or, rejecting both, in terms of their national origin, e.g. Colombian, Guatemalan, and so on. Political discourses, however, are effective, particularly when acceptance of a state constructed identity can increase the probability of finding employment. Political discourses are one among other determinants of identity formation (e.g. experiences, socialisation, adherence to a given political ideology, religion, and so on).

54   Crenshaw 2014, in Grzanka 2014, p. 18.

their experiences in intersectional terms, while at the same time strengthening the capitalist status quo because, as I argued earlier, it reinforces an understanding of oppression that excludes the effect of class location.

In the US, the ideologies and social movement theories fuelling the struggles for social justice, fairness, against gender, racial, ethnic inequality, and so on, are developed within the boundaries of a political discourse in which poverty, low wages, economic disadvantage, unemployment, health and other social and economic problems tend to be perceived as problems of the disproportionately poor, i.e. women, especially single mothers, and non-whites, those whose poverty and near poverty rates and economic and other difficulties and needs are far greater, proportionately, than those that might afflict whites of both genders. To the extent that it focuses on disproportionately disadvantaged women of all races, intersectionality discourse mirrors the dominant ideology in the context of which the disadvantages and problems of poor, homeless, unemployed, underemployed, downwardly mobile men, particularly white men – who are the majority of the male population – become practically invisible. On average, whites are better off than non-whites; they earn higher incomes and have a larger net worth. But wealth and income are highly concentrated and globalisation has had a devastating effect on blue-collar skilled workers, and on the prospects of the people living in small rural communities. This is the material base for the perception, among some sectors of the white working class, that whatever progress women and minorities make, it is at the cost of the economic opportunities for white males and their families.[55] This is why it is not surprising to see the rise of white supremacist ideologies and groups, and the rise of racism, misogyny, and xenophobia.[56] In this context, the results of the November 2016 election in the United States are not surprising either; a majority of white voters, including a large proportion of the white working-class, native-born, living in rural areas and poorly educated,[57] elected someone who started his presidential campaign denouncing Mexican immigrants as rapists and criminals.[58]

It should be clear than I am not excusing white supremacists, nor am I arguing that all disadvantaged, downwardly mobile white workers are white

---

55   See Cherlin 2014a for a detailed study of the declining fortunes of the American working class.

56   Cherlin argues that there is an affinity between downwardly mobile working-class whites who blame non-whites and immigrants for their economic distress and the rhetoric of the presidential candidate, now President Trump (Cherlin 2016).

57   http://www.bloomberg.com/politics/graphics/2016-how-trump-won/?terminal=true.

58   https://www.washingtonpost.com/news/fact-checker/wp/2015/07/08/donald-trumps -false-comments-connecting-mexican-immigrants-and-crime/.

supremacists; I am only offering a plausible account for the tendency, among some, to attribute job losses and economic problems to the relatively meagre gains of women and minority groups. It is true that right-wing politicians exploit the problems of the white working class, exacerbating their anger and misinterpretations about the sources of their economic plight and political invisibility. It is also true that in the United States, until relatively recently, when the plight of the white working class became visible in the media, the sectors of the population with economic and other problems that merited political and public attention were, overwhelmingly, women and minorities. This situation is starting to be publicly acknowledged, as the election results have called attention to the failure of 'identity liberalism'; '[liberals'] own obsession with diversity has encouraged white, rural, religious Americans to think of themselves as a disadvantaged group whose identity is being threated or ignored ... [they] are not actually reacting against the reality of our diverse America ... they are reacting against the omnipresent rhetoric of identity'.[59]

It should be clear also that I am not blaming the hegemony of identity politics in the US on intersectionality. Intersectionality simply uses the same coded identity categories. Is intersectionality a form of identity politics? It might be more accurate to say that it is a framework or 'analytical tool' that serves to reinforce identity politics; its ubiquitous presence in teaching, research and policy making has the unintended consequence of solidifying gender, race, ethnicity, national origin and other sources of oppression in people's consciousness, particularly among students,[60] thus supporting the misleading view of the sources of inequality portrayed in the media and political discourses. Therefore, despite the progressive values of its proponents, it is possible to argue that an important unintended effect of intersectionality in the context of capitalist societies is ideological. There is an 'elective affinity' between the widespread use of intersectional thinking, which spills over beyond academic settings into the media and public discourse, the generalised use of identity categories for the purposes of redressing inequalities and increasing 'diversity' in educational institutions and public and private organisations, and the dominant, misleading view of American society. This is a view that excludes awareness of class as a potential basis for solidarity among workers despite their differences, emphasises racism, sexism and other identity divisions and sources of oppression, and largely ignores or minimises the problems and needs facing a large propor-

---

59   Lilla 2016, p. 4.
60   According to the author of a recent article about college students' activism and unrest, students' 'requisite vocabulary is acquired in college. If the new campus activism has a central paradigm, it is intersectionality' (Heller 2016, p. 30).

tion of the white working class.[61] Intersectionality needs to acknowledge that
exploitation and oppression are not the monopoly of disadvantaged women
and relatively few men. The global capitalist economy has undermined the
employment opportunities and standard of living of the working classes everywhere.[62] In other words, disadvantaged males are not 'occasionally' marginalised; the 'masculinisation of poverty' and the 'feminisation of the proletariat'
are two sides of the same capitalist coin.

Just as feminism has been 'seduced' and co-opted by global elites,[63] it would
seem that intersectionality has also been and co-opted by the neoliberal use
of the language of diversity everywhere, in the academy, in progressive movements and organisations, corporations, workplaces,[64] as if the original goal of
intersectionality had been to facilitate the upward mobility of a few. Carbin and
Edenheim point out that 'intersectional feminism ... has come to signal a liberal
consensus-based project that ignores capitalism as an oppressive structure'.[65]
According to Puar, 'As a tool of diversity management and a mantra of liberal
multiculturalism, intersectionality colludes with the disciplinary apparatus of
the state – census, demography, racial profiling, surveillance – in that "difference" is encased within a structural container that simply wishes the messiness
of identity into a formulaic grid'.[66] In capitalist social formations, no qualitative
structural changes are possible within its material and ideological constraints,
and identity politics, which cannot be totally separated from intersectionality,
can only lead to legal, political and ideological changes that leave the structures of exploitation and domination untouched.[67] That critical inquiries and

---

61   As Lilla points out, 'the fixation on diversity in our schools and the press has produced a
      generation of liberals and progressives narcissistically unaware of conditions outside their
      self-defined groups ... By the time [children] reach college many assume that diversity dis-
      course exhausts political discourse, and have shockingly little to say about such perennial
      questions as class, war, the economy and the common good' (Lilla 2016, p. 2).
62   While women and racial/ethnic minorities are disproportionately poor, in absolute num-
      bers, the size of the white male population that might be considered marginalised and
      oppressed is likely to be larger. In the US, for example, whites comprise close to 63 per-
      cent of the population. Adding up, the number of oppressed, marginalised white and
      non-white males is likely to be large.
63   Eisenstein 2010.
64   Bilge 2013.
65   Carbin and Edenheim 2013, p. 345.
66   Puar 2014, p. 337, in Grzanka 2014; see also Bilge 2013, pp. 407–10.
67   In the essay 'On the Jewish Question' (Marx 1994, pp. 2–39), Marx shows the limitations
      of legal changes that abolish barriers such as birth, education, occupation, religion, and
      so on, to full participation in the political community. The universality presupposed in
      political life, where everyone is equal under the law and has the same rights, presupposes

praxes informed by intersectionality do not and cannot change the capitalist status quo might be a key underlying condition for its phenomenal success.

Conclusion

Intersectionality is an analytical framework that can be used in any discipline, within any theoretical context and at any level of analysis. It is celebrated everywhere as the culmination of 'feminist theory' but, as it is applicable to men and includes, besides gender, a relatively large and variable number of other categories of analysis, to have it so firmly defined as a feminist perspective is confusing to those encountering it for the first time. Feminist theories are about the oppression of women, but intersectionality applies to everyone, male and female, privileged and oppressed and all gradations in between; it is a framework that posits complex identities, inequality and oppression, rather than the oppression of women, as the main subject of theory and research. Essentially, intersectionality as an academic pursuit is an approach to studying inequality in any discipline or field of studies (e.g. history, sociology, queer studies, masculinity studies, legal studies, and so on) from any theoretical perspective *except* Marxism. It is the latest instance of the academic and political 'retreat from class'.

Politically, intersectionality can be used in any political context; e.g. antiracist, anti-sexist struggles and struggles for immigrant rights; neoliberal policies that undermine progressive struggles by promoting 'diversity' in the workplace and elsewhere, and even right-wing anti-immigrant, nationalist and white supremacist movements as well. Progressive proponents of intersectionality, particularly those who use it as tool to influence social policy and make sure that no one remains invisible under the law and in any social or economic context that matters, undoubtedly accomplish a lot in improving the life of those oppressed for a variety of reasons (e.g. gender, disability, race, eth-

---

the continued existence of the material inequalities that characterise capitalist society. In Chapter 1 in this volume, I argued that women's and racial/ethnic minorities' success in civil rights struggles does not alter the situation of the majority, because the class structure remains unchanged. I am not arguing that expanding the scope of civil rights is not important; on the contrary, it benefits many people within the protected groups against discrimination in education, employment, pay, and so on. But legal changes do not alter the normal functioning of the capitalist economy that produces and reproduces the economic distress afflicting the vast majority of the population, or the ideologies about gender, race, ethnicity, ancestry, and so on that fuel discrimination and fragment the working population into antagonistic groups competing for economic survival.

nicity, national origin, immigrant status, and so on). In the European Union, for example, the law protects individuals from 'intersectional discrimination'.[68]

Nevertheless, as I argued earlier, intersectionality is also a discourse in harmony with identity politics; its unintended ideological effect, paradoxically, is to support the status quo that produces the inequality, complex identities and oppressions that are the focus of the discourse.

Like all theories, intersectionality is a product of its time. The effects of globalisation – uprooting millions of workers, triggering the migration of men, women and children from war-torn countries and former colonies to the countries of the former colonisers – are changing the material and social conditions of life, as well as scholars' and activists' consciousness. Such changes will give rise, eventually, to theories aiming to transcend intersectionality's limitations, theorising the systemic connections between the vaunted 'axes of oppression' in ways that may or may not embrace historical materialism. Social reproduction theory is probably such a theory.[69] Alternatively, the intensification of exploitation – manifested in the concentration of wealth and income at the top and the growth of the national and transnational reserve armies of labour – which in the US is already bringing the working class into political and mass media discourse – might eventually bring back the widespread interest in Marxism found in the 1960s and '70s among activists, students and academics. There is already a resurgence of interest in Marxism and Feminism; whether this will entail the demise of intersectionality, its integration with an idealist version of Marxism emphasising racial, gender and other oppressions while minimising the determinant effects of class power and class relations, or a return to historical materialism, will be for the younger generations to decide.

---

68   Lutz et al. 2011, p. 7. See also Crenshaw 2014, pp. 17–22, in Grzanka 2014.
69   See, for example, Ferguson 2016.

CHAPTER 5

What's Material about Materialist Feminism? A Marxist-Feminist Critique

'What's Material about Materialist Feminism?', in *Radical Philosophy*, No. 101 (May/June, 2000): 19–28.

Introduction

It was possible, in the heady days of the Women's Liberation Movement, to identify four main currents within feminist thought: Liberal (concerned with attaining economic and political equality within the context of capitalism); Radical (focused on men and patriarchy as the main causes of the oppression of women); Socialist (critical of capitalism and Marxism, so much so that avoidance of Marxism's alleged reductionisms resulted in dual systems theories postulating various forms of interaction between capitalism and patriarchy); and Marxist-Feminism (a theoretical position held by relatively few feminists in the US – myself included – which sought to develop the potential of Marxist theory to understand the capitalist sources of the oppression of women).

These are, of course, oversimplified descriptions of a rich and complex body of literature which, however, reflected important theoretical, political and social cleavages among women that continue to this day. Divisions in feminist thought multiplied as the effects of poststructuralist and postmodern theorising emerged alongside grassroots challenges to a feminism perceived as the expression of the needs and concerns of middle and upper middle-class white, 'First World' women. In the process, the subject of feminism became increasingly difficult to define, as the postmodern critique of 'woman' as an essentialist category together with critiques grounded in racial, ethnic, sexual preference and national origin differences resulted in a seemingly never-ending proliferation of 'subject positions', 'identities', and 'voices'. Cultural and identity politics replaced the early focus on capitalism and (among Marxist-Feminists primarily) class divisions among women; today class has been reduced to another 'ism'; i.e. to another form oppression which, together with gender and race, integrate a sort of mantra, something that everyone ought to include in theorising and research, though, to my knowledge, theorising about it remains at the level of metaphors (e.g. interweaving, interaction, interconnection, etc.).

It was, therefore, very interesting to read, a few years ago, a call for papers for an edited book on Materialist Feminism (MatFem). The description of Mat-Fem put forth by the editors, Chrys Ingraham and Rosemary Hennessy, was to me indistinguishable from Marxist-Feminism (MarxFem). This seemed such a promising development in feminist theory that I proceeded to invite the editors to join me in creating an electronic discussion list on Materialist Feminism, MatFem. Initially, I thought that MatFem was simply another way of referring to MarxFem, but I was mistaken; the two are distinct forms of feminist theorising. There are, however, such similarities between them in some feminists' work that some degree of confusion between the two is to be expected.

In this chapter, I will identify the differences between these two important currents within feminist theory, and the reasons for the return of feminist appeals to materialism at a time when the theoretical shift towards idealism and contingency seems hegemonic in the academy. Given the conflicting views that co-exist under the materialist cover, I will argue for a clear break between Materialist and Marxist-Feminisms, and for a return to the latter necessitated by the devastating effects of capitalism on women and, consequently, the political importance of a theoretically adequate analysis of the causes of their plight.

What is Materialist Feminism?

To define MatFem is not an easy task; theorists who self-identify as Materialist or as Marxist feminists differ in their understanding of what these labels mean and, consequently, the kind of knowledge they produce. Depending on their theoretical allegiances and self-understanding, feminists may differ in their classification of other feminists' works, so that clear lines of theoretical demarcation between and within these two umbrella terms are somewhat difficult to establish. Take, for example, Vogel's work.[1] I always considered Vogel to be a Marxist-Feminist because, unlike Socialist Feminists (whose avoidance of Marx's alleged reductionisms led them to postulate ahistorical theories of patriarchy),[2] she took Marxism seriously and her analysis of reproduction as a basis for the oppression of women is firmly grounded within the Marxist tradition. However, the subtitle of her recent book (a collection of previously published essays), is 'Essays for a Materialist Feminism'; self-identifying as a socialist fem-

---

1 Vogel 1993 and 1995.
2 See, for example, Firestone 1971; Einsenstein 1979.

inist, she states that socialist feminists 'sought to replace the socialist tradition's theorising about the woman question with a "materialist" understanding of women's oppression'.[3] This is certainly news to me; Socialist Feminism's rejection of Marx's and Marxism's 'reductionism' led to the deliberate effort to ground 'patriarchy' outside the mode of production and, consequently, and from the standpoint of Marxist theory, outside history. Materialism, Vogel tells us, was used to highlight the key role of production – including domestic production – in determining the conditions leading to the oppression of women. Materialism was also used as 'a flag', to situate Socialist Feminism within feminist thought and within the left; materialist feminism, Vogel argues, cannot therefore be reduced to a trend in cultural studies, as some literary critics would prefer.[4] But wasn't Engels's analysis materialist?[5] And didn't Marxist-Feminists (Margaret Benston[6] and Peggy Morton[7] come to mind) explore the ways in which production – public and domestic – oppressed and exploited women?

These brief comments about Vogel's understanding of MatFem highlight some of its problematic aspects as a term intended to identify a specific trend within feminist theory. It can blur, as it does in this instance, the qualitative differences that existed and continue to exist between Socialist Feminism, the dominant strand of feminist thought in the US during the late 1960s and 1970s, and the marginalised Marxist-Feminism. I am not imputing such motivations to Vogel; I am simply pointing out the effects of such an interpretation of US Socialist Feminism which, despite the use of Marxist terms and references to capitalism developed, theoretically, as a sort of feminist abstract negation of Marxism.

Other feminists, for different reasons, would also disagree with Vogel's interpretation. For Toril Moi and Janice Radway, for example, the relationship between Socialist Feminism and MatFem 'is far from clear'.[8] As editors of a special issue of *The South Atlantic Quarterly* dedicated to this topic, they do not offer a theory or a clear definition of the term. Presumably, the issue's content will give the reader the elements necessary to define the term for herself, because all the authors share a commitment to concrete historical and cultural analysis, and to feminism understood as an 'emancipatory narrative'.[9] One of these authors, Jennifer Wicke, defines MatFem as follows:

3   Vogel 1995, p. xi.
4   Vogel 1995, p. xii.
5   Engels 1972. See also Sayers, Evans and Redclift 1987.
6   Benston 1969.
7   Morton 1971.
8   Moi and Radway 1994.
9   Moi and Radway 1994, p. 750.

a feminism that insists on examining the material conditions under which social arrangements, including those of gender hierarchy, develop ... materialist feminism avoids seeing this (gender hierarchy) as the effect of a singular ... patriarchy and instead gauges the web of social and psychic relations that make up a material, historical moment; ... materialist feminism argues that material conditions of all sorts play a vital role in the social production of gender and assays the different ways in which women collaborate and participate in these productions ... there are areas of material interest in the fact that women can bear children ... Materialist feminism ... is less likely than social constructionism to be embarrassed by the occasional material importance of sex differences.[10]

Insistence on the importance of material conditions, material historical moments as a complex of social relations which include and influence gender hierarchy, the materiality of the body and its sexual, reproductive and other biological functions remain, however, abstract pronouncements which unavoidably lead to an empiricist focus on the immediately given. There is no theory of history or of social relations or of the production of gender hierarchies that could give guidance about the meaning of whatever is observed in a given 'material historical moment'.

Landry and MacLean, authors of *Materialist Feminisms*,[11] tell us that theirs is a book 'about feminism and Marxism' in which they examine the debates between feminism and Marxism in the US and Britain and explore the implications of those debates for literary and cultural theory. The terrain of those early debates, which were aimed at a possible integration or synthesis between Marxism and feminism, shifted due to the emergence of identity politics, concern with postcolonialism, sexuality, race, nationalism, etc., and the impact of postmodernism and poststructuralism. The new terrain has to do with the 'construction of a materialist analysis of culture informed by and responsive to the concerns of women, as well as people of color and other marginalized groups'.[12] For Landry and Maclean, MatFem is a

> critical reading practice ... the critical investigation, or reading in the strong sense, of the artifacts of culture and social history, including literary and artistic texts, archival documents, and works of theory ... [it is]

---

10   Wicke 1994.
11   Landry and Maclean 1993.
12   Landry and Maclean 1993, pp. ix–x.

a potential site of political contestation through critique, not through the constant reiteration of home-truths ... a deconstructive materialist feminist perspective.[13]

But what, precisely, does materialist mean in this context? What theory of history and what politics inform this critique? Although they define materialism in a philosophical and moral sense, and bring up the difference between mechanical or 'vulgar' materialism and historical materialism, there is no definition of what materialism means when linked to feminism. Cultural materialism, as developed in Raymond Williams's work, is presented as a remedy or supplement to Marx's historical materialism. There is, according to Williams, an 'indissoluble connection between material production, political and cultural institutions and activity, and consciousness ... Language is practical consciousness, a way of thinking and acting in the world that has material consequences'.[14] Williams, they point out, 'strives to put human subjects as agents of culture back into materialist debate'.[15]

The implications of these statements are that 'humans as agents of culture' are not present in historical materialism and that Marx's views on the relationship between material conditions, language, and consciousness are insufficient. But anyone familiar with Marx's work knows that this is not the case. In fact, it was Marx and Engels who wrote that 'language is practical consciousness' and who posited language as the matter that burdens 'spirit' from the very start, for consciousness is always and from the very first a social product.[16]

Landry and Maclean provide an account of the development of feminist thought from the late 1960s to the present that is divided into three moments: the encounters and debates between Marxism and feminism in Britain and the US; the institutionalisation and commodification of feminism; and 'deconstructive materialist feminism'. These are 'three moments of materialist feminism':[17] a very interesting statement that suggests that MatFem – a rather problematic and elusive concept which reflects, in my view, postmodern sensibilities about culture and about the subject of feminism – had always been there, from the very beginning, just waiting to be discovered. Is that really the case? If so, what is this materialism that lurked beneath the surface of various feminist theories produced on both sides of the Atlantic since the late 1960s?

---

13   Landry and Maclean 1993, pp. x–xi.
14   Landry and Maclean 1993, p. 5.
15   Ibid.
16   Marx 1994, p. 117.
17   Landry and Maclean 1993, p. 15.

Does reference to 'material conditions' in general, or to 'the material conditions of the oppression of women' suffice as a basis for constructing a new theoretical framework, qualitatively different from MarxFem? If so, how? The authors argue that feminist theories focused exclusively on gender and dual systems theories that bring together gender and class analysis face methodological and political problems that 'deconstructive reading practices can help solve'; they propose 'the articulation of discontinuous movements, materialism and feminism, an articulation that takes the political claims of deconstruction seriously ... deconstruction as tool of political critique'.[18] But isn't the linking between deconstruction and Marxism what gives it its critical edge? It is in the conclusion that the authors, aiming to demonstrate that materialism is not an alias for Marxism, outline the difference between MarxFem and MatFem as follows:

> Marxist feminism holds class contradictions and class analysis central, and has tried various ways of working an analysis of gender oppression around this central contradiction. In addition to class contradictions and contradictions within gender ideology ... we are arguing that materialist feminism should recognize as material other contradictions as well. These contradictions also have histories, operate in ideologies, and are grounded in material bases and effects ... [T]hey should be granted material weight in social and literary analysis calling itself materialist ... [T]hese categories would include ... ideologies of race, sexuality, imperialism and colonialism and anthropocentrism, with their accompanying radical critiques.[19]

While this is helpful to understand what contemporary self-identified materialist feminists mean when they refer to MatFem, it does not shed light on the meaning of material base, material effect, and material weight. The main concept, materialism, remains undefined; at times it seems to mean real or objective (e.g. gender and race are as real as class), or central, meaning determinant, having causal effects (e.g. ideologies are just as central or have as much 'material weight' as class). Underlying these ideas lurk the spectres of 'class reductionism' and 'economic determinism', a stereotypical understanding of Marx and the Marxist tradition used to argue for the superiority of claims defined, essentially, as their abstract negation. Also lurking are Althusser's[20] views on the materiality of ideology, now expanded to analyse all forms of

---

18   Landry and Maclean 1993, pp. 12–15.
19   Landry and Maclean 1993, p. 229.
20   Althusser 1971, pp. 127–86.

oppression and oppositional identities, but with a crucial difference: while for Althusser the level of production and, consequently, the contradictions between capital and labour and between the forces and relations of production are determinant 'in the last instance', albeit 'overdetermined' and rendered historically specific and active by the characteristics of concrete social formations,[21] Materialist Feminism appears to rest upon the unsupported claim that there is no hierarchy of causality: all other forms of inequality besides class, and their corresponding ideologies, are equally 'material', meaning they are not only equally real and important but also equal in their causal powers. Such conclusion might be politically satisfying, but it rests upon a functional notion of causality according to which all institutions or elements of the social system mutually interact and affect each other, and none is 'more' causally efficacious than others; i.e. none can set parameters for the conditions of possibility and development of the others. And what is the nature of the other 'contradictions' materialist feminists should recognise? Contradiction is not equivalent to conflict, for conflicts can be resolved within a given system of relations, whereas contradiction can be resolved solely through qualitative social change. Finally, references to ideologies, exploitation, imperialism, oppression, colonialism, etc. confirm precisely that which the authors intended to dispel: materialism would seem to be an alias for Marxism, a Marxism suitably modified, however, to grant materiality (meaning, perhaps, objectivity, reality, and equal causal efficacy) to everything.

MatFem/MarxFem: Same Difference?

Hennessy traces the origins of Materialist Feminism in the work of British and French feminists who preferred the term materialist feminism to Marxist feminism because, in their view, Marxism had to be transformed to be able to explain the sexual division of labour.[22] In the 1970s, Hennessy states, Marxism was inadequate to the task because of its class bias and focus on production, while feminism was also problematic due to its essentialist and idealist

---

21   See Althusser 1970, especially pp. 111–16. Marx had expressed the same idea when he stated that, while the relations of production 'reveal the innermost secret, the hidden basis of the entire social structure ... this does not prevent the same economic basis ... due to innumerable different empirical circumstances ... from showing infinite variations and gradations in appearance, which can be ascertained only by analysis of the empirically given circumstances'. Marx 1968, pp. 791–2.

22   Hennessy 1993, pp. xi–xii.

concept of woman; this is why MatFem emerged as a positive alternative both to Marxism and feminism.[23] The combined effects of the postmodern critique of the empirical self and the criticisms voiced by women who did not see themselves included in the generic woman subject of academic feminist theorising resulted, in the 1990s, in materialist feminist analyses that 'problematize "woman" as an obvious and homogeneous empirical entity in order to explore how "woman" as a discursive category is historically constructed and traversed by more than one differential axis'.[24] Furthermore, Hennessy argues, despite the postmodern rejection of totalities and theoretical analyses of social systems, materialist feminists need to hold on to the critique of the totalities which affect women's lives: patriarchy and capitalism. Women's lives are everywhere affected by world capitalism and patriarchy and it would be politically self-defeating to replace that critique with localised, fragmented political strategies and a perception of social reality as characterised by a logic of contingency.

Hennessy's views on the characteristics of MatFem emerge through her critical engagement with the works of Laclau and Mouffe, Foucault, Kristeva and other theorists of the postmodern. MatFem is a 'way of reading' that rejects the dominant pluralist paradigms and logics of contingency and seeks to establish the connections between the discursively constructed differentiated subjectivities that have replaced the generic 'woman' in feminist theorising, and the hierarchies of inequality that exploit and oppress women. Subjectivities, in other words, cannot be understood in isolation from systemically organised totalities. MatFem, as a reading practice, is also a way of explaining or re-writing and making sense of the world and, as such, influences reality through the knowledges it produces about the subject and her social context. Discourse and knowledge have materiality in their effects; one of the material effects of discourse is the construction of the subject but this subject is traversed by differences grounded in hierarchies of inequality which are not local or contingent but historical and systemic, such as patriarchy and capitalism. Difference, consequently, is not mere plurality but inequality. The problem of the material relationship between language, discourse, and the social or between the discursive (feminist theory) and the non-discursive (women's lives divided by exploitative and oppressive social relations) can be resolved through the conceptualisation of discourse as ideology. A theory of ideology presupposes a theory of the social and this theory, which informs Hennessy's critical reading of postmodern theories of the subject, discourse, positionality, language, etc., is what she calls a

---

23   Hennessy 1993, p. xii.
24   Ibid.

'global analytic' which, in light of her references to multinational capitalism, the international division of labour, overdetermined economic, political and cultural practices, and so on, seems to be at the very least a kind of postmodern Marxism. But references to historical materialism, and Althusser's theory of ideology and the notion of symptomatic reading are so important in the development of her arguments that one wonders about her hesitation to name Marxism or historical materialism as the theory of the social underlying her critique of the postmodern logic of contingency.

To sum up, Hennessy's version of MatFem is a blend of post-Marxism and postmodern theories of the subject and a source of 'readings' and 're-writings' which rescue postmodern categories of analysis (subject, discourse, difference) from the conservative limbo of contingency, localism and pluralism to historicise or contextualise them by connecting them to their systemic material basis in capitalism and patriarchy. This is made possible by understanding discourse as ideology and linking ideology to its material base in the 'global analytic'.

In Hennessy's analysis, historical materialism seems like an ever present but muted shadow, latent under terms such as 'totality', 'systemic', and 'global analytic'. However, in the introduction to *Materialist Feminism: A Reader in Class, Difference and Women's Lives*,[25] written with her co-editor, Chrys Ingraham, there is a clear, unambiguous return to historical materialism, a recognition of its irreplaceable importance for feminist theory and politics. This introduction, 'Reclaiming Anti-capitalist Feminism',[26] is a critique of the dominant feminist concern with culture, identity and difference considered in isolation from any systemic understanding of the social forces that affect women's lives, and a critique of an academic feminism that has marginalised and disparaged the knowledge produced by the engagement of feminists with Marxism, and their contributions to feminist scholarship and to the political mobilisation of women. More importantly, this introduction is a celebration of MarxFem whose premises and insights, they argue, have been consistently 'misread, distorted, or buried under the weight of a flourishing postmodern cultural politics'.[27] They point out that, whatever the name of the product of feminists' efforts to grapple with historical materialism (Matfem, Socialist Feminism or MarxFem), though these names signal theoretical differences and emphases, together they indicate the recognition of historical materialism as the source of emancipatory knowledge required for the success of the feminist project. In this introduction, MatFem becomes a term used interchange-

---

25   Hennessy and Ingraham 1997.
26   Hennessy and Ingraham 1997, pp. 1–14.
27   Hennessy and Ingraham 1997, p. 5.

ably with MarxFem, with the latter being the most prominently displayed. The authors draw a clear line between the cultural materialism that characterises the work of post-Marxist feminists who, having rejected historical materialism, analyse cultural, ideological and political practices in isolation from their material base in capitalism, and MatFem (meaning both MarxFem and Socialist Feminism) which is firmly grounded in historical materialism; 'unlike cultural feminists, materialist, socialist and Marxist feminists do not see culture as the whole of social life but rather as only one arena of social production and therefore as only one area of feminist struggle'.[28] The authors differentiate MatFem from MarxFem by indicating that MatFem is the end result of several discourses (historical materialism, Marxist and radical feminism, and postmodern and psychoanalytic theories of meaning and subjectivity) among which the postmodern input, in their view, is the source of its defining characteristics. Nevertheless, in the last paragraphs of the introduction there is a return to the discussion of MarxFem, its critiques of the idealist features of postmodernism and the differences between the postmodern and the historical materialist or Marxist analyses of representations of identity. Theoretical conflicts, they point out, do not occur in isolation from class conflicts and the latter affect the divisions among professional feminists and their class allegiances. Feminists are divided in their attitudes towards capitalism, their understanding of the material conditions of oppression and the extent to which they link the success of feminist struggles to the success of anti-capitalist struggles. To be a feminist is not necessarily to be anti-capitalist and to be a materialist feminist is not equivalent to being socialist or even critical of the status quo. In fact, 'work that claims the signature "materialist feminism" shares much in common with cultural feminism, in that it does not set out to explain or change the material realities that link women's oppression to class'.[29] MarxFem, on the other hand, does make the connection between the oppression of women and capitalism and this is why the purpose of their book, according to the authors, is

> to reinsert into MatFem – especially in those overdeveloped sectors where this collection will be most widely read – those (untimely) marxist feminist knowledges that the drift to cultural politics in postmodern feminism has suppressed. It is our hope that in so doing this project will contribute to the emergence of feminisms' third wave and its revival as a critical force for transformative social change.[30]

---

28   Hennessy and Ingraham 1997, p. 7.
29   Hennessy and Ingraham 1997, p. 9.
30   Ibid.

In light of the above, given the inherent ambiguity of the term MatFem, shouldn't it be more theoretically adequate and politically fruitful to return to Marxist-Feminism? Is the effort of struggling to redefine MatFem by reinserting MarxFem knowledges a worthwhile endeavour? How important is it to broaden the meaning of MatFem to include Marxist-Feminist contents? Perhaps the political climate inside and outside the academy in the US is one where Marxism is so discredited that Marxist-Feminists are likely to find more professional acceptance and legitimacy by claiming MatFem as their theoretical orientation. I do not in any way impute this motivation to Ingraham and Hennessy whose introduction to their book is openly Marxist. In fact, after I read it and looked over the table of contents I thought a more adequate title for the book should have been Marxist-Feminism. And anyone familiar with historical materialism can appreciate the sophisticated Marxist foundation of Hennessy's superbly argued book.

Materialist Feminist: Am I That Name?

Such positive feminist assessment of the theoretical and political relevance of Marxism is, however, rare these days. Feminists are more likely to share Landry and MacLean's critique of Marxism's alleged economism, class reductionism, and disregard for agency and the effects of culture and ideology. Underlying these and similar feminist criticisms of Marxism's putative shortcomings, there is an economistic and undialectical reading of Marx's work. That Marx may not have addressed issues that twentieth-century feminists consider important is not a sufficient condition to invalidate his methodology as well as the potential of his theory of capitalism to help us theorise and investigate the causes of the oppression of women. This potential, however, was widely recognised in the early stages of the Women's Liberation Movement. It is very interesting, in retrospect, to read the work produced by some British self-defined Materialist Feminists writing in the 1970s, and realise that they were actually using and developing Marxist theory in ways that belied their critical stance towards Marxism. For example, Kuhn and Wolpe, editors of *Feminism and Materialism*,[31] adopted Engels's definition of materialism:

> According to the materialist conception, the determining factor in history is, in the final instance, the production and reproduction of immediate

---

31   Kuhn and Wolpe 1978.

life. This, again, is of a twofold character: on the one side, the production of the means of existence, of food, clothing and shelter and the tools necessary for that production; on the other side, the production of human beings themselves, the propagation of the species.[32]

A materialist problematic entailed, then, recognition of the fundamental importance, for the analysis of human history and social organisation, of the production and reproduction of material life; i.e. the transformation of nature and human nature through labour in the context of changing relations of production and reproduction.[33] For Kuhn and Wolpe, the difference between a Marxist and a materialist analysis hinged upon whether or not analysis went beyond the 'traditional' Marxist focus on modes of production, their tendencies, contradictions and so forth, to incorporate the historical character of the sexual division of labour and the examination of 'the relations of women to the modes of production and reproduction'.[34] It followed that Marxism could not yield a 'correct' analysis of the oppression of women unless it was transformed by including the analysis of the sexual division of labour and all other aspects of the mode of production directly and indirectly affecting male/female relationships. Contributors to their volume attempted in various ways to remedy Marxism's 'failures' by creatively using Marxist theory to explore the relationships between capitalism and institutions that specifically oppressed women; e.g. patriarchy, the family, the state, domestic labour, the sexual division of labour, women's place in the labour force, etc.

MatFem was also associated with the work of French feminists, particularly Christine Delphy.[35] Materialism (i.e. the Marxist method), she argued, is the only theory of history that views oppression as the most fundamental reality; this is why women and all oppressed groups need it to examine their situation: 'to start from oppression defines a materialist approach ... oppression is a materialist concept'.[36] For Delphy, the family or domestic mode of production, analytically independent and separate from production, was the site of patriarchal exploitation and the material basis of the oppression of women. Marriage, she argued, is a labour contract that gives men the right to exploit women, appropriating their labour in the domestic setting or controlling their wages or other market earnings; it is, for all practical purposes, a relationship

---

32   Kuhn and Wolpe 1978, p. 7.
33   Ibid.
34   Kuhn and Wolpe 1978, pp. 7–8.
35   Delphy 1977.
36   Delphy 1980, p. 87.

of slavery.[37] Delphy sought in the organisation of the mode of reproduction the structural basis for gender divisions; rather than inquiring into the social construction of gender or the ways in which individuals acquire gender identities, she sought to identify the material conditions that place men and women in unequal relations. Barrett and McIntosh[38] criticised Delphy on several grounds; e.g. economism (she rejected analyses that gave causal importance to ideology), emphasis on the exploitation of women as wives, overlooking the effects of motherhood and the situation of single women, and for inappropriately applying the concept of mode of production to the family. In postulating the autonomy of the family or domestic mode of production from the mode of production as such, they argued, Delphy isolated it from the dynamics of social change.[39] An acceptable materialist analysis, in their view, should connect the economic and ideological levels of analysis, examining how material (i.e. economic) conditions structure consciousness.[40]

Although earlier self-defined materialist feminists may have understood their work to be one of 'transforming' Marxist theory, they actually demonstrated its fundamental importance for theorising the oppression of women. A theoretical transformation would have entailed a challenge to Marxism's fundamental assumptions, rather than the use of those very assumptions to theorise new phenomena. To demonstrate, as they did, a dialectical understanding of Marxism, introducing in the analysis of the oppression of women the causal efficacy of the state, ideology, the family and other aspects of capitalist society, is to remain faithful its basic tenets, not to transform it.

I too wrote about Marxism and feminism in the 1970s but my approach was different, for I viewed the lacunae in Marx's work simply as results of his immediate political and theoretical priorities. Because Marx's method shows the problems inherent in abstract theories of origins, and reveals the dialectical nature of our categories of analysis,[41] I concluded early on that the notion of patriarchy was descriptively useful, but theoretically unsound because it was intentionally developed to seek the origin of the oppression of women outside history (i.e. independent from the mode of production). I was also critical of the use of 'women' and 'men' as categories of analysis (they ignored class, racial and ethnic divisions, and socio-economic status differences) and the utopian nature of 'sisterhood', given the real contradictions in the material

---

37   Delphy 1977, p. 15.
38   Barrett and McIntosh 1982.
39   Barrett and McIntosh 1982, p. 99.
40   Barrett and McIntosh 1982, p. 103.
41   Marx 1970, pp. 205–6.

interests of capitalist and working-class women. I am originally from Argentina, a society in which, unlike the United States, professional women were not exceptional, class divisions and self-identification prevailed, and the use of domestic servants was widespread (an important reason for the lack of conflict between work and family for professional and employed middle-class women). I was, consequently, unconvinced by theories which overgeneralised about male domination and female oppression and were not sensitive to the realities of life under capitalism, where most men are not powerful and in control over their lives and not all women are powerless. More nuanced theories, differentiating between kinds of oppressions and corresponding levels of analyses were required. This is why, in my work, I sought to identify the historically specific capitalist conditions underlying the observable social and economic inequalities between men and women.

However, I never self-identified as a Materialist Feminist; the label, in my view, misrepresented the dialectical nature of Marxism and obscured the actual Marxist nature of the works thus labelled. While there were some overlaps between my views and those of materialist and socialist feminists of the 1970s, both in terms of topics of analysis as well as in the aspects of Marx's theory of capitalism we considered pertinent to examine the oppression of women, my work differs in the rejection of patriarchy as an explanatory concept, and in the use of Marx's method to identify the capitalist processes that place propertyless men and women in similar class locations while facing different opportunity structures and, therefore, unequal access to the necessary conditions of reproduction.[42] But more important than the differences and similarities between my work and that of other 1970s socialist feminists, here and in Britain, is the issue of the present resurgence of MatFem as a fashionable trend within feminist theory. Why has MatFem reappeared? Why is it a 'hot' commodity, as reflected in the abundance of recent publications with 'materialism' in their title? Is MatFem a positive development in feminist theory? Should Marxist-Feminists struggle to regain political and academic legitimacy, thus striving to differentiate MarxFem from MatFem?

Why Materialist Feminism Now? Does It Matter?

While it is difficult to disentangle Matfem from Marxfem in early feminist works, especially those written by European feminists, today MatFem and

---

42   See, for example, Gimenez 1975 and 1978.

MarxFem are qualitatively different theoretical perspectives, with radically different political implications. That they have become somewhat confused reflects the ideological balance of power in the present political context, in academia and in the publishing business, where 'difference', 'race, gender and class', 'postisms', and, of course, 'materialism' have legitimacy and sell, while historical materialism does not.

Early materialist feminists took Marxism as their starting point. Despite critiques of Marxism's shortcomings, Marxist and materialist feminists agreed on the importance of situating the oppression of women in the context of the capitalist mode of production as a whole, examining how the capitalist organisation of production, the articulation between production and reproduction, ideologies, the state, the legal system, etc. affected and reproduced the unequal relations between men and women within and outside the domestic sphere. Despite disagreements, they shared Engels's conception of historical materialism,[43] which gives a pivotal role in human history to the organisation of production and reproduction and their changing articulation, as the forces and relations of production change and modes of production change accordingly.

Today MatFem is altogether different because it is grounded in the poststructuralist rejection of Marxism. The deconstruction of 'women' as a category of analysis, the focus on 'discursively constructed' genders, sexualities, bodies, and manifold differences among women have severed the links between feminist theory and the actual conditions shaping most women's lives. Today, 'feminist theory has come to mean feminist poststructuralism'[44] and this entails the adoption of principles (e.g. anti-essentialism, contingency, social constructionism, reduction of social reality to discourse, rejection of 'metanarratives', etc.) antithetical to the development of social analyses and political strategies useful for women and all oppressed people.[45] The very idea of women's oppression presupposes the material reality of their plight and the validity of their claims, notions outside the purview of theories for which everything is relative, contingent, and discursively constructed. It is this inability to deal with the material (i.e. objective, independent of the subject's consciousness) conditions affecting real women's lives which, Ebert argues, has produced a crisis in postmodern feminist thought, because the objectivity and forceful impact of historical processes 'cannot be blunted in discourse'; this is why 'historical materialism haunts feminism'.[46]

---

43   Engels 1972.
44   Epstein 1995.
45   Epstein 1995, p. 83.
46   Ebert 1995, pp. 113–49.

In light of the objectively worsening conditions of working people, particularly women, it has become increasingly untenable to hold on to the notion
that everything is socially or discursively constructed, or a localised, contingent story. The oppression of women is not a story, or a text, or a form of
interpreting or reading the world, so that politics is reduced to re-writing or
re-describing the world, a conclusion that follows from the insistence on the
materiality of discourse. Because postmodern materialist feminists have rejected all 'metanarratives', discourses have a contradictory relationship to the capitalist structures, processes and contradictions which are their condition of
possibility; they are only 'contingently' related (thus duly avoiding the spectres
of 'reductionism' and 'economism') to the mode of production but, as they
are considered to be material in their effects, they are *de facto* assumed to be
determinant in their own right, thus resulting in an unacknowledged discursive
reductionism.

Hennessy and Ingraham argue for the need to keep a connection between
discourse, conceptualised as ideology, and the relevant 'global analytics' which
oppress women, patriarchy and capitalism. Their efforts, however, are not sufficient to rescue contemporary MatFem from its clearly anti-Marxist stance,
and only contribute to increase the ambiguity of the concept. Besides, Mat-
Fem has moved further away from the possibility of bridging the gap between
discourses, ideologies and the mode of production; the latest reincarnation of
poststructuralist materialism is not the matter of language, or the text or discourse, but rather 'the resisting "matter" of the non-discursive', with the body
as the matter under consideration. Matter, whether of the body or anything
else, has to be rendered historically specific in order to become theoretically
and politically significant, for 'matter as such is a pure creation of thought and
an abstraction'.[47] This, in turn, presupposes consideration of the characteristics of the mode of production which determine the kinds of labour processes
and other forms of practice which, dialectically, transform nature and human
nature, forms of existence and forms of consciousness, bodies and discourses
about bodies and so forth. This approach to theorising matter and materialism is, however, in contradiction with the assumptions of post-Marxist Mat-
Fem which, consequently, faces an unresolvable dilemma: 'how not to deny the
world outside the consciousness of the subject but not to make that world the
material cause of social practices either'.[48] If materiality implies causality, the
denial of the causal efficacy of the mode of production (e.g. through changes in

---

47   Engels 1940, pp. 322–3.
48   Ebert 1995, p. 117.

the forces of production, class exploitation, class struggles, etc.) while postulating the materiality of language and discourse ends up in a discourse determinism that undermines the very role that the materiality of discourse is supposed to play because, 'if even meaning is material, then there is nothing which is not, and the term simply cancels all the way through'.[49]

Perhaps these theoretical and political dead ends of post-Marxist MatFem are the basis for its academic and commercial appeal. There is an 'elective affinity'[50] between its dominant theoretical assumptions (which essentially 'privilege' agency, embrace contingency, and exonerate capitalism, minimising the pivotal role of class exploitation while emphasising plurality, diversity and identity politics), the dominant ideologies in the advanced capitalist countries, and the lifestyles and worldviews of the middle and upper middle-class professionals and students who have eagerly embraced postmodernism and poststructuralism, including MatFem, in its various manifestations.

Conclusion

MatFem, a term which may have been useful in the past to feminists who, despite their critical stance, remained firmly within the Marxist tradition, denotes something entirely different today. How useful is it to broaden the meaning of MatFem to encompass MarxFem if, at the same time, the term is claimed by cultural materialists and post-Marxist-Feminists whose views are profoundly anti-Marxist? That two anthologies of Marxist-feminist writings have been published under the aegis of materialist feminism attest to the greater market value of 'materialism' and publishers' power to decide what sells, rather than the existence of a theoretical convergence between MarxFem and MatFem. How will the new generations learn about the theoretical and political importance of historical materialism for women if historical materialist analysis is tamed and 'gentrified' under the MatFem label? Marx and Marxism have already been marginalised in academia; the inclusion of MarxFem under the Matfem umbrella would only intensify already widespread misunderstandings among the younger generations of feminists because, as it would call attention to the 'material' in historical materialism, it would strengthen dominant stereotypes about the 'vulgar materialism' presumably inherent in Marxism. It is time, therefore, for Marxist-Feminists to separate themselves from materialist fem-

---

49   Eagleton 1996, p. 75.
50   Weber 1958, p. 284.

inism and assert the legitimacy and political urgency of their approach. Essentially, this would entail a return to Marx whose method and analysis of capitalism, despite its ambiguities, omissions, complexities and nineteenth-century limitations, has far more to offer feminists and all oppressed people than contemporary theories which, having severed the internal relationship between existence and consciousness or between discourse and its material conditions of possibility, postulate the materiality of the discursive and whatever there might be 'outside' discourse (Nature? the Body?) while rejecting as 'economism' the materiality – i.e. the reality, independent of people's consciousness, and causal efficacy – of labour and of the mode of production. As Ebert unerringly points out, Marx's critique of 'Feuerbachian materialism' aptly describes today's MatFem's materialism: 'As far as Feuerbach is a materialist he does not deal with history, and as far as he considers history he is not a materialist'.[51]

There is another reason why I believe MarxFem should 'de-link' from Mat-Fem: Marxist-Feminists are, theoretically speaking, clearer about what MarxFem is all about, politically and theoretically. MatFem, on the other hand, remains a nebulous thing, a place for feminists who are clear about their rejection of Marx and Marxism's alleged flaws, but seem less certain about what they stand for. Feminist scholars, of course, do know what the modern MatFem they theorise is all about, but their work would seem to have difficulties in engaging the consumers of their scholarship. I am grounding these assertions in the very different development of two electronic discussion networks, MATFEM and M-Fem.[52] MATFEM (Materialist Feminism), which I created in December 1994 together with Chrys Ingraham and Rosemary Hennessy, has had for years a stable membership of over 350 (it is currently 363). At the beginning, there were the usual messages of self-introduction but, when those ceased, to our disappointment, no sustained discussions took their place. We once attempted a discussion of an article by Rosemary Hennessy, but this project failed. The list has been mostly silent; once in a while someone will post the announcement of a book, or a call for papers. But MATFEM lacks a sense of community of intellectual and political purpose; there is no sense of urgency in examining, from a materialist feminist standpoint, the various processes that continue to oppress women. M-Fem (Marxism Feminism) is a network I did not create, but help moderate. It was created in May 1997 and its small membership (72) reflects the scarcity of self-defined Marxist-Feminists today. While the volume of mail varies and the network goes through relatively long periods of silence,

---

51   Ebert 1995, p. 125.
52   Unfortunately, these networks are no longer active.

it has produced very lively and useful theoretical and political discussions and altogether a far greater quantity of messages than MATFEM. A substantial portion of this article was, in fact, written as a response to an M-Fem member who asked about the difference between MatFem and MarxFem. I posted it in both lists but drew no reactions from MATFEM (except an enthusiastic, positive response from Rosemary Hennessy) while eliciting a number of comments in M-Fem. The quantitative and qualitative difference between these networks' archives is remarkable; M-Fem archives document the power of Marxism to examine the conditions affecting women's lives today, while the meagreness of MATFEM's archives can be interpreted as resulting from the relative theoretical irrelevance and political sterility of postmodern feminism. MATFEM, in almost five years, has been unable to generate a single sustained theoretical or political discussion, despite its far larger membership. The different trajectory of these networks powerfully illustrates the qualitative differences between MarxFem and MatFem, highlighting the political and theoretical relevance of the former and the scholastic nature of the latter.

Realistically, it can be professionally and politically risky for US academic feminists openly to advocate Marxist-Feminism. Self-identified Marxist-Feminists are likely to face a difficult time, politically and professionally; they would be perceived as 'orthodox' or 'fundamentalist' Marxists and would face difficulties in finding employment, especially at this time when tenure-track jobs are becoming increasingly scarce in US universities. In the short-term, therefore, MatFem's academic dominance might remain unchallenged. In the long-term, and depending on changes in the world capitalist economy leading to transnational political upheavals and organising, and greater awareness, among feminist scholars, of the extent to which most working women's fate is tied to the contradictions of world capitalism, the timeliness and relevance of Marxism might become self-evident again and M-Fem might replace MatFem. In the meantime, as the uneasy and confusing relationship between MarxFem and Matfem illustrates so well, the class struggle at the level of ideology goes on.

PART 2

Capitalist Social Reproduction

∴

CHAPTER 6

Population and Capitalism

'Population and Capitalism', in *Latin American Perspectives*, Vol. IV, No. 4 (Fall 1977): 5–40.[1]

> A man who is born into a world already possessed, he cannot get subsistence from his parents on whom he has a just claim, and if the society does not want his labor, he has no claim of *right* to the smallest portion of food, and, in fact, has no business to be where he is. At nature's mighty feast there is no vacant cover for him.[2]

> Critical flirtation with Malthusianism inevitably results in a descent to the most vulgar bourgeois apologetics.[3]

Marxists have always rejected as unscientific and apologetic the use of 'overpopulation' or the 'population explosion' as the main explanation for the plethora of problems resulting from capitalist development (e.g. unemployment, widespread poverty, famines, environmental pollution, etc.) and as the main barrier to overcoming them.[4] On the other hand, rejection of the Malthusian and neo-Malthusian analyses of the relationship among population growth, economic growth, and the quality of life, has not been followed by the development of an alternative and comprehensive Marxist theoretical framework

---

1   Abridged, with permission from the publishers. For the original version, see Gimenez 1977.
2   Malthus, cited in Meek 1971, p. 8.
3   Lenin, cited in Meek 1971, p. 41.
4   The emphasis given to population as an independent variable was challenged in the United Nations World Population Conference in Bucharest, 1974, which stressed the need for socioeconomic development, the social and economic basis of poverty, malnutrition, and other social problems, and gave population the role of a contributing, rather than determinant, factor in the process of development (Parker Mauldin et al. 1974). The demographic establishment, needless to say, did not react favorably to this standpoint and succeeded in changing the situation in the 1976 conference of the World Population Society: 'Major themes of the World Population Society conference just ended in Washington, D.C., have emerged as the world-wide defusing of the "development must precede family planning" argument (although rhetoric continues, LDCs are weaving family planning programs into their development structures) and the pronounced trend towards sterilisation, with both private and government organisations struggling to keep pace with the current demand for this method of fertility control' (Intercom 1976, p. 11).

for the study of population. I intend to contribute to the elaboration of that framework through the exploration of the relationship between the capitalist mode of production (its structures, processes and contradictions), and fertility, mortality and migration. Because of space limitations, I will not dwell upon the analysis of the political, legal, and ideological determinants of the relationship between mode of production and population. Those superstructural elements as well as the national and international circumstances of each social formation account for the demographic variability found among capitalist social formations. I will restrict my analysis to the level of the mode of production in order to establish a theoretical starting point in the process of developing a Marxist theory of population. With respect to 'overpopulation', I will argue that population growth could become a major problem in the future if qualitative changes in the mode of production were to occur and the satisfaction of people's needs, rather than the accumulation of capital, were to become the goal of production. Contrary to the widespread notion among Marxists that the population issue is a 'paper tiger', I will argue that it is precisely during the socialist transition that population growth will become a major issue.

Capitalism and Population

From a demographic standpoint, there are two basic population processes which determine population size at any given time: the processes of entering and leaving the system – fertility (entrance only), mortality (exit only), and migration (both entrance and exit). The cumulative effect of such processes will also determine the rate of growth of a given population. Assuming a closed population system (without migration), population size will increase if birth rates are higher than death rates, decrease if death rates are higher than birth rates, or remain stationary if birth and death rates are equal. At any given time, fertility, mortality, and migration are a function of the existing age and sex distribution and will determine future population structure. In other words, population structure (i.e. age and sex distribution) is *both* an antecedent or a determinant and a consequence or effect of population processes (i.e. fertility, mortality, and migration).

These basic population structure and processes are the fundamental connection between the demographic system and its natural and social environment; changes in the latter will be reflected in changes in the former. From the standpoint of the social sciences, the issue is relatively simple. For purposes of analysis, population structure and processes can be viewed as dependent (or independent) variables affected by (or determining) a series of independent (or dependent) variables such as food, environmental quality, religion, culture, the economy, social stratification, etc. From a Marxist theoretical standpoint, the issue is more complex because it becomes necessary to explore it in the context of two different levels of analysis: mode of production and social formation. The capitalist mode of production (CMP) affects population structure and processes 'in the last instance' and in historically specific ways common to all capitalist social formations (CSF). On the other hand, the superstructural, national and international features of each CSF will 'overdetermine' (i.e. render historically specific) the impact of the mode of production.[5] In this section I will attempt to make explicit the links between the CMP and population. Because of its crucial role in determining current rates of population growth, I will discuss fertility in greater depth than mortality and migration.

The Capitalist Mode of Production and Population

The overall relationship between the CMP and population is epitomised in the principle of the reserve army of labour or relative surplus population.[6] The logic of capital accumulation implies the creation of unemployed and under-employed sectors of the working class. The relationship between the level of employment and the size of the population is not determined by the latter but by the profit needs of the capitalist class manifested in the organic composition of capital invested at a given time. As Marx clearly indicated, '... the more or less favorable circumstances in which the wage-working class supports and multiplies itself, in no way alter the fundamental character of capitalist production'.[7] This means that capital accumulation is indifferent to and independent from rates of population growth:

---

5   The concept 'mode of production' refers to the historically specific combinations of the elements of the production process (labour, means of production, labourers, and non-labourers) in the context of specific relations and forces of production. Modes of production based upon private ownership of the means of production are characterised by class contradictions and contradictions between the forces and the relations of production. The concept 'social formation' refers to the concrete historical unit where a dominant mode of production is found in a historically specific combination with pre-existing modes. The concept of overdetermination refers to the impact exerted upon capitalist contradictions by the superstructure, and the internal and external situation of a given social formation. Contradictions are thus '... never simple, but always specified by the historically concrete forms and circumstances in which [they are] exercised' (Althusser 1970, p. 106). For further clarification of these concepts as well as the concept of determination 'in the last instance', the reader is advised to consult Marx 1974; 1968; 1970a, pp. 20–1; Engels 1959, pp. 295–412; Althusser and Balibar 1970; Althusser 1970, pp. 89–129.

6   See Marx 1974, Chapter XXV; Braverman 1974, pp. 377–402.

7   Braverman 1974, pp. 640–1.

> The demand for labor is not identical with increase of capital, nor supply of labor with increase of the working class ... That the natural increase of the number of laborers does not satisfy the requirements of the accumulation of capital, and yet all the time is in excess of them, is a contradiction inherent to the movement of capital itself.[8]

Empirically, the operation of the principle of the reserve army of labour in the context of monopoly capital and imperialism results in the internationalisation of the reserve army of labour, the constant presence of unemployment and underemployment in the advanced CSF, and the growth – besides unemployment and underemployment – of 'marginal' sectors in the CSF subject to imperialist domination.[9]

According to Marx, the principle of the reserve army of labour is

> ... a law of population peculiar to the capitalist mode of production; and in fact, every special historic mode of production has its own special laws of population, historically valid within its limits alone. An abstract law of population exists for plants and animals only, and only in so far as man has not interfered with them.[10]

I understand this 'law of population' to mean that, within the CMP, population will always be 'excessive' in relationship to the demand for labour, whatever its rate of growth may be. The principle of the reserve army calls our attention to the *quantitative* aspects of the consequences of capital accumulation; it indicates that unemployment and poverty are inherent features of capitalist social formations rooted in the logic of capital accumulation itself, rather than the effect of '... the constant tendency in all animated life to increase beyond the nourishment prepared for it'.[11] In order to fully understand the relationship between the CMP and population, it is, however, necessary to consider the principle of the reserve army as *one among other* demographically relevant consequences of the process of capital accumulation. The process of capital accumulation is the key determining factor in the analysis that follows and *should not* be confused with the notions of economic development or invest-

---

8   Ibid.
9   Se, for example, Braverman 1974, pp. 377–402; Amin 1976; Mamdani 1974; Castles and Kosack 1972.
10   Marx 1974, p. 632.
11   Malthus 1933, p. 5.

ment as understood in economic theory. The process of capital accumulation is not a purely economic process solely obeying technical criteria of efficiency; it is, above all, the outcome of a political process and, as such, reflects the level of the class struggle as well as the contradiction between relations and forces of production that characterise a given social formation at a given time. Consequently, it is always 'overdetermined' in ways that need to be theoretically and empirically investigated. However, as I am pursuing the analysis at the most abstract level, the level of the mode of production, and therefore seeking to determine the economic and demographic consequences of capital accumulation common to all CSFs, I will not spell out its multiple determinations at each step in the development of the argument. Those economic and demographically relevant consequences are the following:

1) Capital accumulation determines *quantitative* changes in the demand for labour; i.e. it determines the proportion of the labour force which is employed, underemployed, and unemployed at any given time (principle of the reserve army of labour).

2) Capital accumulation determines *qualitative* changes in the demand for labour; old skills become obsolete, new skills are demanded, and the lack of skills becomes, at some points, a skill of sorts. Qualitative changes in the demand for labour imply *changes in the technical relations of production*,[12] i.e. changes in the organisation of the productive process. These changes are reflected in the kinds of skills the agents of production will be required to have.

3) The combined effects of quantitative and qualitative changes in the demand for labour as well as changes in the technical relations of production are manifested in (a) *changes in the articulation between household production and material production*; and (b) *changes in the social division of labour*. (a) The household becomes the main locus for the reproduction (daily and generational biological, physical, and social) of the relations of production (i.e. the capitalist class, intermediate classes, and the working class). This is the material basis of sexism within the capitalist mode of production. The sexes are differentially affected by the processes

---

12   The technical relations of production are the relations that obtain in the context of the production process itself among the agents of production; for example, the relations among workers, managers, and capitalists. The social relations of production or class relations, on the other hand, are the relations among the producers mediated through their relationship to the means of production; e.g. relations between the capitalist class and the working class. See Harnecker 1971, pp. 33–43 and Althusser and Balibar 1970, 231–33.

described above, and female labour becomes primarily defined as household labour. (b) At the level of the social division of labour, sexism and
household specialisation are manifested as processes of sex differentiation and sex stratification which change, historically, in response to fundamental changes in capital accumulation.[13]

4) Capital accumulation determines the *location of investments* and changes
thereof. It can establish the preconditions for further capital accumulation (e.g. through the discovery of new resources, incorporation of new
territories, better exploitation of resources due to technological improvements, development of ports, cities, roads, etc.) and/or take advantage
of pre-existing favourable conditions (e.g. available infrastructure and
labour pool concentrated in metropolitan areas). This implies that it can
also further the decay of cities and regions within a given social formation. Processes of 'urbanisation' and concomitant uneven development
which find their most extreme manifestation in colonial and neocolonial
countries are thus a reflection of specific processes of capital accumulation.

Figure 1 summarises the above.[14] Given those propositions, it follows that capital accumulation will determine the following:

A) *Population distribution* within a given society: population flocks to areas
where employment appears possible and abandons areas where subsistence becomes problematic. Within every social formation some regions
will thus be more densely populated than others and, at the same time,
more 'developed' or 'modern' than others.

B) *Population structure:* the type of demand for labour in a given area contributes to shape the age and sex composition of the population. For
example, demand for male labour can result in places where most of the
population is male (e.g. South African mining areas or Latin American oil
fields).

---

13   There is an abundant literature on this topic. See, for example, Benston 1969; Larguia and
       Dumoulin 1972; Seccombe 1974; and Gimenez 1975.
14   The reader must keep in mind, at this point, that I am developing the analysis at the
       level of the mode of production. Those statements refer or depict structures and pro-
       cesses characterising the CMP after it became consolidated or integrated as a qualitatively
       different mode of production. Historically, the whole family was incorporated in the pro-
       duction process during the earlier stages of capitalist development, and the pace at which
       the demand for female and child labour declined varied from one social formation to
       another.

c)   *Population composition:* qualitative changes in the demand for labour are
     manifested in changing requirements in terms of skills and education.
     This implies changes in the *occupational structure* (e.g. shifts from agri-
     culture to secondary and tertiary sectors); *changes in the educational level
     of the population; changes in income distribution* and, therefore, changes
     in the standard of living and lifestyle of specific sectors of a given pop-
     ulation; and, finally, *changes in the racial and ethnic composition of the
     population* which result also in cultural heterogeneity and the introduc-
     tion of superstructural factors which affect differently the behaviour of
     individuals subject to similar structural constraints. The distribution of
     the members of a given population in the above mentioned categories
     constitute the basis for what sociologists call the *social stratification* of a
     given society.

d)   *Migration processes* within and among social formations: this means that
     population structure, distribution, and composition are always fluctuat-
     ing in response to the economic and demographic processes triggered by
     capital accumulation.

e)   *Household composition in terms of class:* i.e. the proportion of working-
     class, petty-bourgeois, peasant households, etc., found in a given social
     formation at a given time. Household composition thus defined is, of
     course, a counterpart to class structure; it is crucial for understanding the
     impact of qualitatively different contexts affecting mortality and fertility
     rates characterising a social formation as a whole.

On the basis of the above, I conclude that the kinds of migration processes,
household composition, social stratification, population structure, composition, and distribution characterising a given CSF at a given time are all structural effects of capital accumulation; i.e. they are determined 'in the last instance' by capital accumulation. Fertility and mortality vary according to the
characteristics of specific sectors of a social formation (i.e. there are urban-
rural differences as well as differences associated with class, socio-economic
status (SES), ethnicity, etc.). Given that capital accumulation determines the
distribution of a population into all those sectors manifesting differential fertility and mortality patterns, it follows that capital accumulation determines
fertility and mortality at the aggregate level of a special formation through the
complex network of structural effects previously outlined; the same reasoning
can be applied to migration.

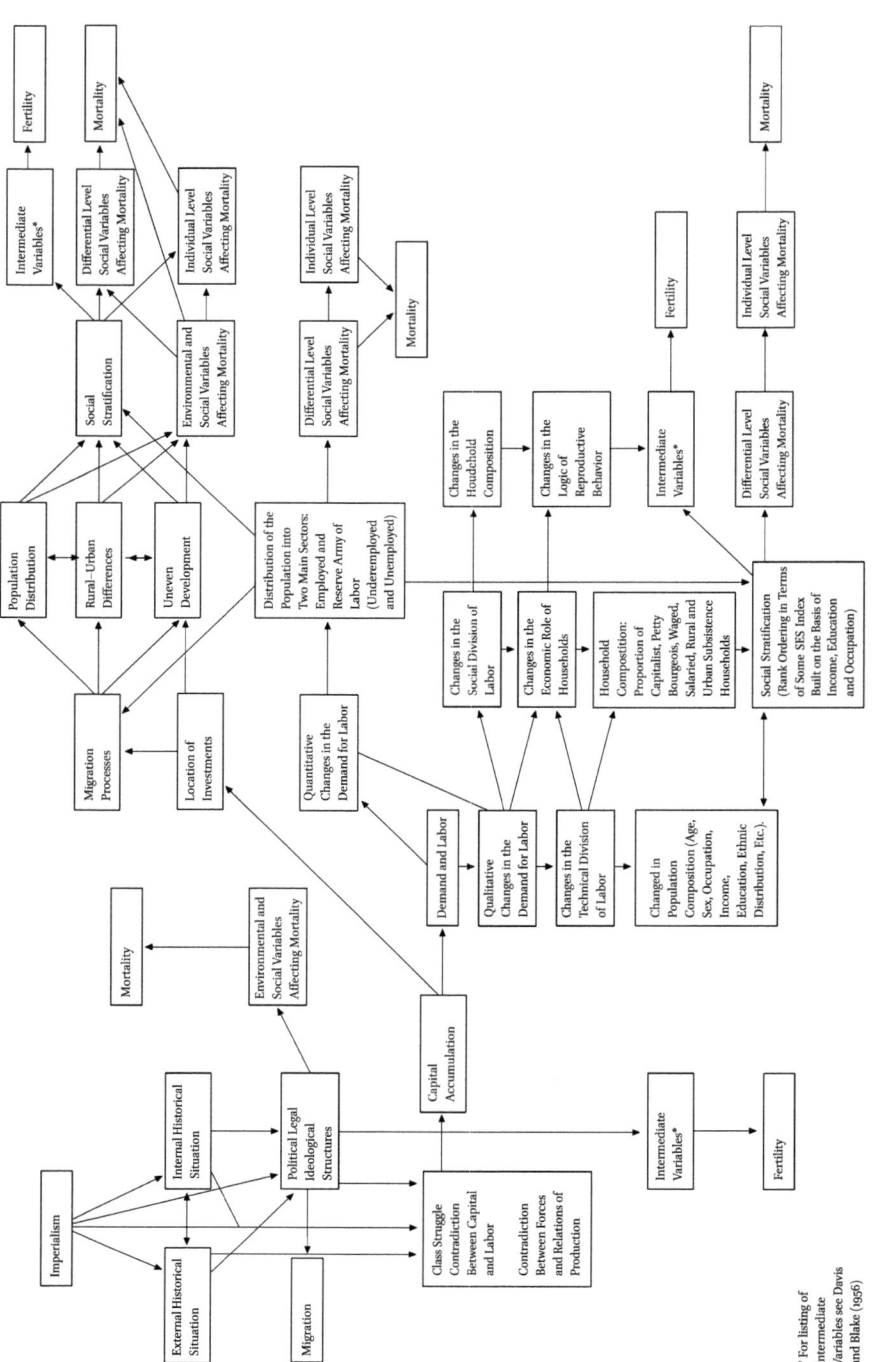

FIGURE 1   Capitalism and population: socio-economic and demographic consequences of capital accumulation

* For listing of
Intermediate
Variables see Davis
and Blake (1956)

Fertility[15]

The issue of the determinants of fertility will be approached from two different angles: first, exploring the general determinants of fertility and second, focusing attention on the rationality of household decision-making processes with respect to reproductive behaviour as it varies according to class and socioeconomic status. Analytically, no theory of structural change can omit considering both the macro and the micro-levels of analysis as well as their interrelationship; Marxist theory is no exception.

The discussion of the general determinants of fertility is facilitated by the pioneer work of Davis and Blake which gives us a classification of the variables through which fertility can be affected by the social structure. These intermediate variables, common to all societies because they stem from the three main stages of the human reproductive process, are factors affecting exposure to intercourse, factors affecting exposure to conception, and factors affecting gestation and successful parturition.[16] Each mode of production affects the characteristics of its corresponding social formations and, through them, the intermediate variables and fertility, in historically specific ways that can be empirically determined. In the context of the CMP, capital accumulation and corresponding changes in the demand for labour, organisation of production, division of labour, social stratification, and so forth are likely to have a direct impact upon variables governing the formation and dissolution of unions in the reproductive period. Involuntary causes affecting fecundity, infecundity, and foetal mortality are indirectly affected by factors determining the health and nutrition levels of the different sectors of the social structure which are, in turn, directly affected by the mode of production. Likewise, the use of contraception, abortion, and sterilisation are affected, in the last instance, by the changing interests of the capitalist class expressed through laws, population policies and ideology.

The positive or negative impact of the intermediate variables on fertility varies according to class and socio-economic status (SES) and results in differential fertility. For example, under certain conditions women belonging to the poorer sectors of the social structure are more likely to enter into sexual unions earlier than women who are better off; they are also likely to deal with contraception (if they use any) in rather ineffective ways and, consequently, start

---

15   Biologically, fertility refers to women's capacity to bear children; family size and the proportion of women who become mothers reflect the historical context shaping reproductive behaviour.
16   Davis and Blake 1956, pp. 211–35.

families earlier. The above is a purely illustrative statement; the actual fertility differentials vary from one social formation to another and must be empirically established in each case.

Current non-Marxist theoretical efforts to explain fertility differentials are based upon the application of economic theory to fertility behaviour. Whether children are viewed as consumer durables,[17] as household produced goods,[18] or as a combination of both,[19] the main theoretical assumption underlying this type of analysis is that households behave rationally, maximising their utility in the context of scarce resources. Basically, the economic theory of fertility states that households with given tastes or preference choose to consume/produce children which are, for purposes of analysis, considered as goods whose utility must be balanced against the utility of other goods. Given that households have limited income and time to their disposal and must take into account market prices, the quantity and quality of children and other goods which they can purchase or produce at home is also limited. The theory of fertility as consumer behaviour gives emphasis to income and price constraints; households with given tastes '... are viewed as maximizing utility subject to the constraints of income and prices. Thus three factors – income, tastes, and prices – are the basic building blocks of fertility behavior'.[20] To those factors, the analysis of fertility as household productive behaviour adds time as a fourth relevant constraint; in this context, the quantity and quality of children and other sources of utility produced in the household will be a function of the amount of time and goods allocated to their production. It is assumed that '... 1) only the husband and wife contribute market earnings to family income; 2) only the wife's time is productive at home; 3) the structure of relative market prices remains fixed; and 4) the joint production of children and utility producing goods is ruled out'.[21] The essence of the economic approach to fertility behaviour resides in the importance given to choice; households *choose* among alternative combinations of goods and children whose utility is balanced so that any given combination may provide a similar amount of satisfaction.

Sociologists have been highly critical of the economic analysis of fertility and have convincingly argued that economists tend to ignore or minimise the social constraints on reproductive behaviour. Sociologically, reproductive behaviour is constrained behaviour; it is rooted in the pronatalist nature of

---

17   Becker 1960; Easterlin 1969.
18   Schultz 1974.
19   Easterlin 1975.
20   Easterlin 1969, p. 128.
21   Willis 1974, pp. 32–3.

adult sex roles and buttressed by a network of social and economic rewards that rule out alternatives to the performance of parental roles. This means that, from a sociological standpoint, parents are not free to choose the quantity and quality of their children. With respect to quantity, normative standards vary from one social formation to another; for example, today in advanced CSFS the established minimum is two children per household; families with one child only and childless couples are, in this respect, 'deviant'. The quality of children defined in terms of socialisation, education, nutritional and health standards, etc., is also largely determined by the expectations corresponding to the different strata of the society. While rich and poor are subject to pronatalist motivational pressures, anti-natalist motivational pressures (e.g. careers, high levels of consumption, etc.) are generally reserved for the higher SES categories; consequently, the commonly observed inverse relationship between income and fertility may be explained by differences in tastes for different quantities and qualities of children.[22] From a sociological standpoint, the existence of pronatalism is explained in terms of functional imperatives developed in high mortality conditions requiring high fertility to ensure the reproduction of the species; under low mortality conditions such as those characterising the world at the present time, universally prescribed reproduction is not only econom-ically and socially unsound but also stands in the way of full and free human development.[23]

From a Marxist standpoint, a full understanding of fertility patterns requires that we move beyond the argument whether reproductive behaviour involves the actual exercise of choice (as economists maintain) or, on the contrary, it is socially determined. Essentially, this involves the development of a Marxist analysis of pronatalism and reproduction. Within the limits of this chapter I will establish at least the theoretical space necessary for the Marxist analysis of those issues.

With respect to pronatalism, which is the universal prescription of parental roles for both sexes as a given dimension of adult roles, I find that the sociolo-gical critique of the economic approach to reproduction has descriptive value; it helps to grasp the social arrangements that lock people into pronatalist roles. I disagree, however, with the broad, ahistorical functional explanation given to account for the persistence of those roles today. To understand the material basis of pronatalism in any capitalist social formation, one must explore its roots in the dominant mode of production, namely, capitalism.[24]

---

22 Blake 1968; 1974.
23 Blake 1974.
24 In doing so, I followed one of Marx's most important methodological injunctions: that of

Alienated labour is the main capitalist ideological support of pronatalism within advanced capitalist social formations. The manifold facets of alienation (from the self, from the labour process, from the product of labour, and from fellow workers) renders people vulnerable to a variety of alienated sources of meaning which further their subordination to capitalist relations of production. Among such palliatives to the consequences of alienated labour, pronatalism figures prominently; as Marx pointed out in a remarkably insightful statement,

> ... [W]e arrive at the result that men and women feel themselves to be freely active only in their animal functions – eating, drinking and procreating, or at most also in their dwelling and in personal adornment – while in their human functions they are reduced to animals. The animal becomes human and the human becomes animal. Eating, drinking, and procreating are of course also genuine human functions. But abstractly considered, apart from the environment of human activities, and turned into final and sole ends, they are animal functions.[25]

From a sociological standpoint, the separation between the world of work (where individuals are forced into constant anxiety, self-denial, and struggle for economic survival) and the world of 'leisure' or 'privacy' (where individuals become consumers of sex, children, hobbies, status symbols of various kinds, etc.) that characterises 'industrial societies' is 'functional for the maintenance of the system'.[26] From a Marxist standpoint, while the ideological and economic role of the family in reproducing the relations of production and labour power have been widely discussed, especially in their relationship to sexism,[27] its pronatalist aspects have been neglected and the implications of pronatalism for sexism are yet to be fully understood. The important point I wish to make, without pursuing that issue because of the limitations of this chapter, is that the antagonism between work and family life created by alienated labour has 'unanticipated' demographic consequences which contribute to exacerbate capitalist contradictions. Because of the special saliency acquired by parental roles, families are both 'functional' to the system in their economic and ideo-

---

giving priority to the analysis of a structure rather than to the genesis of a structure. See, with respect to this point, Marx 1970b, pp. 205–14; and Godelier 1970.

25   Marx 1964, p. 125.
26   See, for example, Greenfield 1969.
27   See Mitchell 1971; Zaretski 1973.

logical roles and 'dysfunctional' in that they produce more workers than they would under other circumstances produce. Consequently, a relative surplus population is being generated by the process of capital accumulation directly ('setting workers free' through technological improvements), and indirectly, because of the pronatalist consequences of alienated labour.[28]

I hypothesise that the overdetermination exerted by the pronatalist implications of alienation is weaker in social formations where capitalism has not yet transformed the great majority of the population into wage labourers: i.e. social formations having large urban subsistence sectors and feudal and semi-feudal agricultural sectors. There, besides the reproductive strategy imposed by the urban subsistence sector and pre-capitalist rural sectors, cultural traditions and religion are likely to play a greater role. On the other hand, in social formations where capitalism has dissolved all other forms of productive and reproductive relations, the drastic division between the ruthless public sphere (market and 'society') and the supportive private family world both generates and perpetuates the phenomena Marx[29] so compellingly described.

Just as pronatalism in CSFs must be understood in relationship to the CMP, reproductive behaviour must also be placed in its capitalist context if it is to be adequately conceptualised. Economic and sociological theories of reproduction are necessarily ahistorical because they view reproduction essentially as a biological activity of individuals through which the survival of the human species is ensured. The task of the social sciences becomes, consequently, that of discovering the universal (e.g. costs, resources, time, etc.) and the socially determined (e.g. pronatalist roles, desired family size, preference systems, etc.) constraints affecting reproductive behaviour.

The economic theory of fertility views reproductive behaviour as formally equivalent to economic behaviour because both are instances of formally rational behaviour.[30] Implicit in sociological and economic theorising and research is the assumption that rational behaviour is synonymous with use of contraception and decline in family size. Some social scientists are, however, careful to point out the independence of formal rationality from any goals

---

28   See Gimenez 1973a.
29   Marx 1964, p. 125.
30   The theory of formal rationality is a general theory of action oriented towards goal attainment in the context of scarce means, and aimed at obtaining maximum efficiency. Formal rationality and economic rationality are the same; specific goals are excluded from the analysis and rationality is defined purely in terms of the efficient use of scarce resources in the pursuit of maximum utility. Readers interested in this issue should consult Max Weber 1969, pp. 82–5; and Godelier, 1972.

except the maximisation of utility and have stressed the importance of changes in the preference system of individuals in order to account for fluctuations and changes in the birth rate.[31]

From a Marxist standpoint, these explanations reveal the two dimensions of capitalist rationality. Formal rationality, while appearing independent from any specific content or any goals, depicts nevertheless, a historical rationality based upon the capitalist relations of production and domination.[32] Changes in reproductive patterns should, therefore, be explained not as the outcome of formally rational behaviour oriented by socially determined preference systems, but in terms of what is objectively required by the capitalist relations of production which are class relations or relations of exploitation and domination. The ideological nature of the economic and sociological analysis resides precisely in the obliteration of the process of capitalist development behind its empiricist fragmentation into a multiplicity of 'factors' likely to produce changes in the preference system and the degree of rationality of the actors. The preference system of individuals cannot be taken for granted but must itself be explained. The different 'tastes' or 'preferences' characterising the various sectors of the social structure (such as desired family size, sex role definitions, desire for children of a given sex, etc.) are a reflection of the articulation between the modes of production and reproduction (in the demographic sense) on the one hand, and its superstructural legitimations. Such preferences smuggle or feed back the requirements of the CMP through the channel of formally rational behaviour that emerges, then, as the main source of explanation of changes in reproductive behaviour at the household level. This requires that we shift the focus of theoretical concern from the rationality of individuals and households to the rationality of the agents involved in the production process. *At the level of consumption, there is formally no difference between capitalists and workers:* both classes confront the same structure of prices and attempt to maximise their utility within the limitations set by their income and according to their preferences. It makes no difference, in the economic theory of fer-

---

31   See, for example, Spengler 1966; Heer 1968 and Easterlin 1969.

32   What brings into the open the ideological nature of formal rationality is its total incapacity to define the social reality it pretends to explain: it takes for granted and can only manipulate social reality in terms of criteria that, in Weber's words, are 'completely indifferent' to its meaning (i.e. the criteria of maximisation are independent and indifferent to their outcome: high or low fertility); it can attempt to explain only through criteria *outside* or *external to* itself (i.e. a given level of fertility is high or low only when considered in a given context) and in doing so, '... this rationality subordinates itself, by virtue of its own inner dynamics, to another, to the rationality of domination' (Marcuse 1968, p. 214).

tility, whether children are conceptualised as household produced goods or as consumer durables; in either case households behave essentially as consumers who 'purchase' children or the goods and services which, in combination with domestic labour time, will result in the 'production' of children. Economists and sociologists acknowledge income differences in a purely quantitative manner; they limit their analysis to the purchasing power linked to those differences as well as to the varying standards about child quality and quantity characterising different income groups. *At the level of production, however, there are qualitative differences between capitalists and workers.* Capitalists' reproductive decisions are not subject to income and price constraints but to constraints that stem from their ownership of the means of production. In general terms, the crucial determinant of capitalists' reproductive behaviour is the maintenance of property in the family. Their behaviour is not formally rational behaviour but can be best understood as value rational and determined by other than purely optimising criteria (i.e. political and economic objectives rooted in the goal to maintain and expand power).[33] On the other hand, the rationality of the workers is

> ... *a complementary, derivative and dependent rationality*, which the worker needs to possess in order that the capitalist's rationality may be fully effective and that, over the head of the individual capitalist, the capitalist system may function without any unsurmountable contradictions.[34]

This dependence and subordination is reflected in the kinds of 'options' which are available to workers at a given time within the capitalist structures of production and consumption. Given their dependence for survival upon the functioning of the CMP, the working classes and dependent salaried sectors must adapt their behaviour in ways that fit with the interests of the capitalist class or pay for their 'deviation' from expected behaviour in terms of their standard of living. The analysis of household reproductive behaviour can now be linked to the previous analysis of the demographic implications of capital accumulation: changes in the process of accumulation will determine changes in the content of the working classes' formally rational reproductive behaviour which will eventually be reflected in changes at the aggregate level. Changes at the level of production, in other words, will be manifested through changes

---

33   For an explanation of different types of rationality, see Weber 1969, pp. 82–5.
34   Godelier 1972, p. 37, original emphasis.

in the demand for labour (quantitative and qualitative); income distribution and the range of 'options' available to the working classes which will be exteriorised, at the level of market and social relations, as changes in their 'taste' for children and consumer goods at a given time. On the other hand, changes in capital accumulation will have a qualitatively different impact on the capitalist classes which, while independent from income and price constraints with respect to their reproductive behaviour, are primordially concerned with the expansion and preservation of property in their family.[35] Because of the limited scope of this essay, it would be impossible to examine the reproductive behaviour of intermediate or contradictory class positions.[36] Nevertheless, two types of households (those of the unemployed and underemployed and those of peasants) are of great importance to an understanding of current rates of population growth in the underdeveloped world and will be briefly examined.

With respect to the households of the unemployed and underemployed, the material basis of their reproductive behaviour differs according to the stage and type of capitalist development characterising specific CSFs. In advanced CSFs, the welfare state pays women a minimum wage to reproduce the unskilled and often unemployable sectors of the working class. Under conditions of extreme poverty, children do not substantially add to household expenditures; on the other hand, they can become the main source of meaning and satisfaction left to the very poor.[37]

In the context of social formations subject to imperialist exploitation, it is necessary to add to the regular reserve army of labour, the 'marginal' or 'appropriated masses'.[38] Capitalist development under those conditions generates a situation in which masses of peasants and artisans are expelled from rural areas without being absorbed by the labour market. The process of uneven development also contributes to the problem through the false promises the urban

---

35   Whether capitalists' concern with expanding and preserving property in the family leads to high or low fertility is an issue that depends on historically specific conditions and can be raised at the level of concrete social formations.

36   Wright 1976.

37   To quote a poverty-stricken Black mother: 'To me, having a baby inside me is the only time I'm really alive. I know I can make something, do something, no matter what color my skin is, and what names people call me. When the baby is born I see him, and he is full of life, or she is, and I think to myself that it doesn't make any difference what happens later, at least now we've got a chance, or the baby does ... If we didn't have that, what would be the difference from death? Even without children my life would still be bad – they're not going to give us what they have, the birth control people' (Dyck 1971, p. 357).

38   Mamdani 1975.

areas hold for the people from the interior. These masses remain 'marginal' to capitalist relations of production in the sense that their livelihood does not depend, primarily, upon wages. Their subsistence is based on

> ... daily casual labor: in construction, in hawking, ... in what is euphemistically called the 'service industry.' But the most important characteristic of the structure of employment as it affects this social group is precisely that it is skewed in favor of child employment ... shoe shining, opening car doors, cleaning cars ... begging ... in slum populations it is not quite unusual to find families where children support adults.[39]

In a situation where the state is unable to contribute to their support through government transfers of various kinds, having a large family is a rational choice for the very poor for it ensures their present and future economic 'security'. Regardless of the precariousness of their standard of living, it would be worse had the existence of large families not created a network of relatives able to provide social and economic support.[40]

The same reproductive logic operates in the context of agriculture: for small farmers, tenants, and sharecroppers, a large family is their only hope for economic survival. Children are all potential workers on the farm, and some will help also with wages earned in the urban centres. As Mamdani clearly shows in his in-depth analysis of fertility in an Indian village, the smaller the holding and the poorer the farmer, the greater the need for labour input from his children. Also, the poorer the craftsman, artisan, and person in service occupations (whose trade is being eroded by technological changes), the more important is the need for large families which benefit from the labour of children and adolescents. The very poor see their children as their only capital, and in the economic context in which they live, their perception is undoubtedly correct.[41]

The two main channels through which capital accumulation influences fertility at the level of the CMP are, first, the intermediate variables, and, second, household reproductive behaviour. In an effort to clarify the theoretical issues involved, the argument is summarised in Figure 1.

It should now be clear to the reader on the basis of the preceding discussion that household reproductive behaviour is far from being homogeneous in the sense of responding to the same constraints. On the contrary, there are qualit-

---

39 Mamdani 1974, pp. 20–1.
40 See also Folbre 1976 for a discussion of this issue.
41 Mamdani 1972.

atively different constraints affecting households in qualitatively different ways which are based on the class structure of the CMP and the operation of the law of capital accumulation. On the one hand, this theoretical insight is important because it indicates the need to explore the class basis of reproductive behaviour as the main context lending meaning to formally rational decision-making processes. On the other hand, this sheds light on the actual meaning of reproduction when viewed from the standpoint of the mode of production rather than from the standpoint of individuals and isolated households. Abstractly considered, reproductive behaviour reproduces the human species. However, if understood concretely and historically, it is a crucial moment of the process of reproduction of all modes of production. Reproductive behaviour reproduces the bearers of the relations of production: capitalists and workers in the CMP, peasants, landlords, and petty commodity producers in pre-capitalist modes of production, and so on. Whether reproduction is materially or ideologically understood depends on the extent to which it takes place under capitalist conditions. Just as the production of surplus is no mystery for direct producers in control of the means of production and the process of production, the productive relevance of their offspring is not lost for them either.[42] It is only in the context of capitalism that the nature of reproductive behaviour becomes mystified in such a way that only its biological and ideological aspects (e.g. the need for an heir to perpetuate the family name, or the need for 'immortality', 'self-fulfilment', etc.) are perceived. When the economic security of the adult members of the household is not dependent upon the actual and future labour input of their children, the latter can easily be perceived as consumer/home produced 'goods', or as indispensable elements of one's 'natural' life, products of one's 'parental' instincts, and so forth. The social sciences simply codify the dominant ideologies about reproduction and remain caught in an individualistic problematic leading to a reasonably adequate account of changes in reproductive patterns to the extent that changes in the mode of production are introduced in the analysis through the back door; i.e. through the changes they produce in individual behaviour.

From a Marxist theoretical standpoint, the key question to be asked with respect to the nature of fertility trends is the following: under what conditions does the reproduction of labour power take place? The investigation of those conditions in the context of capitalist social formations presupposes the study of the specific combination of capitalist and pre-capitalist modes of production characterising specific social formations, the kinds of labour power

---

42   See, for example, Folbre 1977 and Mamdani 1972.

required by the process of capital accumulation at a given time or throughout a given period of time, the place of the social formation in the world capitalist system, the state of the class struggle, etc. The reproduction of labour power is overdetermined by the superstructure, the internal and the international circumstances affecting social formations and a careful investigation of that complex set of elements of the mode of production and the social formation viewed as totalities cannot be overlooked without falling into an economic determinist analysis. The crucial determining element of the process of capital accumulation leading to the reproduction of given quantities and qualities of labour power is the class struggle viewed both in its national and international dimensions. The conditions determining the reproduction of labour power are crucial for understanding fertility patterns because, given the numerical insignificance of the capitalist and intermediate classes, the overall fertility of a given social formation reflects mainly the reproductive behaviour of the great majority whose decision-making processes are 'complementary, dependent, and derivative' from those of the capitalist class. Marx's analysis of the production and reproduction of labour power is extremely important and deserves to be quoted at length:

> Labor power exists only as a capacity, or power of the living individual. Its production consequently presupposes his existence. Given the individual, the production of labor power consists in his reproduction of himself or his maintenance. For his maintenance he requires at given quantity of the means of subsistence ... the value of labor power is the value of the means of subsistence necessary for the maintenance of the laborer ...
>
> The owner of labor power is mortal. If then his appearance in the market is to be continuous, and the continuous conversion of money into capital assumes this, the seller of labor power must perpetuate himself ... by procreation. The labor power withdrawn from the market by wear and tear and death, must be continually replaced by, at the very least, an equal amount of fresh labor power. Hence the sum of the means of subsistence necessary for the production of labor power must include the means necessary for the laborer's substitutes, i.e. his children, in order that this race of peculiar commodity owners may perpetuate its appearance in the market.[43]

---

43   Marx 1974, pp. 171–2.

It follows, from Marx's analysis, that the level of wages/salaries available to specific sectors of the working classes is sufficient only for the continued reproduction of each sector so that specific kinds of commodity owners may continuously appear in the market. It also follows that among the historical and moral elements entering into the determination of the average wage/salary level, those pertinent to parental roles, family formation and family size are very important. After all, the CMP could not function if all workers were to receive less than the minimum necessary for survival and replacement or if, in the context of adequate payments, dominant ideologies, legal structures, economic incentives, etc., were to encourage reproduction below replacement levels. Only under exceptional circumstances will the capitalist classes make direct investments to upgrade the quality of specific sectors of the labour force, and the overall quality of the labour force of a social formation reflects the extent to which investments in 'human capital' are required for the smooth functioning of capitalist accumulation. For example, high illiteracy rates, high mortality rates and an overall low quality labour force reflect the needs of an overall process of accumulation based mainly upon the use of unskilled labour. Ordinarily, that upgrading is financed by the workers themselves who, by investing in their own 'human capital' or by reproducing labour power of quality higher than their own, through the training and/or education of their offspring, give rise to the phenomenon of 'social mobility'. It is through the process of self-upgrading, into which the working classes and salary earners are forced, that differences in reproductive behaviour emerge. Wage and salary earners, subject to income and price constraints as well as to 'overdeterminations' varying from one social formation to another, can 'choose' to reproduce labour power of a quality lower, equal to, or higher than their own. Each sector of the labour force is subject to different kinds of pressures at a given time. Such pressures stem from the process of capital accumulation itself: whether there is a surplus or a deficit in the number of workers of a given quality (unskilled, skilled, professional, white-collar, etc.) depends, in the last instance, upon the dominant interests of the capitalist classes and the extent to which the process of accumulation determined by those interests can operate undeterred by workers' struggles for their rights. The movements of capital are reflected in the movements of population, both geographically and socially. This will become clearer in the following section.

Mortality

Because of the greater complexity of mortality as a phenomenon responding to a variety of direct and indirect causes, it is impossible to develop an analytical framework similar to that already existing for the study of fertility. It would not be possible to identify all the channels through which and only through which the CMP in all its overdetermined complexity may affect the length of human life. The following classification of mortality determinants indicates simply *some* of the possible ways through which the CMP may affect mortality:

1) *Macro-level environmental and social variables:* e.g. availability of natural resources, environmental pollution, territorial size, development of death control technology, organisation of public health services, agricultural policies, defence expenditures, war, internal repression, etc.

2) *Differential level social variables:* e.g. variables determining the differential access of classes, socio-economic status groups, and ethnic groups to adequate housing, diet, healthcare, water supply, etc.

3) *Individual level social variables:* e.g. attitudes towards life and death, food habits, attitudes towards healthcare, etc.

These variables are self-explanatory and their formal links to the CMP are depicted in Figure 1. The discussion that follows is necessarily limited and will be focused upon the overall effect of capitalism on mortality.

Inequality in all its dimensions is inherent in the CMP. The pursuit of profit maximisation at all costs leads to social and economic inequalities which are in turn reflected in differential death rates. Death inequality mirrors social and economic inequality: mortality can be viewed as a 'consequence, correlate, and indicator of social inequality'.[44] The types of mortality which most clearly reflect underlying inequalities are infant and maternal mortality, mortality due to occupational hazards, and mortality due to infectious diseases and environmental diseases (for example, diseases transmitted through insects living in a given environment). While social formations differ widely in their environmental conditions (availability of healthcare, public health services, food, etc.), it is nevertheless possible to identify the structures leading to death inequality which are common to all CSFs. Broadly speaking, the preservation of life requires wholesome food, clean housing and environment, healthcare when needed, and safe and wholesome working conditions. With respect to working conditions, they continue to be one of the key issues of the class struggle because the overall tendency of the capitalist organisation of production is to extract maximum profits with minimum expenditures on labour. With regard to other goods and services needed for health and longevity, it must be taken into account that capitalism presupposes the universalisation of commodity production; this means that food, housing, healthcare, etc. must first become

---

44   Goldscheider 1971, p. 241.

commodities (i.e. must first be sold in the market) before they can satisfy the material needs of the working population. Under capitalist conditions, therefore, all needs must be satisfied through the market; those without sufficient means of exchange are, consequently, unable to purchase the goods and services needed for their physical well-being and that of their offspring. Capitalist production unavoidably results in unemployment and unequal income distribution which place most of the minimum material necessities out of the reach of sizable sectors of the working classes while others are able to purchase food and shelter to the detriment of healthcare. The fact that necessary goods and services are produced on a capitalist basis (i.e. for profit, not for the satisfaction of needs) automatically places them out of reach of the poorer sectors of the working population. Differential access to the necessities of life, which leads to death inequality, reflects not only the contradiction between production and distribution, but also the nature of the class interests served by the organisation of production as a whole and, in particular, the production of health services. Navarro has written an analysis of the production and distribution of health services in Chile before, during, and after Allende's government, which is important because it furnishes insights relevant to the understanding of the issue in all CSFs. Some of Navarro's main points are the following:

1) The class structure is replicated in the structure of the health services; the small middle classes are covered by voluntary insurance while the capitalist sector provides services for the upper classes and the state covers the working classes, peasants, unemployed and the poor. Needless to say, per capita expenditures are lower in the state sector and highest in the private sector.

2) The production and distribution of health services is influenced by the capitalist classes through (a) stress on the market as the mechanism for allocating health services and resources which are thus distributed on the basis of effective demand; (b) control over the medical profession and the type of professionals produced (e.g. surgeons rather than paediatricians and public health experts); (c) the organisation of health services itself and the type of services produced. Following the pattern set by the advanced CSFs, it is oriented toward

> ... (a) specialized, hospital based medicine as opposed to community medicine; (b) urban, technologically intensive medicine in contrast to rural, labor intensive medicine; (c) curative medicine as different from preventive medicine; and (d) personal health services as opposed to environmental health services ... (considering that) malnutrition and infectious diseases are the main causes of mor-

tality and morbidity (in Chile and, I would add, all CSFs subject to imperialism) the best strategy to combat the problems that affect the majority would be to emphasize precisely the opposite patterns of production.[45]

3) Health services are mal-distributed not only socially but also spatially; they are concentrated in the urban areas thus leaving unprotected the rural population.

4) Class interests are also reflected in the allocation of health expenditures with the greater percentage of resources going to individualised, capital-intensive medical care.[46]

Allende introduced some significant reforms in Chile's health sector which were reversed by the military junta with full support from the Chilean Medical Association. All attempts to democratise the system were abandoned, budgets were cut (including the budget of Chile's only school of public health), priorities were changed, the milk distribution programme was cancelled, and the medical opposition was ruthlessly persecuted, '... 21 physicians have been shot, 85 imprisoned, and countless others dismissed'.[47]

The performance of the Chilean military junta in the health sector is, formally, no different from what governments do in all CSFs. The emphasis given to curative, urban-based, capital-intensive and individualised healthcare that characterises CSFs today is tragically reflected in social formations subject to imperialism, in their stubbornly high infant mortality rates, low life expectancy, and the presence of infectious diseases and malnutrition. Such deficient health conditions have drastic repercussions on the overall quality of life and on the efficiency and productivity of the people; it can be argued that those social formations are subject not only to economic plunder but also to the slow physical deterioration of their most valuable resource: their people. Castro[48] and Melotti,[49] among others, have documented the devastating consequences of the different types of chronic hunger. Human life is cheap in the imperialised countries despite the high sounding commitments to its value often uttered by their ruling classes and professional ideologues. The contradiction between bourgeois political and humanitarian ideologies and the inexorable consequences of the CMP is perhaps nowhere more clear than at the level in

---

45   Navarro 1974, p. 103.
46   Navarro 1974, pp. 96–105.
47   Navarro 1974, pp. 118–21.
48   Castro 1967.
49   Melotti 1969.

which the basic necessities of life are priced out of the reach of the labouring masses whose surplus labour has built and continues to build empires.
This contradiction is inherent in the CMP and emerges at the economic level
as unequal income distribution. In their controversial study, economists Adelman and Morris have conclusively shown that economic development, far from
benefiting those who are more needy, increases income inequality. Their findings, which support a Marxist analysis of the relationship between economic
structure and income distribution, indicate that '... hundreds of millions of des-
perately poor people throughout the world have been hurt rather than helped
by economic development'[50] and that 'The record of economic intervention in
underdeveloped countries, good as it is in terms of economic growth, has been
dismal in terms of social justice. Indeed, economic growth, whether planned
or unplanned, has only made things worse'.[51] It is impossible to grasp the
full implications of their findings without taking into account that the demographic dimension of income inequality is the inequality of death and that
both are manifestations of the class struggle and cannot be understood in isolation from it. Wood's research, which examines the relationship between the
Brazilian 'miracle' and the rise in infant mortality in São Paulo and Belo Horizonte, illustrates the real impact of capitalist economic development upon the
Brazilian working class. While Wood is correct in his description of the direct
and indirect effects of rising infant deaths (i.e. losses related to the death of
future members of the labour force as well as physical and intellectual deterioration of those who manage to survive because of the effects of malnutrition),
I want to stress that such effects can be conceptualised as losses only from the
standpoint of a yet unrealised state of affairs: the self-determination of the
Brazilian people. Under capitalist conditions such effects are simply part of
the process of capital accumulation which, for economic and political reasons,
could not proceed smoothly[52] given its capital-intensive nature, in the context
of an increasing and healthy potential labour force.

Throughout this chapter I have focused upon the analysis of the relationship
between capitalism and population, examining the effects of the functioning of
the mode of production upon the socio-economic terrain where people in different class locations make decisions about their reproduction, as households
and individuals and, in the process, reproduce the relations of production.
The postulated determinant relationships between market level changes and
demographically relevant behaviour are overdetermined by the historically

---

50   Adelman and Morris 1973, p. 192.
51   Adelman and Morris 1973, p. 199.
52   Wood 1977, pp. 56–65.

specific characteristics of different social formations; e.g. culture, religion, the balance of power between classes, the place of the social formation in relationship to others, and so on, modify the effects of changes in capital accumulation. The model depicting some of the major effects of changes in capital accumulation is, unavoidably, linear and captures some moments of a highly complex dialectical process. In spite of its shortcomings this chapter offers, however, a Marxist conceptual framework for the study of fertility, mortality and migration, key dimensions of social reproduction in the context of capitalism; it can be taken as a beginning in the development of one of the weakest areas in Marxist thought: population theory.[53] While much of what I have stated here is surely familiar to those fully acquainted with Marxist theory, I have gone beyond the usual emphasis given to the principle of the reserve army of labour and the usual dismissal of population as a pseudo-issue in order to bring attention to the capitalist determinant of fertility, mortality, and migration and, I should add, to the demographic aspects of generational reproduction which play their part in the oppression of women.

Addendum: a Note on the Question of Overpopulation

I became interested in the relevance of Marxism to the study of demography because, at the time I was studying demographic methods, Latin America's poverty and 'underdevelopment' were mistakenly attributed primarily to 'overpopulation'. Today, Malthusian explanations appear to have been discredited. Nevertheless, I decided to include these critical remarks – originally published as part of this chapter, in an extended critique of demographic explanations of Latin American 'underdevelopment' – because it is important for Marxists and Marxist-Feminists to take into account the material reality of demographic processes and their effects on the oppression of women, on the working classes' opportunities for economic survival, and on the problems facing a transition to a mode of production that would place the satisfaction of human needs, rather than the private gain, as the main goal of economic activity.

---

53   Seccombe, writing in 1983, criticised Marxists' neglect of demography: '[they] abandoned the terrain to our enemies' (Seccombe 1983). His discussion of the social context of fertility decisions and of the European demographic transition was, to my knowledge, the first Marxist theoretical analysis of demographic issues published since the publication, in 1977, of *Population and Imperialism*, a section of *Latin American Perspectives* (Vol. IV, No. 4) I edited. Included in this section, besides this chapter, were articles about population growth and capitalist development (Folbre 1977), population control in Puerto Rico (Mass 1977), and infant mortality in Brazil (Wood 1977).

Latin America's 'Population Problem'[54]

Given the logic sustaining the operation of the capitalist mode of production, I will argue that *Latin America has no population problem today*. To argue that Latin America does not have a 'population problem' is not to claim that Latin America has no problems at all, but rather to indicate that such problems are primarily economic and political and stem from the subordinate position of Latin America in the world capitalist system. Essentially, the mechanisms controlling production and distribution are independent from its population size, density, and rate of growth; consequently, the current problems of economic stagnation, unemployment, excessive urbanisation, low agricultural productivity, etc., are not caused by high rates of population growth nor will they wither away with lower rates of growth. Summing up the above, the main reason why there is no such thing as a 'population problem' in Latin America is because, with the exception of Cuba, Latin American social formations are capitalist, and under capitalism population presents no problems at all. The way in which capitalism deals with population growth unsuitable to the political and economic needs of capital accumulation is through furthering reductions in the birth rate (e.g. family planning, sterilisation)[55] and by allowing for the more or less unrestricted operation of the 'Malthusian checks' (presumably based upon 'laws of nature') of malnutrition, '... unwholesome occupations, severe labor and exposure to the seasons, extreme poverty, bad nursing of children, great towns, excesses of all kinds, the whole train of common diseases and epidemics, war, plague, and famine';[56] in other words, through ways which contribute to increase mortality. These ways may be deliberate (e.g. making healthcare unavailable to the poor[57] and too costly for the majority of the population through measures designed to that effect)[58] or unintended consequences of

---

54   Gimenez 1977, pp. 32–4.
55   Mass 1977.
56   Malthus 1933, p. 14.
57   A contemporary example: in the US, 24 Republican governors refused to accept federal government subsidies to expand Medicaid, the government programme providing healthcare to the poor. They preferred to miss out on $423 billion in federal healthcare dollars through 2020 (Holland 2014). According to the US Department of Health and Human Services, it is estimated that the Affordable Care Act has helped 20 million people gain access to healthcare insurance. http://www.hhs.gov/about/news/2016/03/03/20-million-people -have-gained-health-insurance-coverage-because-affordable-care-act-new-estimates#
        The repeal of the Affordable Care Act has been at the top of the agenda of the current Republican administration.
58   See, for example, Navarro 1974.

the process of capitalism accumulation itself operating through the general determinants of mortality.

On the other hand, if Latin America were to become socialist overnight, there would be a population problem of an extraordinary magnitude. *Population problems arise under socialism but do not exist under capitalism.* This apparently bizarre statement has its theoretical foundations on the principles underlying socialism. Marx's guideline 'from each according to their abilities, to each according to their needs' means that, *in practice*, a socialist economy and social organisation would be committed to provide to *all* its members a minimum standard of living that would ensure their survival and growth in conditions suitable for physical and intellectual development. At this point, all the injunctions that non-Marxist economists put forth with respect to the desirability of population control would become an important set of guidelines. Under capitalism, where an individual's 'life chances' are left to the vagaries of the market, it makes no difference how many people there are because the logic of the system is such that even with zero population growth, unemployment and poverty – i.e. 'excess' population – would still be present. Under socialist economic and social organisation, on the contrary, given its political commitment to organise production for the satisfaction of everyone's needs, the population problem would become acute. This argument rests also upon the following assumption: population must be analysed from a materialist standpoint, acknowledging that the problem posed by current rates of growth is real and that no amount of institutional change will do away, overnight, with existing population structure and processes. I am arguing that no Marxist analysis of population can adequately cope with the pressing issues of the times if it falls into the idealist defensive posture of reducing nature to cognition about nature or to a moment in the subject-nature dialectics.[59] Population structure and processes are an obvious aspect of the material constraints imposed by nature on all modes of production and cannot be conceived in purely social terms. A Marxist analysis of population, consequently, cannot be exclusively concerned with the impact which the mode of production has upon population but must also take into account the characteristics of the population itself (e.g. age and sex distribution, median age, percentage of the population under 15, dependency ratio, rate of growth, birth rate, death rate, etc.) and explore their impact upon the options open to the mode of production in a given social formation at a given time. Theoretically and practically, the place of population in the capitalist mode of production as a totality is qualitatively different from

---

59   Timpanaro 1970.

that which it acquires in the process of transitional change from capitalism to socialism. From being both theoretically and practically a 'dependent variable', population becomes an 'independent variable' because the needs of the people, rather than the needs of capital accumulation, acquire first priority in the emergent new mode of social and economic organisation. Conversely, the authenticity of the process of building socialism is revealed by the extent to which the needs of the population are not subordinate to the needs of accumulation.

CHAPTER 7

Feminism, Pronatalism, and Motherhood

'Feminism, Pronatalism, and Motherhood', in *International Journal of Women Studies*, Vol. 3, No. 3 (Summer 1980): 215–40.

Introduction

Motherhood, if conceived as a taken for granted dimension of women's normal adult role, becomes one of the key sources of women's oppression. The notion that *all* women *should* be and *desire* to be mothers has always been used to keep women in a subordinate position while paying lip service to the social importance of their role. In this chapter, I propose to explore the credibility and theoretical relevance of an unusual criticism directed at the mainstream[1] of the US women's liberation movement: the notion that its unqualified support of motherhood as one of the most important women's rights[2] is insufficiently critical of its oppressive dimensions. It is very important to investigate this matter because, to the extent that the current prescriptive nature of motherhood is not theoretically and politically challenged, the struggle for genuine alternatives for women could be self-defeating.

The argument that feminism has not fundamentally challenged the compulsory nature of motherhood has been persuasively developed by sociologist Judith Blake in her research paper on 'Coercive Pronatalism and American Population Policy' prepared for the Commission of Population Growth and the American Future.[3] As a sociologist, Blake is highly critical of the voluntaristic assumptions underlying the ideas of both Family Planning advocates as well as those who fear that population policies aimed at curbing population growth may bring forth coercive measures curtailing individuals' reproductive

---

1 The terms 'women's liberation movement', 'women's movement', or 'the movement', are indistinctly used in a purely descriptive sense to refer to the heterogeneous organisational and ideological mobilisation of women that emerged in the US in the late 1960s. This mobilisation gave rise to an outpouring of literature analysing 'the woman question' from a variety of political and theoretical standpoints, some of which will be reviewed in this essay.

2 Blake 1974, pp. 44–50. Judith Blake is a demographer who has written extensively on the relationship between social structure and fertility. To my knowledge, her systematic analysis of pronatalism and its significance for the status of women is unique in the literature.

3 Blake 1974, pp. 29–67.

freedom. In her view, neither family planners who emphasise parents' right to choose their family size, nor those who assume that smaller families could be attained only by coercion are right in taking for granted the existence of reproductive freedom. On the contrary:

> Neither takes into account that at present, reproductive behaviour is under stringent institutional control and that this control constitutes ... a coercive pronatalist policy. Hence, an effective anti-natalist policy will not necessarily involve an increase in coercion or a reduction in the 'voluntary' element in reproduction, because individuals are under pronatalist constraints right now. *People make their 'voluntary' reproductive choices in an institutional context that severely constrains them not to choose non-marriage, not to choose childlessness, not to choose only one child, and even not to limit themselves solely to two children.*[4]

American society, like all societies, is pronatalist because parenthood is universally prescribed. There are no legitimate or socially rewarded alternatives to the performance of parental roles. Instead, parenthood is a *precondition* for women's and men's adult roles;[5] i.e. the primary basis for achieving full social participation. Deviations from the established role expectations (e.g. homosexuality, childlessness, single status, etc.) are punished by a variety of socio-economic and psychological sanctions.

The essence of Blake's criticism is the following: feminists have overlooked the compulsory nature of parenthood and its relevance for the full understanding of the structural and ideological foundations of women's secondary status. Present-day feminists are uncritically supportive of motherhood as a right and this is reflected in their advocacy of the 'do both syndrome'; i.e. the fact that they posit motherhood and careers not as alternative and equally legitimate choices for women, but as a combination to which all women have a right. The women's liberation movement is implicitly supportive of pronatalism because it has aimed its struggles toward the goal of eliminating the social, economic, legal, educational, and psychological barriers standing in the way of women's ability to 'do both', thus stressing women's right not to have to make a choice.[6] Focusing her analysis on the social constraints that further compulsory parenthood for both sexes, Blake makes a theoretical suggestion that opens the way

---

4   Blake 1974, p. 30, emphasis added.
5   Blake 1974, p. 33, emphasis in the text.
6   Blake 1974, p. 45.

for developing a deeper understanding of the structural basis of sexism. She argues that the barriers women encounter in their efforts to change the existing conditions cannot be exclusively understood as consequences or effects of male dominance; they should also be considered as consequences of '… the intense societal supports for the *family roles* of father and mother'.[7] It would follow, therefore, that male supremacy and female oppression could be viewed as structural effects of social constraints designed to place women *and* men in parental roles.

Blake criticises feminist politics (they have unanticipated pronatalist implications) and suggests an interesting and important direction for theoretical inquiry: the investigation of the relationship between pronatalism and sexism.

My immediate reaction to these criticisms was one of rejection and incredulity. I also found outrageous her argument that the claim for women's right to have a career and a family was tantamount to asking that women should have the right to equally neglect, like men, their family obligations.[8] I re-read feminist literature because I had the overwhelming impression that feminists had subjected every single dimension of the female condition to the most trenchant critical analysis. I believed that the issue of pronatalism and its theoretical and political implications could not have been entirely overlooked. I was, however, disappointed. I had to conclude, for reasons that I will set out later in this chapter, that Blake was basically correct. Furthermore, as I examined more carefully her arguments and their theoretical and political relevance for women, I realised that she had identified a very important issue leading to questions that feminists could not afford to either ignore or consider as already answered:

Why should everyone, regardless of sex, be expected to have children even though their primary commitments and concerns lay elsewhere?

Why should nominal parenthood, for both women and men, be required as a symbol of respectability, normality, or conformity?

What are the social consequences of family formation by persons marginally committed to childbearing?

What is the relationship between social constraints forcing people into parental roles and male dominance?[9]

It is obvious that a critical assessment of the politics of the women's movement in the light of Blake's criticisms and the exploration of the relationship between pronatalism and sexism are crucial for feminist theory and politics.

---

7   Blake 1974, p. 36, emphasis in the text.
8   Blake 1974, p. 47.
9   Blake 1974.

It follows, from her discussion, that *women's liberation from male dominance is inextricably linked to women's and men's liberation from compulsory parenthood.* To the extent that the movement does not subject the dominant pattern of universally prescribed parenthood to thorough analysis and criticism, it unwittingly contributes to consolidation of one of the structural foundations of the situation it aims to change. It is my purpose in this essay to begin that critical and analytical task. I will first present an assessment of the validity of Blake's criticisms through the examination of feminist literature. In the section that follows, I will develop further the theoretical analysis of these issues through the investigation of the capitalist supports of pronatalism and sexism. As I have argued elsewhere, Marxist theory is a source of extremely valuable theoretical and methodological guidelines for feminists.[10] From a Marxist theoretical standpoint, the issues raised by Blake cannot be fully understood if subject only to demographic and functional analysis; they must be examined in their historical dimensions through the investigation of the relationship between capitalism, pronatalism, and sexism.

I should add that I have hesitated a great deal before writing this chapter. Pronatalist structures and ideologies are dominant today; consequently, to appear in any way critical of motherhood in particular or of parenthood in general is threatening to people, particularly to women, most of whom already have or plan to bear children. It might also seem a rather futile concern because, as feminist writings have been so outspokenly critical of the family and sex roles, it would appear as if one were raising a non-existent issue. Furthermore, to subject feminist writings to a critical examination might seem to some unfair given the way in which such writings have contributed to the understanding of women's oppression in capitalist society, and to the articulation of specific political demands. This issue is not, however, one of fairness or unfairness. The topic is far more complex than it seems and criticism of present sex roles and family arrangements are not necessarily criticisms of their pronatalist dimensions if by *pronatalism* one means *the existence of structural and ideological pressures resulting in socially prescribed parenthood as a precondition for all adult roles.*

---

10   Gimenez 1975, pp. 61–80; Gimenez 1978, pp. 301–23.

Pronatalism and Feminism

I proceeded to examine feminist literature under the assumption that it reflects the major concerns of the women's liberation movement. In searching for theoretical arguments, conceptualisation of problems, articulation of policy objectives, etc., I was particularly concerned with the analysis of motherhood and its past, present, and future relevance in determining the status of women. More specifically, I was interested in the definition of reproductive freedom. An analysis of reproduction that took into consideration the universally pre-scribed nature of the mother role and its effects upon the oppression of women would have to define reproductive self-determination as the right of women to choose: a) *how many* children to have; b) *when* to have them; and c) *whether* to have children or not. On the other hand, an analysis of reproduction that did not question the prescriptive nature of motherhood would stress only the first two dimensions of reproductive self-determination: women's right to control their family size and the timing of births. Needless to say, I was also concerned with the place given to the 'do both syndrome' in the articulation of femin-ist demands and goals. More concretely I wanted to find out whether it was presented as the main option, or as one alternative among others also *equally* and *clearly* defined. My examination of the literature, which does not pretend to be anything but exploratory, yielded unexpected and disappointing results. The 'do both syndrome' was the rule, rather than the exception. Reproductive self-determination was defined around the question of number and timing of births; *the right of women not to have any children was not clearly and specific-ally incorporated in the feminist analysis and critique of reproduction*. I had to conclude, therefore, that Blake had been basically correct in her appraisal of present-day feminism.

Before presenting the evidence supporting my conclusions, I will briefly explain the reasoning that led me to them. In contemporary society, prona-talism is structurally and ideologically dominant at the societal and the per-sonality structure levels of analysis. In this context, statements which do not *explicitly* challenge pronatalism become *implicitly* supportive of it because of the objective conditions that determine not only their emergence but also their socially accepted meaning. For example, statements proclaiming women's right to control their bodies or their reproductive behaviour *without* includ-ing in the content or scope of that abstractly defined right the possibility of opting out of motherhood altogether are, *by omission*, supportive of prescript-ive motherhood because they are bound to be interpreted in the context of the dominant ideology surrounding motherhood. There are no neutral statements in the context of ideological and political struggle. By default, unclear, ambiguous, or unspecified concepts support the dominant social arrangements because the latter tend to rule out interpretations of the former that might radically challenge the status quo. The logic underlying my analysis and conclusions is open to two kinds of criticisms: 1) it could be argued that what really matters are the motives of feminist writers and, given their commitment to women's liberation, it would be unfair to suggest that their writings might uphold oppressive structures and ideologies; and 2) it could also be argued that many statements which, in my view, support pronatalism, could be interpreted otherwise. It should be clear to the reader, therefore, that I am not concerned with the motivations of feminist writers, but with the social implications of their writings. The fact that they are open to opposing interpretations only proves that they are essentially ambiguous and, as such, supportive of the status quo. My contention rests upon an assessment of their socially accepted meaning which, as it emerges from the analysis of feminist literature, does not question pronatalist assumptions about motherhood. If that were not the case, childlessness as a legitimate option for women would have appeared in the literature just as frequently as the 'do both syndrome' and this chapter would not have been written.

I will now present a summary of my analysis of feminist literature. I will discuss the insights provided by political statements put forth by various sectors of the movement, significant articles, and theoretical arguments developed in major feminist works.

Statements and Manifestoes

The women's liberation movement is heterogeneous; each sector defines 'the woman question' somewhat differently and offers different explanations and solutions.[11] An examination of manifestoes and statements of principles included in anthologies of women's liberation writings[12] led me to identify the following themes related to reproduction:

1.   A critique of current sex role definitions and expectations. Some writings glorify female attributes at the expense of male traits, although the most frequent vision is that of future androgyny.

2.   A critique of marriage and the nuclear family followed by the proposal of alternatives (e.g. communes, female headed households, etc.) which

---

11   See Deckard 1975 for an excellent overview.
12   MacLean 1976, pp. 39–50; Morgan 1970; Brophy 1971, pp. 73–9; Dunbar 1971, pp. 179–92; McAfee and Wook 1971, pp. 21–38; Tanner 1970, pp. 112–15, 124–6, 129–32.

assume the presence of children. This involves the striving for equalitarian and/or androgynous relations within households where, it is suggested, all members should assume responsibility for housework and childcare regardless of sex.

3. An analysis of the exploitation of women not only sexually and psychologically, but also as housewives, mothers, consumers, and members of the workforce reduced to the jobs with the lowest status and pay.

4. Concern with attaining control of reproduction. With only two exceptions, this meant demand for sex education, inexpensive and safe contraception, and abortion rights.

5. A demand for nurseries and childcare services for working women. As most women work out of economic necessity, this demand is crucial for their economic survival.

Only two manifestoes supplemented the demand to abolish social and legal barriers to contraception and abortion with a call for women's right to choose whether to bear children.[13] In the overwhelming majority of the writings examined, however, there was nothing said, specifically and unequivocally, about the possibility of a 'childfree' status[14] as a legitimate option for women: motherhood was taken for granted throughout. Women's right to control their reproduction was consistently and narrowly defined in relationship to the means of attaining that control (contraception and abortion). There were no clear statements about the meaning of reproductive control beyond the notion that it somehow involved women's access to legal and safe means of controlling their fertility. Such limited notion of reproductive control does not present a radical challenge to the pronatalist institutions in which it remains embedded.

Articles

A review of articles that established the theoretical and ideological basis for developing a scientific and political understanding of women's status in modern society[15] also led me to similar conclusions because of their main general concerns:

---

13   Tanner 1970, pp. 124–6, 129–32.
14   The term 'childfree', which denotes choice rather than the deprivation implied by the term 'childless', is used by Peck and Senderowitz in the introduction to *Pronatalism: The Myth of Mom and Apple Pie*. A childfree status, as a legitimate choice, is advocated by NON, National Organization for Non-Parents.
15   Rossi 1969, pp. 173–86; Dixon 1969, pp. 173–86; Sochen 1971, pp. 87–112 and 149–60; Freeman 1972, pp. 201–16; Dixon 1972, pp. 184–200; Dixon 1975, pp. 56–8; Benston 1969, pp. 13–

1.   the desirability of androgyny;
2.   an awareness of the compulsory nature of motherhood taken as the basis
     for the formulation of alternative ways of coping with childcare and
     housework, and qualitatively different sex roles;
3.   a strong faith in the power of contraceptive technology to determine
     women's control over reproduction.

To acknowledge, no matter how strongly, the oppressive nature of motherhood
(e.g. '... in a woman, not having children is seen as an incapacity somewhat
akin to impotence in a man';[16] '... I think we can defer dropping children on
cultural command ... I am not making a call for eternal celibacy, but for intel-
ligent birth control and a rethinking of the compulsion to have children'),[17] is
not equivalent to conducting a thorough analysis of its consequences if viewed
as a taken for granted aspect of women's lives. These writings do not fully and
comprehensively question the assumption that most women will eventually
be mothers; they question the social arrangements surrounding the practice of
motherhood which interfere with women's ability to participate in the educational and occupational structure. This is reflected in the emphasis given to the
discussion of alternative household arrangements, childcare services, androgyny, and qualitative sex role changes. The possibility that the latter might also
include childlessness is never brought up in the analysis, with only one exception that I will discuss later. I found only one instance of total rejection of
motherhood, in the advocacy of '... the right to artificial reproduction, which
is the key to real control of our own bodies and autonomy to determine our
lives'.[18] It seems unquestionable that the hold of the dominant ideology about
motherhood over people's minds limits their ability to perceive alternatives.
These limits push people into either total acceptance of motherhood or total
negation, thus precluding the emergence of a standpoint which, transcending both, could provide – unlike pure negativity – an effective challenge to the
status quo.

    Cisler's[19] analysis is the only one that suggests, albeit ambiguously, the pos-
sibility that the decision whether or not to bear children might enter into the
definition of reproductive control. In her view, the lack of reproductive control
is at the root of the dominant societal definition of women as childbearers. In

---

27.   Gordon 1970, pp. 193–9; Cisler 1970, pp. 245–88; Salper 1972, pp. 169–84; Brown 1969,
      pp. 222–9.
16   Dixon 1972, p. 189.
17   Brown, p. 226.
18   Salper, p. 184.
19   Cisler 1970, pp. 245–88.

this light, advances in birth control technology are seen as threatening to the maintenance of social control over women's reproductive capacities and the relationship between the sexes based upon that control.

Cisler's analysis gives too much weight to the potential impact of birth control technology and overlooks the strength of existing pronatalist patterns. She argues that the technology of birth control is 'value free' and that '... *people impute meaning to it; people* determine the uses to which it will be put and the consequences of those uses'.[20] Whether birth control leads to the sexual enslavement of women or to their liberation will ultimately depend on women '... actively ... defining the values that surround birth control technology'.[21] Unlike most feminists, she is critical of the fact that among the rationales for allowing women to control their reproduction, '... a woman's own simple wish not to bear any more (*or even any*) children is conspicuously absent'.[22] As she points out, the dominant ideology is such that only 'deserving' women (i.e. those who already have had too many children, or would face death or serious disability if they had a child) are generally considered more suitable recipients of birth control information and technology. On the other hand, 'An undeserving woman ... is one who is concerned with her own self-interest and actively seeks to preserve it by deciding she does not want to bear *a* child'.[23] Her argument, in the absence of further elaboration on the issues of the right of women not to have *any* children if they so desire (as Cisler had intimated earlier), is not strong enough to constitute a clear-cut indictment of pronatalism. Her views, which could have served as the starting point for the development of a revolutionary concept of reproductive control, were not taken up by other feminists.

An interesting reversal in the analysis of motherhood can be found in the work of Alice Rossi, whose early articles were so important to the movement.[24] Initially, she was highly critical of the social definition of motherhood as the major source of women's fulfilment. She condemned American society for having institutionalised motherhood as a full-time occupation for adult women to the detriment of their ability to participate in the social, economic, and political structure.[25] She was also outspokenly critical of the crucial role played by

---

20   Cisler 1970, p. 288, emphasis in the text.
21   Cisler 1970, p. 288.
22   Cisler 1970, p. 248, emphasis added.
23   Ibid, emphasis added.
24   Rossi 1971.
25   Rossi 1971, p. 93.

the social sciences in legitimating the hegemony of that image of women.[26] Her criticisms were exclusively aimed at the full-time pattern of motherhood and, as a solution, she advocated the legitimation of part-time mothering and the development of androgynous sex roles. She was never critical of the prescriptive nature of motherhood as such and that might account for her acceptance of the sociobiological claims about the biological roots of social organisation. She now proposes the existence of a *maternal instinct*, a product of human evolution and, as such, impossible to change through deliberate political action.[27] Her analysis, whose scientific shortcomings and conservative political implications have been effectively singled out and criticised,[28] is perhaps the most blatant and dangerous pronatalist statement to date. In the eyes of the uninformed, the argument's reliance on biology lends it a legitimacy beyond question which is likely to be effectively used by the anti-feminist/pronatalist forces currently struggling against abortion rights and the Equal Rights Amendment.

I should end this section by pointing out that, in her recent and insightful article 'What Does "Control Over Our Bodies" Really Mean?',[29] Moen expands the meaning of the feminist slogan beyond its usual connotations: i.e. women's right to safe and available contraception and abortion to enable them to choose the number and timing of births. She unequivocally includes women's right to bear or not to bear children,[30] and convincingly argues that to be effectively in control of reproduction women should also have economic independence and political control over society itself. Her critical analysis of the meaning of 'control over our bodies' is not aimed at highlighting its shortcomings in dealing with the taken for granted nature of motherhood as a component of the expected female adult role. Instead, she is concerned with the social, economic, and political consequences of aggregate fertility and their implications for women's ability to control reproduction. It is important to note, however, that her explicit consideration of motherhood as an option for women is exceptional in the literature.

---

26   Rossi 1971, pp. 92–3.
27   Rossi 1977, pp. 1–31.
28   The reader is referred to the following excellent critiques of Rossi's arguments: Cerullo, Stacey and Breines 1977–78, pp. 167–77; and Chodorow 1977–78, pp. 179–97.
29   Moen 1979.
30   Moen 1979, p. 136.

Major Feminist Writings

I will now present an in-depth discussion of some major theoretical contributions[31] which not only shed light on the scope and limitations of the feminist analysis of reproduction, but also help to strengthen my conclusions about the adequacy of Blake's criticisms.

One of the first important theoretical attempts to deal with the oppression of women was Juliet Mitchell's article 'Women: The Longest Revolution',[32] later expanded and included in *Woman's Estate*.[33] Mitchell argues that women's role in the family, which appears to be based upon the biological universal of motherhood, is actually determined by the historically specific combination of three structures (reproduction, sexuality, and socialisation) into a monolithic unit: the family or mode of reproduction. In her view, as long as birth control technology was unreliable, the mode of reproduction remained essentially unchanged; until now, reproduction has been defined by '… its uncontrollable, natural character and to this extent has been an unmodified biological fact'.[34] Modern contraception means that '… today there are the technical possibilities for the transformation and "humanization" of the most *natural* part of human culture. This is what a change in the mode of reproduction could mean'.[35] She further develops this point as follows:

> As long as reproduction remained a *natural* phenomenon … women were effectively doomed to social exploitation … They had no choice as to whether or how often they gave birth to children (apart from precarious methods of contraception or repeated abortions); their existence was essentially subject to biological processes outside their control.[36]

Given those premises, contraception is logically hailed as the key for changes in the mode of reproduction: '… what it means is that at last the mode of reproduction *potentially* could be transformed. Once childbearing becomes totally voluntary … [It] need no longer be the sole or ultimate vocation of woman: it becomes an option among others'.[37]

---

31   Mitchell 1969, pp. 19–26; Mitchell 1971; Rowbotham 1974; Gordon 1976; Firestone 1971.
32   Mitchell 1969.
33   Mitchell 1971.
34   Mitchell 1971, p. 107.
35   Mitchell 1971, p. 108, emphasis added.
36   Mitchell 1971, p. 107.
37   Mitchell 1971, p. 108, emphasis added.

Her argument rests upon a questionable assumption: that until the advent of modern contraception, reproduction was a natural fact over which women had little or no control. Granting the greater efficacy of modern birth control methods, social scientists concerned with the study of fertility would disagree with her assumption because no society has abstained from surrounding reproduction with the most elaborate social patterns. Mitchell overlooks both the existence of pronatalist pressures and the existence of ways to regulate fertility which have been present in all societies. The evidence from the social sciences suggests that women in pre-capitalist societies had greater control over reproduction than feminists generally seem to admit, and that modern women have far less autonomy in reproductive matters than feminists would like to believe.[38] In my view, the availability of contraception has indeed the potential to modify the mode of reproduction, but it is not sufficient to trigger drastic changes in reproductive patterns. In order for childbearing to become 'totally voluntary', 'one option among others', radical changes in the capitalist modes of production and reproduction would have to occur; i.e. changes in the relations of production and in the relations of reproduction.[39] Although Mitchell is critical of Firestone's biological determinism,[40] she seems to share it to the extent that she appears to overestimate the power of contraceptive technology to give women control over their reproductive lives, while underestimating the power of pronatalist social and psychological structures that contain and modify its potentially revolutionary effects. Her analysis is, however, unusual in its straightforward advocacy of childbearing as one option among others.

There is another sequel to the availability of contraception: the separation of sexuality from reproduction. Feminists, for reasons that deserve careful investigation, seem to have given greater theoretical consideration to the analysis of sexual exploitation. This standpoint is conducive to a relative theoretical neglect of reproduction which is thus unwittingly or deliberately relegated to the realm of nature, to biology. Consequently, the complex pronatalist patterns conditioning reproduction are not scrutinised as thoroughly and the notion of women's control over their reproductive lives remains bound to the dominant pronatalist alternatives. Rowbotham, for example, greatly stresses the impact of contraception on sexuality: '... contraception lays the basis for a great explosion in the possibility of female pleasure'.[41] The grounds contraception

---

38   See, for example, Davis and Blake 1956, pp. 211–35.
39   For an understanding of the concept 'mode of production', see, for example, Althusser and Balibar 1970.
40   Mitchell 1971, p. 90.
41   Rowbotham 1974, p. 114.

establishes for 'a great explosion' in alternatives with respect to childbearing remain unexplored in her discussion of women's control over reproduction.

Linda Gordon's work is unique in its grasp of pronatalist structures. It would be impossible to dwell on all the valuable insights she offers in *Woman's Body, Woman's Rights*;[42] my remarks will be based primarily on the last chapter, 'Sexuality, Feminism, and Birth Control Today', which summarises her main points and is most relevant to the present chapter.

In Gordon's view, reproductive freedom is a dimension of human freedom and is thus affected by all the institutions which, in one way or another, curtail that freedom. For example, class structure affects the reproductive pattern of all classes which thus seek in family formation goals as varied as the maintenance of political and economic power, meaning and satisfaction to compensate for the consequences of alienated labour, economic and social security, etc.[43] Unlike most feminists, Gordon correctly acknowledges the existence of pronatalist pressures affecting all adults which:

> ... make children potentially the victim of adults' unsatisfactory lives. These pressures systematically push reproduction *beyond* the reach of technological solutions. Only the liberation of children from the burdens of being useful to adults can make childbearing a free choice, emanating from the desire to perpetuate human life, not oneself.[44]

She points out that, although men and women are subject to those pressures, reproduction creates more difficulties for women who are given, whether they are employed outside of the home or not, sole responsibility for childcare.

Feminists have consistently denounced the negative psychological, social and economic consequences of socialisation patterns stressing motherhood as women's major social role. Gordon expands that critique to include the analysis of the pronatalist dimensions of the motherhood mystique. Socialisation creates a female personality structure for which motherhood becomes a need not easily rejected. To be childless becomes synonymous with failure and those feelings are reinforced by cultural and social pressures which evaluate childlessness negatively. The equation of motherhood with self-realisation in conjunction with the lack of desirable alternatives to motherhood and the enhanced opportunities for sexual exploitation resulting from a 'sexual revolution' in the midst of sexual inequality, make women's attainment of reproduct-

---

42   Gordon 1976.
43   Gordon 1976, pp. 404–5, emphasis added.
44   Gordon 1976, p. 405, emphasis added.

ive freedom structurally impossible: 'Self-determination cannot exist if none of the options is attractive. Reproductive options cannot be separated from economic, vocational, and social choices'.[45] Under these conditions, Gordon argues, women 'fall into motherhood' for, in spite of its problematic aspects, it is not only more creative and rewarding than most alternatives but also it is a source of meaning and comfort that compensates for the alienating features of the work most women have the opportunity to do.

Gordon's critique of motherhood is important because she does not share the optimistic view on the liberating power of contraceptive technology that characterises most feminist analysis of reproduction. On the contrary, she outlines the variety of pronatalist pressure, which, operating at the social and psychological levels, '... push reproduction beyond the reach of technological solutions'.[46]

Her concept of reproductive freedom remains ambiguous: it *does not* mean population control, birth rate reduction or family planning.[47] What *does* it mean? It would seem, deducing from the text, that it means voluntary childbearing:

> Involuntary childbearing has burdened all women ... poor women most, and the sexual inequality that resulted has helped perpetuate all other forms of inequality and weakened struggles against them. Reproductive self-determination is a basic condition for sexual equality and for women to assume full membership in all other human groups.[48]

The concept of voluntary childbearing is simply the negation of the present situation in which childbearing is determined by pronatalist constraints. It is not concretely defined, specifying the choices women would have if they were to attain reproductive self-determination and remains, therefore, an empty, abstract statement of freedom. At this point, Gordon's argument takes a surprisingly voluntaristic and idealistic turn that contrasts with her previous research and understanding not only of the pronatalist pressures underlying reproductive behaviour today, but also of the *social nature of reproduction* whatever its historical context. For example, she suggests that women could resist current population policies by using contraceptive knowledge '... to help

---

45   Gordon 1976, p. 408.
46   Gordon, p. 405.
47   Gordon 1976, p. 414.
48   Gordon 1976, p. 417.

make *their own decisions* about childbearing'.[49] Given that individual decisions *always* have a social content, because of the dominant social arrangements that rule out childlessness as a desirable option, such 'voluntary' decisions would most likely be limited to establishing the timing and frequency of childbearing. This lack of specificity blunts the potential effect of this work in increasing women's awareness of the full dimensions of pronatalism.

The only feminist work which not only recognises pronatalism as a barrier to women's liberation but also advocates non-procreative lifestyles is Firestone's *The Dialectic of Sex*.[50] Hers is a biological determinist analysis of women's oppression that considers sexual inequality as the first 'class' antagonism arising from the biological fact of reproduction. Her main argument is that 'sex class' is directly determined by biological imperatives: a) the subordination of women to their biology prior to the development of birth control technology; b) the special mother/child relationship created by the long time required by humans to grow up; and c) the biological difference between the sexes giving rise to the first division of labour.[51] This biological family is a constant that underlies, in her view, all institutional variations which, in the best bourgeois tradition, she dismisses as mere proofs of the 'flexibility' of 'human nature'.[52] Having established a biological premise for her argument which relegates reproduction, again, to the realm of nature, she proceeds to argue – predictably – that the 'natural' (i.e. biological reproduction) is not a 'human' value.[53] Technology is again endowed with the power to 'humanise' nature; women must seize control over reproduction and the final goal would be the elimination of sex as a social category. Technology would break the tyranny of the biological family and:

> The reproduction of the species by one sex for the benefit of both would be replaced by (at least the option of) artificial reproduction: children would be born to both sexes equally, or independent of either, however one chooses to look at it; the dependence of the child on the mother (and vice versa) would give way to a greatly shortened dependence on a small group of others in general ...[54]

---

49   Gordon 1976, p. 418, emphasis added.
50   Firestone 1971.
51   Firestone 1971, pp. 8–9.
52   Firestone 1971, p. 9.
53   Firestone 1971, p. 10.
54   Firestone 1971, p. 11.

On the issue of reproduction, her analysis is challenging although faulty in its exclusive and utopian reliance on technology. She succeeds, however, in raising the issue of motherhood as a possible option rather than as a prescriptive role and part of the value of her analysis lies precisely in that recognition of the need to free women from compulsory motherhood. As she indicates, the myth of motherhood as some kind of inherent attribute of all women is so powerful that women who dare to challenge it are likely to be punished:

> Artificial reproduction is not inherently dehumanizing. At the very least, development of an option should make possible an honest examination of the ancient value of motherhood. At the present time, for a woman to come out openly against motherhood on principle is physically dangerous. She can get away with it only if she adds that she is neurotic, abnormal, child hating, ... 'unfit' ... This is hardly a free atmosphere of inquiry. Until the taboo is lifted, until the decision not to have children or not to have them 'naturally' is at least as legitimate as traditional childbearing, women are as good as forced into their female roles.[55]

Firestone not only unerringly identifies the compulsory nature of motherhood and the current 'deviant' status of non-motherhood, but also questions the existence of a parenthood instinct affecting women and men. She argues that it is difficult to establish whether the fact that most people want children at the present time stems from 'an authentic liking for children' or 'a displacement of other needs'.[56] To avoid the suffering that ensues when children are used as a means to fulfil their parents' needs, she suggests a number of alternatives predicated upon the social recognition of reproduction as a real option for women and men: single, couple, and group living arrangements with or without children, through which adults and children could freely move at a pace imposed by their own developmental needs.

Her overall analysis of the oppression of women rests upon biological and technological determinism and, as such, it is inherently conservative in its theoretical assumptions and political implications. Her work is uniquely important, however, because of its outspoken and radical critique of reproduction and the taken-for-granted nature of parental roles. The fact that her work attracted more theoretical criticisms with respect to her theoretical foundations than attention and praise for some of her insights about the nature of reproduc-

---

55   Firestone 1971, pp. 199–200.
56   Firestone 1971, p. 299.

tion and parenthood is in itself a manifestation of the ideological hegemony of pronatalism in American society.

This admittedly incomplete review of the literature lends support to Blake's[57] criticism. The idea of optional motherhood is presented either casually, as if it were an already agreed upon objective; as a matter of political expediency; or as a drastic rejection of biological reproduction calling for at least the option of artificial reproduction. Needless to say, such approaches are not likely to have major theoretical or political impact. The rejection of biological motherhood calls forth visions of test tube babies and the horrors of conditioning as depicted in *Brave New World*[58] and similar dystopias: the genuine concern for freedom and self-realisation inherent in those suggestions becomes necessarily lost in the technological nightmare they evoke. On the other hand, abstract statements about the desirability of reproductive freedom are no substitute for well-developed theoretical and political arguments.

Pronatalism, Sexism, and Feminism

The possibility of developing an effective challenge to pronatalism rests upon the political and theoretical starting points provided by the gains of the women's movement and by feminist theory. On the other hand, the fact that feminist writings do not deal critically and specifically with pronatalism, do not examine its relationship to sexism, and do not clearly posit a childfree status as another real and legitimate option for women *tacitly* and unwittingly supports the dominant pronatalist ideologies and practices that take motherhood for granted.[59] This theoretical shortcoming reflects the experience and needs of the movement's constituency: women brought up in a pronatalist context who, in their overwhelming majority, are or expect to be mothers. Their concerns are reflected in the primacy given to the in-depth analysis of sexual and psychological oppression while the oppressive aspects of reproduction are viewed at a different level, as if it were possible to overcome them through practical measures: abortion, contraception, childcare. The conscious form in

---

57   Blake 1974.
58   Huxley 1969.
59   It is true that to overlook pronatalism is not the same as to actively support it. On the other hand, neutrality is impossible in situations of power inequality. In the arena of ideological struggles, to have low consciousness about crucial issues that challenge the status quo has the unintended effect of lending support, albeit unwillingly so, to the dominant views sustaining the status quo.

which women's oppression has been experienced and acted upon has been, ultimately, one in which women (and their children) gather together to support each other in their struggle against male supremacy inside and outside households. The fact that, because of a variety of factors, the fastest growing type of household in the US is the female-headed household may have contributed to highlight the problems confronting women as working mothers, thus overshadowing other aspects of reproductive oppression.[60] Concern with economic discrimination and the conditions supporting it, and concern with the exploitation of women as 'sex objects' have obscured the exploitation of women as 'reproductive objects'. Women's oppression was analysed primarily from the general vantage point of women and, more specifically, from the vantage point of present and future mothers. As motherhood was taken for granted, the main issue became one of finding ways to combine it with an active working life. The issue of parenthood was considered in the context of role sharing and developing ideologies about the benefits and desirability of androgyny. Ideologically, reproduction was conceptualised as a female issue; structurally, sexual inequality led to the identification of men as the main source of oppression. Given those ideological and structural boundaries determining the historically specific form in which women's oppression under advanced capitalism is experienced, the issue of pronatalism, which questions not just compulsory motherhood but compulsory parenthood and considers reproduction as a process affecting both women and men, could not possibly emerge as a paramount issue. On the other hand, *the lack of specific theoretical and political concern with pronatalism among women at this time does not invalidate its existence and its negative impact among all women*. Given the present material conditions, working mothers (whatever their socio-economic status) face a series of social, economic, and psychological obstacles. The situation is worsened in the case of women who are the sole support of themselves and their children. Many of those women might not have become mothers and would have today considerably better opportunities if pronatalism had not impelled them into motherhood. In a sense, pronatalism compels women to handicap themselves, sometimes very early in their lives, and a similar argument could be made with respect to men. As Blake pointed out, pronatalist reward structures impel women and men marginally committed to parenthood to form families because that is the price to be paid for normality, respectability, credibility, and fulfilment of adult sex role expectations.[61] The high incidence of child abuse

---

60   The reader can find a thorough study of this trend in Ross and Sawhill 1975.
61   Blake 1974.

and battered wives, the high divorce and remarriage rates, the high increases in illegitimacy and teenage pregnancy, and the growth of female headed households are phenomena which should highlight the importance of investigating the negative consequences of prescriptive parenthood. I am *not* arguing that pronatalism is their only cause or even their major cause; I am suggesting that it is likely to be a strong contributing factor because it pressures women and men, sometimes at very early ages, to enter into relationships for which they might not be entirely suited and under conditions that turn those relationships into mere means to accomplish personal goals. A drastic change in the social organisation of reproduction is not likely to do away with those processes entirely, but it is very probable that it may drastically reduce their incidence. What follows is an attempt to theoretically examine the relationship among capitalism, sexism, and pronatalism in an effort to clarify some of the issues raised in the preceding discussion.

Capitalism, Pronatalism, and Sexism

Demographically, pre-capitalist societies were characterised by high rates of death, birth and infant mortality, in addition to low life expectancy. Under these conditions, social mechanisms ensured – through complex networks of rewards and punishments – that most adults engaged in reproduction to ensure societal survival. This is a functional argument advanced to explain the *demographic origins* of pronatalism: the answer to high mortality conditions is universally prescribed parenthood. From the standpoint of Marxist theory, a demographic functional explanation is adequate only to account for pronatalism *abstractly* and *in isolation from any historical determinations*: i.e. as a universal feature of all societies. A purely functional explanation, however, is in itself insufficient to account for the *origins* and *variations* of the pronatalist institutions operating in concrete social formations at a given time. Such institutions (e.g. values, sex roles, norms about family size, etc.) must be linked, *structurally* and *historically*, to the mode of production dominant in a given social formation at a given time. Given the world dominance of the capitalist mode of production, to develop a Marxist theoretical analysis of pronatalism it is necessary to identify its *capitalist origins* and the *capitalist structures and processes* that *support* it. *I am not arguing that pronatalism originated with capitalism.* Following Marx's[62] methodological principles, I am arguing that a functional

---

62   See Marx's important methodological considerations in Marx 1970, pp. 188–214; Godelier 1970, pp. 340–58.

explanation (i.e. the need to ensure societal survival) cannot explain the historically specific form taken by pronatalism under capitalism nor the specifically capitalist institutions that support it.

Capitalism emerged in a social context where high birth and death rates were dominant, and capitalism inherited a variety of pronatalist institutions. Research would show that the features pronatalism acquired in the capitalist mode of production are likely to be qualitatively different from those characteristic of pre-capitalist social formations. A thorough comparative analysis is beyond the scope of this chapter for it would require well-developed theoretical frameworks providing specific hypotheses about the origins and determinants of pronatalism, about its relationship to sexism, and about its relationship to the organisation of production within the capitalist mode of production and within pre-capitalist modes of production. Such frameworks are yet to be developed. I have limited my contribution to that task by developing a very general theoretical argument outlining my understanding, at this point, of the relationship between sexism, pronatalism, and capitalism. For reasons of space I will not examine the impact of pronatalism upon the capitalist class; my analysis will be restricted to the working class.

The impact of the process of capitalist development upon the family resulting in the division between private and public spheres of production and social life has been amply documented.[63] This is the material basis for women's oppression under capitalism.[64] Women are segregated in the home as reproducers of the present and future generation of workers. Their participation in the public sphere is subordinate to their household role and they, and their children, are economically dependent on men. Although increasing numbers of women have been drawn into the labour force, women have not been successful in their struggle for equal jobs with equal pay. The material constraints on women's labour force participation result from the contradictions of the capitalist mode of production and the changing strategies with which the capitalist

---

63   See, for example, Zaretski 1973, pp. 69–125; Secombe 1974, pp. 3–24; and Ryan 1976.

64   I am making here a theoretical point similar to that previously developed about pronatalism. *I am not arguing that sexism originated with capitalism.* From a Marxist standpoint, knowledge of the 'origins' of sexism – in chronological terms – is not very helpful for understanding how it operates today, what are its institutional supports, and how to fight effectively against it (and this principle is relevant for the study of any other issue). In order to understand how sexism operates under capitalist conditions, it is necessary to identify its capitalist 'origins' and functions: i.e. the specifically capitalist processes that incorporated sexism into the fabric of capitalist structures and ideologies, and the uses of sexism in the interest of the capitalist class. For a detailed development of this argument, see Gimenez 1975 and 1978; for methodological sources, see footnote 63.

classes attempt to resolve those contradictions. Such strategies determine fluctuations in real wages as well as fluctuations in the quantity and quality of the
demand for labour which in turn determine the size and composition of the
reserve army of labour. These material constraints have been justified in a variety of ways. While feminists have identified sexism as one of the most powerful
justifications, Blake suggests that the maintenance of family roles may be just
as important:

> The difficulties women experienced who wished to challenge the identity
> of sexual and parental roles have not been simply 'male dominance' or
> 'male power,' but rather the intense societal supports for the *family roles*
> of mother and father. The opposition to women working thus stemmed
> fully as much from the obligatory nature of family formation (and the sex
> differentiation of parents) as from fear for the diminution of male author-
> ity generally.[65]

This is an important theoretical insight suggesting that sexism could be productively analysed as a result of pronatalist structures and ideologies aimed at
placing men and women in family roles. Blake's argument rests upon an analysis of the social processes through which men and women are recruited into
family roles. She points out that, contrary to the dominant feminist assumptions, family formation entails direct costs and opportunity costs not only for
women but also for men; '... men's chances for social and personal mobility,
for education, for promotion, etc., may be impaired by parenthood'.[66] Male
supremacy is the main social inducement pressuring men into domesticity. The
social and economic advantages it brings to them compensate for the opportunities they may forego, and for the problems, humiliations, and setbacks
experienced in the labour market and in their jobs. In turn, women are pushed
into family roles not only by institutionalised sexism, but also by the social and
psychological rewards attached to those roles.

Blake discloses a complex interrelationship between sexism and pronatalism. Pronatalism places women and men into family roles through structures and ideologies that reward the latter while punishing the former: sexism. This inherently unstable situation is stabilised by pronatalist ideologies
about motherhood that reward women's compliance with pronatalist and sexist sex role expectations. Sexism obscures the costs of parenthood for men

---

65   Blake 1974, p. 36, emphasis in the text.
66   Blake 1974, p. 49.

while the motherhood mystique obscures the costs of parenthood for women; both reflect pronatalist social constraints supporting family roles as a taken for granted component of adult roles.

To establish the relevance of Blake's insights for the understanding of sexism under capitalist conditions, it is necessary to investigate the relationship between pronatalism and the capitalist material basis of sexism. If sexism is structurally supported by the specifically capitalist division of production into a public and a private sphere, where does pronatalism fit? The answer to that question might be found in the relationship between alienated labour and reproduction depicted by Marx in his early writings on alienation.[67] Capitalist production rests upon the exploitation of labour. All labour is, thus, alienated labour; i.e. instead of furthering self-realisation labour becomes a process of self-degradation and, conversely, everything else becomes a means of self-realisation.[68] In Marx's graphic terms, '... man [the worker] feels himself to be freely active only in his animal functions – eating, drinking, and procreating, or at most in his personal adornment – while in his human function he is reduced to an animal'.[69]

Marx has vividly portrayed the dichotomy permeating social life under capitalism which has enshrined 'personal life' while destroying the possibilities for fruitful and creative public life. The full meaning of alienated labour involves the alienation of the workers from themselves, from their work, from the product of their work, and from their fellow workers.[70] Women and men are compelled to seek meaning, under such conditions, in a variety of individual pursuits; some constructive (among which family roles are the most important) and some self-destructive. Social scientists investigating the determinants of fertility patterns have documented the significance of family roles as the major source of individuals' satisfaction in contemporary society, as well as the relationship between high fertility and feelings of alienation, powerlessness, isolation, and failure to achieve occupational success.[71] It would appear that, in the context of advanced capitalism, family formation patterns as well as fertility patterns reflect pronatalist constraints supported by the alienating and exploitative nature of the economic and social organisation.

---

67   Marx 1964, pp. 120–34. See also Gimenez 1973, pp. 74–88, and the section on 'Fertility' in Gimenez 1977, pp. 5–40.
68   See, for example, US Department of Health, Education and Welfare 1973; Braverman 1974.
69   Marx 1964, pp. 124–5.
70   Marx 1964.
71   See, for example, Groat and Neal 1973, pp. 83–8, and 1975, pp. 46–59; Blake 1965 and 1968; Blau and Duncan 1975, pp. 427–8.

The specific features characterising pronatalism and sexism under capitalist conditions are the result, at different levels of analysis, of capitalist structures, processes, and contradictions. The strategies for capital accumulation followed by the capitalist classes at any given time are the product of the contradiction between capital and labour, and the contradiction between the forces and the relations of production.[72] One important consequence of the accumulation process, at the level of the overall organisation of production, has been the division of production into a domestic and a public sector; this is the key underpinning of sexism under capitalist conditions. At a different level of analysis, looking at the relations of production within each sector, the most prominent phenomena that emerges is that of the exploitation and alienation of labour; this is the key underpinning of pronatalism under capitalist conditions. Alienation and exploitation of labour, and the separation between household and public production are two aspects of the same process which are important to differentiate analytically in order to establish their different modes of affecting sexism, pronatalism, the nuclear family and family relations and, most importantly, the status of women in capitalist society.

Sexism and pronatalism are two qualitatively different sets of oppressive structures and ideologies which are supported by the overall capitalist organisation of production and by the nature of the relations of production. They are reproduced by the process of capitalist accumulation which constantly reproduces their structural underpinnings and by the pertinent ideologies that contribute to their reproduction at the level of the personality structure of women and men living under capitalism.

Sexism and pronatalism are mutually interrelated and support each other by providing compensatory ideologies and practices that relieve the tensions and contradictions they bring about in the relationships between the sexes and between generations. For example, the exploitation of male workers is made more bearable by male supremacy and its attendant social, economic, and domestic privileges. Because of their secondary status in production, women are exploited in the labour and sexual markets while experiencing economic and reproductive oppression at home. On the other hand, pronatalist ideologies about family roles, the nature of motherhood, the meaning of children, etc. compensate for a great deal of the oppression women experience inside and outside their homes. The alienation women and men experience in their lives is resolved in the idealisation of the family which is structurally supported by the contradictions inherent in capitalist relations operating directly, through

---

72   For a clear explanation of these concepts, see Therborn 1976, pp. 353–86.

the organisation and relations of production and indirectly, through pronatalist and sexist constraints. As feminists have pointed out, the ideological construction of the family as a place of total peace and refuge constantly breaks down for it reproduces the contradictions of the mode of production in ways that are ultimately destructive to its members.[73] Nevertheless, although the problematic nature of family relations in contemporary society has been widely acknowledged, families continue to be formed. Why? Not only because they fulfil important structural and ideological functions for the capitalist mode of production but also, and this is where Blake's contribution sheds light, because parental roles are a taken for granted aspect of adult roles. Structurally and psychologically, family formation is not a choice for either women or men.

The development of the productive forces has brought about a decline in the death rate which has rendered obsolete not only the high fertility previously required for societal survival but also the pronatalist constraints that went with it. Advanced capitalism has created the material conditions necessary to undermine prescriptive parenthood in the context of advanced capitalist societies, and allow for the emergence of a qualitatively different form of institutionalised pronatalism that would make optional motherhood possible. On the other hand, advanced capitalism continues to reproduce the material conditions that make prescriptive parenthood (as well as sexism) an important tool for maintaining social control and the exploitation of labour. The contradiction between the demographic consequences of the development of the productive forces and the pronatalist and sexist implications of the capitalist organisation and relations of production is reflected in the mutually reinforcing and, at the same time, contradictory relationship between pronatalism and sexism. For example, capitalism tends to undermine sexism by allowing greater economic and educational opportunities for women, but at the same time, supports sexism through pronatalist ideologies that compel women to subordinate their social and economic self-reliance and advancement to family roles. Capitalist processes undermine pronatalism by creating the material conditions for a qualitatively different form of reproductive freedom while at the same time supporting it by: a) denying real, desirable options to women so that family roles remain more appealing whatever gains women may experience in labour force participation; and b) strengthening sexist relations between women and men that interfere with women's ability to use contraception effectively and consistently.

---

73   Mitchell 1971, Ch. 8, offers an excellent analysis of this topic.

Bringing pronatalism into the theoretical analysis of sexism is helpful not only for understanding the structural underpinnings of sexism, but also for devising effective measures against it. Sexism is not likely to disappear as a result of changes in the mode of production unless such changes also lead to the demise of pronatalism as currently structured. While pronatalist constraints ensuring population replacement are a given in all modes of production, the analysis so far developed in this essay has led to the following general theoretical insights: 1) In modes of production based on class and the private appropriation of the surplus, pronatalist constraints are linked to the oppression of women and class exploitation in ways that are yet to be investigated; 2) In transitional socialist societies, characterised by heightened class struggles aimed at abolishing the old institutions and creating the material and subjective conditions for a classless society, pronatalism and sexism are likely to persist to the extent that changes in the material conditions and 'socialist accumulation' are emphasised to the detriment of changes in the subjective conditions and in the quality of life. The persistence of sexism in transitional socialist societies today might be partially explained by the fact that reproduction is held subordinate to production requirements,[74] and alienating labour conditions have not yet been superseded;[75] 3) In classless modes of production based upon the collective ownership of the means of production and the collective appropriation and enjoyment of the surplus, pronatalist constraints will change their theoretical and empirical location in the mode of production. From being part of the structural constraints determining the behaviour of individuals independently of their will, they will become part of the conscious effort of the collectivity to achieve mastery over its own processes of production and reproduction, both in terms of the production of goods and services as well as in terms of generational reproduction. The collective will be able to choose its replacement rate in accordance to a rational assessment of its material constraints and possibilities while giving maximum freedom of choice to its individual members.

---

74   In the Soviet Union, for example, concern with declining birth rates and future labour shortages overrides considerations about women's rights to control their reproductive lives. In an effort to encourage women to bear more children, the state attempted to discourage pre-marital sex (separate from reproduction) and extolled the joys of marital sex and childbearing. Blatant pronatalist arguments are used for that purpose; it is suggested, for example, that the birth of the first child is the best cure for female frigidity ('Russia Battles Birth Rate with Sex Education', *Intercom*, 4, 2 (1976), p. 14). Also, pronatalist rewards and penalties were instituted to foster childbearing: 'Women still receive medals for having more than ten children, and a couple pays a penalty tax of 6% of their salaries until they have their first child' ('Liberated Women in Russia? Nyet', *Intercom*, 4, 9 (1976), p. 14).

75   See, for example, Mandel 1971, pp. 187–210.

In this section I have explored the relationship between capitalism, pronatalism, and sexism, and I have briefly touched upon the changing nature of pronatalism and sexism under different modes of production. In light of the experiences of the women's movement since the 1960s and the resurgence of right-wing anti-feminist forces in the late 1970s, pronatalism and sexism emerge as tools of class domination which capitalist processes tend to undermine in times of economic prosperity and reinforce in times of economic downturns, when women's increased pressure for full socio-economic participation serves to exacerbate the contradictions of the system.[76]

I have discussed these issues at the highest level of analysis, the mode of production. The empirical manifestations of the issues examined above will vary from one social formation to another according to their historically specific characteristics.[77] My intention has been not to present a theory of pronatalism under capitalist conditions, but simply to suggest a useful framework for future investigation.

Conclusion

Present pronatalist structures and ideologies that rule out a childfree status as a legitimate and desirable option for women as well as for men have undesirable social and demographic effects; more importantly, they play a key role in supporting sexism and, as such, they deserve serious consideration by feminists. In arguing that feminists should take pronatalism seriously, I am *not* suggesting that they should take an 'anti-child' stance. I am, however, suggesting that reproduction be considered *one among other options* rather than *the main option*, the focal point determining the range of other possible options for

---

76 For an up-to-date and comprehensive account of processes aiming to undermine abortion rights, see Glen 1978, pp. 1–26; for an excellent theoretical and empirical analysis of the relationship between the capitalist economic cycle and the politics of feminist repression, see Dobbins 1977, pp. 53–68.

77 While the capitalist structural supports of pronatalism and sexism are the same in all social formations where the capitalist mode of production is dominant, their empirical manifestations will be modified in historically specific ways that vary with the characteristic of each social formation (e.g. the kinds of pre-capitalist modes of production with which capitalism is combined, the ethnic composition of the population, the kinds of economic opportunities determined by the natural environment, etc.), their legal, political, and ideological structures, and their dominant or subordinate place in the world capitalist system. For a theoretical discussion of these issues see, for example, Althusser 1970, pp. 80–128 and 162–218.

women. This implies giving to the loosely defined 'right to control one's body' a concrete content: women's right to determine not only *how many* children they want and *when* they want them, but also *whether* they want *any* children at all.

The reader should be aware of the limitations of this expanded concept of reproductive freedom. Present capitalist constraints determine the emergence and dominance of an abstract notion of reproductive freedom as the pure negation of constraint. I have argued in this chapter that the apparently radical advocacy of reproductive freedom in the abstract, without specifying a content including the option to remain childfree, remains trapped in the dominant pronatalist problematic and unwittingly lends support to it. On the other hand, while positing a more concrete and effective challenge to pronatalist and sexist institutions, this expanded notion of reproductive freedom is itself conditioned in its scope and relevance by the nature of the present social arrangements. It is formulated as a woman's right and, as such, it remains caught in the individualistic approach to rights that characterises the capitalist legal and political traditions, and in the dominant approach to reproduction that views it as a purely female concern. As Blake pointed out, pronatalism has also oppressive consequences for men. Furthermore, from a Marxist theoretical standpoint, reproduction is more than the reproduction of the human species; reproduction is a class strategy for survival and the study of changing reproductive patterns cannot adequately proceed in the absence of an analysis of their roots in class relations and class struggles.[78] This involves, in turn, the analysis of the specific ways in which sexism and pronatalism operate in the context of different classes and sectors of classes. I have not pursued these lines of inquiry not because I do not consider it important to explore the meaning of reproductive freedom as a man's right as well as the relationship between class reproductive strategies and concrete manifestations of sexism and pronatalism; these issues would have taken me beyond the limited objectives of this chapter which was to determine the adequacy of Blake's criticisms and to explore the theoretical and political importance of pronatalism for the feminist struggle. In spite of its limitations, nevertheless, this concept of reproductive freedom, which presents a childfree status as a legitimate option for women, is in itself an important advancement that needs further consideration and elaboration by feminists and should be incorporated as a specific goal of the present struggle for reproductive self-determination.

---

78   For further elaboration of this point see, for example, Gimenez 1977, pp. 5–40, and 1979, pp. 17–24; and Weiss-Altaner 1977, pp. 65–75.

Both the early feminist standpoint according to which women should have to opt between spinsterhood and careers *or* motherhood, and the modern feminist support for women's right 'to do both' are uncritically built around motherhood as an ascriptive status, as a taken for granted aspect of women's lives. Awareness of pronatalism and its relationship to sexism would lead one to critically question prescriptive motherhood and the oppression of women as 'reproductive objects' just as deeply and systematically as women's oppression as 'sex objects'. Unless a critical examination of parenthood is accomplished and clear alternatives to it are outlined, discussed, and brought into the open, lip service to women's right to control their reproductive lives will not suffice to free women from present pronatalist constraints. *Theoretically*, the task is to develop a thorough analysis of the relationship between capitalism, pronatalism, and sexism. The different ways in which pronatalism affects the sexes, classes, sectors of classes, and ethnic groups should be empirically established, thereby providing a sound basis for political action. *Ideologically*, the advocacy of clearly defined alternatives for women that go beyond the 'do both syndrome' to include, among others, a childfree status as well as full-time motherhood as legitimate options, would not only contemplate the needs of all women at this time, but also present younger women with options that challenge the pronatalist orientation of the society.

Marx argued that, in the process of studying social transformations,

> ... it is necessary to distinguish between the material transformation of the economic conditions of production, which can be determined with the precision of natural science, and the legal, political, religious, artistic or philosophic – in short, ideological forms in which men become conscious of this conflict and fight it out. Just as one does not judge an individual by what he thinks of himself, so one cannot judge such a period of transformation by its consciousness but, on the contrary, this consciousness must be explained from the contradictions of material life.[79]

Current contradictions in the material conditions of production and reproduction have made possible the rise of feminist and anti-feminist political forces as well as the theoretical analysis of sexism and pronatalism from a variety of standpoints. Blake approached these issues as a demographer concerned with not only the excess population generated by pronatalist patterns, but also their individual and social costs. Like her work, mine too is a product of its time and

---

79   Marx 1970, p. 21.

could not have been written without her valuable insights, and without the groundwork prepared by feminist theory and feminist struggles. However, it must be acknowledged that most feminist analyses depict the ideological forms in which women have become aware of these contradictions and have fought them. The present mainstream consciousness of the movement is a product of the dominant contradictions affecting women for whom the most pressing problem is that of combining home and work. The ideological hegemony of pronatalism makes it difficult to perceive its contribution to the existence of the problems affecting women; as Blake pointed out, social pressures ensuring the performance of parental roles are generally perceived as men's efforts to keep women in their place. The reality of male supremacy overshadows the reality of pronatalism as well as the connections between the two.

It might be argued that it would be unrealistic and perhaps counterproductive to criticise pronatalism on the grounds that, at the present time, most women are or plan to be mothers. That argument would be as self-defeating as the suggestion that one should not combat sexism because, after all, we have all been socialised in a sexist society and everyone is sexist in one way or another. Without denying the legitimacy, validity, and timeliness of the dominant concerns of the present generations, it must be acknowledged that *theory cannot be entirely subordinate to practical concerns without becoming a mere reflection of dominant interests rather than a scientific effort to disclose the nature of social reality*. Lenin's oft-quoted statement, that '... without revolutionary theory there can be no revolutionary movement',[80] is pertinent here. A revolutionary theory of the oppression of women, i.e. one that uncovers all the manifold determinations of sexism in the capitalist mode of production in order to effectively struggle against it is one that goes beyond the immediate forms in which sex and class struggles are perceived and fought. Awareness of pronatalism and research on its relationship to sexism is an important step in that direction.

---

80   Lenin 1975, p. 369.

CHAPTER 8

Reproduction and Procreation under Capitalism: a Marxist-Feminist Analysis

'The Mode of Reproduction in Transition: A Marxist-Feminist Analysis of the Effects of Reproductive Technologies', in *Gender & Society*, Vol. 5, No. 3 (September 1991): 334–50.[1]

'Die Heraufkunft der kapitalistischen Fortpflanzungsweise-Umbruche der Reproduktion im 21. Jahrhundert', in *Das Argument*. Zeitschrift fur Philosophie und Sozialwissenschaften 242 (Jahrgang Heft 4/5, 2001): 657–70.

Introduction

The development of reproductive technologies have introduced changes in the social organisation and in the very experience of reproduction: the biological processes have been fragmented and opened to manipulation, thus bringing about unforeseen changes in the social relations within which children are brought into the world. Given women's key role in biological reproduction, and the importance in women's lives of the ability to decide the timing and number of births and whether or not to become mothers, attaining a modicum of control over reproduction has been a key component of women's liberation struggles. Feminists have not greeted the emergence of reproductive technologies without ambivalence, for whether they further or hamper women's autonomy, self-realisation and ability to control their lives depends on the social context within which they are deployed. Women's class location, in conjunction with racial and ethnic divisions affect their access to all reproductive technologies and the effect of these technologies on their lives: '... the critical issue for feminists is not so much the content of women's choices, or even the "right to choose," as it is the social and material conditions under which choices are made. The "right to choose" means very little when women are powerless'.[2]

A brief description of these technologies offers a glimpse of their potential to alter taken for granted social relations. There are four kinds of reproductive

---

1   This chapter is an updated and expanded version of Gimenez 1991 and 2001b.
2   Petchesky 1980, p. 674.

technologies: those designed 1) to control fertility (e.g. birth control pills); 2) to monitor the quality of the foetus and provide prenatal and neonatal care (e.g. ultrasound and amniocentesis); 3) to monitor and control labour and child-birth (e.g. caesarean sections); and 4) to help infertile and sub-fertile people to have children who are genetically their own (e.g. in-vitro fertilisation (IVF) and artificial insemination).[3] In my earlier work I referred to the latter as New Reproductive Technologies (NRTs), though surrogacy and artificial insemina-tion were not new. The novelty resided in their increasing demand and use in combination with the more recently developed IVF and related technologies. These technologies are no longer new and in the literature they are called ARTs, Assisted Reproductive Technologies.[4]

In this chapter I will present some feminist perspectives on reproductive technologies and their implications for women. I will describe some effects of AID and AIH (artificial insemination by donor or by the husband) and ARTs on the consciousness of the users and the changing discourse on the meaning of motherhood, parenthood, and family. Finally, I will use Marxist-Feminist the-ory to explore the impact of these technologies on the social organisation of reproduction arguing that these technologies, as they split intergenerational social reproduction from procreation, give rise to the capitalist mode of pro-creation.

Feminist Perspectives on Reproductive Technologies

Despite their theoretical differences, feminists share a common concern with the effects of these technologies on the status of women and on the quality of women's lives. Central to all feminist analyses is the intent to demonstrate that the issues surrounding these technologies, women's exposure and access to them, their effects on women's lives, etc. are not purely technical and med-ical but unavoidably and essentially political issues.

Earlier writers[5] stressed the role of patriarchy, or the interaction between patriarchy and capitalism, in oppressing women through the practices entailed in the use of ARTs. On those grounds, most feminists reject conceptive, ARTs,

---

3 Stanworth 1987, pp. 10–11.
4 According to the Center for Disease Control and Prevention, ARTs include 'all fertility treat-ments in which both eggs and sperm are handled (i.e. intrauterine – or artificial – insem-ination) or procedures in which a woman takes medicine only to stimulate egg production without the intention of having eggs retrieved', http://www.cdc.gov/art/whatis.html.
5 See, for example, Arditti et al. 1984.

and prenatal technologies.[6] Feminist critics argue that these technologies place women under male control because they reflect the values of a male medical, legal and pharmaceutical establishment.[7] Furthermore, the technological fragmentation of the biological process of reproduction is mirrored in the depersonalisation and fragmentation of women's experience of reproduction (i.e. as sources of eggs for personal use, donation, sale and, often unwittingly, experimentation; as sites for embryo development or transplant, or environments for foetal growth), as well as in the objectified ways their bodies are perceived.[8] This fragmentation, which makes it possible for individuals or couples to purchase the different elements of the reproductive process to 'build', eventually, a baby for themselves,[9] and for fertility specialists to create embryos outside women's bodies, is the material basis for the subordination of women's needs and rights to foetal needs and rights protected by the medical establishment and the state.[10] Other feminists, however, have tempered their critique, arguing that ARTs and other technologies satisfy some women's legitimate needs.[11]

Reflecting the 'postmodern turn' in contemporary scholarship, some feminist writings about ARTs tend to examine the culture, narratives, and discourses about reproduction, rather than the relationship between the structures of inequality and domination (patriarchy and/or capitalism) and the implications of conceptive technologies and ARTs. For example, they analyse changes in cultural representations and social constructions of reproductive roles, the micro-politics of reproduction and the 'deconstructive' effects of ARTs upon the reproductive process, parenthood and kinship. They also stress the role of the mass media as the main source of public and common sense awareness, understanding and knowledge about ARTs and the problems (i.e. infertility, childlessness) they presumably are intended to solve. The availability and use of ARTs are replacing 'old stories' about reproduction – whose main characters are families constituted by heterosexual parents and their genetically related children, conceived out of love and in the privacy of their homes – with 'new stories' where, besides parents, we find other social actors: medical professionals, sperm and/or egg donors, buyers and sellers, consumers and surrogates,

6   See most of the essays in Arditti et al. 1984; also Corea 1985; Spallone and Steinberg 1987; McNeil et al. 1990; Birke et al. 1990; Holmes 1992; Raymond 1993; Ginsburg and Rapp 1995. For a different view, sceptical of feminist condemnation of men and their intentions, see Purdy 1992.
7   Steinberg 1990, pp. 74–5.
8   Crowe 1990, pp. 28–34; Steinberg 1990; Shachar 2001.
9   Saul 2009.
10   Spallone and Steinberg 1987; Corea 1985.
11   Petchesky 1987; Rapp 1984; Rothman 1987a.

and conception is a public, outside a woman's body, event.[12] Women's, gays' and lesbians', and single persons' reproductive rights were excluded within ARTs emerging discourse about the biological and social forces compelling people to want genetically related children, for marriage and heterosexuality are considered to be the only legitimate basis for using ARTs. Women are socialised to base their identity around their ability to reproduce and become mothers; this is, presumably, the reason why IVF was developed, as a remedy to infertility viewed as a medical problem requiring a scientific or technological, medical solution. In turn, IVF contributes and reinforces the social construction of women as mothers.[13]

An unexpected consequence of ARTs and other reproductive technologies is the weakening of the sociological critique of socio-economic theories of fertility that view children as consumer durables or as home produced goods.[14] From the standpoint of these theories, within the constraints of income, prices, taste and time, households or individuals are free to maximise their utility in any way they choose; e.g. choosing consumer goods rather than children; choosing to have only one 'high quality' child or several 'lower quality' children, and so forth. From the standpoint of sociology, however, reproductive behaviour is socially determined behaviour, woven into people's identity – particularly women's – and a necessary condition for the fulfilment of adult roles and social expectations. Unlike consumer durables, children cannot [legally] be purchased; furthermore, parents cannot freely choose the quantity and quality of their children because in every society there is a normatively established family size, and socially expected standards of child quality.[15] Finally, consumer durables that do not meet the buyer's expectations can be easily returned or exchanged for different, better products. Parents, however, regardless of their children's physical and/or mental problems and the economic and psychological hardships those problems might cause, have the ethical and social obligation to keep their children.

Reproductive technologies have altered some of these social constraints. Parents can choose some of their children's qualities[16] and prospective parents can purchase children (through surrogacy) and/or elements of the reproductive process (sperm and/or eggs). Parents can exert control, through various

12   Franklin 1992, pp. 75–91 and 1995, pp. 333–4; Farquhar 1996.
13   Bartholet 1992, pp. 254–6.
14   See, for example, Becker 1960, pp. 209–31 and Easterlin 1969, pp. 127–55. For a Marxist critique of these theories, see Chapter 6.
15   Blake 1968; also Chapter 7.
16   Rothman 1987a, p. 2, and 1987b; Arditti 1984, p. 4.

preconception and prenatal techniques, over the foetus's sex and quality; prenatal diagnosis allows women to know whether they are carrying a foetus with genetic defects, and to choose a healthy foetus of the desired sex. This choice, however, entails a late abortion; the painful 'tentative pregnancy' is the price to be paid by women in doubt about the viability of their foetuses. Once technologies are developed, their use becomes socially and medically expected and the right to know or not, to use them or not, might be lost in the future. For example, reproductive technologies open and close doors; they both increase and narrow the choices women face, while changing the relationship between parents and children.[17]

While some feminists are critical of the practice of surrogacy and the commodification of all facets of the reproductive process, other feminists see in these technologies and practices benefits for infertile women and couples and, for some women, the opening of economic opportunities and even empowerment. For example, women planning demanding careers can choose to freeze their eggs in advance, so they can attain their goals without having to interrupt their advancement because of an untimely pregnancy.

To those who would argue that surrogacy is degrading and alienating labour, Purdy's answer is that such views show 'ignorance of the kinds of risks working class people routinely face ... [and] a refusal to take seriously the fact that circumstances ought to make a difference in whether a given act is judged prudent or moral'.[18] Radin argues that, as we live in a society characterised by wealth and power inequalities, the pursuit of ideals such as social justice, gender, racial and ethnic equality, and the market inalienability of persons, their attributes and social relations inexorably lead to a double bind: for example, it can be argued that the commodification of things we deem inalienable (e.g. sex, babies, wombs, eggs) threaten women's personhood because

> essential attributes are treated as several fungible objects, and such treatment denies the integrity of the self. But if the social regime prohibits this kind of commodification, it denies women the choice to market their sexual or reproductive services and, given the current feminisation of poverty and lack of avenues for free choice for women, this prohibition also poses a threat to the personhood of women ... thus the double bind: both commodification and non-commodification maybe harmful.[19]

---

17   Rothman 1984, pp. 23–33; 1987a, pp. 3–9; Browner and Press 1996.
18   Purdy 1992, p. 315; see also Purdy 1989.
19   Radin 1996, p. 126. For a powerful critique of the notion that women have a choice in marketing sexual services, see Raymond 2013.

Radin calls attention to the importance of understanding different women's choices, needs, and behaviours in the context of the social, economic and political inequalities that shape their lives. The 'social regime' she alludes to is capitalism; under capitalist conditions, women made vulnerable by their class location and family responsibilities are often coerced to 'choose' between poverty, unemployment, selling their labour for low or insufficient wages, or selling sexual or reproductive services, or their eggs, for higher payments.

There are also conflicting views about the meaning of motherhood in the feminist literature about ART, views which capture the divisive effects of the historical context within which women act, make choices and understand the effects of those choices. Some feminists stress the social, not natural or instinctual basis for motherhood, and are critical of women with such a strong need for children that they are willing to accept the economic and psychological costs inherent in the use of IVF. Surrogacy is the basis for the fragmentation of motherhood into women with different 'mother' roles; e.g. egg donors, biological carriers (who may or not be genetically related to the foetus) and social mothers who raise the child born from a surrogate. The need to mother of the women who pay for eggs or surrogacy to have a child receives the medical, legal and social approval denied to the egg donors (or sellers) and surrogates who, in most cases, are also the genetic mothers.[20] Some argue that surrogates are the 'real' mothers although technology has effectively 'deconstructed' motherhood and could eventually abolish it biologically with the development of artificial wombs.[21] The sharp division in feminist thought about these issues is captured in these two different assessments of Mary Beth Whitehead's[22] claim to the child she bore under contract:

According to one assessment,

> When she claimed her intimate connection to the child, claimed that it is a part of her, it grew out of her flesh, in her body ... then she was accused of biological determinism ... is there no language we can use to express the particular, unique relationship that is pregnancy? Has feminism nothing

20   Corea et al. 1987, p. 4; Raymond 1987, p. 62.

21   Stanworth 1987, p. 16.

22   Mrs. Mary Beth Whitehead entered into a surrogacy contract in 1985; a couple, Mr. and Mrs. Stern, paid her $10,000 to bear a child through artificial insemination with the husband's sperm. Genetically, the child was hers and she claimed it as such, thus leading to the widely known 'Baby M' case. For an account of this case see, for example, Spar 2006, pp. 69–71.

to offer Mary Beth Whitehead here? So often ... we have found ourselves defending women's rights to be like men ... to work at men's jobs for men's pay. But what of our rights to be women?[23]

According to the second assessment,

Parenthood is not essentially biological. It is social: it comes about when people develop social expectations and assume responsibilities. Eliza-beth Stern was an expectant mother during the nine months of Mary Beth Whitehead's pregnancy ... To privilege Mary Beth Whitehead's claim is to support the biological essentialism that justifies the sexual division of labour and the definition of women first as child bearers.[24]

These views capture two different forms of social consciousness that reflect social and political divisions among US women, as well as radically different theoretical assumptions about the nature of motherhood: motherhood as a primarily social bond or as a biologically grounded reality.

Feminists ask important questions and offer important insights into the con-sequences and implications of reproductive technologies, especially ARTs. Do these technologies enhance or hamper reproductive rights and freedom, i.e. women's right to control their bodies? Do they liberate or impose new pressures on women? Do they reflect women's interests or the interest of the medical and business interests that benefit from their commercialisation? Are these tech-nologies designed to strengthen male domination? Feminists have also probed into the portrayal of these technologies by the media, the various ways they are constructed within different political discourses, and their ideological effects on the family and the meaning of family roles, particularly motherhood which, because of the fragmentation of the biological process of reproduction, has become a contested terrain. Who is the 'real' mother? The surrogate, or the woman who paid the surrogate to carry her embryo? What if the surrogate provided her own egg? Isn't she, genetically, the mother, with a right to the child that supersedes the right of the woman who paid her? Is motherhood a social or a biological relationship? In the absence of government regulations controlling the use of reproductive technologies across the nation, the important theoret-ical and political issues raised by feminists identify points of contention and sources of potential conflict among the women placed in different roles in the

23   Rothman 1987b, pp. 314–15.
24   Brenner 1987, p. 4.

technologically assisted reproductive process, and between consumers of these technologies (couples or individuals), medical providers and the corporations that often mediate the relationship between women and infertility specialists.

A Marxist-Feminist Perspective on Reproductive Technologies and Their Effects

Approaching the development of reproductive technologies and their effects from a Marxist-feminist theoretical standpoint leads me to consider it as part of the overall development of the productive forces or *forces of production*.[25] Reproductive technologies, ranging from their earlier forms to the latest advances in IVF and genetic testing, can be fruitfully viewed as part of the process of development of the *forces of reproduction*, i.e. the combination of science, technology, skilled and specialised labour in the context of professional, social and market relations. I argue that the concept of forces of reproduction is similar, in its theoretical importance for the study of social change, to the concept of forces of production. And, as the forces of reproduction develop and change, the *relations of reproduction* and corresponding forms of consciousness change in profound ways. The concept of *social relations of reproduction* refers to the relations between adults and between adults and children who engage in the labour necessary for their ongoing physical and social reproduction within households. In this form of labour it is women who work more heavily, though sometimes households rely on varying quantities of paid forms of this labour; e.g. nannies, maids, housecleaners, cooks, etc.[26]

To speak of forces of reproduction does not entail a form of technological determinism. The development and use of new technologies always takes place in the context of class and other unequal social relations, ideologies, and power struggles which render historically specific their economic, ideological and social effects. Under capitalism, the nuclear family is the more widespread observable form of the *mode of reproduction*. This family form is characterised by the unity or confluence of relations of sexuality, reproduction (physical and social), and economic cooperation between men and women.[27] Capitalist

---

25   Forces of production is a complex concept that includes science, technology, combined within a specific social and political organisation of production; see Althusser and Balibar 1970, pp. 233–5.

26   See Chapter 10.

27   The mode of reproduction refers to the historically specific combination of labour and the material basis of physical and social reproduction. This material base includes the means

development, however, at the same time it selects this family form as the most 'functional' for daily and intergenerational reproduction, constantly undermines it through changes in the productive forces in the realms of production and reproduction. These changes – e.g. de-industrialisation, outsourcing, economic recessions, changes in the quantity and quality of the demand for labour, increase in the use of AI and ARTs – create the material conditions for divorce and the emergence of other social relations of reproduction such as families headed by single parents, mostly by women, children raised by same-sex parents, grandparents or other family members, and foster families.

Reproductive technologies, particularly ARTs, have qualitatively changed the material biological conditions of reproduction by separating procreation from sexuality and opening up the possibility of parenthood for individuals and couples who, because of infertility or other biological reasons, are unable to have children, and for gay and lesbian individuals and couples. ARTs are the result of the overall process of development of the forces of reproduction which, in changing the biological conditions of intergenerational biological reproduction, have established the material basis for the structural and functional differentiation within the existing mode of reproduction. For most people, sexual relations and procreation are a presupposed aspect of the social relations of reproduction which, in the vast majority of cases,[28] result in pregnancy and childbirth. The use of ARTs leads to the separation of procreation from the social relations of reproduction and the emergence of *relations of procreation*. Sometimes these are relations between donors and recipients who could be known or related to each other. But the main form relations of procreation take are market relations between buyers (couples or individuals) and sellers of professional services or of elements of the reproductive process (i.e. sperm, eggs, embryos, wombs). These are not, however, purely exchange or monetary relations, for they establish genetic connections among people which have, up to now, been considered the biological basis for kinship relations. Examining these issues from an anthropological standpoint, a feminist anthropologist concludes that ARTs not only assist people in their quest for becoming parents

---

of reproduction (e.g. household goods, raw materials, the household infrastructure, etc.) and the biological conditions of reproduction. Labour and the material basis of physical and social reproduction are combined or brought together through relations of physical and social reproduction; i.e. relations between people mediated by their relationship to the material conditions of reproduction. See, for example, Gimenez 1973b; Seccombe 1973; Chapter 2 in this volume.

28   In any population, between 10 and 15 percent cannot, for a variety of reasons, have children. Spar 2006, p. 31.

but entail also the production of 'assisted kinship'.[29] However, as these genetic bonds are unlikely to be automatically acknowledged as social bonds, 'more kinship does not necessarily lead to more relatives'.

A new theoretical concept is needed to capture the social impact of these changes: I propose the *mode of procreation*,[30] i.e. the combination of the biological elements of the process of reproduction through *relations of procreation* independent from sexual relations and from the social relations of reproduction. Taken for granted, obvious or 'natural' meanings of motherhood are undermined by changes in the material conditions of procreation which determine their real (i.e. material, objective) 'deconstruction' or structural and functional differentiation first in practice (e.g. the material fragmentation of motherhood among women with competing social, genetic and biological claims over a child) and then in thought (i.e. the emergence of competing concepts of motherhood). Dominant ideas about motherhood acquire their social power or efficacy from the unity of biological and social reproduction that underlies the experience of most people. Conceptive technologies and surrogacy shatter that unity and several kinds of woman-child relations have now become possible: a) genetic, gestational, and social; i.e. the 'natural' relationship; b) genetic and gestational but not social, the result of surrogacy with AI, e.g. artificial insemination by the genetic and social father; c) genetic and social, but not gestational woman-child relations entailing womb leasing and embryo transplant to a surrogate; d) gestational and social but not genetic woman-child relations through egg donation or purchase, and embryo transplant; e) genetic, but not social or gestational woman-child relations resulting from egg donation or sale; and g) exclusively social woman-child relations made possible through surrogacy, embryo donation or purchase, adoption or step parenting.[31] Fatherhood, in turn, can be genetic and/or social, the latter the effect of AID (artificial

---

29   Strathern 1992, pp. 148–69.
30   An emergent way to call these relations is 'biomedical mode of reproduction' (Floyd 2016, p. 62).
31   More problematic in their consequences are the mitochondrial manipulation technologies, which 'involve removing the nuclear material either from the egg or embryo of a woman with inheritable mitochondrial disease and inserting it into a healthy egg or embryo of a donor whose own nuclear material has been discarded'. The outcome would be a baby genetically related to three people, for he or she would carry 'the nuclear DNA of the mother and father and the mitochondrial DNA of the donor'. How can this biological relationship between the child and donor be labelled? More importantly, there is uncertainty about the long-term effects this genetic manipulation could have for children thus engineered, and for the human species. Scholars and scientists oppose the genetic manipulation of the elements of the reproduction process. Darnovsky 2014.

insemination by donor or through the purchase of sperm from a sperm bank) or embryo donation (or purchase). Social fatherhood is also possible through adoption and step parenting. These are only some of the possibilities opened up by reproductive technologies, for the relations of procreation become more complex when surrogates, sperm, eggs or embryo donors are genetically related to the individual or couple seeking to have a child.[32]

Acknowledging that everything people do is social by definition, in the taxonomy presented above I have qualified as social those relations between parents and children embedded in relations of physical and social reproduction usually, but not necessarily, based on marriage. The opposite of social, in this sense, is not asocial but *procreational*. My argument is that the reproductive technologies, particularly ARTs, establish the material conditions for the structural and functional differentiation between *relations of procreation*, and *relations of social reproduction*. Unlike the latter, the relations of procreation are relations between people mediated by their relationship to the biological and technological conditions of reproduction. People enter into these relations compelled by:

a)   biological conditions (e.g. female or male infertility, difficulties in carrying a pregnancy to term, etc.);

b)   pronatalist ideologies (e.g. cultural or religious expectations that stigmatise infertility and privilege biological over social parenthood; in such a context, ARTs appears as the only solution to infertility);

c)   economic need, which prompts some men to sell sperm and some women to sell eggs or agree to a contract pregnancy;

d)   profit seeking: ARTs are very expensive and very profitable for the corporations and experts of all kinds – scientists, doctors, lawyers – involved in their development and sale;

e)   the availability of these technologies themselves, whose very presence makes such behaviours possible.

These relations of procreation do not entail the social expectation of a concomitant involvement of gestational and/or genetic donors or sellers in the process of physical and social intergenerational reproduction; i.e. in the process of caring and rearing the child or children produced via their input. In other words, they only generate biological, not social, kinship ties unless the donors, sellers or surrogates are already socially related to the buyers (e.g. a mother becoming pregnant with her daughter's embryo and giving birth to her own grandchild). Whether people entering in these relations of procreation

---

32   See, for example, Haimes 1992, pp. 119–22.

will claim social kinship status is not determined by the biological connection, but by social and individual factors contingent on the needs and interests of the parties involved. Given that the ideological connection between biological and social parenthood is still dominant, because the material conditions that sustain it are still prevalent, it is to be expected that people entering in these relations, particularly women, might find it difficult, afterwards, to relinquish their claim on the child thus produced.

Depending on their own experiences with children, childhood memories and experiences, social class, and political views, some women might perceive parenthood as essentially social. Most women, however, are likely to adhere to a biologically based concept of motherhood rooted not only in ideology, but also in their own experience of pregnancy and childbirth. Their adherence in this respect is forcefully stated by Rothman: 'What of our right to be women?'[33] Empirical research is likely to show a gap between most women's views on the significance of pregnancy and childbirth as a basis for their sense of motherhood and personal identity, and feminist and scholarly perspectives which stress the social construction or socially determined meaning. This gap – similar in its social determinants and political significance to that which Luker[34] identified between pro-life (working-class, less educated) and pro-choice (college-educated, professional) women's views on sexuality, contraception, abortion and motherhood – is likely to narrow as women's level of education and economic opportunities improve. It is not likely to disappear in the near future because, at this time, the use of ARTs – which alter the biological basis for feelings and experiences – is so expensive that it is not likely to become widespread any time soon and, consequently, as most women will continue to experience pregnancy and childbirth in the usual way, they will continue to be subject to the limits that biological experience imposes upon the 'social construction' of motherhood.[35] Furthermore, most women are relegated to lower paid, often unrewarding jobs, a situation intensified by deepening economic inequality in the aftermath of the great recession of 2008. Such conditions heighten the importance of motherhood and family life as sources of meaning for women.

---

33 Rothman 1987b, pp. 314–15.
34 Luker 1984.
35 I not arguing that biology determines the meaning of motherhood but that the very experience of pregnancy – at this time in history when the use of ARTs is the exception, not the rule – conspires against the acceptance of a purely social understanding of motherhood.

I base my understanding of the conditioning that nature exerts upon consciousness and experience of social reality on the work of Timpanaro,[36] a
Marxist scholar critical of the tendency in Western Marxism to adopt idealist philosophical and methodological standpoints in its efforts to avoid 'vulgar
materialism'. If compared to changes in modes of production, he argues, nature
changes very slowly; for all practical purposes it can be taken as constant. The
fact that we are biological beings, however, remains. As such, we have strengths
and frailties (e.g. the capacity for pleasure, the experiences of pregnancy, childbirth, disability, pain, illness, aging, death) that affect our experience and consciousness:

> To maintain that, since the 'biological' is always presented to us as medi-
> ated by the 'social,' the 'biological' is nothing and the 'social' everything
> would ... be idealist sophistry. [If we agree], how are we to defend our-
> selves from those who will in turn maintain that, since all reality (includ-
> ing economic and social reality) is knowable only through language (or
> the thinking mind), language is the sole reality and the rest abstraction.[37]

Since the time Timpanaro's work was published in English, what he warned
us about has happened: it became intellectually fashionable to reduce social
reality to a text; it is legitimate to invoke the materiality of discourses and bodies, while reference to the materiality of biology leaves one open to charges
of biological reductionism or 'orthodox Marxism'. But current debates about
the meaning of motherhood, fatherhood and kinship cannot be reduced to
debates about competing narratives, discourses or social constructions; I argue
that they capture, at the level of ideology, the effects, in people's consciousness, of material changes in the biological conditions of reproduction and,
consequently, changes in men's and women's experiences of reproduction, as
well as material transformations in women's relations to pregnancy and childbirth.

Feminist arguments that support the notion that motherhood is essentially
social are correct from a social scientific standpoint. Motherhood and fatherhood are socially defined. The extent to which genetic bonds are legally and
socially recognised varies historically and by social class.[38] Politically, the issue
is more complex. Feminists have critiqued the dangers of biological essential-

---

36   Timpanaro 1975.
37   Timpanaro 1975, p. 45.
38   See, for example, Smart 1987.

ism. But those who defend the claim of biological mothers who find themselves unable to fulfil a surrogacy contract also acknowledge a realm of bodily experience which is the material condition for the persistence of a biological or 'natural' understanding of motherhood. Court decisions and changes in women's lives and in social and political perceptions of motherhood cannot fully eradicate the effects of that material condition because, 'although the biological level has virtually no importance in determining traits distinguishing large human groups ... it does again have a conspicuous weight in the determination of individual characteristics'.[39]

In addition to class, socio-economic status, and racial/ethnic differences, differences in women's biological history are also extremely important to understanding how individual women experience sexuality, pregnancy, childbirth, and the effects of ARTs.[40] Writing courageously about her feelings in dealing with the negative results of amniocentesis, Rapp tells us: 'having spent fifteen years arguing against biological determinism in my intellectual and political life, I'm compelled to recognize the material reality of this experience'.[41] Reproductive experience is not 'imbibed raw'.[42] On the other hand, it is irreducible to thought about it and the historically specific cultural meanings and social relations that mediate it have developed precisely on its terrain. This terrain, as reproductive technologies – particularly ARTs – demonstrate, is not immutable. It constitutes the material base for new biologically grounded experiences and emergent forms of consciousness.

Current changes in the material conditions of biological reproduction reflect the development of the forces of reproduction under capitalism. This is why it is necessary to identify the capitalist structural determinants of the problems, experiences, cultural representations and ideological conflicts that feminists so eloquently write about. Rather than attribute, a priori, the developments and effects of ARTs to patriarchy or to the presumably patriarchal intentions of male experts, it is important to differentiate between levels of analysis:

1) concrete instances of ARTs use and abuse – at the level of analysis of social and market relations and specific settings (e.g. hospitals, infertility clinics, etc.) – where male dominance, profit seeking, and class and racial/ethnic differences may be the most important factors in determining how ARTs are used and how they affect individual women;

---

39 Timpanaro 1975, p. 45.
40 Petchesky 1987, p. 76.
41 Rapp 1984, p. 323.
42 Petchesky 1987, p. 73.

2) the capitalist structural and ideological determinants of scientific and technological change and ensuing changes in social relations of reproduction and procreation, which are irreducible to micro-level explanations based on the motivations of the men and women who participate in these relations as scientists, doctors, lawyers, buyers, sellers, etc.

This distinction is important theoretically, methodologically, and politically because it helps clarify research goals and set political aims.

The Mode of Procreation and the Oppression of Working-Class Women

It is helpful to theorise these processes that separate biological kinship from the family to identify and differentiate the empirical referent of the *relations of social reproduction*, i.e. the relationship between adults and children within a family, whatever its form, from the *relations of procreation* (whether they involve economic and, perhaps, genetic links between one or both parents with the child or children resulting from the use of reproductive technologies, and the economic and sometimes genetic relations between parents and the person or persons who sold or donated the missing elements for biological reproduction). The *relations of procreation* establish biological kinship relations and economic relations which may or may not overlap with the *relations of social reproduction*. These relations include not only those between the family made possible by ARTs and those who contributed eggs, sperm or a womb to the process of procreation, but also those between these social agents and the medical specialists and legal/commercial intermediaries that made the whole process possible. Who can enter in these relations, under what conditions, who profits, is not entirely under the control of the direct participants but is largely determined by the class location and socio-economic status of the buyers and sellers, and the profit seeking organisations of infertility scientists, doctors and the corporations through which they sell their services. Under capitalism, all needs must be satisfied through the market and some people's need for children, particularly children genetically related to them, is no exception. True, sometimes the elements of the reproduction process are actually donated, i.e. freely given without financial remuneration, by friends and/or relatives. But, as demand for these technologies has increased, markets developed and all the elements of the reproduction process and its final outcome, one or more children, have become commodities: 'When parents buy eggs or sperm; when they contract with surrogates; when they choose a child to adopt or an embryo to implant, they are doing business. Firms are making money, customers are making choices, and children – for better or worse – are being sold'.[43] Class differences and racial/ethnic inequality determine access to reproductive technologies. The selling of reproductive technologies, especially ARTs, has become a big and lucrative business, 'the industrialization of reproduction ... the reproductive supermarket'.[44] ARTs remain a privilege of the wealthy and those in the higher income brackets. In the late 1980s, the cost of a surrogate or 'contract pregnancy'[45] in the US was between $30,000 and $50,000.[46] The Centre for Surrogate Parenting (CSP) estimated, in May 2000, a total cost of $66,975 (US median income for all races was 43,965 and for whites, $41,591[47]). In December 2014, the CSP page indicating the estimated costs of gestational surrogacy (IVF) offers a great deal of itemised information that includes some set fees (e.g. a $20,000 initial fee; $1,000 discretionary fund for personal expenses of the surrogate mother; a surrogate mother compensation that ranges from $25,000 to $30,000 in all states except California, where it is a bit higher, ranging from $28,000 to $35,000, etc.). This CSP page also indicated many estimated medical, personal, legal and other expenses, some monthly, others per medical procedure. While this makes it difficult to figure out the total cost, given that the initial fee and the surrogate's compensation alone can add up to $50,000, it is possible to surmise the total cost to be anywhere between $80,000 and $100,000, perhaps more.[48] According to Reproductive Possibilities, the home page of a company offering to match prospective parents with women willing to be surrogates, in December 2014, the 'total expenses for a successful IVF pregnancy (*excluding medical costs for the IVF procedure and pregnancy*) [was] $60,000 – $80,000+'.[49] It could easily reach $100,000 or more if medical costs are included, beyond the possibilities of most families. In 2013, the US median income for all races was $51,939, according to the US Bureau of the Census. Adjusting for inflation, it was 8 percent lower than it was in 2007, before the recession started.[50]

Theoretically, the relations of procreation are market relations between free agents, who freely buy and sell elements of the biological reproductive process to their own advantage. The markets for those elements are differentiated,

43   Spar 2006, p. xi.
44   Corea, cited in Spar 2006, p. 77.
45   Purdy 1992, p. 305.
46   Nelson 1992, p. 299.
47   US Bureau of the Census 2014.
48   http://www.creatingfamilies.com/intended-parents/?Id=44#.VIIdbU1oypo.
49   http://www.reproductivepossibilities.com/parents_exp.cfm.
50   US Bureau of the Census 2014. http://fivethirtyeight.com/datalab/five-years-of-recovery -havent-boosted-the-median-household-income/. Last retrieved in 2014.

so prospective buyers can buy eggs or sperm of individuals with the personal characteristics (e.g. race, ethnicity, education, height, hair colour, skin colour, IQ, SAT score, etc.) they deem desirable.[51] The higher the social status and educational attainment of the 'donors', the higher the price their 'donation' commands in the market. Wealthy buyers pay thousands of dollars per 'donation' and most of that money does not go to the actual 'donor' but to the fertility clinics where they are sold.

These market relations, however, are not between free and equal individuals, but between individuals divided by class, race, ethnicity and national origin. Most buyers are either very wealthy, for whom prices do not matter, or affluent enough to afford these technologies without having to borrow a great deal to pay for them. But the wish for a genetically related child or the experience of childbirth can be strong enough to induce less affluent couples or individuals to risk bankruptcy. The sellers, on the other hand, tend to be men and women for whom the money to be earned matters. The organisations that mediate between buyers and sellers operate in the context of an ideology of altruism, calling the sellers of eggs and sperm 'donors', even though at the same time they name a price for the commodity they will be buying and then selling to prospective parents. For example, the NW Cryobank home page offers sperm 'donors' up to $1,000 per month, plus free tests to make sure the 'donor' is healthy and not a drug user;[52] and 'Columbia University Medical Center pays "donors" $8,000 per egg retrieval cycle'.[53]

The capitalist *mode of procreation* makes visible and rests upon class divisions and other forms of economic and social inequality among women. All women are not oppressed by the current *relations of procreation*; women located in the capitalist class or in the upper income levels, use their economic power to their advantage, to purchase the elements of the reproductive process they need, or to lease or rent the womb of working class, often non-white women. They may use gestational surrogates either because they cannot themselves carry a foetus to term, or because they want to avoid the changes in their bodies resulting from pregnancy and childbirth.

Economic necessity pushes young women to endure procedures designed to force their ovaries to hyper-ovulate, thus producing a large number of eggs at the time. The long-term health effects of these procedures are not well-known at this time. Economic necessity pushes working-class women, white and non-

---

51   For a detailed discussion of these markets and niches within markets, see Spar 2006, pp. 35–46.
52   https://www.nwcryobank.com/sperm-donation/.
53   Saraceno 2015, p. 24.

white, to rent their wombs to bear children often genetically unrelated to them. Depending on their class position and economic resources, some women can outsource not only all or most of their domestic labour (e.g. childcare, cooking, cleaning, etc.) but also the very process of biological reproduction.

It is important to distinguish between traditional and gestational surrogacy.[54] In traditional surrogacy, birth mothers provided their womb and their own egg; they were, genetically, the mother of the child to whom they gave birth. Consequently, prospective parents were exceedingly concerned with the birth mother's physical and mental health, appearance, behaviour, education, etc. They sought a birth mother as similar to themselves as possible. In gestational surrogacy, birth mothers provide only their womb; they give birth to a child genetically unrelated to them because the prospective parents provide the embryo. The change to gestational surrogacy was facilitated by the development of the market for eggs, which quickly fragmented into different niches, offering eggs of different qualities and prices and catering to the needs and income of different buyers (e.g. couples, single women, lesbians, etc.). Parents now focused their attention and concern upon the egg donor's genetic, personal and social attributes; the appearance, race and social attributes of the birth mother no longer mattered. All that mattered was the surrogate's health and healthy behaviour (e.g. abstention from drugs, alcohol, and tobacco) prior to the birth; everything else became irrelevant.[55]

Both types of surrogacy are controversial; one, because surrogacy contracts oblige women to give up a child who is, genetically, their own, a fact that leads some women to claim the child and break the contract; the other, because it further objectifies women, reducing them to interchangeable wombs. Their identity, race, nationality, social class, etc. no longer matter; the buyers are only interested in a healthy body which can produce a healthy baby. Whereas traditional surrogacy necessitated a birth mother not only healthy but, in some ways, resembling the buyers, thus limiting their options, gestational surrogacy has expanded the supply of potential surrogates within and across national boundaries.

Paid surrogacy has been banned in many countries.[56] In the United States, however, there are no federal laws regulating the industry; instead, states vary

---

54   Twine 2011, p. 11; Spar 2006, p. 81.
55   Spar 2006, p. 81.
56   Countries which banned surrogacy include Australia, Austria, Belgium, Canada, China, the Czech Republic, Denmark, France, Germany, Italy, Mexico, Netherlands, Norway, Portugal, Spain, Sweden, Switzerland, Taiwan, and Turkey; it is also banned in several states within the US Sorenson and Mladovsky 2006, pp. 6–7; Twine 2011, p. 15. Surrogacy in the United Kingdom is allowed but subject to a number of restrictions; see Preston 2013.

in the extent to which they restrict or allow it, so prospective parents must face a multiplicity of different and contradictory regulations.[57]

The high cost of dental and medical services in the US pushes many people to seek care abroad, thus leading to the emergence of 'medical tourism' and 'dental tourism'; likewise, the high cost of reproductive services has pushed less affluent couples and individuals to engage in 'reproductive tourism', travelling to purchase what they need in poorer countries, where sometimes there are fewer regulations and the cost of reproductive services is far lower. At the same time, as some Western European and other countries restrict access to reproductive technologies to heterosexual couples, while banning commercial surrogacy, single individuals, gay and lesbian couples from wealthy countries travel to the United States, where access to these technologies, though expensive, is largely unregulated. The development of a global capitalist market for reproductive services opened up profitable opportunities for individuals, businesses and countries seeking to benefit from local customers and the influx of reproductive tourists. India legalised commercial surrogacy in 2002 and has become, since then, an 'international magnet for surrogacy services due to the high quality of the medical clinics, the supervision of the gestational surrogates and low cost relative to the United States and Europe'.[58]

The mode of reproduction remains, then, localised; the social relations of reproduction take place within households located within a given country. The mode of procreation, however, encompasses biological and economic relations among agents whose location varies, depending on whether buyers of the elements of procreation can find what they need and can afford nearby, or in a different city, province or state, or in a different country. The relations of procreation and ensuing biological kinship connections among social strangers can, therefore, be local or dispersed within and across countries. The oppression of the women who enter into these relations as sellers of eggs or as renters/leasers of their wombs is thus not only obscured by the apparent egalitarianism characteristic of market exchanges but by the vast social and sometimes geographical distance between them and the buyers.

---

57   The most lenient state is California; 'Arizona and the District of Columbia ban all commercial surrogacy contracts, while other states ban payments but allow for services', see Twine 2011, p. 9.

58   Twine 2011, p. 17.

Conclusion

As abundantly documented in the feminist literature, reproductive technologies have contradictory implications. Feminists have been primarily concerned with their effect on individual women, whatever their participation (as buyers or sellers) in the reproductive process might be. These technologies can be viewed positively, because they allow individuals and couples, regardless of sexual orientation, to form families and raise genetically related children. They can be viewed as empowering women, because they allow them to become mothers on their own and at a suitable time, without a pregnancy conflicting with personal goals. For example, technology allows women who can afford to pay thousands of dollars for this technology, to freeze their eggs and go on with their lives until they consider it is the right time for them to become pregnant.[59] Some employers are now offering to pay the costs of egg freezing (oocyte cryopreservation) to employees that choose to do so.[60] Portrayed as a form of equalising men and women, and a 'progressive' policy decision by employers, this possibility can be viewed also as a manipulative decision by employers who do not want to pay future expensive infertility treatments and seek to benefit from employees' uninterrupted productivity. Furthermore, this procedure entails the same health risks to which egg 'donors' are subject (discussed earlier in this chapter) and does not guarantee success; it is not endorsed either by the American College of Obstetricians and Gynecologists or the American Society for Reproductive Medicine.[61]

Reproductive technologies might be empowering to those who can afford to use them but they can also be oppressive, especially but not only for working-class and minority women. Women, both buyers and sellers, are exposed to painful procedures and they are open to public scrutiny, medical manipulation and intervention. The very existence of the technologies compels some women to use them, though they might be far better off adopting a child or remaining child-free. Employers who offer to pay for egg freezing today might make it a condition for employment in the future.

While I share the feminist concern about the oppressive effects of these technologies, in this chapter I have given more attention to the implications of the processes of structural and functional differentiation these technologies have produced in the mode of reproduction under capitalism, processes that result in the separation between reproduction – understood as the unity

---

59   Rosenblum 2014.
60   Bennett 2014.
61   Johnston and Zoll 2014.

of social and physical reproduction – and procreation, understood as the bio-logical side of physical reproduction. There is, I have argued, an emergent cap-italist *mode of procreation* which operates as another corporate profit seeking component of the capitalist economy. This establishes limits to the influence that feminist and other critiques (e.g. ethical, religious) of these technologies might have. These macro-level structural changes and their unintended effects on the lives of individual women, and on the split between reproduction and procreation, are unlikely to be substantially modified through changes in the ideology or the gender of those at the top of the research and medical organisa-tions and businesses within which these technologies are used. It is possible to envision, in concrete instances, infertility clinics or small surrogacy businesses controlled by female or male professionals mindful of the concerns of women and ethicists, whose values might make a difference to them. In the society as a whole, and in the globalised 'baby business', however, the process of sep-aration between reproduction and procreation is likely to continue unabated, unless it runs into structurally generated conflicts and effective political oppos-ition seizing the opportunity provided by those conflicts. For example, given that those who avail themselves of ARTs are likely to be people with consid-erable economic and social resources relative to those of their 'shadow' bio-logical kin, unless legislation unambiguously defines and limits the rights of purely biological kin, there is the possibility that a conflict of interests may arise between families and their socially acknowledged kin, and their unac-knowledged, 'shadow', biological kin. Because ARTs users are a relatively small proportion of the population, and because providers of the elements of procre-ation are sometimes friends or relatives, it is not likely that these kinds of con-flicts might become widespread in the near future. But it is possible to envision a quantitative change in the use of IVF and contract pregnancy prompted by drastic increases in infertility brought about by environmental degradation and exposure to toxic chemicals and radiation. This change could be accompan-ied by the 'democratisation' of ARTs, as their use becomes widespread among the less affluent, subsidised by the state to ensure the supply of labourers, fol-lowed by the concomitant growth in the proportion of families with unknown or unacknowledged biological relatives located in a lower class or social strata. Furthermore, to the extent that the current trend toward deepening economic inequality continues, there is the potential for conflict between former 'test tube babies', now affluent adults, and their unacknowledged and economically disadvantaged biological parents or siblings. In other words, if in the emergent mode of procreation, the buyers are likely to be always the haves, and the sellers always the have little or the have-nots, and if the separation between social reproduction and procreation becomes widespread, this situation is likely to strengthen the deep economic divide already existing between the two main classes and among women, thus becoming a source of endemic social, economic and personal conflict. This divide is likely to be aggravated by the use of prenatal testing[62] by those who are better off, thus ensuring that their offspring, born 'naturally', or with the help of ARTs, are healthier, and free from the possibility of developing hereditary diseases. The already existing health gap based on class and racial/ethnic inequality could be deepened by deliberately created genetic inequality between classes.[63] In a dystopian capitalist future, class divisions would be thus strengthened and deepened by the potential effects of ARTs and technologies of genetic modification.

I have focused primarily on conceptive technologies. But the development of genetic engineering and biotech industries, the possibilities open by the decoding of the human genome, stem cell research, prenatal diagnosis and selective abortion of those afflicted with severe congenital anomalies, or the potential for developing an incurable disease, altogether constitute a source of transformation in the material conditions of human reproduction whose implications we have hardly begun to explore. These technologies have the potential to take procreation entirely out of the 'private sphere', transforming it into another capitalist industry. While this seems farfetched, rising healthcare costs might make the use of some of these technologies mandatory. But the capitalist production of human beings would enter into contradiction with core tenets of capitalist ideologies about the worth and uniqueness of human life. These are just speculative reflections which highlight the importance of going beyond the analysis of gender implications and social constructions of the effects of ARTs to investigate also the complex social and ideological implications of the separation between sexuality and procreation, and of the emergent network of social and economic relations that the use of ARTs necessitates, i.e. the emergent mode of procreation, which is not only subtly altering the meaning of kinship and kinship relations but also opening up new venues for the oppression of working-class and poor women, and new possible ways to deepen and strengthen class inequality.

---

62 For example, Preimplantation Genetic Diagnosis or Embryo Screening, 'a screening test used to determine if genetic or chromosomal disorders are present in embryos produced through in vitro fertilization'. http://www.pennmedicine.org/fertility/patient/clinical-services/pgd-preimplantation-genetic-diagnosis/.

63 There is a genome editing technique, Crispr-Cas9, which is currently used to explore possible ways to treat, or even cure, some diseases, but scientists worry that it could be used to 'alter genes in human embryos, sperm or eggs in ways that can be passed from generation to generation ... [thus creating] an elite population of designer babies with enhanced intelligence, beauty or other traits' (Doudna 2015).

CHAPTER 9

The Feminisation of Poverty: Myth or Reality?

'The Feminization of Poverty: Myth or Reality?', in *The Insurgent Sociologist*, Vol. 14, No. 3 (Fall 1987): 5–30.

The 'feminisation of poverty' is currently a phenomenon of great concern to the government, social scientists, politicians, and feminists of all political persuasions. This phrase attempts to capture the essence of the following facts: in the United States, the fastest growing type of family structure is that of female-headed households and, because of the high rate of poverty among these households, their increase is mirrored in the growing numbers of women and children who are poor; almost half of all the poor in the US today live in families headed by women. In 1984, 16 percent of all white families, 25 percent of all families of Spanish origin, and 53 percent of all black families were headed by women.[1] In the same year, the poverty rate for white, Spanish-origin and black female-headed households was 27.1 percent, 53.4 percent, and 51.7 percent respectively.[2] Poverty affects not only young and adult women with children, but also older women; in 1984, the median income of women 65 years and over was $6,020 (while it was $10,450 for men in the same age category) and 15 percent of all women aged 65 and over had incomes below the poverty line.[3] The poverty of women is reflected in the poverty of children. There are almost 13 million poor children in the US; 52 percent of them live in families headed by women and the poverty rate for white, black, and Spanish-origin children living in female-headed households is 46 percent, 66 percent, and 71 percent respectively.[4]

The facts and figures documenting the increased immiseration of women and children can be found in many recent publications,[5] together with analyses that put forth the notion that it is women, *as women*, who are peculiarly vulnerable to poverty. Poverty is being 'feminised' and this idea is nowhere expressed more clearly than in an oft-quoted statement from the President's National Advisory Council on Economic Opportunity (1981):

---

1   Rodgers Jr. 1986, p. 5.
2   Rodgers Jr. 1986, p. 12.
3   Sidel 1986, p. 158.
4   Rodgers Jr. 1986, pp. 32–3.
5   See, for example Rodgers Jr. 1986; Sidel 1986; Stallard et al. 1983.

All other things being equal, if the proportion of the poor in female-householder families were to continue to increase at the same rate as it did from 1976 to 1978, the poverty population would be composed solely of women and their children before the year 2000.[6]

Critics have rightly pointed out that this statement suggests that 'by the year 2000 all of those men who are presently poor will be either rich or dead'.[7] While those who quote it acknowledge that society does not stay still, that poverty affects men also and falls more heavily among non-whites, nevertheless the main thrust of the analysis of present trends continues to interpret them as the 'feminisation of poverty'.

Is this a theoretically adequate notion? What can we learn from it? What are its shortcomings? Does it adequately convey the nature of the processes it describes? Is the 'feminisation of poverty' a real phenomenon or a mystification that obscures the unfolding of other processes? These are some of the questions I will seek to answer in this chapter. I will examine, from the standpoint of Marxist-feminist theory, the strengths and shortcomings of current explanations to establish whether recent changes in the size and composition of the poor population, growth in female-headed families, and the increased vulnerability of women to poverty can be adequately understood as the 'feminisation of poverty'.

Factors Accounting for the Feminisation of Poverty

The definition of a social phenomenon shapes the questions that can be asked about its possible determinants and, of course, the questions in turn shape the answers. In this case, it is unavoidable to centre such questions around women: why are women more likely to be poor than men? Why are female-headed households and families more likely to be poor? Why is the number of those households and families increasing? This leads researchers to focus on factors which are specific to the situation of women in modern society and conclude that women, as a group and regardless of class, are more vulnerable to poverty than men and that, consequently, women's poverty has different causes than the poverty of men. These are some representative statements of this view:

---

6   Rodgers Jr. 1986, p. 7.
7   Alliance Against Women's Oppression 1983, p. 6.

While there is clearly much truth to the statement that race and class have been major determinants of poverty in this country, women as a group, including middle- and sometimes even upper-middle-class women, have recently become more vulnerable to poverty or near poverty than their male counterparts ... It is clear that some of the key causes of poverty among women are fundamentally different from the causes of poverty among men.[8]

There is a fundamental difference between male and female poverty: for men, poverty is often the consequence of unemployment and a job is generally an effective remedy, while female poverty often exists even when a woman works full time ... Virtually all women are vulnerable – a divorce or widowhood is all it takes to throw many middle-class women into poverty.[9]

Race may well be the principal determinant of poverty in this country ... And it is redundant to say that class causes poverty ... To account for a trend that specifically involves women, we need an explanation in which gender is the determining factor ... To explain the feminisation of poverty we have to invoke some of the things that many women have in common – such as motherhood and low paying jobs.[10]

The conceptualisation of women *as a group* characterises most discussions of the feminisation of poverty. This tendency is encouraged by the manner in which poverty statistics are compiled. Census data do not differentiate between social classes; researchers have information about income, sex, racial and ethnic categories of analysis and this reinforces the tendency to frame the discussion in terms of statistical rather than theoretically significant categories of analysis. The determinants of women's poverty, it is therefore implied in the analysis, are factors that affect *all* women and place *all* women at risk.

What are these factors? Changes in mortality and marriage rates, divorce and separations, and out of wedlock births contribute to the increase in female-headed households.[11] Women's higher life expectancy contributes to the increasing number of women over 65 years of age living alone and a substantial proportion of these women are poor. Younger women become heads of house-

---

8   Sidel 1986, p. 25.
9   Stallard et al. 1983, p. 9.
10   Ehrenreich 1987, p. 12.
11   Rodgers Jr. 1986, pp. 38–42.

holds through out-of-wedlock childbearing, separation, divorce, or the decision to live alone while they work and postpone marriage until they consider it appropriate.

Needless to say, while young and old single women are found among poor female-headed households, the majority of these households consist of women and their children. Poor young women, particularly minority women, are more likely to become single mothers and teen-age motherhood is one of the most important correlates of poverty. The sex-segregated nature of the labour market contributes to the poverty of women; most women work in low-paid, low-status jobs with little or no prospects of promotion, lacking good pension and retirement plans. Poverty is also the result of unemployment; many women cannot find jobs while others cannot work because of their childcare responsibilities and the lack of affordable and reliable day care.

Male unemployment, lay-offs, and decline in wages are also crucial correlates of women's poverty. Such factors correlate with marital stress and violence, separation or divorce, and can make family formation impossible. Poor men who are chronically unemployed or underemployed cannot form families or stay with their families, particularly in states where welfare policies deny eligibility to two-parent families. Because of the heritage of racial and economic discrimination, these factors are intensified in the black and Spanish origin populations which have a higher proportion of poor female-headed families than the white population. This situation leads Ruth Sidel to ask whether present trends depict the feminisation or the minoritisation of poverty; her conclusion is that both phenomena are taking place because, like blacks, women are also an oppressed group.[12] Acknowledging that the poverty of men is correlated with the poverty of women, Sidel is critical of policy makers who avoid the cause-effect relationship between extremely high rates of male unemployment and a high percentage of female-headed families within minority populations, calling the attention of those concerned with the feminisation of poverty to 'the *obvious correlation* between the lack of economic opportunities for millions of American men ... and their lack of commitment to and steady participation in family life'.[13]

In addition to these structural factors and the lack of adequate welfare policies, Sidel argues that women's poverty is also the result of ideological and structural constraints peculiar to women. Women socialised to put family obligations first, to see themselves primarily as wives and mothers and seek

---

12   Sidel 1986, p. 24.
13   Sidel 1986, p. 110, my emphasis.

in marriage and the family their fulfilment as adult members of society are likely to neglect or overlook the need to develop occupational and educational skills that will help them support themselves if they remain single or their marriage breaks up. Women's domestic activities, in spite of their social, economic, and psychological significance, are devalued and time consuming, and interfere with their full participation in the labour force. The domestic division of labour thus interacts with the sex-segregated nature of occupations to restrict the economic and educational opportunities of women. The negative effects of this situation become more salient once women become single heads of families.[14]

As the preceding discussion indicates, the feminisation of poverty is associated with many interrelated structural and ideological variables. Stallard et al. sum up the determinants of the feminisation of poverty as follows:

> It is a direct outgrowth of women's dual role as unpaid labour in the home and underpaid labour in the work force. The pace has been quickened by rising rates of divorce and single motherhood, but the course of women's poverty is determined by the sexism – and racism – ingrained in an unjust economy.[15]

It would seem that recent literature has produced not only a detailed description but also some plausible and, some may even say, obvious explanations of the feminisation of poverty. That this is really the case, in spite of the impressive documentation and well-developed arguments, is not as self-evident as it may seem. The identification of the determinants of the feminisation of poverty in sexism, racism, and the operation of the economy does not really tell us much beyond that which is empirically obvious and observable. What is questionable is the meaning given to the trends: are we witnessing the feminisation and the minoritisation of poverty or something else? I will introduce some additional facts and figures about poverty to highlight the complexity of these issues, and the problems inherent in the 'feminisation of poverty' perspective.

Who Are the Poor?

A recent analysis of poverty in the US indicates that, while it is the case that women are more likely to be poor than men and that, in absolute numbers, there were more poor women in 1983 than men (20,084,000 vs. 15,182,000), 'the

---

14   Sidel 1986, pp. 25–35.
15   Stallard et al. 1983, p. 51.

female share of the overall poverty population was the same in 1983 as it was in 1966 [the earliest available data] – 57 percent.[16] Poverty trends since 1983 have modified this conclusion only slightly. Between 1983 and 1986, the female share of the poverty population increased slightly from 57.0 percent to 57.6 percent.[17]

The female and male shares of the poverty population from 1966 to 1986 show remarkable stability: the female share increased gradually, rising to 59.1 percent in 1978, declining to 57.0 percent in 1983 and 1984, rising to 57.6 percent in 1986. If only adults over 21 are considered, in 1983 – *as it was in 1966* – women comprised 62 percent of the poor.[18] This percentage increased to 62.1 in 1984, 62.7 in 1985, and 64.2 in 1986.[19]

Mortality differentials increase the numbers of older women living alone, and 27.7 percent of the 6.7 million women age 65 and over who, in 1983, lived as 'unrelated individuals' were below the poverty level. In 1984, the number of women in that category increased to 6.8 million, but the percent below the poverty level declined to 25.2 percent.[20]

By comparison, in 1984 20.8 percent of 'unrelated males' age 65 and over fell below the poverty level. The differences between the poverty rate of younger 'unrelated' women and men is reflect the sharp fluctuations associated with the 1981–82 recession.

The overall poverty rate increased most sharply between 1978 and 1983 (from 11.4 percent to 15.2 percent of the total population), declining to 13.6 percent in 1986. Between 1978 and 1983, poverty increased faster for the 18–44 age category (70 percent) than for the 45–64 or the 65 and over age categories (26 percent and 14.8 percent respectively). Taking into account male/female differences, *between 1978 and 1983 the number of poor men increased faster than the number*

---

16   O'Hare 1985, p. 18, my emphasis. The lower proportion of poor men in the population below the poverty level might be partially correlated with sex differential mortality. This is a complex issue that cannot be fully examined here, but it is possible, nevertheless, to present some pertinent observations. Occupationally caused mortality and disability are disproportionately high among working-class men and women (Berman 1978; Chavkin 1984). Death rates among working-age males (15–64) are considerably higher than among females of the same age. Death rates from accidents and violence are also exceedingly high for younger males, particularly for blacks (US Bureau of the Census 1986c, pp. 72, 76). As mortality varies inversely with socio-economic status, it is reasonable to suppose that death rates for occupational accidents, disease and violence are likely to be higher for working-class men, than the reported rates which do not take class differences into account.

17   US Bureau of the Census 1987b, p. 30.

18   O'Hare 1985, p. 18.

19   US Bureau of the Census 1974–87.

20   US Bureau of the Census 1985, p. 41; 1986a, p. 29.

of poor women at all ages (51.6 percent versus 38.7 percent), ages 18–44 (93.3 percent versus 56.9 percent), and ages 45–64 (33.0 versus 22.5 percent). Among those of age 18 and under, the percent increase for males and females was relatively similar (40.0 percent versus 38.1 percent). Only among those 65 and over was the percent increase in the number of poor women slightly higher (15.7 percent versus 12.7 percent).[21]

Given the mortality differentials between the sexes, it is to be expected that poverty among the elderly would increase faster for women. On the other hand, the fact poverty increased faster for men in the other age groups, particularly among those between 18 and 44 years of age, is somewhat surprising, given of the public and scholarly concern with the 'feminisation of poverty,' which gives the impression that the growth of poverty has been primarily among women and that men have been less affected by the structural transformation of the economy. In actuality, between 1978 and 1983 the increase in poverty affected primarily younger people, particularly men. For example, the number of men aged 18–44 below the poverty level almost doubled between 1978 and 1983, increasing from 2,832,000 to 5,474,000. One could thus make a case for considering age, rather than sex, the defining feature of recent poverty trends.

It might be argued that the higher percent change in male poverty between 1978 and 1983 is an artefact of the particular years chosen for comparison. O'Hare's analysis reflects the sharp fluctuations associated with the 1981–82 recession. However, an examination of the average annual percentage changes in the number of men and women below the poverty level between 1975 and every year until 1985, for all ages, shows a greater increase in male poverty in every year from 1982 on. At ages 18–44, there is a higher rate of increase in male poverty for every year from 1979 on.[22] The lower proportion of men below the poverty level makes the percent changes in male poverty higher than what they would have been had sex ratios been closer to unity. On the other hand, the higher percent changes in male poverty cannot be dismissed lightly as statistical artefacts; and it must be remembered that male poverty is an important correlate of female poverty. The sharp increases in male poverty between 1978 and 1983 were real and seem to have lingered on after the 'economic recovery'

---

21   O'Hare 1985, p. 14.

22   The decline in the poverty rate after 1975 is reflected in the decline, for all ages and both sexes, in the numbers below the poverty level during the next four years. In 1978, the year chosen by O'Hare as the base year, the poverty rate was low (11.3 percent) and the number of poor men of all ages (10,017,000) was the lowest ever since 1966, while the number of poor women (14,381,000) was relatively low if compared to most of the preceding years, but certainly higher than the lowest number recorded since 1966: 13,316,000 in 1973.

that followed the 1981–82 recession. They reflect the vulnerability of men to unemployment at times of rapid economic decline, whereas women tend to work in more 'recession proof' sectors of the economy.[23]

As indicated earlier, the proportion of men and women in the 18–44 age group who become poor has been steadily increasing. While in 1983 the poverty rate for families with a householder aged 45–64 was 8.7 percent (up from 6.4 percent in 1978) and 14.2 percent (up from 10.2 percent in 1978) for families with a householder age 25–44, it was 29.5 percent (up from 18.5 percent in 1978) for families with a householder under 25.[24] In 1984, the poverty rate for householders under 25 remained practically unchanged at 29.4 percent, while the rate for householders aged 25–44 declined slightly to 13.2 percent.[25]

The faster increase in the poverty rate of younger workers of both sexes indicates that the working class is experiencing substantial downward mobility.[26] The increase in the poverty of children, usually linked to the increase in the number of female-headed families, is actually the result of the increase in poverty among young adult workers. While in 1983, 49 percent of poor children lived in female-headed households, 81 percent of poor children lived in families where the householder was under 45. Between 1978 and 1983, 4 million children under 18 joined the poverty population and only 25 percent of them lived in female-headed households.[27]

Real average earnings of young male workers aged 20–24 have declined 30 percent since 1973. A comparison between the earnings of men who turned 30 in 1973, and in 1983, shows that the average real income of the older men kept pace with inflation while that of the younger men declined 35 percent.[28] Income inequality among young men is related to education; those without a college degree are reduced to taking whatever the economy offers them, which, in these days, are jobs that pay relatively little. While college attendance by low income men is declining, the gap in earnings between college graduates and high school dropouts is growing: 'in 1973, the average earnings of a 20 to 24-year-old male high school dropout were three-quarters of the earnings of a college graduate. By 1984, this fraction dropped to two-thirds'.[29]

---

23   Sparr 1987, p. 11.
24   O'Hare 1985, p. 13.
25   US Bureau of the Census 1986a, p. 14.
26   O'Hare 1985, pp. 13–14; Harrington 1984, pp. 46–8.
27   O'Hare 1985, pp. 13–17.
28   Dollars & Sense 1987, p. 10.
29   Dollars & Sense 1987, p. 11.

In light of this information, it must be acknowledged that the 'feminisation of poverty' is only one dimension of a broader process that also affects men, children, and the elderly in different degrees and for reasons that are fundamentally interrelated. *Just as an exclusive focus on 'women' leads to a one-sided analysis that seems to give lesser importance to other dimensions of poverty, it would be equally misguided to focus on the poverty of 'men' or of 'young adult workers'.* These are simple descriptive categories that indicate the composition of the poor population, but cannot serve as the basis for developing a theoretical analysis of the meaning of present poverty trends. Poverty is, furthermore, only a descriptive concept that does not help us understand the nature of the phenomena captured by these and many other statistics.

An important statement critical of the 'feminisation of poverty' perspective[30] convincingly argues that it offers an inaccurate empirical and political analysis of the situation because it ignores, for all practical purposes, the class differences between women and the common basis for class, racial and ethnic solidarity between men and women. Because the focus of analysis is the poverty of women *as women*, their class and race are not considered as crucial in determining their poverty as the fact they are women. It is the case, however, that not all women are in danger of becoming poor; only those who are working-class or members of racial and ethnic minorities are thus threatened. Many women are becoming richer and, of course, ruling class women have never been at risk if becoming poor.[31] Poverty is not a phenomenon affecting primarily women; it is a structural component of the capitalist economy that affects people regardless of age and sex and falls disproportionally upon minorities. It is racism, more than sexism, that determines who works in the worse sectors of the economy. Racism excludes large numbers of minority men from employment and the possibility of forming families, thus changing the conditions faced by working-class women of colour in ways which the 'feminisation of poverty' perspective cannot adequately account for as long as it views all women as an oppressed class.[32]

This critique of the 'feminisation of poverty' interpretation of current trends identifies important issues for further theoretical and empirical investigation. These insights, as well as those presented previously, have to be connected to their underlying capitalist structural determinants in production and reproduction, to more clearly understand the significance of these empirically

---

30   AAWO 1983.
31   AAWO 1983, p. 2.
32   AAWO 1983; Center for the Study of Social Policy 1985; Sparr 1987.

observable phenomena. This process entails the examination of the relationship between capitalist structures, processes, and contradictions, which are not readily observable, and empirically observable changes in the size and composition of the poverty population. *It is my contention that the feminisation of poverty is an important dimension of a larger process: the immiseration of the working class brought about by the profound structural changes undergone by the US economy during the 1980s.* It would be beyond the limits of one book chapter to do justice to the complexity of these issues. The remarks that follow ought to be taken as tentative statements that will provide guidelines for future theoretical and empirical investigation.

Beyond Women as a Category of Analysis: Class Differences among Women and Their Impact on Poverty

The feminisation of poverty perspective focuses mainly on the poverty of women *as women*. This starting point introduces problems in understanding why some women become poor, while others do not. In this section, I will argue that gender related factors are relevant correlates (not determinants) of poverty only among women whose class location already makes them vulnerable to poverty. If no class differences (in the Marxist sense) are taken into account in the analysis of the feminisation of poverty, it does appear as if it were caused primarily by sexism. It is necessary, therefore, to examine the concept of social class and explore its implications for the life chances of women in different social classes.

From the standpoint of Marxist theory, class is a relation between people mediated by their relationship to the means of production. Ownership of means of production, even on a modest scale, gives political and economic control over others, and economic independence. Lack of means of production places workers – male and female – in a dependent situation, vulnerable to the decisions taken by those who, in controlling capital, control their access to the conditions indispensable for their physical and social daily and generational reproduction: employment. Changes in the occupational structure and quantitative and qualitative changes in the demand for labour divide the propertyless class in terms of occupation, income, and education, which are precisely the building blocks with which the average person and most social scientists construct socio-economic status categories.[33] This is the material basis

---

33   I am aware of the complexity of the issue of class and class structure within Marxist and

for the common sense division of people into a variety of 'classes', in a ranking that ranges from 'the poor' and the 'lower class' at the bottom, to the 'upper class' at the top, with the 'working class', 'middle' and 'upper-middle class' in between. This is an empiricist understanding of social class that mystifies the sources of women's poverty; it is a simple ordering or gradational concept of class, that focuses only on the different power and resources individuals bring to the sexual and economic markets.[34] It is a central contention in my argument that, if the social class location of women (not their socio-economic status) is taken into account, it becomes obvious that it is not sex but class that propels some women into poverty.

Capitalist Women and Petty-Bourgeois Women Are Not at Risk of Becoming Poor

Being a capitalist or a petty-bourgeois woman entails, theoretically, having capital of one's own and, therefore, a source of income *independent* from marriage or from paid employment. Women who own wealth are unlikely to become poor for gender-related factors, though inheritance practices and family accumulation strategies might deny them full control of their property.

Of the top wealth-holders with gross assets of $300,000 or more in 1982, 39.3 percent (1.85 percent of the total female population) were women. Between 1985 and 1986, the proportion of women aged 21 and over in the poverty population rose 1.5 percentage points (from 62.7 percent to 64.2 percent); in the same period of time, the number of women workers (full- and part-time) earning more than $35,000 increased 32 percent; those earning between $50,000 and $75,000 increased 34.5 percent, while the number of full-time women workers earning more than $75,000 increased 55.4 percent. As some women fell into poverty, others certainly became more affluent, although only 3.2 percent of all women workers earn more than $35,000 a year and only 0.3 percent of full-time working women earn more than $75,000.[35] Women earning over $35,000 a year are certainly far less likely to fall into poverty if they become single mothers, divorce or separate. On the other hand, if they lose their jobs, *lack an independ-*

---

neo-Marxist theory. Nevertheless, for the purposes of developing my argument in this chapter, I consider that it is enough to point out the crucial differences between classes defined at the level of production relations and classes defined at the level of market relations. If relationship to the means of production is overlooked, it is possible to argue that most women, regardless of social class, could become poor; if the impact of propertylessness is taken into account, it becomes obvious that is working-class women who are at the greatest risk of becoming poor.

34   Ossowski 1963, pp. 41–57; Weber 1982, pp. 61–2.
35   US Bureau of the Census 1987, p. 19; 1986c, p. 447.

ent source of income, and are unable to find a job with similar pay, they will experience downward social mobility and might even become poor.

Patterns of income distribution and wealth ownership indicate the existence of extreme socio-economic status differences (based on income) and class differences (based on wealth ownership) among women, which constitute the underlying material basis for the notion that virtually all women are vulnerable to poverty: that is so because most women (and most men as well) are propertyless.

Propertyless Women (and Propertyless Men) Are Always at Risk of Becoming Poor

As economist Ferdinand Lundberg has trenchantly observed: 'anyone who does not own a substantial amount of income-producing property, or does not receive an earned income sufficiently large to make substantial regular savings or does not hold a well-paid securely tenured job is poor ... By this standard at least 70 percent of Americans are poor, although not all of these are by any means destitute or poverty stricken'.[36]

Propertyless women may attain, at the level of market relations, through family-transmitted advantages (e.g. real estate property, higher education) and/or marriage, a socio-economic status that appears to place them above the working class. When it is argued that the feminisation of poverty places all or most women at risk, including 'middle', and 'upper-middle class' women, a very important observation is made which does not apply to women across social classes. The often made statement, 'most women are just a man or a divorce away from poverty', reflects the conditions of existence of most *propertyless* women whom the capitalist organisation of production and reproduction makes dependent on marriage and/or employment for economic survival.

Working-class women with substantial 'human capital' of their own are still a tiny minority; they, and women with stable jobs face a lower probability of poverty than women with less skills or with precarious working conditions. Data on women's income and employment indicate that the vast majority of propertyless women are working class, not only in terms of their location in the relations of production (i.e. they are propertyless and depend on a wage or salary for the economic survival of themselves and their families) but also at the level of socio-economic stratification (i.e. the vast majority of women work in low paid, low status, blue- or white-collar jobs). Of the 39,214,000 women who worked full-time in 1986, 72.3 percent earned less than $20,000; 32.3 per-

---

36   Lundberg 1969, p. 23.

cent earned less than $10,000.[37] On the other hand, there are more men than women in 'middle class' and 'upper-middle class' occupations and in the better paid skilled blue-collar jobs. Consequently, most women experience some form of 'upward mobility' through marriage and, if they lack skills or resources of their own, are likely to return to their previous place in the socio-economic structure in case of separation, divorce, or widowhood.

Most of the 'social mobility' propertyless men and women experience in their lifetimes is not social class mobility in the Marxist sense (e.g. changing from being propertyless to becoming petty-bourgeois, small or big capitalist) but occupational mobility. It is important to realise that men and women can experience mobility at the market level while remaining, at the same time and whatever their socio-economic status may be, located in the working class or propertyless class. Intra-class differences (i.e. differences within the propertyless class) in the socio-economic status and individual resources that men and women bring to the market is at the core of women's greater vulnerability to poverty and the transformation of marriage into the major source of economic survival for vast numbers of women.[38]

The feminisation of poverty is a market level structural effect of intra-class differences in male and female socio-economic status and mobility; it is fundamentally a class issue although it is experienced and analysed as an effect of sex and race discrimination. Sexism and racism unquestionably intensify the effects of economic changes upon the more impoverished layers of the working class.[39] Nevertheless, the ultimate determinant of individuals' relative vulnerability to poverty is their class location: 'if sexism [and, I add, racism] were eliminated, there would still be poor women [and poor non-whites]. The only difference is that women [and non-whites] would stand the same chance as men [and whites] of being poor'.[40]

The Immiseration of the Working Class

Capital is indifferent to the reproduction of the working class as a whole; the extent to which workers can have access to the means necessary for their own

---

37   US Bureau of the Census 1987, p. 19.
38   Intra-class differences in the market resources of propertyless men and women reflect, in turn, differential patterns in the intergenerational transmission of socio-economic status which, in turn, are determined by the articulation of production and reproduction within the propertyless class, a topic which cannot be examined within the limitations of this chapter.
39   AAWO 1983; Sparr 1987.
40   Sparr 1987, p. 11.

reproduction and that of the future generation of workers is very much constrained by the demand for different kinds of labour power. The demand for certain kinds of skilled labour power may lead not only to good wages and salaries but also to special subsidies like public and private funding for the development of special training and educational programmes and, sometimes, the establishment of day care facilities at the workplace. In general, however, the social and physical reproduction of the working class on a daily and generational level is left to the ingenuity of the workers themselves. Those whose skills are no longer needed or whose birth in the reserve army of labour deprived them of the opportunity of developing any skills are left behind in poverty.

In the US, the working class has suffered enormous setbacks in the last 15 years, reflected in high rates of unemployment, an overall decline in real wages, the demise of the 'family wage' for most workers, and qualitative changes in the economy and the organisation of work that have significantly reduced the number of full-time, skilled and relatively well-paid blue-collar male jobs that constituted the backbone of the US 'middle class'. The 'new poor' include not only working-class women but a substantial number of working-class men and their families as well. According to a 1982 survey of the US Conference of Mayors, the 'new poor' were created by economic decline, high unemployment and cuts in federal programmes: They are 'people who are losing their jobs, exhausting their financial resources, exhausting their unemployment benefits and losing their hopes'.[41] According to the Bureau of Labor Statistics:

> Only 65 percent of the 3.8 million experienced workers aged 25 to 54 laid off between 1979 and 1983 were employed in January of 1984, some 25 percent were still unemployed, and 10 percent had dropped out of the labor force altogether.
>
> They averaged 23 weeks of unemployment and only half of them earned as much after their reemployment as they had earned before.[42]

In such times of economic crises, the illusory nature of 'middle class' and 'upper middle class' statuses is clearly revealed when social class reasserts itself through the powerlessness and untold suffering heaped upon men, women, and children by unemployment, underemployment, and cuts in social services.[43]

---

41   Congressional Quarterly 1983, p. 129.
42   Rose 1986, pp. 24–5.
43   See Parker 1972 for an excellent discussion of the distorted way in which social class is commonly perceived by social scientists and the general public.

Conclusion

The data discussed earlier in this essay show that the sex ratio of the poverty population has changed little since 1966; its age composition, however, did change. Today, the majority of the poor are children under 18 and adults under 44. While, in absolute numbers, there are still more poor women than poor men, the dramatic increase in poverty between 1978 and 1983 was felt more heavily among men than among women. Since 1983, the modest decline in poverty has also been more rapid among men than among women.

Theoretically, these trends are empirical indicators of the immiseration of the working class. The essence of this argument is that people do not fall into poverty because of their age, sex, or racial/ethnic characteristics, but because of their social class. Age sex, and ethnic/racial groups are not socially homogeneous; they are divided into social classes which, in turn, are stratified on the basis of income, education and occupation. The fact that poverty falls disproportionately upon the young, women and minorities does not invalidate the analysis; those who become poor share a common relationship to the means of production that cuts across age, sex, and racial/ethnic differences.

Sexism and racism are important in determining who gets the worst jobs or is most likely to be affected by unemployment.[44] But sexism and racism are not unchanging entities standing on an independent material base; they are shifting structural effects of capitalist processes of labour allocation designed to increase profit margins and enhance economic and political control over the working class. The general determining dynamics of poverty are, from this standpoint, located in capitalist processes which racialise, ethnicise and sexualise the workforce on national and world-system levels – processes whose ideological, political and legal effects, in turn, perpetuate them through time, endowing them with a deceptive universality and antiquity.[45] The specific determinants of recent poverty trends are to be found in the interplay between the historical effects of sexism and racism and recent political and economic changes which have drastically altered the US economic structure. Some sectors of the capitalist class, to become competitive at the international level are lowering the average price of labour; cuts in wages, union busting, right to work laws, 'give backs', cuts in social services, and recent changes in immigration laws that allow the legalisation of undocumented workers under certain conditions are all efforts aimed at cheapening the overall costs of labour.[46]

---

44   AAWO 1983.
45   Wallerstein 1983; 1985.
46   Piven and Cloward 1986; Harrington 1985.

Lacking access to the material conditions for their physical and social reproduction on a daily and generational level, over 32 million members of the working class below the poverty level[47] barely survive under the restrictive conditions imposed by the welfare state. Altogether, 43.4 million people live below 125 percent of the poverty level; this includes 9.4 million families (45.9 percent headed by women) and 15.5 million children under 18 (51.1 percent of which live in families headed by women).[48] Nutrition levels and health among the poor have deteriorated; between 1982–85, the food-stamp programme was cut by $7 billion and child-nutrition programmes by 5 billion. In spite of the large number of people below the poverty level, only 19 million today receive food stamps; 12 million children and 8 million adults suffer from hunger.[49]

Lack of access to the basic material conditions necessary for physical and social reproduction on a daily and generational basis threatens the intergenerational reproduction of the working class among all races, particularly among racial and ethnic minorities. The immiseration of the working class culminates in the breakdown of its intergenerational reproduction. Poor parents, particularly poor single mothers, are placed under conditions that deprive them of their ability to reproduce people with marketable skills. This situation may be 'functional' for the economy, insofar as the demand for skilled and educated workers is not likely to rise dramatically during the near future. From the standpoint of the working class and minorities, in particular, this is a very serious situation which civil rights, better educational opportunities, and measures designed to help women combine work and parenting, *in themselves*, cannot possibly solve.

William Julius Wilson has written of the 'declining significance of race' and the need to recognise the primarily economic and class-based determinants of the poverty and deprivation of most black Americans.[50] By the same token, *the recent increase in both male and female poverty should alert us to the declining significance of sex as a cause of women's poverty*. The feminisation of poverty reflects the fact that women are more than half of the US propertyless class and that the standard of living of this class is noticeably declined in the last ten years.[51] The media, social scientists, politicians and activists give – depend-

---

47   45.3 million in 2013, https://www.census.gov/content/dam/Census/library/publications/
      2014/demo/p60-249.pdf.
48   US Bureau of the Census 1987, p. 28.
49   Brown 1987, pp. 37–41.
50   Wilson 1978.
51   For a thoughtful statement about the need to overcome the limits of an exclusive focus
      on sex, to the detriment of class and race, as sources of women's oppression, see Dill 1987,
      pp. 204–13.

ing on their specific concerns, political agendas and the theoretical commitments – greater importance to different sectors of the poor. The notoriety of the
'feminisation of poverty', the poverty of the minorities, the elderly, or children
contrasts with the relative silence over the erosion in the standard of living and
the growing poverty of the working class. While it is important to uncover the
correlates of poverty pertinent to each of these sectors, to the extent the analysis stops there it can lead to the development of theoretically flawed explanations and policies that pit the interests of women against the interests of men,
the young versus the old, whites versus non-whites.

Stress upon the poverty of those who are disproportionately poor produces
a misleading perception of poverty as something that affects mainly women,
the elderly, ethnic/racial minorities, and welfare recipients and could, theoretically, be effectively dealt with by measures addressing the needs of women
workers, civil rights enforcement, and the welfare reforms. In fact, most of the
poor are white (69 percent in 1986); most of the poor between the ages of 22
and 64 are working or looking for work, and only 35 percent of the poor families receive welfare benefits.[52] Only 10.5 percent of the elderly aged 65 and over
are poor and 55 percent of the poor who live in families do not live in families headed by women.[53] Furthermore, of the 2,453,000 families between the
poverty level and 125 percent of the poverty level, only 30 percent are headed
by women.[54]

To speak of the immiseration of the working class does not entail the adoption of a mindless economic reductionism or the callous denial of the plight
of minorities, women, children, and the elderly. It simply entails recognition
of the fact that those sectors of the poor population, including men, do not
live as isolated individuals but are linked to each other through common relations of production and reproduction. The fate of each sector is tied to the fate
of the others because they are all part of the same social class, just as the fate
of individuals is tied to the fate of those with whom they share a kinship or
emotional and social bonds. People are 'an ensemble of social relations'[55] and
cannot be meaningfully understood in isolation of those relationships that give
them their historically specific place in the world they live.

It is not by reducing people to age, sex, racial or ethnic categories that
poverty and its determinants can be best understood; people are poor or be-

52   O'Hare 1985, p. 4.
53   US Bureau of the Census 1986b, pp. 22–4.
54   US Bureau of the Census 1987, pp. 28–9.
55   Marx and Engels 1947, p. 198.

come poor because they are subject to common socio-economic and political processes that deprive them of access to their material conditions of existence, tear families apart, or make family formation impossible for vast numbers of working-class men and women, particularly those who are also members of racial and ethnic minorities. Placed in its historical context, the feminisation of poverty is a real, important, albeit partial dimension, of a vast process of social transformation resulting in a drastic decline in the overall level of wages and standard of living of the US working class, a significant increase in the size of the reserve army of labour, the intensification of the proletarianisation of women,[56] and the undermining of the material conditions necessary for the maintenance of 'middle class' illusions and for the intergenerational physical and social reproduction of the lower strata of the working class – particularly its racialised, ethnicised, and feminised sectors.

Addendum

Thirty years after Chapter 9 was originally published, women continue to earn less than men, and are more likely to be poor. The data indicate that the *sex composition* of the poverty population in the US has not changed a great deal since then. The *female proportion of all ages* of the population below the poverty level had remained relatively constant since 1966, when it was 57.1 percent, fluctuating between 57 and 58 percent in the 1970s and early 1980s, but remaining mainly a little over 57 percent since 1982. It declined to 56.1 percent in 1987 and its highest peak (59.1 percent) was reached in 1978; 20 years later it was 57.3 percent.[57] It was 56.5 percent in 2001.[58] From 2001 to 2013, the data show that the female proportion of all ages of the population below the poverty level contin-

---

56   This process is not equivalent to the 'feminization of the proletariat' (Ehrenreich 1987, p. 12). Because of demographic reasons (high male mortality) women have always been more than half of the proletariat, whether they were aware of it or not. I refer here to the erosion of 'middle class' and 'upper-middle class' statuses among growing numbers of propertyless women. It is also true that working women are concentrated in the more poorly paid jobs and the demand for female (and male) cheap labour is increasing. These trends can be best understood not in demographic terms (giving emphasis to the sex or age composition of the proletariat), but as effects of current processes of wealth concentration and class proletarianisation.

57   US Bureau of the Census, 'Historical Poverty Tables – Table 7', http://www.census.gov/hhes/poverty/histpov7.html. Last retrieved in 2014.

58   http://bls.census.gov/macro/032002/pov/new01_001.htm. Last retrieved in 2014.

ued to remain relatively constant; it fell below 56 percent in 2003 and 2004, and again after 2008, remaining constant, at 56.6 percent between 2011 and 2013.[59]

Women's poverty rates continue to be higher than men's: In 2013, the overall poverty rate was 14.5 percent; the poverty rate for women was 15.8 percent, compared to 13.1 percent for men;[60] when differences by age and gender are taken into account, the poverty rate for women aged 18–64 was 15.3 percent (compared to 11.8 percent for men), and for women 65+ was 11.6 percent (compared to 6.8 percent for men). The poorest women are members of racial and ethnic minorities. In 2013, the poverty rate for white, non-Hispanic women age 18+ was 10.7 percent, compared to Black women (25.3 percent), Hispanic women (23.1 percent), Asian women (11.0 percent), Native American women (26.8 percent), and foreign-born women (19.0 percent).[61]

The poverty of women is, of course, the cause for the poverty of children. There were 14.7 million poor children in 2013, and the child poverty rate was 19.9 percent.[62] Children's poverty rates differ by race and ethnicity: in 2013, the rate was 36.9 for African-American children; 30.4 percent for Hispanic children and 10.7 percent for non-Hispanic white children.[63]

The rise of global capitalism intensified the economic changes in the US that since the late 1970s brought the feminisation of poverty to the consciousness of scholars and the media. It is in the context of deepening inequality, falling incomes,[64] and a polarised labour market[65] favourable to the college-educated and to women with a high school education, that working-class women's current opportunities and risk of becoming poor must be understood. Men without a college education fare poorly, even if they have a high school education. Young women, who are more likely to graduate from college than young men, are better able to take advantage of opening opportunities in professional and managerial occupations.[66] These differences in education

---

59   https://www.census.gov/content/dam/Census/library/publications/2014/demo/p60-249
      .pdf.
60   https://www.census.gov/content/dam/Census/library/publications/2014/demo/p60-249
      .pdf.
61   National Women's Law Center 2014.
62   http://aspe.hhs.gov/hsp/14/PovertyAndIncomeEst/ib_poverty2014.pdf.
63   Hispanics can be of any race.
64   National Women's Law Center 2014; Kotkin 2014.
65   'In the future ... there will be many high-education professional and managerial jobs (involving abstract tasks) and low-education service jobs (involving manual tasks), with fewer jobs involving routine tasks and paying middle class wages', in National Research Council 2008. See also Boehm 2014.
66   'By 2013 ... 37 percent of twenty-five to twenty-nine-year-old women and received a bachelor's degree or more compared to 30 percent of men of comparable age' (Cherlin 2014,

and employment opportunities are reflected in their earning capacity; 'among young adults without bachelor's degrees, the earning prospects for women and men diverge markedly. Women are still paid less than men, on average, but their earnings have been trending upward'.[67] College-educated women have benefitted the most but even women with only a high school diploma fare better, in terms of economic opportunities, than men with a similar qualification. During the postwar economic boom, working-class men with high school education or less could find well-paid, secure jobs in manufacturing. Today, as most of those jobs have been automated or outsourced, they can find mainly poorly paid employment, often temporary, at the bottom or near the bottom of the occupational structure.[68] On average, young men without a college education saw their earnings decrease whereas among women, only those who dropped out of high school found themselves worse off. Working-class men with only high school education are no longer able to find secure jobs earning a family wage, or close to it;[69] as Coontz points out, 'between 1970 and 2010 the median earnings of men fell by 19 percent and those of men with just a high school diploma by a stunning 41 percent'.[70]

Because young working-class women with a high school diploma only, or a year or two of college, are likely to earn more than young working-class men with a high school diploma or less,[71] they are less inclined to marry such men; hence the increase in cohabitation, out-of-wedlock childbearing, and the rise of what social scientists call 'fragile families'. Cohabiting relations tend to be unstable; as men and women become involved with other partners, they may have additional children. Pregnancy might lead a couple in a cohabiting relationship to marry, but such marriages are unstable and likely to end in divorce.[72] As the earnings of working-class men decline, the marriage rate

p. 125); 'women accounted for 51 percent of all workers employed in management, professional and related occupations, somewhat more than their share of total employment (47 percent)', in Bureau of Labor Statistics Report 2014, p. 2.

67   Cherlin 2014a, p. 125.

68   Cherlin 2014a, pp. 124–5.

69   Cherlin 2014a, p. 125. See also Autor and Wasserman 2013.

70   Coontz 2014a.

71   'Real wages for men under age 35 have fallen almost continuously since the late 1970s, and those with only a high school diploma have experienced the sharpest losses. Between 1979 and 2007, young male high school graduates saw a 29 percent decline in real annual earnings – an even steeper decline than the 18 percent drop for men with no high school diploma' (in Coontz 2014b).

72   For social science research about these issues, see Cherlin 2014a; Carlson and England 2011; and Sawhill 2015.

declines accordingly; marriage has become unaffordable for those without a college education, hence the rise of the so-called 'marriage gap'.[73]

The economic changes of the last few decades have undermined the economic foundations of marriage for low income, less educated people; they have produced, as sociologist Cherlin argues, 'the fall of the working-class family in America'.[74] Families headed by women are more likely to be poor;[75] as cohabitation replaces marriage among the working poor and those who without being poor do not earn enough to afford the long-term economic responsibilities linked to marriage, the proportion of women and children in the poverty population is likely to increase. When I wrote Chapter 9 in the mid-1980s, although single mother heads of households could be and continue to be found across the socio-economic spectrum, this type of family was associated with poverty, unemployment, and racial and ethnic minorities, *which are disproportionately poor*. Today, this pattern, i.e. cohabitation eventually resulting in single mothers and fathers with children from more than one partner, is now found also among low income, working women from the less educated sector of the white working class.[76] Few cohabiting unions end in marriage; most dissolve after a few years, women and men find new partners, more children are born and this gives rise to what researchers call 'multi-parent fertility', 'family complexity', or 'the family go-round'.[77] Young children are thus growing up in the midst of an unstable context, as their mother's or father's partner changes, and other children also come and go as parents separate, becoming single parents or finding new partners.

This trend toward family instability and out-of-wedlock births among low income women and men, a trend based on men's declining economic prospects, could be interpreted as a continuation and, perhaps, an intensification

---

73   See, for example, http://www.usnews.com/news/articles/2014/12/16/marriage-gap-widens -with-income-inequality.

74   Cherlin 2014a, Chapter 5; he defines class in terms of income and education.

75   In 2013, the poverty rate for married couple families with children was 7.6 percent; for all female-headed families with children it was 39.6 percent. The rates differ by race and ethnicity: the poverty rate for white non-Hispanic female-headed families with children was 31.6 percent, compared with 46.3 percent for black and 46.5 percent for Hispanic female-headed families with children. National women's Law Center 2014.

76   'Middle America, meaning women with at least a high school degree and often some college as well, are now having children outside marriage. In 2010, 58 percent of first births to women with either a high school degree or some college were out of wedlock, while for those with a college degree the comparable statistic was only 12 percent. The group of women without a college degree is large; it includes about two-thirds of the population' (in Sawhill 2014, pp. 68–70).

77   Sawhill 2014, p. 71.

of the 'feminisation' of poverty. Using also the gender lens, however, Coontz argues that 'since the 1980s there has been a "defeminisation" of poverty, as a growing proportion of men have fallen in hard times ... Millions of men face working conditions that traditionally characterized women's lives: low wages, minimal benefits, part-time or temporary jobs, and periods of joblessness. Poverty is becoming defeminised because the working conditions of many men are becoming more feminised'.[78] Coontz's analysis illustrates the limits inherent in examining social trends solely on the basis of gender identity, female or male; the working conditions she describes characterised *working-class* women's lives, and the men facing similar conditions today are *working-class* men. The same critical observations I made when the feminisation of poverty emerged as a new way to talk about women's poverty continue to be relevant today. I argued then that it is not gender but class that places most women in poverty or at the risk of becoming poor, because most women (like most men) are propertyless, working-class, and depend on a job or on marriage for their economic survival. Today, under changing economic conditions, low income working-class women and men find it more difficult to build stable families; this is why low income working-class women find themselves at the risk of becoming poor single mothers.

A focus on the identity of those who are poor, or at the risk of becoming poor, overlooks their class location and, consequently, the main causes of their poverty. It would be equally misleading if increases in male economic vulnerability and poverty were to lead to a widespread concern with the 'masculinisation' of poverty. Nevertheless, it is important to pay attention to the effects of global capitalism on the economic prospects of working-class men. In the US, a large proportion of poor working-class men are in jail. Concomitant with the rise of global capitalism, neoliberalism and the dismantling of the welfare state in the US, there is also the rise of the 'penal state', i.e. the 'criminalisation of poverty' and rapid growth of the incarcerated population; in the year 2000, there were 6.5 million people under criminal justice supervision.[79] In the US, one adult man in 20 and one young black man in three are in prison.[80] By 2010, the prison population had reached about 1.6 million, 90 percent of which are men.[81] Working-class men who are not in jail, particularly those without

---

78   Coontz 2014a.
79   More precisely, 1,312,000 in state and federal prison; 621,000 in county jail; 726,000 on parole, and 3,840,000 on probation; Wacquant 2009, p. 134.
80   Wacquant 2009, p. xv.
81   http://www.prb.org/Publications/Articles/2012/us-incarceration.aspx.

education and marketable skills, are likely to be engaged in illegal activities, unemployed, often unemployable and, if employed, living precariously, on the edge of destitution.

That the economic prospects for male workers without a college education have been declining in the last 40 years is not a phenomenon unique to the United States. For example, in a discussion paper entitled 'The Masculinisation of Poverty: Gender and Global Restructring [sic]', the author points out that 'changes in the world economy have resulted in the erosion of the work and life prospects for an increasing share of the male population in both core and peripheral regions', and argues that 'the growth of male poverty as a global phenomenon is a function of the shift in the gendered division of labour and illustrates the intersection between changes in the international division of labour and transformations in the sexual and racial division of labour'.[82]

These changes in the relative position of some working-class men and women in the occupational and income structures, which from the standpoint of identity politics can be described as changes in the 'gender order', are the outcome of class struggles in which the world's working classes have been overpowered by capital. *Underlying phenomena such as the 'feminisation', 'masculinisation' and 'juvenilisation'[83] of poverty, and other identity ways to describe segments of the poverty population such as the poverty of the elderly, or the 'feminisation of the proletariat', the 'feminisation of migration', or the disproportionate poverty of racial and ethnic minorities, is the impoverishment the working class, the deterioration in the working class's standard of living and family stability.* Consequently, while policies targeted at different poverty populations are important to help and improve the lives of those who are already poor, it must also be recognised that poverty is not uniquely a women's issue, or a men's issue, and so forth: *poverty is a class issue* which can, at best, be ameliorated – not resolved because it is endemic to the capitalist mode of production – through labour's collective action, through unionisation and struggles for job training and job creation aimed at creating employment for manual, skilled and unskilled labour, in addition to programmes intended to enhance the health and educational opportunities for everyone, regardless of gender, race or ethnicity. In the present historical conjuncture, however, acknowledgement of the class (in the Marxist sense) nature of poverty and the problems facing the lower strata within the working class is beyond the limits of political

---

82   Nurse 2003. Nurse explains that he uses the term 'masculinisation of poverty' to 'exemplify this transition in the global gender order', and that use of this term should not be seen 'in competition with the "feminisation of poverty"'.

83   Bianchi 1999. Bianchi uses this term to refer to the increase in children's poverty.

action and discourse in the US. The trends identified 28 years ago leading to the impoverishment of the working class continue unabated, as well as the politicians' and the media's refusal to acknowledge the class nature of poverty. Consequently, it is to be expected that identity based descriptions of current and future changes in the poverty population, such as the 'feminisation' of poverty, will continue to dominate social science, media, and political discourse.

CHAPTER 10

The Dialectics of Waged and Unwaged Work: Waged Work, Domestic Labour and Household Survival in the United States

'The Dialectics of Waged and Unwaged Work: Waged Work, Domestic Labor, and Household Survival in the United States', in *Work Without Wages. Domestic Labor and Self-Employment Under Capitalism*, edited by Jane C. Collins and Martha E. Gimenez, New York: State University of New York Press, 1990, pp. 25–45.

Theoretically, the accumulation of capital on an ever-expanding scale entails the proletarianisation of the population and the universalisation of commodity production. This should lead to the centralisation and concentration of capital in very few hands and the concomitant transformation of the rest of the population into a propertyless class whose only source of survival is its ability to sell its labour for a wage. Historically, this process is far from being completed and, within the world capitalist system, the degree of proletarianisation in each country is determined by its unique insertion in the world economy and its corresponding place in the core or the periphery.

Proletarianisation is least advanced in the periphery, where the presence of rural and urban subsistence sectors and relatively widespread cottage industries lowers the cost of labour power. Cheaper labour (and other incentives, of course) attracts capital from core to peripheral countries, where it is able to realise higher profits while maintaining the structural conditions that brought it there. Abundant unwaged labour engaged in the production of food and services (legal and illegal) keeps wages extremely low and profits high for those able to take advantage of these conditions. On the other hand, the flight of capital from core countries, particularly in recent years, has very important effects upon the quantity and quality of the demand for labour, and the relative input of unwaged labour in the reproduction of the labour force within core countries. Those effects have been intensified by the present crisis of accumulation and the adoption of economic and public policies designed to lower the labour costs of production regardless of social costs.

In this chapter, I intend to explore the impact of this crisis, and the concomitant transformation of the economy in the United States, on the changing significance of waged and unwaged labour in the reproduction of the labour force. It will be my contention that the role of certain forms of unwaged labour in the reproduction of the labour force is relatively less important here than in the periphery because of the greater scale with which proletarianisation proceeded in this country. I will also argue that the relative importance of unwaged labour as a source of household income and well-being in the United States varies directly with the value of the labour that is being reproduced. Finally, I will argue that the historically specific conditions that led to the structuring of unwaged domestic labour in the United States have been crucial for determining both the specifically capitalist basis for the oppression of working women and the conditions for generating the political and ideological awakening and mobilisation of women. The dialectics between waged and unwaged labour are, after all, the empirically observable form – at the level of market and social relations – of the dialectics of production and reproduction under capitalist conditions; their study can shed light on the political significance of changes in the conditions under which unwaged domestic labour is performed.

Forms of Unwaged Labour

The transformation of labour power into a commodity on a large and expanding scale is one of the essential features of the capitalist mode of production. Historically, proletarianisation has been most advanced in the core countries, a fact that meant the near universalisation of wage labour and the drastic decline in the proportion of independent producers. By 1974 in the United States, only 8.2 percent of all workers were self-employed, and only 8.8 percent were salaried managers and administrators; the rest were all non-managerial waged and salaried employees having no other source of income than the sale of their labour.[1]

Unwaged labour, on the other hand, comprises different kinds of labour. It is, in fact, not always perceived as labour, given dominant ideologies defining as 'real work' only that which is exchanged for a salary or a wage. The most important kind of unwaged labour under capitalist conditions is domestic household labour, which has been and continues to be the primary responsibility of women. Domestic labour is engaged in the physical and social, daily and generational reproduction of the labour force; it entails the daily and generational maintenance of the domestic worker herself, her children, and her husband

---

1   Reich 1978, pp. 180–1.

and, sometimes relatives or friends.[2] Households differ in size and structure, ranging from single-person households to urban or rural communes or 'collectives' including more than one 'nuclear family' and a number of unrelated people. Consequently, households differ in the amount of domestic labour at their command; I am referring here to the labour of children, husbands, and other household members who, in addition to the labour of the main domestic worker, can under some conditions become an important source of non-market income.

In addition to the production of goods and services for internal consumption, household labour may produce for the market. Unwaged labour – usually women's labour – can turn to the production of goods or services of varying quality which, although reaching a relatively unstable and narrow market, can become another source of household income, supplementing and sometimes replacing wage or salary income. Homes become small cottage industries supporting themselves on a regular basis or during times of low wages, unemployment, or underemployment. This kind of household activity partially accounts for the low level of wages in poor nations, where wages are seldom the major source of income ensuring the survival of vast sectors of the population.

In the core countries, there is a specific kind of unwaged labour that is becoming increasingly noticeable – empirically – although it is by no means a new development; what is new is the fact that it seems to be growing by leaps and bounds. I am referring to the work involved in the process of consumption: 'The clear trend is for producers to work less and for consumers to work *more. The consumer, ultimately, will have to choose between hiring a robot and hiring himself*'.[3] 'Self-service' in retailing entails work; food stores, discount stores, and department stores can sell at lower prices because customers do a great deal of work in the process of purchasing commodities. This work often includes evaluation, selection, weighing, wrapping, and carrying, and it almost always, of course, includes delivering the goods to the customers' homes. Self-service has become predominant in vast department stores and most clothing stores (except those for the very wealthy), as well as in gas stations; the proliferation of electronic tellers, catalogue showrooms, computerised and televised education, vending machines, salad bars and other forms of food self-service are just a few of the additional ways in which customers are forced to work in order to consume. Most of the shopping for food and clothing is done by women, although most people, regardless of sex, at times have to do this kind

---

2   Seccombe, 1974; Gimenez 1978.
3   Burns 1977, p. 191, emphasis in the original text.

of work. Glazer, in her research on the emergence of self-service in retailing, has convincingly argued that this is 'involuntary unpaid labour'.[4] Although it is perceived as privatised work done by women for the benefit of their families, it is work that benefits commercial capital by drastically lowering its distribution and retail costs. Under such conditions 'women's unwaged work can be understood to be appropriated by capital'.[5]

The notion that capital actually appropriates consumers' unwaged labour is, in my view, a powerful metaphor emphasising the fact that capital unquestionably benefits from this primarily female labour. However, capital can appropriate surplus value *only* through the exploitation of wage labour; the effect of unwaged consumption work is to allow capital to lower the overall level of wages and increase the rate of exploitation, as the reduction in the costs of consumer goods made possible by self-service in fact cheapens labour power.

This kind of unwaged labour takes place, therefore, outside the household and entails – from the standpoint of capital – a process of *work transfer* from the realm of waged labour to that of unpaid labour. From the standpoint of households, on the other hand, it entails a transfer of unwaged labour from the 'private', to the 'public' sphere. This transfer, as Glazer points out, is part of a general process designed to lower both the costs of retailing and the cost and quality of healthcare and other services which were, in the past, performed by waged workers. Given that most of those services were performed by low-waged female labour, the present trend leading to their transformation into 'family responsibilities' essentially means that it is the unpaid labour of women which will fill the gap in the necessary services needed for childcare, care of the elderly, care of the sick in hospitals, etc. As is obvious, this process of transformation of waged into unwaged labour generates unemployment, lowering the bargaining power of workers and contributing to the ability of capital to lower the level of wages. Growth in unwaged consumption work, therefore, allows capital to reap greater profits through two channels: the cheapening of labour power, and the increase in its ability to discipline the labour force and impose lower wages.

Another form of work transfer takes place when manufacturers not only reduce the costs of distribution but also the assembly costs; increasing numbers of household goods (furniture, exercise equipment, toys, etc.) require not only that the customer work at the place in which the goods are sold and take care of their delivery, but also that they be assembled at home. The high cost

4   Glazer 1984.
5   Glazer 1984.

of paying wage workers a living wage is thus reduced for manufacturers, while customers must spend some of their 'free time' doing unpaid assembly and finishing work under the guise of consumption.

Renting equipment to do some kinds of household work or home improvements, instead of calling for the services of a company, is another form in which people perform unpaid labour; in this case, however, it is for themselves, not for capital. Only exceptionally wealthy households can afford to pay a living wage for services; those who can pay only for equipment, tools, and other materials use their own labour to produce many of the goods and services that enhance their standard of living. The home improvements industry has thus become 'a subcontractor to the producing household'.[6]

Waged Labour as a Necessary Condition for Unwaged Labour

In the United States today, what is the economic and political significance of the process whereby paid labour is replaced by unpaid labour? How does it affect the reproduction of various kinds of labour power? How does it affect workers' ability to struggle for higher wages? Can unpaid labour be a basis for the sustenance of households, as some would want to believe in their celebration of 'household capitalism?'[7] Could workers turn to their useful labour as a source of subsistence in these times of high and persistent unemployment? Could unemployed workers, in other words, use some of the survival strategies of workers in the periphery, transforming their households into small commodity-production units or small-scale food or services providers? Could the intensification of unwaged domestic labour contribute to stretch low wages?

The present crisis of accumulation has reduced millions of persons to poverty or near-poverty levels. The poverty rate reached 15.2 percent in 1983, the highest level since 1966, while the number of people below the poverty level, over 35 million, was the highest since 1964.[8] By 1986, the poverty rate had declined to 13.6 percent and the number of people below the poverty level reached 32.4 million.[9] The persistence of high unemployment rates in many parts of the country during the last few years, however, has had a devastating

---

6   Burns 1977, p. 43.
7   Burns 1977, especially Chapter 3.
8   O'Hare 1985, p. 8.
9   US Bureau of the Census 1987b, p. 1.

impact upon millions of families and their communities.[10] Sluggish economic recovery has been accompanied by the increased immiseration of the working classes. This is reflected primarily in the decline in real wages, especially among young male workers,[11] and the enormous increase in the labour force participation of married women, particularly those with small children – 54 percent of women with children under six were working in 1985, up from 34 percent in 1976[12] and 12 percent in 1950.[13] In 1984, 53 percent of all married women and 65 percent of all married women with school age children (ages six to 17) were in the labour force, up from 24 percent and 28 percent respectively in 1950.[14]

The greatest declines in employment during the late 1970s took place in the manufacturing and construction industries, which offer the best wages for blue-collar workers. As the economy slowly recovers, it does so through sectoral changes and changes in the division of labour which offer relatively few opportunities for most of the presently unemployed. A recent study by Bluestone and Harrison[15] indicates that over 50 percent of the eight million net new jobs created in the United States between 1979 and 1984 paid less than $7,000 a year, well below the 1983 official poverty threshold of $10,178 for a family of four.[16] The decline in the demand for skilled blue-collar labour has been accompanied by some increases in the demand for technical and scientific labour and for relatively unskilled and low-paid production and service labour. According to the Bureau of Labor Statistics, for example, the fastest job growth between 1984 and 1995 is likely to occur mainly in occupations at the top (e.g. lawyers, physicians, and surgeons) and bottom of the occupational hierarchy (waiters and waitresses, janitors, cleaners, etc.) with very few jobs in between:[17]

> Between 1973 and 1986, the number of blue collar workers ... increased by
> only 4.4 percent. In contrast, men's employment in service occupations –
> for example, security guards, orderlies, waiters, day care workers, and jan-
> itors – increased by 36.7 percent.[18]

---

10   See Bluestone and Harrison 1982; Buss, Redburn and Waldron 1983; Piven and Cloward
      1985; Patton and Patton 1984; Congressional Quarterly 1983.
11   Dollars & Sense 1987, pp. 10–11.
12   O'Connell and Bloom 1987, p. 7.
13   Baldwin and Nord 1984, p. 18.
14   Ibid.
15   Bluestone and Harrison 1986.
16   O'Hare 1985, p. 6.
17   US Bureau of the Census 1987a, p. 384.
18   Dollars & Sense 1987, p. 10.

Consequently, large numbers of men are unable to find jobs similar in pay and skills to those they have lost and thus are unable to support their families as in the past. Most working-class households today need the wages of at least two adults to keep above the poverty line; the 'family wage' is no longer a realistic possibility for most workers. This problem has been exacerbated by the fact that employers, to cut labour costs, impose wage cuts at the time new contracts are negotiated and/or demand a lower starting salary for many blue- and white-collar jobs. Working-class poverty is further intensified by cuts in the federal budget which affect badly needed social services. In turn, these cuts generated enormous pressures on state and local budgets which now have to cope with substantial increases in the demand for their help.

The effects of these changes on the lives of millions of people is shown by the evidence beginning to emerge from a variety of reports from special interest groups, research institutes, and congressional documents. Most waged and salaried workers have few if any savings, and their major assets are their homes and cars. Unemployment forces them to cut expenses in food, medical, and dental care. Once unemployment insurance, compensation, and severance pay are exhausted, many go on welfare or have to rely on food stamps; they use up their savings and, eventually, after missing payments on cars or other credit purchases, they lose these goods. Many also lose their homes when the new jobs they are able to get do not pay enough to keep up mortgage payments. A new category of poor appears in the soup lines; the 'new poor', who until recently had been relatively prosperous, now join the ranks of those in need of food and shelter. The estimated national total homeless population ranges between 240,000 to 1,000,000.[19] Long-term unemployment also has devastating effects on people's physical and psychological well-being; domestic violence of all kinds, alcohol abuse, insomnia, depression, and suicide increase under these conditions.[20]

I have described in some detail the consequences of unemployment to highlight the vulnerability of working class households in this country. Among vast sectors of the labouring masses in the periphery, households may be appropriately conceptualised as 'income-pooling units' only partially dependent on a wage for their survival.[21] In the context of the United States, the degree of proletarianisation of the population has led to a situation in which the concept of 'wage-dependent households' might be more appropriate to characterise the

---

19   Congressional Quarterly 1983, p. 135.
20   Congressional Quarterly 1983, p. 129; see also Buss et al. 1983.
21   For a thorough exploration of the significance of this concept, see Smith, Wallerstein and
        Evans 1984.

conditions under which most workers live. Given that all households – regardless of class – include as a component of their total income goods and services produced by domestic labour (which is paid labour in its entirety only in the households of the very wealthy), there is a general abstract sense in which all households can be viewed as income-pooling units. But the experience of the unemployed in the United States shows their virtually *total* dependence on wages for basic survival. This is exactly what advanced proletarianisation means: the separation of the vast majority of the population from any access to viable means of production which, unavoidably, generates total dependence on wage income.

While some households may have some resources which allow them to survive without a wage or salary input (e.g. rental income, income from farms or from other businesses), it is unlikely that the vast masses of the unemployed will be able to pull themselves up by their bootstraps through the use of their own labour. It is the case that when real wages begin to fall, some households can stretch their wages through an intensification of domestic labour. Women work harder, things are repaired and mended, and all household members make do with less. This is contradicted, however, by the fact that drastic declines in real wages, such as those that have taken place in recent years, have been reflected in the enormous increase in female employment and 'dual-pay-check' families. As is obvious, women's employment, especially when it is full time, reduces women's ability to intensify home production of use values to stretch the wage.[22] Furthermore, while women's wages keep households afloat while their unemployed husbands seek work, their lower salaries are frequently not sufficient, in the long-run, for mortgage payments and other debts. Once unemployment benefits are exhausted, households are left in a desperate situation unless other members can find paid employment.

The preceding discussion highlights the fact that, in the circumstances created by advanced capitalist development, the sale of labour power by at least one wage earner is *the* major condition that allows for the productive use of unwaged labour in the household – for the production of goods and services for internal consumption and for the market as well; 'reproductive activities are possible only insofar as they come in contact with the capitalist wage relationship'.[23] In wage- or salary-dependent households, waged labour is the condition for the productive combination of unwaged labour and means of household production.[24] A second important condition for the productive use of unwaged

22   Waite 1981, pp. 11–12; Smith 1990, pp. 128–41.
23   Smith 1984, p. 67.
24   Gimenez 1982.

labour is the possession of skills. Proletarianisation, as Braverman and others after him have shown, entails a constant process of skilling and deskilling of workers.[25] As new skills emerge commanding high wages, in time they are fragmented into their component elements, lowering workers' skills and wages.

The universalisation of commodity production also implies, at this level of analysis, the relative deskilling of domestic workers. While what Cowan has called the 'industrialisation of housework'[26] entails the learning of new skills to use modern household technology, it also entails the loss of skills that could have been used to turn domestic labour towards market-oriented production. What is more important, the cheapening of some basic subsistence goods – food and clothing – through mass production, self-service, and the availability of cheap imports makes it impossible for home-produced goods to compete in the market with mass-produced goods, even if people still had the necessary skills. Most working-class households in the United States could not become cottage industries when unemployment strikes, not only because of the lack of financing the household's wages could initially provide, but also because market conditions and the relative lack of skills of most people would make that transition extremely difficult. This is in clear contrast to the countries of the periphery, where cottage industries continue to flourish as a crucial source of supplementary income. In the United States, even if unemployed workers have skills (furniture making and repair, auto repair, dressmaking, etc.), the average salaried or waged household cannot afford such services and opts for mass produced goods or the use of domestic unwaged work to repair cars and some appliances. The very high (from the standpoint of working-class households) hourly wages of service people have pushed more and more people to learn how to do those things themselves. The peculiar dialectics of waged and unwaged labour under conditions of extreme proletarianisation as in the United States have thus led to the relative economic uselessness of unwaged useful labour. The production of use values (for household consumption or for the market) via useful unwaged labour is thus subordinate to the production of exchange values via waged or salaried labour.

The rule of capital is thus manifest in the subordination of unwaged to waged labour, of useful labour to abstract labour. Unemployment would not be a threat if households were only partially dependent on wages or salaries and could switch their income from wage to non-wage income when unemployment strikes. The success of proletarianisation is the stripping of households of

---

25   Braverman 1974.
26   Cowan 1983.

their income pooling capacity insofar as it could be used to ensure economic survival outside the wage relation. Production, therefore, determines reproduction in ways that vary with employment status and location within the various strata in which propertyless workers are distributed. Total dependence on a wage or salary to survive means that employment and wage/salary levels condition the ability of households to engage in some or all the forms of unwaged labour previously discussed:

a) domestic labour engaged in the production of use values for household consumption (i.e. labour that enters in the process of physical and social reproduction at the daily and generational levels),

b) domestic labour engaged in consumption work (shopping, self-service, and transportation of purchases),

c) domestic labour engaged in the production of use values for home maintenance and improvements (i.e. labour that reproduces households' 'infrastructure'), and

d) domestic labour engaged in the production of goods and/or services for the market (e.g. 'cottage industries' of all kinds, word processing, childcare).

Class and Intra-class Differences in the Use of Unwaged Labour for the Process of Physical and Social Reproduction

How does the differential ability of households to take advantage of their unwaged labour affect the reproduction of the capitalist class and of the various socio-economic strata (i.e. 'poor,' 'working class,' 'middle class,' 'upper-middle class,' etc.) in which the working class (i.e. the class of propertyless waged/salaried workers) is fragmented at the level of market relations?

Recent economic changes in the United States resulting in declining living standards in the working class have been accompanied by an increase in the concentration of income at the top, the growth of a small but privileged 'upper-middle class sector' (with incomes above \$47,000), and the 'shrinking of the middle class'.[27] Upper and upper-middle class sectors represent a growing market for specialty stores; for hand-made, labour-intensive and relatively unique goods (e.g. pottery, 'wearable art'); and for expensive personal services. Those who can use type *d* unwaged labour to take advantage of these narrow markets are generally persons with specialised skills from 'middle class' back-

---

27   Rose 1986, pp. 9–11.

ground; they may be suddenly unemployed professionals or skilled workers who can successfully use their skills, often blessing the day they lost their jobs. But my major concern in this essay is not with the small 'cottage industry' sector catering to the needs of the privileged. Instead, I am concerned with the conditions that affect the ability of wage-dependent households to use their labour resources to survive, to engage in the tasks of physical and social reproduction, and to improve their quality of life.

The dialectics of waged and unwaged labour among the steadily employed and more affluent sectors of the working class are quite different from those which obtain among the poorer sectors, particularly those afflicted with periodic lay-offs, unemployment or underemployment. Among the employed and relatively affluent working classes, households have the ability to use types *a*, *b* and *c* unwaged labour to produce a standard of living that would be unaffordable at market prices. As indicated earlier, because of market conditions that make it difficult for most households – except those of the very wealthy – to pay a living wage for labour needed for household repairs, cleaning, improvements, etc., and because of manufacturers' and retailers' cost-cutting strategies, most adults in the United States engage in increasingly larger quantities of unwaged labour inside and outside their homes. These forms of unwaged labour are wage or salary-dependent; the amount of unwaged labour time households can generate to their advantage depends on their levels of income and the amount of labour time already exchanged for that income. There is, in other words, a direct relationship between income level, the quantity and kind of unwaged labour households can generate, households' standard of living, and the quality of labour power they reproduce.

Given that women are the major providers of types *a* and *b* unwaged labour, their employment lowers the amount of housework they do, as time-use surveys show.[28] When real wages fall and married women enter the labour force, and when single mothers work, the quantity of type *a* unwaged labour available falls (e.g. fast foods replace homemade meals); type *b* declines in some respects (e.g. food shopping); and the overall quality of life may decline, particularly for single mothers. Depending on the size of their combined income and stage in the life cycle, working couples might experience a decline in the quantity of home-cooked meals and housecleaning, and increases in types *b* and *c* unwaged labour resulting in home improvements and repairs. In low-income dual-earner working-class households, the quantity of waged-labour time required for basic survival increases without providing the monetary basis

---

28   Waite 1981, pp. 11–12.

for the use of unwaged labour to their advantage. Under these conditions, the quantity of types *a*, *b*, and *c* unwaged labour these households can use is likely to decline, especially type *c* labour because it requires money for the purchase or rental of tools, materials, etc. While affluent 'dual-career' households can simply purchase domestic labour and other services, low-income 'dual-pay-check' working-class households have to make do with less, sacrificing standards of consumption and childcare. 'Dual-career' households and, in general, affluent upper-middle class households are able to substitute services purchased directly from individuals (e.g. servants, baby-sitters, gardeners) or from companies that provide services (housecleaning, lawn care, childcare, repair of household appliances, etc.), for some of the socially necessary labour time that would have to be spent in types *a* and *b* unwaged labour. At the same time, they can increase the quantity of time spent in less arduous and more appealing forms of *b* and *c* unwaged labour, thus improving considerably their home environment and their quality of life. On the basis of the preceding discussion, it is possible to make the following generalisations pertinent to households of waged and salaried workers who are, in terms of their location in the relations of production, propertyless workers (i.e. they do not own income-producing property or capital):

1) Dual-earner households – given time constraints and women's primary responsibility for domestic labour – are likely to experience a decline in the quality of life if their ability to use type *a* unwaged labour to their advantage declines, without being accompanied by the ability to substitute market services.

2) The higher the total household income, the greater the ability of households to substitute (at least on a part-time basis) purchased services for type *a* unwaged labour and to use types *b* and *c* unwaged labour to their benefit.

3) The higher the socio-economic status (i.e. ranking based on levels of income, education, and type of occupation) the greater the ability of households to substitute purchased services for most or all of the most arduous and less creative forms of types *a, b* and *c* unwaged labour, and the greater the ability to use all three types of unwaged labour primarily for the considerable improvement of their quality of life.

The ultimate product of unwaged domestic labour, in its three forms, is the physical and social reproduction of social classes on a daily and generational basis. As income levels rise, householders tend to relieve themselves of the labour that enters into physical reproduction, by purchasing services through the market, or through relations of personal dependence with servants. In other words, the greater the household's income level, the greater the ability

of people to spend 'quality time' with their children, and the better able they
are to concentrate on the pleasant tasks of social reproduction through enhancing their personal development, social life, and home environment. This process of structural and functional differentiation[29] in the context of unwaged
domestic labour relations is fluid and its outcome fluctuates, in propertyless
households, with socio-economic status, the number of adults who work, and
marital status.

Unless income levels are high, single parents – especially single mothers –
are less likely to be able to focus on the social dimensions of domestic unwaged
labour. In very affluent single- or dual-earner households, women and men are
unlikely to engage in unwaged labour, except those types dealing with social
reproduction. And in very wealthy households (i.e. capitalist households), in
contrast to what takes place in working class households, even household management can be left to butlers and housekeepers, while the lady of the house is
concerned exclusively with the tasks of social reproduction on a daily and generational basis (and even those are likely to be shared with social secretaries,
governesses and tutors).[30]

Among the propertyless classes[31] – regardless of their 'socio-economic status' at the level of market relations – waged/salaried labour is the necessary
condition for people's access to the material conditions required for their physical and social reproduction on a daily and generational basis. The class that
controls the means of production also controls people's access to the conditions of reproduction. At the level of market relations, this means that employ-

---

29   By process of structural and functional differentiation I mean the process whereby house-
     hold structure changes to incorporate other people who, on a temporary or semi-perman-
     ent basis, carry on activities that were previously the sole responsibility of the adult mem-
     bers of the household.

30   Gimenez 1978, pp. 315–19.

31   Throughout this chapter I make a distinction between *social classes*, based on house-
     holds' and individuals' relationship to the means of production (a concept of social class
     based on Marxist theory), and *socio-economic status*, the ranking of individuals on the
     basis of indices arbitrarily constructed using type of occupation, income and education
     (a concept based on sociological theory). From the standpoint of Marxist theory, those
     who own nothing but their labour power – no matter how skilled that labour power may
     be – are members of the working class. At the level of the market, the differences in socio-
     economic status *within* the working class are large: people who are working class in terms
     of their location in the relations of production can be 'middle class' or 'upper-middle
     class' in terms of socio-economic status. I chose, therefore, to use the concept of prop-
     ertyless class to indicate that households dependent on wages or salaries for survival face
     common constraints, despite socio-economic status differences in their standard of liv-
     ing.

ment conditions the exercise of unwaged labour; in the absence of a wage, unless the state intervenes, people are left to fend for themselves in ways that vary according to the place of their countries in the world-system.

In core countries, there are welfare systems that make it possible for the unemployed, and those unable to participate in the labour force, to survive at a minimum level of subsistence. The welfare state intervenes to pay for the physical (but not the social) reproduction of the labour force at substandard levels – so that many households are forced to reproduce the unemployable layers of the reserve army of labour. Even when the welfare check and other government transfers are combined with domestic labour, they are frequently insufficient to allow for the economic recuperation of households, and for the reproduction of labour power in a marketable form. In fact, an important effect of long term unemployment and welfare dependency in core countries is the stripping of a large proportion of poor households from their last important economically productive role: the reproduction of labour power. Instead, they simply reproduce people; and people, in themselves, without marketable skills, have no value under capitalist conditions. Each crisis of accumulation increases the population of the unemployed and the unemployable by expelling from the work force – sometimes forever – millions of workers and their families. Their numbers are augmented also through natural increase, thus presenting a problem insurmountable within the parameters of the system.

On Domestic Labour and the Oppression of Propertyless Women

As shown so far in this chapter, the dialectics of paid and unpaid labour in the propertyless class are such that unpaid labour is thoroughly dependent on paid labour for its utility to the household. By propertyless class I refer to the vast majority of people in the United States who depend on wages or salaries for survival; this propertyless class is stratified on the basis of income, education, and occupation. It would be out of place here to enter into the debate about the class location of the so-called middle classes. For the purposes of developing my argument, I will point out that it is possible to differentiate strata at the level of market relations (e.g. working, middle, upper-middle classes), based on individuals' income, education, type of occupation, place of residence, and overall standard of living. On the other hand, at the level of relations of production, these 'classes', insofar as they share a similar relation to the means of production (i.e. they are propertyless), are subject to the constraints inherent in the nature of domestic labour. All households, regardless of socio-economic status, are faced still with the fact that domestic labour is socially necessary and cannot be indefinitely postponed, particularly in the case of childcare or the care of the sick or elderly.

Feminist thinking to date has been focused primarily on the fact that domestic labour is defined as *women's labour* and has, as such, important and real negative effects on the lives of women and on their ability to attain economic and social equality. Even when working full time, women continue to be responsible for most of the housework and childcare. To change this situation, feminists have advocated, in addition to equal opportunities for women in the economic sphere, childcare services and changes in the sexual division of labour in the home. Some have perceived both waged and unwaged women's labour as labour controlled by men for their benefit – the material basis of patriarchy.[32]

The origins of the oppression of women today cannot be sought in primordial relations between the sexes or in male conspiracy theories, but in the historically specific ways in which the relationship between men and women are structured as agents of production and reproduction in different social classes and strata within classes. Under capitalism, the class that controls the means of production also controls and determines the relative access of the propertyless classes to the means and conditions for their social and physical reproduction. The development of capitalism, the tendency towards the universalisation of commodity production, and the proletarianisation of the labour force have indeed structured the relations of physical and social reproduction between the sexes and, therefore, domestic labour, in historically specific ways.[33] One important dimension of these processes has been the 'industrialisation of housework'[34] and the erosion of the ability of working-class households to use domestic labour for stretching the wage. A second and relatively overlooked consequence of those processes, with momentous significance for most propertyless women, has been the relative eradication of the servant strata as a stable and widespread participant in the relations of physical and social reproduction. In countries of the periphery, domestic service is still one of the major sources of men's and women's employment, particularly in Latin America.[35] Not only the rich, but also middle- and working-class families have access to domestic servants often on a full-time, live-in basis. The rich and the affluent can afford skilled servants; others can have as live-in servants, in exchange for board and room, orphan girls or the daughters of the rural or the urban poor.

---

32   Hartmann 1981, p. 18.
33   Gimenez 1982 and 1987; Smith 1990, pp. 50–69.
34   Cowan 1983.
35   Boserup 1970; Rollins 1985, pp. 38–48.

In the United States, on the other hand, 'at no time ... have even half of the households in the nation been able to have such help full time'.[36] In the nineteenth century young unmarried women and immigrant women worked as maids, and the 1870 census shows that about one million women – half of the women employed for wages – were domestic workers. During the early twentieth century, decline in immigration and growth in other employment opportunities led to a decline in the number of white women willing to do domestic work: from white and single, the domestic labour force became black and married. The inclusion of domestic work under government regulations requiring the payment of income taxes, social security, and contributions to unemployment funds, increased the cost of domestic servants beyond what most households could afford, pushing such employment underground and making it hard to estimate accurately the number of participants. While having at least a full-time maid was the acknowledged symbol of middle class status in the nineteenth century, today the number of domestic servants has declined drastically (from 28.7 percent of the female labour force in 1900 to 5.1 percent in 1970), and a maid is certainly not required for middle class status.[37]

The hiring of domestic workers on a part-time basis, however, is relatively widespread in the United States. Part of the supply of domestic labour comes from people who work on a temporary, part-time basis (e.g. teenagers, students, housewives who might need extra money for a while, etc.), in addition to those who support themselves through such work. Domestic work is also provided by commercial enterprises who hire wage workers to provide housecleaning services to those who can afford them. Only the very affluent and the capitalist class, of course, can afford full-time, live-in servants. Furthermore, there is a qualitative difference between the hiring of temporary and sporadic domestic help (e.g. baby-sitters, biweekly cleaning women, etc.) and the practice, common among the affluent and the wealthy in core countries and vast sectors of the population in periphery countries, of having live-in domestic servants, or servants who come daily and stay from morning to night.

The examination of the dialectics between waged and unwaged labour sheds light on the fact that *domestic labour*, widely held as one of the material conditions that determine the oppression of women, has a *dual nature* grounded in the material conditions in which it takes place in different social classes. As structured by capitalist development in core countries, *domestic labour is unwaged labour among the propertyless classes*; it is not only one of the historically specific material conditions that determines the oppression of propertyless

---

36   Cowan 1983, p. 119.
37   Cowan 1983, pp. 120–2; Rollins 1985, pp. 53–7.

women under capitalism, but *owes its specificity to the fact that capitalism has eroded the material basis that made possible the existence of a servant strata catering to the needs of vast sectors of the propertyless class during the early stages of capitalist development.* This fact, which is the inexorable outcome of the process of capitalist development as a whole, is also one of the crucial *structural determinants* of the emergence of the women's liberation movement in core countries, of the positive reception of the movement among middle and upper-middle class upwardly mobile, career-oriented white women, and of the directions taken by the feminist analysis of the family and the sexual division of labour.

The women's movement of the late 1960s and 1970s, like all political movements, had in addition to political and ideological determinants, structural, objective determinants. The latter had to do with demographic and economic changes resulting in the presence of a larger-than-ever number of adult and young women in the labour force and in higher education, higher divorce rates, and the military draft which pushed many married women to the labour force. *Another important structural condition was the fact that most propertyless women, regardless of their socio-economic status and level of education were, for all practical purposes, servants in their own homes.* This, in combination with the other factors listed above, was a powerful determinant of the positive acclaim with which Betty Friedan's *The Feminine Mystique* was received.[38] This is a book that captured the discontent of white, affluent, and educated middle class women with the narrowness of their lives as domestic workers secluded in their suburban, appliances/filled homes. This book, which has been called 'the single inspiration of the movement'[39] could not have experienced the success it did if it had not reflected the experiences of millions of women; furthermore, it could not have been written if the material conditions for the 'problem that had no name' not only existed but were widespread. In other words, it would not have been successful if the vast majority of relatively affluent middle class housewives had had access to permanent domestic help on the scale it is available to the upper classes in core countries and to vast sectors of the population in periphery countries.

The other side of the 'industrialisation of housework', which enables women to do what would have required the help of husbands, children, and/or servants in the past, is the demise of domestic servants as regular, expected members of middle class and even working-class households. This has entailed the structural and functional transformation of *all* propertyless women, except the most

---

38   Friedan 1963.
39   Mitchell 1971, p. 52.

affluent, into domestic servants themselves; that is, they are transformed – for all practical purposes – into servants in their own households, servants who, as feminists have pointed out, are not only on call twenty-four hours a day but are also unpaid, engaged in invisible and seemingly valueless labour. Sociologically, one could refer to this process as one of functional integration in which – among the 'middle classes' – two roles, the role of servant (primarily engaged in tasks of physical reproduction) and the role of 'lady of the house' (primarily engaged in management and tasks of social reproduction) became fused into one single role, the housewife. It is, on the other hand, obvious that the vast masses of working class women never played the role of 'lady of the house', while many poor immigrant and non-white women (especially black women) were forced into the servant role.[40]

The ideological construction of domestic labour emphasises the tasks of social reproduction and minimises those of physical reproduction. This, and the fact that feminist analysis tends to focus on the oppression of women 'as women', minimising class differences, has resulted in an analysis of domestic labour that neglects the differential impact upon women's consciousness and political interests of the fact that the tasks of physical and social reproduction do not constitute a monolithic unit oppressing all women. It neglects the variation – within the propertyless class – in the degree of differentiation of such tasks, i.e. the extent to which some housewives must do both or can concentrate mainly on social reproduction, while women from the less privileged strata of the propertyless class must earn a living working for low wages or for other women, neglecting, to some extent, their need to use their labour for their own households.

The structural and functional differentiation between the servant role and the wife role is permanent in the households of the capitalist class and the most affluent strata. Among the propertyless, it varies according to levels of income and education. In capitalist and very affluent households, domestic labour engaged in the tasks of physical reproduction is paid labour; that which deals with social reproduction is partially paid labour. Among most propertyless households, domestic labour is unwaged. As socio-economic status increases, households are more likely to substitute paid labour for their unwaged domestic labour in the less pleasant tasks of physical reproduction. The ability of working women, particularly of career and professional women, to work and have families, depends more on their ability to purchase domestic labour

---

40   These 'roles' are the empirically observable effects of processes of structural and functional differentiation at the level of market and individual relations which, in turn, rest upon underlying capitalist processes and contradictions.

than on a radical reorganisation of the household division of labour.[41] Most working-class women, however, have managed with little or no extra help, to the detriment of the quality of working-class life. While the *need* for childcare services, for example, was always there, the *demand* (backed with money) became visible and grew as middle and upper-middle class women entered the labour force.

The impact of *The Feminine Mystique*, the appeal of the women's movement among white-collar workers and professional women, and the feminist demand for nurseries and childcare services that could allow women to have careers and families at the same time, all reflect the realities of the structure of domestic work in the core capitalist countries. The demand for childcare itself reflects the options open to a society in which an ideological commitment to political equality makes the call for more and affordable servants a political impossibility, at least at the level of public utterance. But practice tends to differ from theory, and in practice those who can afford it hire domestic labour in the quantity and quality they can afford. In fact, the 'liberation' of professional and career women and the ability of vast numbers of working women to work is predicated on the labour of other women, a large proportion of which are immigrant and non-white women.

One of the topics that has occupied a central place in the context of feminist writing, both theoretical and political, has been the domestic conflict emanating from men's resistance to do their fair share in domestic work. The material basis of this conflict (i.e. the fact that most propertyless households rely primarily in the unpaid domestic labour of wives and daughters) is absent from households where most of the tasks of physical reproduction are done by servants or by the waged workers employed by companies providing cleaning and childcare services for a fee. To make the point differently, to the extent feminism in the periphery may be limited to the left or to the scholarly concern of a few – generally foreign-educated – women, this may reflect the widespread availability of domestic servants who work for full-time housewives as well as for working women. In fact, from the standpoint of the average middle class or professional woman from the periphery, the lot of their US counterparts leaves much to be desired, to the extent that they lack permanent domestic help. These remarks, tentative as they are, should highlight the complexity of the structural determinants of the oppression of propertyless women in core and periphery countries while placing at their centre the dialectics between waged and unwaged labour.

---

41   See, for example, Holmstrom 1972.

Conclusion

This chapter has focused on the changing relationship between paid and un-paid labour, and on the significance of the latter for capital accumulation, household survival, and the oppression of propertyless, especially working-class women. Unwaged labour – as a quantity of labour that benefits capital by cheapening the value of labour power and undermining the relative power of the working class – takes place in a variety of settings. At the *level of circulation* of commodities, it is embodied in the vast amount of time consumers spend in self-service activities of all kinds. At the *level of production*, unpaid labour takes place at home; it is labour primarily, but not exclusively, executed by men in the process of assembling and finishing goods. At the *level of physical and social reproduction* (daily and generationally) of different social classes and strata within classes, I also examined the usefulness of unwaged domestic labour for the economic survival of households. I argued that the intense proletarianisa-tion that has taken place in the United States, as a core country, indicates that a conceptualisation of working class households as wage-dependent units would be more useful than the notion of income-pooling units. Proletarianisation and universalisation of commodity production in the United States have abolished the conditions that would, theoretically, allow households to use domestic labour for market-oriented production. Wage-labour is the condition for the usefulness of unwaged labour and, paradoxically, the higher the wage or salary, the greater the contribution of types *b* and *c* of unwaged labour to a household's quality of life. On the other hand, the lower the wage, the greater the eco-nomic importance of type *a* unwaged domestic labour, particularly in families with two adults where only one works outside the home. In dual-earner house-holds (currently the most numerous in the United States), the quantity of type *a* unwaged domestic labour actually declines. The decline in real wages, the fact that women's jobs are generally low-paid, and the lack of affordable child-care force many single mothers to become wards of the state. Their situation highlights the problems created when the price of unskilled labour falls below the cost of its daily and generational reproduction. Under those conditions, given the socially necessary nature of domestic labour, women become full-time domestic workers paid by the state and, in that sense, unwaged domestic labour becomes, for all practical purposes, exceedingly low-paid waged labour.

I have linked the dialectics of waged and unwaged labour to the oppres-sion of women through the analysis of the relationship between the capitalist structuring of the relations of physical and social reproduction between the sexes, and the eventual demise of the servant strata. If domestic servants had continued to be available on a permanent basis for vast sectors of the propertyless class, the women's movement – had it emerged at the time it did – might have taken a different direction, and the content of its ideology and theories might not have been the same. It is not a collusion between men, either individually or collectively, which placed propertyless women into the location of domestic unwaged workers, but the structural effects of the laws of capital accumulation, the secular trends towards a relative decline in the demand for labour combined with the universalisation of commodity production and proletarianisation, mediated by the material conditions of physical and social reproduction. Finally, I have shown the theoretical importance of examining class differences and intra-class differences, not only in the relative ability of households to use unwaged domestic labour for their benefit, but also in the extent to which the tasks of physical and social reproduction become structurally and functionally differentiated or integrated.

Integration entails the oppression of women as full-time domestic servants in their own households. Theoretically, this could be ameliorated by men agreeing to shoulder part of the burden (becoming part-time servants themselves), with help from friends and relatives, or with inexpensive paid full- or part-time domestic servants. I use the word 'servant' not pejoratively, but to call attention to the fact that most of the tasks of physical reproduction are menial work, something that tends to be obscured when euphemisms such as 'housekeeper' are used. While people in the core countries may treat their domestic help in ways far more democratic than in periphery countries, the social differences and the differences in social and economic power between those who hire and those who do the work do not disappear.

Differentiation, on the other hand, increases with level of wages and socioeconomic status, resulting in substitution of unwaged for paid domestic labour within the sphere of physical reproduction, while householders reserve for themselves the more pleasurable aspects of social and physical reproduction. While within the propertyless class differentiation fluctuates according to many factors impossible to examine in this chapter (e.g. the level of education of women, age, stage in the life cycle, etc.), it is institutionalised within the capitalist class and the top layers of the petty bourgeoisie and socio-economic stratification: here, domestic labour in charge of physical reproduction is always paid labour, while the tasks of social reproduction are shared in ways likely to vary with age, number of children, level of education, social expectations, and so forth.

Given the fact that the socialisation of housework and childcare is unlikely to become a reality in the near future, the conflict between waged and unwaged labour as it exists today could theoretically be resolved, in the absence of widespread affordable quality childcare and provision of reliable and inexpensive housecleaning services, by the development of a new servant class, this time composed of immigrants whose willingness to work for low wages, or even for board and room, might make them accessible to working-class households. Women's rate of labour force participation of over 50 percent in the United States is high if compared with past rates, but relatively low if compared to some western and eastern European countries; in 1980 it had reached 54 percent in Austria and the United Kingdom, 56 percent in Denmark, 60 percent in Finland, 71 percent in the USSR, and 69 percent in eastern Europe.[42] Using 1982 data on women's labour force participation, it has been estimated that child-care facilities would considerably increase those rates (e.g. from 47 percent to 59 percent among white women and from 56 percent to 79 percent among black women).[43] Hypothetically, similar increases could be expected to the extent affordable immigrant domestic servants were available. While the percentage of black domestic servants has considerably declined, their place is being taken by immigrant women, especially from the Caribbean and Latin America.[44] The extent to which the increased labour force participation of US women, especially at the upper echelons of the occupational structure, is *already grounded* in the use of domestic servants (many of them immigrant and, perhaps, undocumented) has yet to be empirically established. Their number, however, is likely to be considerable. The uncertain immigration status of many domestic servants renders them vulnerable to exploitation and makes it difficult to find out their numbers and location. This is not pure speculation. Dill alerts us to these possibilities by suggesting that the self-interest of middle class women who want to work could lend support to proposals similar to that made by Anne Colamosca in *The New Republic*, which would seek to increase the availability of household help 'with a government training program for unemployed alien women to help them become "good household workers"'.[45] Clearly, the dialectics of waged and unwaged labour place the issue of domestic servants at the heart of 'the woman question', highlighting the presence of social class contradictions and status antagonisms among women which are generally unacknowledged in the literature. This should call our attention to trends already in the making which reflect, in unexpected ways, the effects of the operation of the world-system upon both core and periphery countries through processes which might reproduce, in the future, periphery patterns in the core (i.e. the

---

42 Sivard 1985, pp. 39–40.
43 O'Connell and Bloom 1987, p. 8.
44 Rollins 1985, pp. 56–7.
45 Cited in Dill 1987, p. 212.

widespread use of domestic servants) while undermining them in the periphery, through proletarianisation and political changes placing domestic servants beyond the reach of the average housewife.

CHAPTER 11

Loving Alienation: the Contradictions of Domestic Work

'Loving Alienation: The Contradictions of Domestic Work', in *The Evolution of Alienation: Trauma, Promise, and the Millennium*, edited by Lauren Langman and Devorah Kalekin-Fishman, Rowman & Littlefield, 2006, pp. 269–82.[1]

Among the many issues that fuelled the development of feminist theory and politics since the late 1960s, domestic labour remains one of the most important, contentious, and seemingly intractable. Scientific and technological change have affected sexuality and reproduction in ways previously thought possible only in the realm of science fiction; and increases in women's labour force participation, levels of education, and political involvement have challenged traditional gender roles and the sexual division of labour. Domestic labour, however, remains a perennial source of household conflict, as well as the basis for sharp theoretical and political debates about its nature and its economic and political significance. Questions – such as is domestic labour enslaving? Empowering? Does it only produce use values? Surplus value? Is it paid? Unpaid? Alienated? Fulfilling? – and many others have answers that vary with feminists' theoretical and political allegiances and, to some extent, with the historical conditions within which they are asked.[2]

In this chapter, I will examine some of these issues from the standpoint of Marxist theory because, as long as capitalism prevails as the dominant mode of production, Marx's work, and the Marxist intellectual and political heritage remain necessary to understand the world in which we live and the processes and contradictions that affect our lives. I will use Marx's theory of alienation to examine the changing nature of domestic labour today, as its commodification deepens among the upper-middle classes in the advanced capitalist countries, while in the vast majority of households its basic features remain relatively unchanged. Domestic labour, I will argue, should be conceived dialectically, as

---

1 This chapter builds upon the analysis of the different types of domestic labour and the depiction of class and intra class variations in domestic labour presented in Chapter 10.

2 For a useful bibliography of the domestic labour debate, see 'Appendix', pp. 467–9 in Hamilton and Barrett 1986.

a unity of opposites, characterised by negative and positive features whose saliency and effects vary according to households' location in the class structure and the socio-economic stratification system.[3]

Conflicting views about domestic labour, consequently, reflect its contradictory nature and the experiences and perceptions of women in different socio-economic strata. The structural and ideological complexity of domestic labour needs to be acknowledged in order to understand its manifest and latent effects upon people's consciousness and development, its political and ideological significance, and the potential political implications of its growing commodification. I will also argue that, objectively and in light of Marx's theory of alienation, domestic labour is not alienated labour; however, under certain historical conditions it does become alienated labour, with important political and ideological effects.

Alienation and Domestic Work

As the vast literature on alienation shows, there is no agreement about its meaning, causes, and nature. Alienation has been conceived as an inherently subjective phenomenon, as a set of psychological states, as observable behaviour, or as an objective phenomenon, inherent in specific macro-level social processes and social relations, independent of the subjective feelings that may be correlated with it.[4] Following Seeman, who defined alienation as feelings of 'meaninglessness', 'normlessness', 'powerlessness', 'isolation', and 'self-estrangement',[5] sociologists tend either to psychologise alienation, or to see it mainly as the subjective effect of social conditions. Objective and subjective analyses of alienation, however, can be combined in ways that vary with researchers' aims and theoretical perspectives. In this essay, I will rely on Marx's theory of alienation, which defines it as an objective phenomenon with important, but not predetermined subjective effects, and identifies its objective basis within the core structures and relations of the capitalist mode of production. Marx's theory of alienation is both a philosophical anthropology – for Marx grounds the genesis of humanity in the dialectical relationship between people

---

3   I will develop my arguments at the highest level of abstraction, the level of the mode of production. I am fully aware that, at the level of analysis of concrete social formations, the meaning and organisation of domestic labour vary also according to historically specific sources of inequality, such as culture, race, ethnicity, national origin, immigrant status, and so forth.

4   For an excellent and comprehensive examination of theories of alienation, see Israel 1971.

5   Seeman 1959.

and nature through labour – and a critique of capitalism as a mode of production that subverts the self-realising potential inherent in labour, interposing between people and nature the capitalist organisation of production and mode of surplus appropriation.[6] Capitalism is the culmination of historical processes through which ownership of the means of production became eventually concentrated in a few hands, while the vast majority of people became propertyless, reduced to having to support themselves by selling their labour power. Under these conditions, labour is objectively alienated because all workers, whether wage or salary earners, are: a) alienated from nature; i.e. from the means of production, the material conditions necessary for their physical and social reproduction; b) alienated from their own selves, because they not only must tailor their education and skills to whatever sells, but also because a vast proportion of workers are deprived of even the possibility of developing skills, let alone finding out what their inclinations and talents might be; c) alienated from the labour process itself, now controlled, organised, and reorganised by their employers; d) alienated from their fellow workers, because they are forced into relentless competition within and outside the work place; and e) alienated from their products, which are not of their own choosing and do not belong to them, but to the owners of the means of production.[7]

The physical and psychological effects of alienated labour are such that workers live a divided existence, feeling really alive when not working and not really living while at work. As Marx notes,

> man [the worker] only feels himself freely active in his animal functions of eating, drinking and procreating, at most also in his dwelling and dress, and feels himself an animal in his human functions. Eating, drinking and procreating, etc. are indeed truly human functions. But in the abstraction that separates them from the other round of human activity and makes them into final and exclusive ends they become animal.[8]

Marx's statement captures some of the effects of the profound division between work and life that is the lot of most working people in advanced capit-

---

6   The main elements of the theory are found in Karl Marx's *Economic and Philosophical Manu-scripts*, of which there are a variety of translations. I have used in this chapter the section on 'Alienated Labor', in McLellan 1977, pp. 77–87, but there are important elaborations and insights in the rest of Marx's work. The best Marxist secondary sources are Ollman 1971 and Mészáros 1970.

7   Marx 1977, pp. 81–7.

8   Marx 1977, p. 81.

alist countries; it is a powerful indictment of alienated labour, useful to understand some of the problematic aspects inherent in domesticity. It is, however,
somewhat limited in its scope because it undialectically stresses the negative
dimensions of private life and domestic activities and overlooks their potential
for generating, as I will argue later in this chapter, experiences, social practices,
and forms of consciousness antithetical to capitalism.

Underlying Marx's concept of alienation is the assumption that labour plays
a fundamental role in human development, for in the process of transforming nature, people transform themselves, developing new talents and needs, in
a never-ending cycle of change and expansion of human knowledge, powers,
and self-awareness. Free, non-alienated, self-directed labour, however, is structurally impossible for everyone within capitalism, while alienation is inherent
in the objective conditions within which most people work. Alienation, therefore, is an objective attribute of waged and salaried labour; it is independent
of individuals' perceptions and feelings about their work experiences because
it is grounded in the material social relations through which labour power is
partially produced,[9] sold, bought, and used. It follows that the state of non-
alienation is not synonymous with workers' subjective feelings of happiness
or job satisfaction; it presupposes qualitatively different relations of production, which, while objectively non-alienated, may or may not be perceived
as such. Marx's conception of the relationship between objective conditions
and subjectivity is thoroughly dialectical. We must be aware, he argues, of the
difference between objective processes and the forms in which people understand those processes and their effects: 'It is always necessary to distinguish
between the material transformation of the conditions of production, which
can be determined with the precision of natural science, and the legal, political, religious, artistic, or philosophic – in short, ideological forms in which
men become conscious of this conflict and fight it out ... Consciousness must
be explained from the contradictions of material life'.[10] In light of these meth-

---

9   Against the widespread view that domestic labour reproduces mainly labour power, I
        argue that it primarily reproduces the members of different social classes; e.g. the own-
        ers of capital, or the labourers themselves, the present and future generations of owners
        of labour power, and only partially produces labour power by instilling capacities, beha-
        viours, attitudes, etc. which become then reinforced or undermined by the institutions
        where concrete labour powers are produced such as schools, colleges, the workplace, gov-
        ernment training programmes, etc.

10   Marx 1970a, p. 21. Whether alienation is universal under capitalism, i.e. whether non-
        alienated social relations, experiences and forms of consciousness are possible in cap-
        italist society is a matter scholars continue to debate. In this chapter, I rely on Marx's
        dialectic and materialist conception of the relationship between material conditions and

odological principles, it is possible to understand some of the paradoxes of the work experience under capitalism: not all objectively alienated workers (e.g. factory workers, teachers) are unhappy, subjectively alienated (though the vast majority might be so), and not all objectively non-alienated workers (e.g. most domestic workers, the self-employed) are subjectively fulfilled and happy about what they do. It is through the analysis of the contradictory conditions within which people work that we can seek to understand their subjective positive or alienated feelings and perceptions.

Waged and salaried labour are not the only forms of labour under capitalism. Domestic labour is just as important and even more widespread because, while at any given time a proportion of the population is partially or fully outside the workforce (e.g. the unemployed, the elderly, part-time workers, children, people on welfare, etc.), most individuals engage in some form of domestic labour for themselves and their families, and/or for others. Domestic labour is necessary labour; no mode of production is conceivable without it because it comprises basic tasks involved in the social and physical, daily and generational reproduction of social classes and strata within classes, tasks that have been and continue to be primarily the responsibility of women. In capitalist societies, domestic labour refers to a range of diverse activities which fall within these categories:

1) the production of use values (goods and services) for household consumption in the process of physical and social reproduction at the daily and generational levels (e.g. housecleaning, cooking, childcare, play, adult sexuality, and psychological/emotional support, etc.);

---

consciousness: 'It is not the consciousness of men that determine their existence, but their social existence that determines their consciousness' (Marx 1970, p. 21). Changes in material conditions, for example, experiences possible outside the workplace, have the potential for generating forms of consciousness critical of taken for granted capitalist social relations and possibilities. This is why I argue that the kinds of experiences possible in the processes entailed in the domestic production of use values to be shared with family, friends, neighbours, and so on, are non-alienated experiences that give a glimpse of what an alternative form of social organisation could be. Capitalism exploits and alienates, but also allows for experiences that generate resistance and, sometimes, political mobilisation and collective organisation, depending on the balance of power among classes, the political culture, the historical conditions at that moment, and so on. Capitalism is full of contradictions; as it constantly changes social relations and experiences, it also allows for people's ability to carve spaces for self-direction, for creative and artistic endeavours and community building, with the potential to generate forms of consciousness, experiences and social relations antithetical to capitalism. Self-directed domestic work has the potential to produce one of those spaces.

2) consumption work (e.g. shopping, self-service, consumer self-education, transportation of purchases, unpacking, etc.);

3) production of use values for home maintenance and improvements; and

4) production of exchange values, or goods and/or services for the market (e.g. 'cottage industries', word processing, piecework, etc.).

Domestic activities produce some of the necessary subjective and objective conditions within which social classes and strata within classes are partially reproduced.[11] The network of social relations within which people engage in domestic work can be fruitfully conceptualised, at the highest level of abstraction, as the 'domestic mode of social reproduction'. The Marxist concept of the mode of production refers to the historically specific combination of the elements of the production process – labour, the subject of labour, and means of production – through social relations between the agents of production (e.g. relations between capitalist and workers), mediated by their relationship to the means of production.[12] The concept of the domestic mode of reproduction, in turn, refers to the historically specific combination of labour and the material basis of physical and social reproduction through social relations between the agents of reproduction; i.e. relations between people mediated by their relations to the material conditions of reproduction.[13]

These relations of production and reproduction are not purely voluntaristic and intersubjective, because they rest upon a material base that exerts its effects whether or not those affected are aware of them or believe in them.[14] Regardless of whether or not individual women believe in it as an element

---

11   All modes of production presuppose a mode of reproduction; i.e. a set of social relations within which the present and future members of the different classes, strata within classes and other relevant social locations are reproduced daily and generationally. Within capitalism, for example, besides households of various kinds (e.g. nuclear families, single-parent families, extended families, etc.), schools, churches, factories, eating facilities, etc. enter into the process of reproduction. This is why I state that domestic labour, despite its crucial importance, is *partially* responsible for the process of social reproduction because it shares that task with other institutions in ways that cannot be theoretically predicted but need to be historically and empirically established.

12   Althusser and Balibar 1970, pp. 173–5.

13   The material conditions of reproduction refer to the biological conditions of reproduction, to the dwelling or household infrastructure, and the durable and perishable goods that enter into domestic activities. Just as capitalists' ownership of the means of production is the basis of their power over the propertyless, in the context of domestic relations the balance of power rests usually with men, for they are more likely to provide most of the economic resources with which households are set up and the commodities necessary for the household's upkeep are purchased.

14   Althusser and Balibar 1970, p. 173.

of the social structure, gender inequality underlies all relations of reproduction. It could thus be argued that domestic workers, who are generally women, work under exploitative and, by implication, objectively alienating conditions. Some feminists have argued that the very basis of gender inequality is located in male control over women's labour power, sexuality, and reproductive capacity, resulting in women's economic dependence and primary responsibility for domestic labour, including childcare.[15] This is a one-sided, undialectical analysis of domestic relations which ignores variations in the organisation of domestic labour related to social class and socio-economic status, and does not acknowledge its contradictory nature. It underestimates women's agency and the benefits (not just economic, but social, psychological, and emotional) that might accrue to them and their children from a stable domestic setting, and overestimates men's agency, interpreting the unanticipated and objectively structured effects of gender inequality as a principle of social organisation, as if they were the intended effects of individual men's actions, thus underestimating men's genuine needs for affection and caring and non-utilitarian reasons for entering into domestic relations of reproduction. Furthermore, this view does not allow for the possibility of relations that are both objectively unequal, given men's usually greater economic resources, and at the same time objectively complementary, the basis for economic cooperation and reciprocity and, subjectively and in practice, rewarding, the material basis for non-market, non-utilitarian, caring forms of social relations, consciousness, and experiences. Besides inequality, other criteria would have to be met to conclude that domestic labour is alienated labour. But it is not possible to argue that all women subordinate their personal development to the acquisition of domestic labour skills in order to survive, lack control over the domestic labour process, do not decide what they will produce, and find themselves in permanent competition with other domestic workers. Domestic labour might be objectively oppressive because it is grounded in unequal relations, but it usually lacks the main features of objectively alienated labour in the Marxist sense. The issue of the ownership of the products of domestic activities is more difficult to theorise because most of what domestic workers produce is intangible; its consumption is a social, rather than an individual act, embedded in networks of social relations that cannot be deduced purely from gender inequality because they may include domestic workers related to the household only through market relations. Although 'the family' is the most prevalent form of the domestic mode of

---

15   These ideas are typical of the socialist feminist literature of the 1970s and early 1980s. See, for example, Eisenstein 1979.

reproduction in advanced capitalist societies, it is not the best point of departure to establish whether or not domestic labour is alienated labour because
it directs attention to intimate relations, conflicts, etc., thus reducing domestic
labour primarily to a couple/family issue. Intimate relations are indeed significant for any analysis of domestic labour, but they are a subset, albeit the most
prevalent, within the larger set of domestic relations of reproduction historically possible in capitalist societies. Domestic relations of reproduction vary
according to household composition, the relationship between the mode of
production and the domestic mode of reproduction, and the location of households in the class structure and the social stratification system.

Household composition affects the combination of domestic labour power
and the means of reproduction in deceptively obvious ways; for example,
single persons and single parents are likely to have less time for domestic
work than couples, extended families, or groups of families or of related and
unrelated persons who decide to live communally. And gender inequality,
just as obviously, affects that combination through a sexual division of labour
that allocates to women primary responsibility for domestic work. But neither
gender inequality nor household composition, either in themselves or together,
account for the relations of reproduction that might be found in a given household, for those relations are also determined by the household's class location
and location in the socio-economic stratification system that divides classes
in strata of different socio-economic status (SES). Under capitalism, the basic
necessities of life, the material conditions for physical and social reproduction, are commodities; i.e. they have to be purchased in the market. Consequently, the mode of production determines the mode of domestic reproduction because access to the means or material conditions of reproduction
requires either economic self-sufficiency (which capitalism precludes for the
vast majority of the people), the ownership of capital (or, at least, enough inherited wealth to be economically independent), or the sale of labour power in
exchange for wages or salaries. Whether people marry or form stable unions,
with whom, when, the number of related or unrelated adults who live in a
household, how many are employed, family size and, therefore, the kinds of
division of labour and relations of domestic reproduction they enter into are
matters significantly shaped by their social class and SES and by the effects
of the ups and downs of the capitalist economy. To be sure, other important factors affect the conditions within which people are able to engage in
domestic labour – such as race, ethnicity, culture, age, and so forth – which,
in turn, modify, often in very significant ways the effects of class and gender
divisions. But I am developing my argument at the highest level of abstraction, theorising the ways in which the capitalist mode of production affects the

domestic mode of reproduction, and the set of structurally possible relations of reproduction within which people engage in domestic labour. The underlying premise of my argument, as stated above, is that these relations vary according to class and SES, variations that can be captured in ideal types useful to identify the different networks of social relations within which people do domestic labour.

1.   Among the homeless and the extremely poor, who lack access to most of the material conditions of reproduction, domestic labour is reduced to a minimum. It is often replaced, however, by networks of mutual aid and caring which help people survive.

2.   The propertyless population (i.e. those who depend on the sale of their labour for economic survival) is heterogeneous; the vast majority is employed and objectively located in the working class. There are, however, vast income, educational, and occupational (i.e. SES) differences within this class, as well as differences in household composition (e.g. nuclear families, single-parent families, extended families) and the number of working adults (e.g. one- or two-pay-check families, dual- or single-career families, etc.). A small proportion lives below or near the poverty level, some primarily on welfare, others earning minimum wage or close to it.

   a.   Given their meagre economic resources, and the likelihood that it is with the wages of two adults that those households make ends meet, the working poor and near poor are likely to spend far less time in domestic labour than the more affluent, with childcare comprising the bulk of domestic activities. They are also likely to be far less skilled in all domestic tasks, for domestic labour, like all forms of labour, is an acquired skill. A significant proportion of the poverty and near-poverty population are households headed by single women with children, many of them depending on public assistance (e.g. welfare, food stamps) for survival. In these households, state policies determine access to the material conditions of reproduction, and domestic labour takes place in a context of oppressive relations in which women's ability to acquire domestic labour skills and use them productively, for themselves and their families, depends on political and economic processes beyond their control. On the other hand, as domestic labour is not just about the production of use values and services, but about the expression of feelings, caring, and solidarity, economic scarcity does not necessarily deprive the poor of taking care of others within their possibilities and within a broader social space, through networks of mutual help that take domestic relations of reproduction outside their privatised setting, opening up the opportunity for community organising and the emergence of various forms of political consciousness.

b. In households above the poverty level, the quantity and quality of domestic labour people are able to deploy varies with level of income and number of adult wage/salary earners and this, in turn, affects their standard of living and their quality of life. Households with the resources necessary to engage in the production of abundant and quality use values for themselves (types 1, 2, and 3 above) can theoretically attain a standard of living above what they could afford at market prices. As capitalists cut labour costs and replace waged labour with self-service, domestic work expands and spills outside the household into the time and work involved in self-service, transportation of goods, assembly of unfinished goods at home, etc. Ultimately, however, the quantity and quality of domestic labour adults do depend on their wage/salaried work demands and their income levels. As women increase their labour force participation, the time they can dedicate for the type of domestic work they generally do (1 and 2) declines and with it, the standards of cleanliness and overall quality of life. The range of use values domestically produced has narrowed in the last 100 years, as the commodification of food, clothing, washing, and the expansion of self-service have resulted in the deskilling of domestic labour and the transformation of most domestic workers into consumers of commodities rather than the producers of use values.

Affluent, 'upper-middle class' (single-career or dual-career) households, on the other hand, tend to substitute increasingly large proportions of their socially necessary domestic labour time with the labour of others, paying others for producing and/or purchasing the goods and services they need.

3. Among the wealthy (i.e. the capitalist class, upper class, the elites), domestic labour is primarily something that paid workers do; the wealthy hire some domestic workers to do the work, and others (e.g. butlers, housekeepers, secretaries, etc.) to manage and supervise to make sure the work gets done.

These admittedly sketchy vignettes intend to capture the enormous variety of social relations within which the many tasks that comprise domestic work are done or barely done, as the case may be. Domestic labour has enjoyable, creative, and boring, unpleasant, routine aspects, which closely but imperfectly overlap with the tasks of social (mostly pleasant) and physical (mostly unpleasant) reproduction. Who does what and how varies not only according to gender but, most fundamentally, according to social class and SES. At one extreme, the owners of capital, or of enough wealth to live free of economic worries, are free from alienated labour and from domestic labour. At the other extreme, those who are 'free' from alienated labour, because they are homeless and/or unemployed or unemployable, are also, for all practical purposes, 'free' from domestic labour and unable to attend to their basic needs except at a minimum level. For most people, alienated labour, meaning employment for a wage or a salary is, then, the necessary condition of possibility for domestic labour. This is why domestic labour is, in many respects, a 'middle class' issue, meaning by 'middle class' the vast majority of the people who are neither paupers nor wealthy, among whom a variety of trade-offs and accommodations are made to combine the need to sell labour with the need to allocate some time to domestic labour. People have to carry on the socially necessary tasks of reproduction in their own time, with whatever resources they are able to attain through their labour force participation. It is in this context of relative economic and time scarcity that domestic labour emerges as an ever-present and controversial issue in people's lives, especially among women, who, depending on their class, SES, and degree of labour force participation, are divided about its meaning and significance. Some women consider domestic labour demeaning, degrading, a waste of their valuable time, while others view it as a source of pleasure, creativity, and an expression of love. For most working people who cannot afford domestic help on a frequent, expanded, and permanent basis, despite its shrinking nature due to the inroads of commodification into domestic, everyday life, domestic labour is an ever-present source of stress and conflict between intimate partners and between parents and children. Among full-time housewives it can be experienced as a source of satisfaction and even pride or, as the case may be, as an intolerable burden. Among the more affluent and educated (e.g. in 'dual career' households), domestic labour becomes an inconvenience, something people pay others to do in ways and quantity directly related to their income. It is, therefore, impossible to identify relations of domestic reproduction transcending class and SES differences, which could be used to build a case for considering domestic labour objectively or even subjectively alienated labour. There are no theoretical or empirical grounds to argue that all domestic workers are objectively or subjectively alienated from themselves, from the domestic labour process, from other domestic workers, from the product of their labour, and from species life. When class and SES differences in the organisation of domestic labour are taken into consideration, however, it is clear that domestic labour is alienated labour, in the Marxist sense, only when domestic labour power becomes a commodity and domestic workers become wage workers, employed directly or indirectly (i.e. when their wages are paid by the corporation that sells their services, not by the people whose houses they clean) by those who prefer other uses for their time. Generally (with the exception of the wealthy few who hire full-time, often live-in, domestic workers), people hire domestic workers on a part-time basis, to do mainly tasks of physical reproduction (cleaning bathrooms, appliances, dusting, mopping floors, etc.) widely regarded as unpleasant, routine, and 'never done'. They tend to reserve for themselves the more pleasant tasks of physical and social reproduction, such as childcare, socialisation, play, cooking, entertaining, decorating; i.e. tasks conducive to reproducing class and status, daily and generationally, which can be sources of creativity and self-realisation.

Waged domestic workers are alienated from their own potential, and are exploited by the companies that sell their services, which set rigid routines for the domestic work process, forcing them to work in a pre-established pattern and at a speed calculated to allow them to clean a given number of houses per day; they do not control their labour process, and do not own the product of their labour. Independent domestic workers who sell their labour on their own are oppressed by their employers and sometimes subject to sexual and other forms of abuse.[16]

Domestic labour is not alienated labour, in the Marxist sense, when people do it for themselves, their families, and others who share their lives; they control their work process, they share in the goods and services they produce, and the use values and services they produce are for themselves and people who matter to them. Their activities are not just expenditures of labour time, but are embedded in emotion-laden relationships, thus becoming expressions of marital and parental love and, depending on the task, opportunities for creativity, for parenting, for teaching and learning skills, for self-expression and the building of rewarding kinship and social networks. In the process of working together, adults and children, whatever their education and intellectual interests might be, can engage in various forms of manual labour and learn from each other. Understood holistically, in its material and emotional, physical and social dimensions, domestic labour is an important material base for the persistence and strengthening of intimate caring bonds.

But isn't private life the sphere of 'animal functions'? In the early manuscripts, Marx presents a thoroughly bleak picture of workers' lives, divided between exploited, alienated labour and alienated (i.e. inimical to self-development) fulfilment in 'animal functions' and consumption. However, he acknow-

---

16   Ehrenreich 2002.

ledges that 'eating, drinking and procreating, etc. are indeed truly human functions. But in the abstraction that separates them from the other round of
human activity and makes them into final and exclusive ends they become
animal'.[17] Clearly, by 'the other round of human activity', Marx means labour,
indicating that a truly human, non-alienated life should be a rounded life where
work is part of people's enjoyment and satisfaction of their other needs, so that
work should be embedded in a larger network of social relations. While presci-
ently identifying the separation between work and life that was to characterise
capitalism, and the extent to which the pleasures of private life became a form
of compensation for the indignities of alienated labour, Marx overlooked –
from his own theoretical standpoint – the obvious: people unavoidably experience those pleasures within a network of social relations, some impersonal,
exploitative, and commodified, and some, like intimate, domestic relations,
which partake of both oppressive and humanising features and could potentially transform such activities into truly 'human functions'. Domestic labour is,
consequently, a unity of opposites: objectively, it is oppressive labour because
of the structured inequality between men and women which love, affection,
and intimacy lack the power to abolish, so that it exerts its effects through
women's economic, social, and psychological dependence on their partners,
the unequal division of domestic labour prevalent in most households, and
the detrimental effects upon women's educational and occupational choices
that domestic responsibilities may have. Subjectively, domestic labour may be
evaluated in positive and in negative ways. In contrast to the demands and
stresses of waged, salaried, and even professional work, domestic labour, especially as it pertains to intimate relations and parenting, may be experienced as
a relief from alienated work, as a set of activities that give intimate partners
the opportunity to be creative, to express their love for each other, for their
children and other close relations and friends. Domestic labour can include
activities and experiences of agency, self-realisation, caring, reciprocity, and
cooperation, which are the material basis for the emergence of needs and values critical of the selfish, competitive, and dehumanising world of capitalist
work and social relations. Is domestic labour alienating or fulfilling? Is love an
ideological ploy through which men extract women's labour to their advantage? Is domesticity a pseudo *'Gemeinschaft'* – a set of ideological constructs
that strengthen male domination? There are no true or correct answers to those
questions; they reflect important class and SES divisions among women which
result from ongoing and uneven processes of socio-economic change that open

17   Marx 1977, p. 81.

opportunities for some while, for all practical purposes, denying them for most of the female population. Depending on the kind of work women do, their education, the demands paid work imposes on their time, and the amount of pleasure and opportunities for self-realisation they find in their work, their views of domestic labour will be shaped accordingly. Subjective feelings of alienation can be elicited by the contrast between rewarding aspects of waged/salaried work and the banal, routine dimensions of domestic work, but even the latter might seem appealing, because of their ideological significance as ways of enacting feelings and constructing a life, in relationship to undesirable working conditions. Female and male workers might feel, at different points in time and regardless of the objective conditions within which they work, that one kind of work is, subjectively, more alienating than the other, especially when the more creative aspects of domestic work are contrasted with the alienating features of waged/salaried work. Underlying changes in the ways households allocate time to paid and unpaid work and corresponding changes in people's practices and perceptions, there are macro-level processes resulting in greater wealth and income polarisation, a division in the labour force between the overworked and the underworked, an increase in the number of dual-pay-check and dual-career households, and an intensification in the commodification of the material conditions of reproduction and domestic work.

Conclusion

Dialectically, domestic labour is neither total drudgery, oppression, the terrain of 'animal functions', nor the main destiny to which all women should aspire; it is a set of socially necessary contradictory activities, some unpleasant and some enjoyable and constructive, which allow people to experience and learn a variety of behaviours and expectations that have the potential to fuel the emergence of a critical consciousness, antithetical to the alienated world of capitalist economic and social relations. Following Marx's view of labour as the material source of human development, I argue that domestic labour, undertaken by people on their own behalf, leads to the production of one of the few spaces in capitalist societies where people can labour freely and experience, albeit sporadically, 'species life', meaning the kind of self-directed, free, self-actualising activities that non-alienated labour presupposes.[18] One of the achievements of feminism has been the identification of the unequal,

---

18   See footnote 10.

oppressive relations between men and women, parents and children, which underlie this space and often turn it into a place of exploitation and abuse. The ideologies of love and family responsibilities that compel women to do most of the work need to be demystified, but this critique must be accompanied by the recognition of the positive aspects of domestic relations and activities. The persistent negative evaluation of domestic work nicely complements the increased commodification of domestic work and everyday life, and contributes to strengthen the process of universal commodification in the collective consciousness, so that people increasingly tend to perceive all their personal attributes, feelings, and intimate relations as market transactions.[19] Liberation from domestic responsibilities is a necessary condition for women's ability to attain parity with men, but it is necessary to question whether the commodification of domestic labour is the only and final form that liberation should take. Unavoidably, under capitalism, the ability of some women to fulfil their employment or career goals is predicated on the oppression and exploitation of domestic workers, most of whom are women. The commodification of domestic labour, which is apparently a benign phenomenon fully justifiable in terms of people's 'opportunity costs' and women's needs to develop their potential, has far from benign latent ideological and political effects. The growing servant class strengthens class and status differences, as well as racism, as most domestic workers are women of colour; it fosters feelings of entitlement among the privileged, as well as a 'trained incapacity' to take care of their needs and of their homes among the young; most important, it detaches parenting from shared household activities with children[20] which are an important material base for non-commodified social relations and channels for the meta-communication of culture and social values.

The contradictions of domestic labour, the qualitatively different social spaces that its commodified and non-commodified practices produce, and the conflicting views about its significance rest upon the intensifying contradiction between the changing economy, the growing commodification of domestic activities, and the continuing privatised nature of the reproduction of classes and fractions of classes. The capitalist solution so far has been the intensification of work demands together with the fast growing commodification of the material conditions of reproduction (fast foods, prepared 'gourmet' foods, paid services such as home delivery of dry cleaning, consumer goods, wardrobe coordination and shopping, etc.) and the commodification of domestic

---

19   Radin 196, pp. 1–8.
20   Ehrenreich 2002.

work, including the capitalist provision of domestic services.[21] In the process, the material basis for the development of strong social bonds of love and friendship, especially, but not exclusively, among intimate partners and parents and children, is unavoidably undermined. The feminist solution has been so far the continuing struggle for flexible working hours, legislation supporting parental leaves, and greater equity in the domestic division of labour, an alternative that seems reasonable but which in practice is defeated by the impossibility of satisfying the demands of paid work and domestic work at the same time. The processes of commodification of domestic labour have positive latent effects, such as the demystification of domestic work, separating love for others from the process of surrendering women's selfhood and personal needs, as well as negative latent effects; i.e. the erosion of an ever-shrinking space for the actual experience of concrete labour and cooperation with others in non-market relations which have the potential for generating new needs and visions of a different, more caring, and socially responsible form of social organisation. The Marxist-feminist alternative should be to rescue the positive elements of domestic work, seeking to transcend the real material difficulties most working people face in trying to combine work and family through the development of cooperative solutions (e.g. the creation of partial communities, like cohousing; sharing domestic tasks with friends, relatives, and neighbours, etc.), expanding the sphere of non-instrumental relationships beyond the household, and self-consciously engaging in the historical process of struggles toward placing social reproduction and the satisfaction of human needs, instead of production and the accumulation of capital, as the central goals of economic activity.

---

21   See, for example, Schorr 1991.

CHAPTER 12

Self-Sourcing: How Corporations Get Us to Work without Pay!

'Self-Sourcing. How Corporations Get Us to Work Without Pay!', in *Monthly Review*, Vol. 59, No. 7 (December 2007): 37–41.

The expansion of the capitalist world economy, which accelerated after the fall of the socialist bloc, has produced everywhere drastic changes in the division of labour, occupational structure, and the quality and quantity of labour that is in demand. In the United States, public awareness about the causes of job losses (downsizing, capital flight, offshoring, and outsourcing) has vastly increased since it became widely known that these processes caused the loss not only of blue-collar but also of 'middle-class' and 'upper-middle-class' jobs; i.e. jobs requiring some degree of education and technical competence.

Politicians, academics, the media, and job seekers focus on downsizing, offshoring, and outsourcing as the main causes of unemployment and declining opportunities, even for college graduates. They neglect, however, the impact of *self-sourcing*, a term I apply to the complex and relatively unnoticed effects of the radical reorganisation of our working and non-working time due to the widespread use of information technologies. In this essay, I will explore the significance of self-sourcing, which I define as the intensification of the process of transferring work from the sphere of production, where it is visible and paid, to the sphere of consumption, where it is invisible and unpaid. This process is not new and it is commonly understood as self-service. It is my contention that self-sourcing signals a qualitative change in the forces and the relations of production, consumption, and circulation, which merits theoretical and empirical investigation.

Self-sourcing is a relatively unnoticed basis for the growth of business profits even as average wages and salaries decline; it is an important contributor to unemployment and underemployment. Consumption increasingly requires the performance of tasks previously done by paid workers. Jobs are not disappearing just because of automation, downsizing, and outsourcing; they disappear because they are increasingly done without pay by millions of consumers while the people who previously held those low-paid service and clerical jobs find themselves unemployed and perhaps unemployable.

I first became interested in these issues when, in the mid-1980s, the university where I worked subsidised the faculty's purchase of personal computers, a practice that still continues. As computers were quite expensive in those days, I wondered about the reasons for the university's decision. True, computer use enhanced faculty productivity, as word processing accelerated the writing process. Computers were fun to use and quickly become addictive, the source of a new 'trained incapacity' which made previous forms of writing seem clumsy and cumbersome.

More importantly, the use of computers changed the organisation of intellectual production and the conditions for the reproduction of intellectual labour power. Computers created the need to use them and increased the ability of one person to do many things which, in 'the old days', would have been time-consuming and would have required the labour of staff workers. Faculty members were not given paid time off to retool themselves; instead, they spent a great deal of their theoretically 'free' time learning new skills and reproducing their labour power at higher and higher levels of competence. Through speedup, they increased their future productivity on a scale that would have been difficult to attain without having access to research funds, research assistants, and secretaries. It also became easier for faculty to use the computer for all the paperwork associated with teaching (e.g. bibliographies, memos for students and colleagues, syllabi, letters, book requests, handouts for students, exams, etc.) than to type or write by hand a draft to be typed by department secretaries.

In the last 25 years, computers have become smaller, ubiquitous, inexpensive, and far more efficient. Faculty have become their own typists, secretaries, research assistants, computer experts (to some extent), and webmasters; they hold virtual office hours, teach virtual courses, and increasingly incorporate information technologies in the classroom. The ease with which computers have become integrated into the processes of intellectual production and teaching masks the intermingling between professional and clerical work. The consumption of information technologies by faculty has long-term implications not only for their overall productivity but also for the employment of non-faculty personnel at the university. Faculty have taken on some of the work formerly done by research and teaching assistants, secretaries, typists, data analysts, work-study students, proofreaders, library employees, and others I may not have thought about.

The transfer of unpaid clerical labour to the faculty is irreversible, and its quantity varies with the relative power of individuals and departments. These two kinds of labour, unpaid clerical labour and paid professional labour, are inextricably combined and may not appear as separate domains in the consciousness of most faculty who simply enjoy their self-sufficiency and the ease with which work is done, without reflecting about the kind and quantity of work they do. These observations, which relate the use of computers to a process of speedup or intensification of professional labour via its combination with labour previously done by clerical workers and graduate students in various capacities, might be received with derision, as manifestations of elitism. What is at issue, however, is not what is proper or improper work for somebody with a PhD, but the implications of these changes for the skills, wages, and employment of staff workers. Speedup for the faculty means that, though their job description does not openly state it, they are now expected to perform a variable quantity of unrecognised and unpaid computer-related clerical labour which expands their working day without expanding their pay checks. Faculty speedup, as well as the speedup inherent in most clerical jobs, also means long-term changes in the employment prospects for people who, given their levels of education and training, can only aspire to middle- and low-level clerical employment.

An examination of self-sourcing in the context of educational institutions is a good starting point for theorising the nature of this phenomenon. It is, in some ways, an extension of the now familiar practices of self-service and do-it-yourself, and the uncritical acceptance of the work entailed in many instances of consumption. While these practices are not new, in creating the concept of self-sourcing I want to call attention to the qualitative changes in the amount of work required by consumption. Feminists have called attention to the ways capital benefits from women's unpaid labour within and outside the household.[1] Others have written about the increase in household production, where mostly male unpaid labour enters into the process of delivery and assembly of unfinished goods and materials used in building, remodelling, repairing, and so forth.[2] But the development of online shopping for goods and services, and online self-management of finances, employment benefits, health insurance, etc. have taken self-service to a different plane. Cumbersome and maddening phone menus were an early stage in the process of replacing the paid labour of customer service employees with standardised information often irrelevant to the callers' problems. Phone menus are still there but increasingly direct people to websites where they can find or do what they need by themselves, without the paid labour of someone guiding them through the process.

I still refuse to get an ATM card, because there are people, mostly working women, who need jobs at the bank; and it is only recently that I learned how to pump gas into my car because I thought the teenager who did it needed the

---

1   See, for example, Glazer 1984 and Gimenez 1990.
2   See, for example, Burns 1977.

job. Now the service station, recently purchased by BP, charges $2.50 for full-service. But these, as well as the salad bars and self-service supermarkets, are the earliest forms of a process of transformation in the consumption process which increasingly demands more unpaid work from the consumer while jobs quietly disappear. Supermarkets are now diminishing the number of cashiers while replacing them with self-checking machines.

Consumers now work not only as they select their groceries but also as they bag and check them out, guided by a creepy mechanical voice that instructs them how to do it in alignment with the machine's requirements. Self-service check-in machines are not just in the airports (where passengers, after purchasing tickets online, pay for and receive boarding passes from a machine), but in hotel lobbies (where they dispense room keys and can be used by customers to check themselves out), theatre lobbies, the post office, and, increasingly, in most settings where consumers do what was previously done by paid workers. The last time I travelled by air, the airline employee wanted me (and other passengers as well) to print the baggage claim and attach it to the suitcase! We, the passengers, had no idea how to do it and we had to complain loudly until someone finally took care of our luggage.

The growth of self-service online transactions covering every conceivable consumer need, the use of self-service kiosks in large, big box stores, and the technological upgrading of self-service everywhere can be experienced as fun and self-empowering. The concept of self-sourcing, however, calls attention to the actual significance of these applications of information technologies; they not only restructure occupations through the blurring of job descriptions but also displace paid labour with unpaid labour. The fact that this unpaid labour is, depending on the context, blended in with paid labour (as in the case of teachers), or of such short duration as to be practically invisible, just one more aspect of a pleasurable consumption experience, obscures its significance as a source of profit – corporations and businesses of all sizes save money when they cut labour costs by having the consumers' unpaid labour replace the paid labour of retail clerks, cashiers, travel agents, hotel clerks, bank clerks, etc. While the unpaid labour time of each consumer is minimal, adding up the unpaid labour time of millions of consumers yields substantial cuts in labour costs for businesses, which see their profits grow through their appropriation of unpaid consumption labour.

It may be argued that the lost jobs, which are generally low-skill, low-paid jobs, should not be saved, and that automation opens up jobs with higher skills and better pay. Those better jobs, however, are usually beyond the skills of those who self-sourcing technology replaces and a large proportion of the jobs are likely to be outsourced to countries where labour is cheaper. While the process of self-sourcing is irreversible, it should not be accepted uncritically. Self-sourcing is an important aspect of the 'hollowing out' of the job market, which entails the creation of jobs at the top and the bottom of the occupational structure, while the jobs in the middle are increasingly outsourced, or self-sourced.

Consumers do not know that they are doing more than just consuming goods and services: they are working without pay, entering into relations of circulation and distribution independent of their will and outside their consciousness of themselves as free, self-empowered consumers. If the trend of the future is, as Scott Burns suggested, for consumers to do more of the producers' work, it is important to raise awareness of the productive moment of consumption or 'productive consumption'.[3] While it might provide 'middle-class' consumers with great satisfactions, it turns them into a vast reservoir of unpaid workers who contribute to capital accumulation while consciously reproducing themselves as consumers and objectively reproducing themselves as unpaid workers. At the same time large numbers of working-class people fall between the cracks of the system, condemned to menial, poorly paid jobs, permanent underemployment, or unemployment.

---

3   For an illuminating discussion of the dialectical relationship between production and consumption, see Marx 1970, pp. 193–9.

CHAPTER 13

From Social Reproduction to Capitalist Social Reproduction

Introduction

My work, considered as a whole, is a contribution to Marxist-Feminist theory. Because the concept of 'social reproduction' is present throughout this book in different contexts, my work could also be interpreted, at least in part, as a contribution to social reproduction theory (SRT). After a brief survey of SRT literature, I concluded that some chapters could be considered as a contribution to *capitalist social reproduction* theory. To explain how I arrived at that conclusion, I will first present some general considerations on reproduction and social reproduction, SRT definitions, assumptions, main points, and so on, taken from several representative publications. I will then offer a critical assessment of some SRT theoretical assumptions and claims. Finally, I will proceed to identify points of convergence and divergence between my work and social reproduction feminism.

Social Reproduction Theory: Definitions, Theoretical Assumptions, Purpose, Claims

Reproduction and social reproduction are concepts of long standing in the social sciences and feminist theory. Edholm, Harris and Young, writing in the late 1970s, offered a detailed critique of social reproduction, a concept they consider problematic because, they argue, in feminist theory it tends to be used ahistorically, in a universalising manner, without attention to its multiple meanings and the different levels of analysis they presuppose.[1] Reproduction can refer to human biological reproduction, to the reproduction of the labour force, and to social reproduction.[2] The latter, to be useful as a concept, 'must refer to the reproduction of the conditions of social production in their totality and not to the reproduction of only certain levels of the total social system ...

---

1 Edholm, Harris and Young 1977, p. 103.
2 Edholm, Harris and Young 1977, pp. 105–16.

Any theory of social reproduction has ... to reveal what the basic structures of a given mode of production are, and then to demonstrate the necessity for their continued existence in order to ensure the continued existence of the mode of production itself'.[3] They argue, then, that a theory of social reproduction ought to be comprehensive, covering *all* the conditions and social levels conducive to the reproduction of a given mode of production as a whole, an objective difficult to attain, indeed.

Writing in the mid-1980s, Dickinson and Russell observed that political economy 'failed to consider seriously the question of social reproduction' of capitalist social relations in general and, particularly, the reproduction of labour power.[4] It was only with the rise of conflict theories, feminist theories and the opening of sociology to the theories of political economy and theories of class rule, class power, and so on that a theory social reproduction emerged, according to which social reproduction is

> an outcome of the relationship or interplay between three major institutional realms: the productive consumption of capital by labour within the economy; the formation and maintenance of working class households through individual consumption; and the social interventions of the modern state which constitute collective or social consumption. These three basic institutional realms constitute the productive and reproductive moments of capitalist society, and if we are to grasp modern society as a totality, we must delineate the essential interconnections between these spheres and describe the part they play in the reproduction of labour power as a commodity.[5]

Those early views about social reproduction influenced how I used to understand the concept, as a social science umbrella term covering a variety of social phenomena – the subject matter of different disciplines (e.g. political economy, population studies, social demography, public health, sociology of the family, feminist family history, and so on) and late 1960s and early 1970s Socialist and Marxist-Feminist theories[6] – useful for teaching the sociology of the family from feminist and Marxist perspectives.

---

3 Edholm, Harris and Young 1977, p. 105.
4 Dickinson and Russell 1986, pp. 2–3.
5 Dickinson and Russell 1986, pp. 5–6.
6 See, for example, Morton, 1972; Benston 1969; Larguia and Dumoulin 1972; Seccombe 1973; Gardiner 1975; and Molyneux 1979.

Today, while feminists tend to coincide in their appreciation of the centrality of the 'production of human beings' and the reproduction of labour power for the reproduction of capitalism, and for buttressing the oppression of women, they theorise these and related matters in somewhat different ways, as shown in the following presentation of key points from several approaches to SRT. I will start with Vogel's work, originally published in 1983, which offers the first fully developed theory of social reproduction.[7]

Vogel, writing at the level of analysis of class societies, developed a theory that identifies the basis for the oppression of women in the relationship between surplus production and one of the essential conditions for its continuous reproduction: the production and reproduction of labour power. Rejecting dual systems perspectives, she places her analysis within a theoretical perspective she calls social reproduction. According to this perspective, 'women's oppression in class societies is rooted in their differential position with respect to generational replacement processes'.[8] Under capitalism, the daily and generational reproduction of labour power occurs mainly,[9] but not exclusively, in the context of working-class households where the combined purchasing power of male workers' wages is supplemented by women's domestic labour. The burden of domestic labour falls disproportionately on women, Vogel argues, because of the 'historical legacy from oppressive divisions of labor in earlier class-societies ... strengthened by the particular separation between domestic and wage-labour generated by capitalism'.[10] The working-class household is likely to be riven by conflict, given men's economic dominance, women's dependence, particularly at the time of childbearing and rearing and, I would add, appropriation of women's unpaid services. The material basis of women's oppression, however, is not to be found in male supremacy or in the sex-division of labour in the household: 'it is the responsibility for the domestic labor necessary to capitalist social reproduction ... that materially underpins the perpetuation of women's oppression and inequality in capitalist society'.[11] To sum up, Vogel's social reproduction theory articulates the implications, for the oppression of women, of the dependence of capital accumulation on the continued production and reproduction of labour power.

---

7   Vogel 2014.
8   Vogel 2014, p. 135.
9   It could also take place in other institutions such as orphanages, prisons, labour camps
     and others (Vogel 2014, p. 159).
10   Vogel 2014, pp. 160 and 188–9.
11   Vogel 2014, p. 177.

Feminist political economists are critical of neoclassical economics, and of Marxist political economy as well because they take for granted the production of people, thus failing to recognise the importance of social reproduction.[12] Political economy, they argue, should acknowledge 'the centrality of social reproduction ... [because] the production of people, meeting human needs, and fostering their wellbeing should be the driving force of economics rather than production for markets and private profits'.[13] The study of social reproduction should be 'integrated centrally into theories of how societies work'[14] [because] 'social reproduction is fundamental to human survival – all societies have to organize the labor involved in maintaining and renewing the population'.[15] Luxton describes social reproduction as a perspective that entails 'at least human biological reproduction, the production of the laboring population, and the reproduction of the social relations, community or society as a whole ... the work of social reproduction is essential to the process of capital accumulation ... and places reproduction at the heart of the class struggle'.[16] This emphasis on class and recognition that class struggles (in the absence of revolutionary conditions, I should add) are struggles for basic conditions of reproduction is very important, particularly in today's political and academic context in which feminists seem more open to theorise any number of oppressions, besides gender and race, rather than deal with class in the Marxist sense: 'By developing a class analysis that shows how the production of goods and services and the production of life are part of one integrated process, social reproduction does more than identify the activities involved in the daily and generational reproduction of daily life. It allows for an explanation of the structures, relationships, and dynamics that produce those activities'.[17] Luxton also argues that a social reproduction perspective is useful to illuminate the ways in which imperialism affects the reproduction of labour, creating 'global relations of reproduction' that affect all countries which open up to international migration flows that benefit corporate profits, to great detriment to the standard of living of the local labour force. In the process, migrant workers are racialised and racism reinforced, thus affecting gender and other forms of oppression.[18]

---

12   Luxton 2017, p. 1.
13   Ibid.
14   Beneria 1979, cited in Luxton 2017, p. 2.
15   Brenner 2014, cited in Luxton 2017, p. 2.
16   Luxton 2017, p. 3.
17   Luxton 2006, pp. 36–7.
18   Luxton 2006, pp. 38–9. I have examined the racialisation and ethnicisation of immigrants in the United States in Gimenez 1989.

Turning now to the introduction to a special issue of *Historical Material-ism*,[19] dedicated to social reproduction, I find a definition that gives social reproduction a foundational role; from this perspective, social reproduction is primary with respect to the functioning of the economy as a whole: '[social reproduction] encompasses the activities associated with the maintenance and reproduction of people's lives on a daily and generational basis. By cent-ralising these activities as the *foundation* on which markets, production and exchange rest, the social reproduction perspective conceptualizes the "mater-ial foundations of social relations as an integrated and unified process"'.[20] The thrust of this statement is clear: social reproduction is given the primary, determining role in the totality encompassing production, markets and ex-change.

The lines between early Marxist-Feminist theoretical analyses of domestic labour in the 1970s and 1980s and current theorising about social reproduc-tion are 'blurred',[21] as Ferguson et al. point out. I agree; a great deal of what I read today under the heading of social reproduction brings back elements from earlier conceptual frameworks, and reminds me also of basic sociology and an abundance of 'radical' and Marxist social research and theorising about wel-fare, public health, labour markets split on the bases of gender and race, migra-tion, imperialism, colonialism, and so on. They argue, however, that earlier fem-inist frameworks were flawed because of limitations identified – in my view – from the standpoint of intersectionality's strictures about complexity and the multiplicity of oppressions. From their perspective, earlier Marxist-feminist work was developed within 'limited terms of reference; i.e. the binary concepts of class and gender', limited in comparison to 'the multi-faceted complexity of real world relations and political struggles as well as the ways in which racial oppression intersects with gendered forms of domination and class exploita-tion'.[22] Today such limitations are replicated to the extent that proponents of 'social-reproduction feminism'[23] continue to view social reproduction labour exclusively as gendered, household labour. The social reproduction of labour power, however, takes place outside the household as well, in other institutions, through gendered, racialised and other kinds of relations.[24] It would seem,

---

19   Ferguson et al. 2016, p. 28.
20   Ferguson et al. 2016, p. 28.
21   Ferguson et al. 2016, p. 28.
22   Ibid.
23   This term is used throughout the special issue of *Historical Materialism*; In this chapter I
      will use it only when discussing work published in that issue.
24   Ferguson et al. 2016, p. 30.

in light of this reasoning, that blending intersectionality[25] and social reproduction theory is the way to leave behind 'one of Marxist-Feminism's greatest weaknesses [i.e.] ... to begin theorizing within a binary framework which privileges issues of gender and class, and to investigate these in isolation from race, sexuality, colonialism and other constitutive social relations'.[26] That is precisely the approach taken by Ferguson, who states that social reproduction feminism offers 'a way to theorise the integral unity of the diverse, differentiated social relations that intersectionality feminism foregrounds'.[27]

According to Ferguson, 'At the heart of social-reproduction feminism is the conception of labour as broadly productive – creative not just of economic values, but of society (and thus of *life*) itself'.[28] Taking Brenner and Laslett's definition of social reproduction[29] as her point of departure, Ferguson argues that 'broadly productive labour' is 'the "practical human activity" that creates all the things, practices, people, relations and ideas constituting the wider social totality – which Marx and Engels identify as "the first premise of all human history"'.[30] We all engage in such activities and, therefore, we all 'partake of a wider reality – both in the sense of expressing that reality, and helping to create

---

25   For a critical assessment of Intersectionality, see Chapter 4.

26   Ferguson et al. 2016, p. 30. I do not understand this criticism of Marxist Feminism, though Gunnarson's observation, that 'among feminist theorists the endeavour of transcending binaries or dualisms has become something of a given imperative', is helpful (Gunnarsson 2013, p. 13). At the time Marxist feminists started developing their theories of the oppression of women, they did so – as it could not have been otherwise – by examining the relationship between gender inequality, capitalism and capitalist class relations, postulating dual system theories or unitary theories. The intersectional turn, introducing other relations of oppression besides gender, blurs the boundaries between feminist theory and social stratification theory. See Chapter 4 for an examination of these issues.

27   Ferguson 2016, p. 48.

28   Ibid.

29   'By social reproduction we mean the activities, attitudes, behaviours and emotions, responsibilities and relationships directly involved in maintaining life on a daily basis and intergenerationally' (Brenner and Laslett 1991, p. 314, cited in Ferguson 2016, p. 48).

30   Ferguson 2016, p. 48. Marx and Engels's 'first premises of human history' were formulated as a critique of idealism; used today to turn all activities into the sources of 'all things ... the wider social totality' is a form of elisionism according to which society is what it is because of the people who are now present, acting, reproducing it, 'constructing' or 'constituting' it on an ongoing basis. For a critique of ontological individualism and elisionism (which conflates structure and agency while privileging the latter), see Gimenez 1999 and Archer 1995. To make the point in a slightly different manner, 'People and society are not ... related "dialectically". They do not constitute moments of the same process. Rather they refer to radically different things' (Bhaskar 1979, p. 33, cited in Archer 1995, p. 63).

it anew. Work – broadly conceived – is the ontological premise of an integrated (albeit diverse) unity'.[31]

Ferguson criticises Marx because he considers labour only as it enters into the production process and does not take into account the contribution of reproductive labour to the reproduction of capital. A consequence of Marx's exclusion of reproductive labour from the theory of capital is that 'the full rich diversity of labour and labouring bodies is sidelined from Marx's theory of capitalism. Social-reproduction feminism restores that diversity developing the conceptual apparatus to understand labour as a differentiated-yet-shared experience, a concrete, diverse unity ... labour is a concrete, embodied experience ... i.e. labouring bodies are differently sexed and gendered ... racialized ... differently spatialized in a geographic and social sense'.[32]

Finding a convergence between intersectionality's ontology, such as the mutual constitution or co-constitution of all forms of oppression (which Ferguson expands to the co-constitution of [all?] social relations) and 'the Marxist-Hegelian conviction that *everything* is *socially* mediated', she credits intersectionality for 'having pushed Marxist-Feminism to acknowledge a much more complexly-organized social totality'.[33] It is not her argument that intersectionality supporters have adopted a concept of the totality based on Ollman's Hegelian interpretation of Marx,[34] but that social reproduction feminism offers intersectionality a 'possible theoretical resolution' to its lack of theoretical foundations. The basis for this resolution is the expanded concept of labour as human practical activity that creates and recreates social reality, and as an 'embodied, spatially-located practice underpinning the reproduction of that totality ... labour as a *diverse unity*'.[35] Labouring bodies are gendered, racialised, sexualised, and so on in their nature and this is why they are *diverse*. Ferguson views gender, race, sexuality and other characteristics of labouring bodies as 'discrete moments' which are also 'complexly unified', as 'every differently constituted labouring body participates in the reproduction of a shared social reality and is an expression of that social whole ... There is no labour (or "work") outside of gender, race or ability, just as there is no gender outside of race, labour or sexuality'.[36]

---

31   Ibid.
32   Ferguson 2016, p. 51.
33   Ferguson 2016, p. 54, emphasis in the text.
34   Ollman 1971.
35   Ferguson 2016, p. 54 emphasis in the text.
36   Ferguson 2016, pp. 54–5. The statement is confusing; it can be interpreted as a sociological truism, meaning that in all societies its members – workers, for example, whether or not

I have quoted extensively from Ferguson's work to convey the substance and effects of the integration of social reproduction feminism and intersectionality in the context of a Hegelian-Marxist notion of the capitalist totality

So far, the authors whose work I have examined built their understandings of SRT in dialogue with the work of earlier Marxist-Feminists. Bhattacharya, on the other hand, takes as her starting point the crucial political issue of our times: the multiple divisions in the global working class and the difficult task of surmounting those divisions. Arguing against those who dismiss the working class as reactionary, disappearing or hopeless, narrowly defining it in terms of the type of jobs people have, she argues that 'the key to developing a sufficiently dynamic understanding of the working class is the framework of social reproduction'.[37] According to Bhattacharya, Marx's concept of reproduction applies not just to the reproduction of labour power but to the reproduction of society as a whole, i.e. of the *capitalist system* as a whole, including the reproduction of labour power and the ways capitalist production influences or conditions the rest of the society or sphere of the non-economic, meaning other institutions such as the state, the legal system, and so on.[38] Indeed, Marx does offer a relational view of production and reproduction as a '... a continuous process ... every social process of production is, at the same time, a process of reproduction'.[39] Marx did not theorise, however, the processes and conditions surrounding the reproduction of the working class. Wage labour is among the topics Marx intended to write about, but he never did.[40] Lebowitz's work,[41] which fills that gap, informs Bhattacharya's perspective on SRT. According to Lebowitz, capitalist production as a whole is constituted by the production of capital and by the production of wage labour, which are distinct moments of the totality; the circuit of capital *necessarily* implies a second circuit, the circuit of wage labour.[42] From this perspective, production and reproduction do not constitute separate spheres, and this integration means that workers' subordination to the rule of capital does not end outside the workplace. The reproduction of capital depends as much on the reproduction of the working class as the repro-

---

they view themselves in terms of all or some of those categories – can be characterised by the identity categories prevalent in that society. It could also be interpreted as assuming the universality of those categories.

37   Bhattacharya 2015, p. 2; see also Bhattacharya 2013.
38   Bhattacharya 2013, p. 10, emphasis in the text.
39   Marx 1974, p. 566.
40   Marx 1970, p. 214.
41   Lebowitz 2003.
42   Lebowitz, cited in Bhattacharya 2015, p. 11, emphasis in the text.

duction of the latter depends on the former. The class struggle is central to this continuous process; capitalists, pursuing their interests, seek to pay as little as possible while workers struggle for employment and better wages which, for them, imply access to the necessary conditions for their own reproduction and self-transformation. The working class includes the employed as well as 'everyone in the producing class who has in their lifetime participated in the totality of reproduction of society – irrespective of whether that labor has been paid for by capital or remained unpaid'.[43] This broad concept of the working class helps us to understand that struggles for the conditions of reproduction go beyond workplace struggles and entail struggles for housing, better schools, safe neighbourhoods, against police brutality, access to higher education, and so on. Workers continue to be workers outside the workplace and, I would add, whether they are employed or unemployed. Working and non-working lives are interrelated and it is through the framework of social reproduction that this relationship, fundamental to the future of the class struggle, can be understood.

According to Cammack, from the very beginning, globalisation was 'built into' Marx and Engels's framework; their approach to social reproduction was 'parsimonious, restricted to the role of the family unit (in its variety of forms) in the material production and reproduction of labour power on a daily and generational basis', located in a 'broader global social production complex whose logic was that of the world market brought into being by the industrial revolution'.[44] From this perspective, the tendency in recent SRTs to examine social reproduction in the context of global capitalism has a historical antecedent in Marx and Engels's work, which anticipated the spread of capitalism all over the world. Worldwide, the reproduction of labour power today takes place in unstable households; because of changes in the division of labour, the fragmentation of production, and the decline in the demand for skilled labour, the majority of global labour force is female, engaged in low-paid, temporary and precarious work, often migrating across the globe to find employment. In these conditions, the formation of stable households is impossible. These changes, Cammack argues, make unnecessary – within capitalist social formations – the division between production and reproduction; what has emerged is a 'social reproduction complex' in the context of which it is possible to find the meaning of a variety of 'thoroughly gendered'[45] social phenomena, many of which are

---

43   Bhattacharya 2015, p. 27.
44   Cammack 2015, p. 17.
45   In the social reproduction literature, as in feminist theory – Marxist or otherwise – 'gender' is coded to mean female.

related to changes in reproduction technologies, the birth rate, working-class women's migration patterns, and so on.[46]

SRTs have been criticised on the grounds of biological determinism and functionalism.[47] Defending SRT from its critics, Arruzza argues that SRT has the potential to avoid the problems inherent in dual or triple systems theories that postulate some form of relationship between capitalism and patriarchy, or between those systems and racism. Identifying a theoretical impasse in the standard explanations for the relationship between gender, race and capitalism (e.g. 'relative autonomy', their 'reciprocal articulation or intersection', or their 'consubstantiality'), Arruzza argues that SRT does not share in their weaknesses and 'has the potential to avoid this impasse, while at the same time suggesting a non-reductionist account of the capitalist mode of production: one in which capital is not seen as the subject of a strictly "economic" process'.[48] Against an understanding of capital accumulation solely in automatic, mechanical terms, a unitary theory of social reproduction would understand that the automatic aspects of the processes of capitalist reproduction 'are constantly combined with human agency within the process of total reproduction'.[49]

Capital accumulation indeed imposes limits on what capitalists have to do to remain capitalists, i.e. to ensure their investments are profitable. How capitalists go about their business, however, is not predetermined, as demonstrated by the success of some and the failures of others. In other words, this functionalist, automatic, machine-like understanding of how capitalist accumulation works is far from Marx's dialectical, contradictory and dynamic theory of capitalism, a theory that does not preclude the 'agency' of individual, historical capitalists who are 'free to choose' what to do with their capital within the parameters set by the mode of production and in the context of the opportunities and resources available in the capitalist social formations where they may reside. Likewise, workers can and do use their agency in various ways and within the historically specific conditions of the capitalist social formations where they may reside. It would seem, however, that social reproduction feminists oppose an abstract, ahistorical notion of agency, unencumbered by social determinations, to a deterministic and mechanical understanding of social structures and, more specifically, of capitalism as a mode of production and its effects on capitalist social formations.

---

46   Cammack 2015, pp. 19–20.
47   See Arruzza 2016 for an examination of some critical assessments of SRT.
48   Arruzza 2016, p. 27.
49   Arruzza 2016, p. 28.

Social Reproduction: a Critical Assessment

All approaches to social reproduction, with the exception of Cammack's, share the same starting point: *Marx failed to integrate the question of the reproduction of labour power into the theory of capitalism and took for granted its availability.* This criticism is misplaced; it overlooks the distinction between the levels of analyses – *mode of production* and *social formation* – which Marx considered appropriate for different kinds of social phenomena: the reproduction of the *wage* labourer, as a social category, takes place at the level of the mode of production, whereas the reproduction of the working class, the owners of labour power, takes place at the level of social formations.

Capital is a theory that elucidates how the *capitalist mode of production* (CMP) works, how surplus is appropriated when the means of production are owned by a class while the direct producers' economic survival depends on the sale of their labour power. At this level of analysis, class relations function independently from the personal characteristics of their bearers; they are identity blind, indifferent to 'the full rich diversity of labour and labouring bodies'[50] and to the diversity of capitalists' 'bodies' as well. Class relations are part of the theory Marx developed in *Capital*, which explains the visible or observable aspects of the changing economic, social and political landscape within which people live in *capitalist social formations* (CSFs), including changing relations of oppression based on gender, race, ethnicity, immigrant status, and so on, and including the reproduction of labour power and its owners. CSFs are the historical terrains, shaped by the CMP instantiated in their 'economic basis',[51] where gender, racial and other oppressions matter, as capitalists pit workers against each other, creating and recreating economic and ideological divisions. This distinction between the 'economic form', captured in the theory of the CMP, and its empirical, historical effects in CSFs, is expressed by Marx as follows:

> It is always the direct relationship of the owners of the conditions of production to the direct producers ... which reveals the innermost secret, the hidden basis of the entire social structure, and with it the political form of the relation of sovereignty and dependence, in short, the corresponding specific form of the state. This does not prevent *the same economic basis –* the same from the standpoint of its main conditions – due to innumerable different empirical circumstances, natural environment, racial relations,

---

50   Ferguson 2016, p. 51.
51   Marx 1968, p. 792.

external historical influences, etc., from showing infinite variations and gradations of appearance, which can be ascertained only by analysis of the empirically given circumstances.[52]

Marx included racial relations among the variable empirical circumstances; we can add gender relations and other relations of oppression and, equally important, *the reproduction of the working class*. Harvey, for example, addresses this issue in terms of the distinction between *capital* and *capitalism*, which he defines as 'any social formation in which processes of capital circulation and accumulation are hegemonic and dominant in providing and shaping the material, social and intellectual basis for social life'.[53] I agree with Harvey when he argues that gender relations, racial relations and other relations of social oppression are indeed important but 'not specific to the form of circulation and accumulation that constitutes the economic energy of capitalism';[54] they are part of the organisation of social, economic and political life within CSFs (e.g. nation states, regions within nation states, and so on), where they acquire features reflecting the historical specificity of the economic, political, legal and ideological context characterising each social formation. This theoretical standpoint does not deny the 'centrality of gender and race to capitalism'[55] but argues that gender, race and other forms of oppression and inequality are not central to the logic of capital accumulation as such: they are central to the operation of concrete, historical capitalist economies – the 'same economic basis', in Marx's terms – and the organisation and functioning of CSFs.

In *Capital*, in the chapter on Simple Reproduction and *at the level of analysis of the capitalist mode of production*, Marx states: 'if production be capitalistic in form, so, too will be reproduction'.[56] Reproduction, in this context, refers to the reproduction of the conditions of production. As the reproduction of labour power is an essential condition for the reproduction of capital, it is logical to assume its inclusion in the theoretical analysis of the mode of production and *it is*, though not in the way feminists usually think about it: 'The labourer ... constantly produces material, objective wealth but in the form of capital, of an alien power that dominates and exploits him; and the capitalist *as constantly produces labour power, but in the form of a subjective source of wealth*, separated

---

52   Marx 1968, pp. 791–2, emphasis added.
53   Harvey 2014, p. 7.
54   Harvey 2014, pp. 7–8.
55   Luxton 2017, p. 6.
56   Marx 1974, p. 566.

from the objects in and by which it can alone be realized; *in short he produces the labourer, but as a wage labourer*.[57] In the theory of the CMP, Marx *includes* the production and – given that production is a continuous process – reproduction of the labourer *as a wage-labourer*, just as the labourer, through the labour process constantly produces and reproduces capital and, therefore, the capitalist. The production and reproduction of capital entails the production and reproduction of the relations of production or class relations – the relations between capitalist and wage-labourers – which is a social relation with a material base, i.e. their respective relationship to the means of productions. *This is a process of social reproduction within the capitalist mode of production.* At the same time, Marx *excludes*, from the theory of the CMP, the physical reproduction of the labourers, the owners of labour power: 'The maintenance and reproduction of the working class is, and must ever be, a necessary condition for the reproduction of capital. But the capitalist must safely leave its fulfilment to the labourer's instincts of self-preservation and propagation'.[58] The reason why Marx allocates the social and the physical reproduction of the working class to different levels of analysis is clear: the structure, social relations and contradictions characterising the CMP are *invariable* and present in all its observable instantiations in the economic organisation – i.e. the 'economy' – of CSFs which, otherwise, show 'infinite variations and gradations of appearance'.[59] The maintenance and physical reproduction of the working class, therefore, takes place in a variety of historically specific relations of reproduction and social contexts.

Marxist feminists and social reproduction feminists sought to fill this perceived omission in *Capital* in several ways: *First*, as in early Marxist-feminist theories, theorising the reproduction of labour power and women's role in its reproduction as the material basis for their oppression under capitalism; *secondly*, expanding the concept of social reproduction to include practically all of social life outside the sphere of production; i.e. social relations, institutions and conditions that in one way or another contribute to the social reproduction of labour power and life in general; *thirdly*, broadening the scope of social reproduction even more to include the effects of global capitalism on workers' migration flows, the heterogeneity that relations of oppression create in the national and global working classes, and so on; and *fourthly*, arguing that social reproduction is 'foundational', i.e. the material *foundation* on which

57   Marx 1974, p. 571, emphasis added.
58   Marx 1974, p. 572.
59   Marx 1974, p. 792.

markets, production and exchange rest.[60] The unintended overall effect of this evolution of SRT is tantamount to arguing that Marx failed to include, within the theory of capital, a theory of CSFs because it is within CSFs – differentially located in the global capitalist economy and characterised by a multiplicity of institutions, oppressive relations, and repressive and ideological state apparatuses[61] – that labour power and other essential conditions for capital accumulation, including the natural environment, are reproduced or non-reproduced, as the case might be.[62]

Feminists do not differentiate between those two levels of analysis and the result is an exceedingly broad conceptualisation of the scope of social reproduction, now rendered equivalent to the reproduction of CSFs in their entirety. When this view of social reproduction is combined with the abstract premise, often found in Marx and Engels's work, that 'every process of production is simultaneously a process of reproduction' (or words to that effect), there is but a short step to reducing both levels of analysis to social relations and processes, as a way to integrate the reproduction of labour power with the production of things: 'if Marx's interrogation of capitalism is understood as being a discussion of social relations and processes, *as opposed to a static thing – the economy* – then the "social production of people" must be included within the social processes and not assumed'.[63] This unaccountable reduction of capitalism, unquestionably the most dynamic engine of change in history, to a 'static thing', highlights the problematic theoretical assumptions underlying some versions of SRT. Ferguson clarifies the implications of this shift towards eliminating structural determinants and reducing everything to some form of praxis: Marxists, instead of narrowly focusing on abstractions such as 'households' or 'economies', need 'to start with the concept of labour as lived, creative experience, and train [their] analytic lenses on the "survival strategies" and not just formal paid labour'.[64] This argument prefigures Ferguson's 'broadly productive' concept of labour, cited earlier in this chapter, and adherence to the presentist or elisionist ontology underlying her view of the totality.[65]

The 'privileging' of 'agency' in feminist theories is, in my view, an effect of the power of capitalist ideologies about individualism and freedom – and avoid-

60   See footnote 22.

61   Althusser 2001.

62   Environmental destruction, pollution, denial of healthcare to the poor, commodification of healthcare, people who cannot afford it have to do without it, and so on, are instances of non-reproduction in the context of CSFs.

63   Leach 2016, p. 120, emphasis added.

64   Ferguson 2008, p. 49, cited in Leach 2016, p. 21.

65   Ferguson 2016, p. 48.

ance of Marxism's alleged 'determinisms' – that influence self-understanding and theoretical developments in CSFs. Marx and Engels developed their historical materialist 'premises of all human history' as a critique of idealism. Those premises also entail, I argue, a critique of ontological individualism and theories that deny the materiality and effectivity of structures and foreshadow Marx's dictum, 'Men make their own history, but they do not make it just as they please ... under circumstances chosen by themselves, but under circumstances directly encountered, given, and transmitted from the past'.[66] Enduring structures, like the capitalist mode of production, the state and other institutions within capitalist social formations, are the effect of the activities of past generations: 'the tradition of all the dead generations weighs like a nightmare on the brain of the living'.[67] Consequently, agency is always historically circumscribed and challenged: the scope of human practical activity, and its potential effectivity reproducing or challenging existing social arrangements, has to contend with the structural constraints transmitted from the past such as, for example, 'the economic basis' or mode of production itself, the effects of the class structure and class relations, the population structure, the repressive and ideological state apparatuses, the heritage of slavery, the presence of colonised minorities, the balance of power between the classes, and so on. Capitalist contradictions create spaces for practices and forms of consciousness with the potential to challenge the status quo, but effective struggles require full awareness and knowledge of the obstacles they face in addition to beliefs in the effectivity of agency as such. Structural determinants, however, are outside the purview of an ontology according to which everything is 'co-constitutive' of everything else. Ferguson does acknowledge the determinant effects of capitalism, stating that the capitalist totality or 'capitalist social formation' has such effects that it makes it very difficult to challenge it, favouring, for example, certain kinds of gender relations[68] and, I would add, other kinds of social relations as well: however, she also argues that 'those gender relations – reciprocally determinative of, and determined by, racial and other relations – *constitute* cap-

---

66   Marx 1969, p. 15. Underlying my understanding of Marx's dictum is Archer's 'analytical dualism' according to which social reality is stratified, so that the emergent properties of structures and agents are irreducible to one another ... and given structures and agents are also temporally distinguishable. Ontological dualism allows for the examination of the interplay between agency and structure over time, and the conceptualisation of different time scales within which either agency or structure play the most salient role, without *a priori* privileging one or the other. See Archer 1995 and Gimenez 1999; see also footnote 31.

67   Marx 1969, p. 15.

68   Ferguson 2016, p. 51.

italism'.[69] This conclusion conflates mode of production and social formation: according to Marx, however, 'the economic basis' is invariant, hence impervious to the variety of gender and other relations that can be found in different social formations.

The use of abstract premises characterising the universal human condition, as the basis for theorising social phenomena taking place under capitalist, i.e. *historically specific conditions*, bypasses their historical, material conditions of possibility, and reproduces the limitations inherent in social science theories about the universal features of all societies. Such abstract formulations, however, are compatible with the abstract notion, social reproduction, used in SRTs. Like 'society' or 'economy', social reproduction is an abstraction;[70] it denotes a universal feature of all societies without which they would cease to exist. As Marx observed in 1868, 'every child knows that a social formation that did not reproduce the conditions of production at the same time as it produced would not last a year'.[71] What matters are the specific capitalist forms in which the reproduction of labour is organised in capitalist social formations.

According to Marx, though the reproduction of labour power is a 'necessary condition for the reproduction of capital, the capitalist may safely leave [the maintenance and reproduction of the working class] to the labourer's instincts of self-preservation and propagation',[72] which, he assumes, will be sufficient to ensure its availability. His assumption is based upon his analysis of the effects of capital accumulation on the working class: as the productivity of labour grows, the demand for labour declines, and an ever-growing mass of surplus population is generated:[73]

> The labouring population therefore produces, along with the accumulation of capital produced by it, the means by which itself is made relatively superfluous, is turned into a relative surplus-population; and it does this

---

69 Ibid. Emphasis in the text, but see footnotes 31 and 67 for critiques of the elisionist assumptions underlying that conclusion.

70 Just as *'production in general'* is an abstraction, albeit a 'sensible' one, so is social reproduction. It is its divergence from '... general and common features' that constitutes the historical specificity of the phenomenon, the 'essential differences existing despite the unity that follows from the very fact that the subject, mankind, and the object, nature, are the same'. Marx 1970, p. 190.

71 Althusser, paraphrasing Marx's views, stated in the 11 July 1868 letter to Kugelmann. Althusser 2014, p. 47.

72 Marx 1974, p. 572.

73 The arguments are exceedingly complex and need not be summarised in this chapter. I refer the reader to Marx 1974, Chapter XXV.

to an always increasing extent. This is a law of population peculiar to the capitalist mode of production; and in fact every special historic mode of production has its own special laws of population, historically valid within its limits alone. An abstract law of population exists for plants and animals only, and only in so far as man has not interfered with them.[74]

There is no reason, then, for capitalists to worry about the availability of labourers and labour power. Against Malthus's explanation of poverty and unemployment as effects of a 'natural law' (namely, the tendency of humans to multiply beyond the means of subsistence available to them), Marx argues that unemployment and poverty are the historical effects of capital accumulation.

Ferguson and McNally argue that this is a 'significantly flawed' account because it rests upon a 'naturalistic premise'; Marx's view of procreation is purely biological, not social, and expected to yield – though 'Marx does not provide any *social* account as to why this should be so – an unchanging rate of biological reproduction'.[75] From their perspective, Marx did not take into account that generational reproduction, though grounded in biology, is 'socially mediated and historically variable'.[76] Marx's 'naturalistic' assumption, they argue, has been 'empirically refuted' by fertility declines brought about by working-class women's ability to take control over their reproduction, thus leading to declines in the supply of labour, state controls over contraception and abortion, and immigration policies designed to replenish the reserve army of labour.[77]

This is a very interesting interpretation. Though I have theorised the effects of capital accumulation on fertility, migration and mortality,[78] I have always interpreted this insight – that capitalists may 'safely' leave their maintenance and reproduction to the workers themselves – politically, not in terms of demographic assumptions; to me, this claim meant that capitalists are indifferent to the workers' fate *except when it may impinge on their own safety and ability to accumulate*. Workers are left to their own devices, to survive as best as they can within conditions set by the ebb and flows of capital accumulation and the success or failure of working-class struggles. When growth in productivity

---

74   Marx 1974, p. 632.
75   Ferguson and McNally, p. 4.
76   Ibid. But see Gunnarsson's critique of the prevalence of 'nature phobia' in feminist theory; she argues, and I agree, that any coherent account of how social systems work requires the acknowledgement of nature's limiting force (Gunnarsson 2013).
77   Ibid.
78   See Chapter 6 in this volume.

made it necessary to expand internal markets, having a better educated labour force able to consume more than basic necessities, universal public education was established. But a system based on exploited, alienated labour with a complex and changing division of labour is in contradiction with the development of a highly educated, knowledgeable citizenry. Hence the way class inequality is reflected in unequal education, and other problems facing a large proportion of the working classes such as inequality in access to employment, healthy food, adequate housing, good schools, healthcare, and in overall health, life expectancy and mortality rates.[79] Altogether, they demonstrate capital's indifference to the physical and social reproduction of most workers, and the utter dependence of working-class reproduction on the mode of production. This is why in CSFs there is always a great surplus of what Marx called 'ordinary labour', produced in the homes of the poor and the near poor and augmented by the immigration of manual workers from abroad.[80] At the same time, the more powerful and wealthier CSFs import skilled and professional workers, a 'brain drain' that appropriates the labour that entered in their production while depriving poorer CSFs of their potential contributions.

Even though Ferguson and McNally's interpretation is thought-provoking, I disagree with it. Throughout his work, Marx criticised the 'naturalistic mystifications' of bourgeois thought.[81] As a historical materialist, however, he did not reduce the materiality of nature to its social construction, instead pointing out how the same biological drives can be satisfied in historically specific ways.[82] It is as unrealistic to assume that Marx would think that biological drives were the only factors determining the reproduction of the working classes and fertility would remain unchanging as it would be to assume that he was unaware of the manifold ways in which women, and men, of all classes, sought to control biological reproduction,[83] and of the various material and ideological constraints affecting sexual activity and procreation. Finally, CSFs are not closed systems where labour force size and rate of growth depend only on their popu-

---

79   See, for example, Watson 2011.

80   When skilled labour of a given kind is needed, there will be investments to produce it, or immigration quotas to bring skilled professional workers from abroad, thus profiting from other countries' investments in their own labour force.

81   Mills 1985, pp. 472–83.

82   'Hunger is hunger: but the hunger that is satisfied by cooked meat eaten with knife and fork differs from hunger that devours raw meat with the help of hands, nails and teeth' (Marx 1970, p. 197).

83   Historically, women have used a variety of methods to control biological reproduction – some effective, some ineffective – ranging from abortion and death by exposure of unwanted children to child spacing, prolonged breastfeeding, and sexual abstinence.

lations' rate of natural increase.[84] The world is awash today in surplus workers, even though in many CSFs aging populations together with below replacement fertility rates and other concerns lead states to encourage immigration and institute pronatalist policies. Further changes in the forces of production, already the source of long-term unemployment, are likely to increase the size of surplus populations in the future even more. This situation confirms, rather than refutes, Marx's 'law of population',[85] namely, that the working classes will always be redundant as long as capitalism is the dominant mode of production,[86] not because of Malthusian 'natural laws', but because *the demand for labour is not identical with increase of capital, nor supply of labour with increase of the working class* ... That the natural increase of the number of labourers does not satisfy the requirements of the accumulation of capital, and yet all the time is in excess of them, is a contradiction inherent to the movement of capital itself'.[87] Consequently, the effects of capital accumulation unavoidably undermine the conditions for the economic survival and flourishing of a substantial proportion of the world working classes.[88]

Capitalist Reproduction: an Alternative to Social Reproduction?

When I chose Marxism as the theoretical foundation of my work, I did not consider Marxist theory as something to be fixed, or supplemented, but as a source of theoretical insights that would help identify the capitalist determinants of social phenomena in capitalist social formations, starting with the oppression of women. This volume is not intended to fill a gap, but to demonstrate, through 'theoretical practice', the continuing relevance of Marx and Engels's work. As a Marxist feminist, I did not start from an abstract, ahistorical question. I did not seek to find out why men oppressed women; rejecting ahistorical theories of patriarchy, I sought to identify the capitalist processes that, in the context of CSFs, placed men and women in unequal power relations.[89] I used the concept, social reproduction, to describe the effects of domestic labour in the process of

---

84   Natural increase is the difference between the crude birth rate and the crude death rate.
85   Marx 1974, pp. 631–2.
86   Technological developments, particularly Artificial Intelligence, are intensifying the processes whereby machines replace living labour; see, for example, Rainie and Anderson 2017.
87   Marx 1974, pp. 640–1.
88   Furthermore, future technological changes leading to 'human disposability' are likely to trigger deep economic and social crises; see Harvey 2014, pp. 91–111; Avent 2016.
89   See Chapters 1 and 2, for example.

reproducing labour power, and the ways in which workers' needs are met or not, in CSFs, through a combination of domestic labour and wages. I did not use it as part of an overarching SRT about the reproduction of labour power, capitalism, or society as a whole. Many of the topics I examine in this volume, however, fall under the scope of social reproduction, meaning the various processes through which labour power and social classes are reproduced; it would be understandable, therefore, if my work were to be considered a contribution to SRT literature. This interpretation would not be entirely accurate and I will now proceed to explain why.

Until recently, had someone asked me to characterise my work, I would have replied: Marxist-Feminist Theory. Only in the process of engaging with SRTs, and critically assessing their theoretical assumptions, have I come to the realisation that a substantial proportion of my work reflects a perspective I will call *capitalist social reproduction* because, under capitalist conditions, social reproduction takes on historically specific characteristics.[90] This is the fundamental principle underlying the approach I call *capitalist social reproduction*: in the social formations where capitalism is the dominant mode of production, the structure, processes and contradictions of the mode of production *determine* the social organisation (i.e. establishes historical limits for its variability) and the material basis of the mode of reproduction feasible for the social classes and strata within classes.[91] Access to the material conditions of reproduction is secure for the capitalist class, small business owners, rentiers and the more privileged stratum within the working class; it is variable and insecure for the working class, particularly the lower strata constituted by temporary workers, underemployed, unemployed and the poor. The reproduction of the propertyless classes is subordinate to and dependent upon the reproduction of the propertied classes; i.e. the capitalist class and intermediate strata whose economic survival does not depend on the sale of labour power.[92]

---

90   This observation may seem so obvious that it is unnecessary to make it. Nevertheless, in light of the idealist interpretations of Marxism that seem to inform social reproduction theorising, it is important to stress that the historically specificity of social reproduction under capitalist conditions stems from the *determinant* role of class power upon the economic survival and physical and psychological well-being of the majority of the population.

91   I define the mode of reproduction as the historically specific combination of labour, and the conditions and means of reproduction (the material basis – biological and economic – for the performance of reproductive tasks) in the context of relations among the agents of reproduction. I elaborate this concept in the Introduction to this volume, and in several chapters, e.g. Chapters 2, 7 and 8.

92   I substantiate this point in a variety of contexts and at different levels of analysis through-

The key differences between my view of social reproduction and that of SRTS – in addition to the theoretical and methodological differences sketched earlier – are as follows:

First, the emphasis on the *determinant* role of capital accumulation, the class structure, and the state of the class struggle underlying capital accumulation, upon the conditions of reproduction of the social classes.[93] SRTS postulate 'a non-determinist conceptualisation of the social', the interrelation, interdependence or integration between production and social reproduction, giving equal weight to each or viewing social reproduction as 'foundational'.

Secondly, the emphasis on the reproduction of the working class[94] as a whole, including the reproduction of the various strata that fragment the working class, and taking into account the effects of economic changes upon the extent to which working-class men are able to participate in the process of reproduction. SRTS' emphasis on gender (women) and the racialised and gendered (feminised) nature of the labour force leads one to wonder about the fate of working-class men and their place in SRTS. Are they staying home taking care of children? Are they living off remittances from female relatives or wives? Are they engaged in illegal trades? Are they mercenary soldiers? Are they migrant workers? In the US, a large number of poor, mostly non-white men end up in jail; poverty is being criminalised.[95] They cannot all be out of the labour force, although capital's need for cheap labour prefers women's labour and the labour of children if it can be obtained. And what are the consequences for the social reproduction of the working classes if most men are either out of work or poorly paid? Sex and procreation will go on regardless. These are rhetorical questions intended to highlight SRT's somewhat one-sided focus on women; even if it is women who bear children and reproduce labour power, they may have husbands or partners and even if they do not, a male fathered their child or children, who might or might not be involved in their upbringing

---

out this volume; see, for example, Chapters 2 and 3, the chapters in the section on Capitalist Social Reproduction, particularly Chapter 9, and Chapter 16, where I recapitulate and refine arguments presented earlier in Chapter 2. The theoretical and methodological assumptions underlying my work are briefly discussed in several chapters and presented at length in Chapter 2. With respect to the ways in which the mode of production determines the mode of reproduction, I have found useful Wright's methodological guidelines (Wright 1978, pp. 9–29).

93   See, for example, Chapter 16.

94   The reproduction of the capitalist classes and intermediate classes (e.g. small businesses, independent professionals) also fall within the scope of capitalist reproduction; in this chapter, however, I will focus on the reproduction of the working class.

95   Wacquant 2009.

but with whom they might keep in touch and even support with remittances.[96] The focus on the reproduction of labour power and on the female members of the labour force neglects the fact that the working classes are composed of men and women workers who – whatever their racial, ethnic and other identities might be – are 'ensembles of social relations', i.e. they have families and friends with whom they share their lives, resources however meagre they might be, and struggles for social reproduction.

Thirdly, the emphasis on the contradictions of capitalism that constantly alter and disrupt access to the conditions of reproduction for different sectors of the working class. Social-reproduction feminists correctly argue that social reproduction is 'at the heart of the class struggle';[97] I prefer, however, to be more specific and say that the economic survival of the working classes, and their physical and social, daily and generational reproduction, is at the heart of the class struggle. Class struggles are an expression of class contradictions; unlike social reproduction feminists, I view the relationship between capitalist production and reproduction as an inherently contradictory process, characterised by the subordination of the reproduction of the working classes to the power, interests and reproduction of the capitalist class.

How does capital accumulation affect the reproduction of social classes? As I argued in 'Population and Capitalism',[98] the process of capital accumulation is not a purely economic process; it is the outcome of political processes; changes in capital accumulation and location of investments, themselves influenced by the state of class struggle, capitalist contradictions and the historical characteristics of social formations, produce changes in the quantity and quality of the demand for labour which, in turn, affect the division of labour, social stratification within classes, changes in the reserve army of labour, and so on, thus altering the context within which people work and have access to their conditions of reproduction.[99] The working classes are always in a crisis of reproduction because wages, except under exceptional circumstances (e.g. US economic prosperity after WWII), are seldom sufficient to cover the cost of daily and generational reproduction. Working-class relations of reproduction are, consequently, fragile, unstable and, for unskilled workers, impossible to sustain and yet they are also a survival strategy. Under capitalist conditions of unemployment, job scarcity and universalised commodity produc-

---

96   I examine these issues in Chapter 15. See also Ehrenreich and Hochschild 2002.
97   See Luxton 2017, p. 3.
98   See Chapter 6 in this volume.
99   This is a very simplified statement about a complex network of relations; see Figure 1 outlining the theoretical framework in Chapter 6.

tion, which requires the prior sale of labour power to satisfy most basic needs, working-class men and women enter into relations of reproduction in a context that places those agents of reproduction who are also wage earners in a position of power over those who are only domestic workers, and turns the position of domestic worker into a structural alternative to that of wage worker. Domestic labour becomes an economic 'option', an alternative to wage labour for working-class women, which places them in a dependent position with respect to men.[100]

Family formation as a survival strategy, however, is withheld from the lower strata of the working class. In the US, for example, the effects of the 2008 recession undermined the possibilities for family formation for some sectors of the mostly white working class, as employment opportunities for poorly educated men declined, at the same time that women's levels of education and employment opportunities rose.[101] Low-income men who cannot support families do not marry, and working women are less likely to marry men who cannot earn at least as much as they do. Men and women eventually marry, but after having had children with more than one partner. In 2012, almost 41 percent of all births were out of wedlock.[102]

These differences in the relations of reproduction within different strata of the working class illustrate the determinative effect of their differential access to the conditions of reproduction which varies according to the historically specific characteristics of social formations such as political and legal institutions, dominant ideologies about gender, race, ethnicity, immigrant status, the balance of power between classes, and so on. The fragility of the working-class family, entirely dependent on the employment of at least one wage earner and often two, and its collapse or instability when wages are too low, so men and women become single parents, in and out of unstable relations, indicate that the material basis for the oppression of working-class women is to be found in the effects of the permanent crisis of reproduction caused by the overall indifference of capital to the physical and social reproduction of the workforce. Racism and xenophobia intensify this crisis among non-white and immigrant members of the working class.

Under capitalism, the needs of reproduction are subordinate to profit making; the welfare state subsidises reproduction among the unemployed and

---

100   I have developed this argument in Chapter 2, also in the Introduction and elsewhere in this volume.
101   See, for example, Addendum to Chapter 9.
102   I have discussed these issues in greater detail in the Introduction and in the Addendum to Chapter 9.

the unemployable within limits that do not threaten capital accumulation by providing an incentive to choose unemployment. To attribute the oppression of working-class women solely to childbearing and their responsibilities for daily and generational reproduction, or their responsibility for the reproduction of labour power, for example, *obscures the effects of class location* on the kinds of relations of reproduction feasible for workers with different skills and wages; it *naturalises the effects of the expropriation of the means of production* and the complete dependence of working-class men and women on the sale of their labour for a wage. The work of physical and social reproduction of labour power, daily and generational, is labour intensive, demanding, and unpaid; working-class women's main responsibility for it is a source of oppression not just because of its characteristics, but because it has to be done privately and, among the majority of working-class households, in unstable economic conditions and with generally insufficient resources both in terms of money and time, often when women also work full- or part-time outside the home. This is why, when income allows it, the tasks of daily and physical reproduction are outsourced to baby sitters, nannies and house cleaners.[103] The extent to which working-class women, and even 'middle-class women' working for salaries, not wages, are oppressed because of their domestic responsibilities is inversely related to income (which allows them to outsource some that work to other women less privileged than them). The relative 'liberation' of some working-class women, then, is predicated on the oppression of other working-class women who tend to be non-white, often immigrant undocumented women.

According to Marxist-feminist and social reproduction theories, women reproduce 'labour power' daily and generationally, and it is understood that, at the same time, they reproduce the labour force and, therefore, the members of the working class. This emphasis on the reproduction of social categories obscures the theoretical and political importance of: a) the materiality of human biological reproduction and the effects, on women's consciousness, politics, decisions, of the actual experiences of sex, pregnancy, childbirth, miscarriage or abortion; b) the variety of ideologies and forms of legal and social control surrounding sexuality and procreation,[104] which impinge upon men's and women's behaviour, opportunities, self-understanding and, crucially, upon women's ability to control their reproductive lives (e.g. number and timing of pregnancies, decision to remain childfree, and so on); and c) the actual material physical needs of human bodies that have to be fulfilled for the healthy

---

103   See Chapters 10 and 11, where I examine these issues in some detail.
104   I have examined some of these issues in Chapters 7 and 8.

development of the existing and future generation of 'owners of labour power' and the proper care of the elderly, those who are ill and those who, for a variety of reasons (e.g. autism, Down's syndrome) cannot take care of themselves. The oppression of working-class women is based on not only their primary responsibilities for reproducing labour power, often under difficult social and economic conditions, but also the extent to which they are able to control their sexuality and their reproductive life in ways conducive to their own and their family's well-being.

Does the reproduction of labourers *always* entail the reproduction of labour power? As Marx points out, human organisms need to be 'modified' to acquire the skills appropriate to different branches of industries; 'special education and training are required' and these costs enter in the calculation of the costs of reproducing labour power, though 'ordinary labourers' cost very little.[105]

If marketable labour power is largely reproduced outside the family, what is it that domestic labour – which is primarily women's labour – actually reproduces at home? The concept mode of reproduction allows for the formulation of that question in a different way: what do the agents of reproduction do and where? The family is only one of the forms that the mode of reproduction takes, the more prevalent indeed, but not the only one. The agents of reproduction are not only parents or, in some instances, grandparents or other relatives, but also teachers, scientists, managers, supervisors, and so on, who educate and train the future members of the labour force in the myriad of institutional locations where labour power of different kinds is reproduced. Parents, especially mothers, socialise the new generations, but their inherent, abstract or *generalised capacity* to labour[106] can be developed in *particular, concrete*, i.e. *historically specific*, marketable ways, in other settings where future workers acquire the kinds of knowledge, training, and skills that changing patterns of accumulation demand.

There is an important distinction between the reproduction of specific kinds of intellectual and manual skills – i.e. concrete kinds of labour power – in a variety of institutional contexts, and the reproduction of labour power as a *generalised capacity* to work, which requires attention to the material conditions infants require to develop their cognitive and social skills, language, and so on. The latter is a condition for the former and it is usually, but not always,

---

105   Marx 1972, p. 172.
106   Marx defines labour power or capacity for labour as 'the aggregate of those mental and physical capabilities existing in a human being, which he exercises whenever he produces a use-value of any description' (Marx 1974, p. 167).

reproduced in domestic settings where parents and other family members may foster or dampen children's intellectual development and ability to learn, and may or may not actively intervene so that their talents can be identified and nurtured, and so on.

The distinction between the reproduction of labour power as a generalised capacity and as a specific type of labour power sheds light on the significance of the differentiation between physical and social reproduction. I argue that, theoretically and at the highest level of abstraction, domestic labour enters into the daily and generational *physical* reproduction of *basic labour power*,[107] meaning the maintenance or replenishment of the physical and psychological health and capacities of current and, through procreation, potentially future members of the labour force. Historically, whether or not households actually enhance or undermine the maintenance and/or reproduction of *basic labour power*[108] and the reproduction of specific kinds of labour power depends on the economic and cultural resources available to the agents of reproduction, i.e. on their location in the class structure and socio-economic stratum within the class.

The oppression of the poorer sectors of the working class entails, among other things, the relative inability of adults – whether for lack of skills themselves, lack of time, or both – to develop adequately their children's capacity for learning and developing intellectual skills. This is not a 'blaming the victim' analysis but an indictment of a system of exploitation that deprives so many people of the opportunity to develop and activate their own capacity for learning. *The correlation between poverty and very low incomes with children's poor school performance suggests that there are sectors of the working class that have also been expropriated from the capacity to reproduce basic labour power, so they reproduce potential labourers who might, in the future, become at best 'ordinary labourers'.*

As human beings, we are part of nature and ought to acknowledge the conditioning that nature exerts on us, individually as well as collectively, and on the social worlds we create: 'man is conditioned by his own physical structure and

---

107   This concept, basic labour power, refers to the transhistorical capacity of human beings to transform nature through their labouring activity; 'basic labour' is not synonymous with 'human labour in the abstract', i.e. 'homogeneous human labour' which, as the 'substance of value', is a property common to all commodities regardless of their qualitative differences as use values (Marx 1974, pp. 38–9).

108   Agents of reproduction (parents, relatives, foster parents, older siblings, for example) vary in the extent to which they foster the healthy development of children's bodies and minds, language and vocabulary, capacity to learn, and so forth.

the natural environment'.[109] My standpoint is based on Timpanaro's materialist philosophy and defence of materialism against the idealisms that characterise bourgeois culture; 'every exploiting class always needs a discourse on "spiritual values"'[110] and, I add, discourses 'privileging agency' such as those that consider labour as the source of all wealth while excluding the contribution from nature. According to Timpanaro, people enter into relationship with nature not only through work, as Marx and Engels state in their first premises of human history, but also 'through heredity and, even more, through the innumerable other influences of the natural environment on his body and hence on his intellectual, moral and psychological personality'.[111] We are historical, social and biological beings, who grow old and die, with various hereditary characteristics that affect individuals' life span, propensity to certain illnesses, and quality of life. A great deal of what happens to individuals in the course of their lives is influenced by their genes, inherited from both parents; in addition, women's health, habits, nutrition, and so on influence the future health of their offspring. While nature changes imperceptibly and, for all practical purposes, appears to be constant, in comparison to historical transformations, biology has important material effects on individuals, and such effects are irreducible to social constructions.[112]

As Gunnarsson argues, 'Acknowledging that nature underpins the social is not only compatible with theorising social change but *necessary* for any tenable account of how social processes work'.[113] A materialist standpoint is therefore necessary to take into account the ways that the physical and social reproduction of the working class, generational reproduction in particular, are affected by the lack of adequate conditions for reproduction inside and outside the workplace such as lack of housing, exposure to asbestos, toxic waste, factory fumes, lack of adequate food, healthcare, and so on. This is why class inequality and socio-economic inequality are reflected in unequal mortality rates, incidence of chronic diseases, suicide rates, maternal mortality and lower life expectancy. The still unresolved water crisis in Flint, Michigan, where in 2014 the water supply of drinking water was contaminated with lead and other chemicals, is a case in point.[114]

---

109   Timpanaro 1970, p. 33. See also Gunnarsson's critique of 'feminist nature-phobia' (Gunnarsson 2013).
110   Timpanaro 1970, p. 31.
111   Timpanaro 1970, p. 41.
112   Timpanaro 1970, pp. 43–5.
113   Gunnarsson 2013, p. 5.
114   http://www.cnn.com/2016/03/04/us/flint-water-crisis-fast-facts/ see also https://en .wikipedia.org/wiki/Flint_water_crisis.

Capitalist social reproduction refers not only to workers' access to basic and other necessities for physical and social, daily and generational reproduction, but also to their ideological reproduction through the ideological state apparatuses i.e. the family, the educational system, the media, political discourse, religion, establish the boundaries within which people come to understand themselves.[115] In his essay, 'Ideology and Ideological State Apparatuses',[116] Althusser illuminates the role of power and ideology in the reproduction of the conditions of capitalist production, including the reproduction of labour power. The latter is secured through wages, which allow for the purchase of the means of subsistence, the acquisition of knowledge and techniques, and 'the reproduction of its submission to the rules of the established order ... *subjection to the ruling ideology* or the mastery of its "practice"'.[117] The ideological reproduction of the working class is functional to capital accumulation; in the US, it has replaced class politics with identity politics, and erased, for all practical purposes, knowledge of the US history of labour struggles, awareness of class location, class interests and potential for collective organisation and political action; awareness of exploitation and workers' right to a share of the wealth they produce; and awareness of the functional importance of all types of work as contributions to the collective well-being.

The hold of capitalist ideology cannot always withstand the undermining effects of the contradiction between the growing concentration of wealth and concomitant stagnation of wages, poverty, long-term unemployment, and widespread deterioration in the standard of living of the working classes, as demonstrated by anti-austerity movements like Occupy, Podemos, social movements against the privatisation of water, environmental racism, police brutality, and movements for better schools, housing, healthcare, and so on. Challenges to the power of ideology emerge also from the effects of capitalism itself, as it propels changes in the forces of production and searches for sources of profit all over the globe, altering traditional ways of life, fuelling scientific and technological development, changing patterns of consumption and communication and, in the process, altering the way people relate to each other and to nature. Such changes are subtle and do not affect everyone equally; some, like the environmental movement, concern for climate change, animal rights, fair trade products, anti-nuclear movements, peace movements, and so on, are more likely to emerge from the more privileged strata of the working class,

---

115   Althusser 2001, pp. 87–90.
116   Althusser 2001, pp. 85–126.
117   Althusser 2011, pp. 87–90.

the 'middle-class', but not exclusively so. Like working-class social movements for better schools, community safety, against gentrification, against racism, for example, these 'middle-class' movements arise from changes in consciousness prompted by experiencing and/or learning about the effects of capitalism on people's lives and on the environment. Capitalism is inherently contradictory; it relentlessly exerts its power and, in the process, it transforms the material conditions underlying people's experiences at all levels (family, work, consumption, recreation, and so on). Such changes sometimes tighten its ideological hold, but they can often undermine it, as critical forms of consciousness, political objectives and social movements emerge. The rise of its 'gravediggers' is far in the future but, in the meantime, its constant revolutionising of production and experiences triggers ever present challenges to its domination.

Conclusion

This *capitalist social reproduction*[118] perspective I have hastily constructed has no pretention to being a fully fledged theory. It is only the sketch of an analytical framework foreshadowed in my work and in the preceding critical assessment of SRTs theoretical assumptions. Although capitalist social reproduction and SRTs focus on capitalist phenomena, they differ in theoretical assumptions, as indicated earlier, and in the dimensions of social reproduction they consider important.

The differences between *capitalist social reproduction* and *social reproduction* signal two alternatives to the future of feminism and feminist theory. Will feminism place the oppression of women in the context of the exploitation of the working class in the workplace and working-class oppression outside the workplace, and become a working-class women's feminism in solidarity with the working class as a whole, theoretically engaged in seeking ways to develop solidarity across gender, racial, ethnic and other differences and politically supportive of working-class struggles whatever the gender and identity of the workers engaged in those struggles? Will feminism leave identity politics behind and, bringing class out of its stigmatised 'reductionist' or 'determinist' status, start using 'hyphenated-identities' such as working-class women,

---

118   The opposite of *capitalist social reproduction* would be *socialist social reproduction*, where the satisfaction of the material needs and self-development of the direct producers would determine the objectives of production; under socialism, reproduction would become *foundational* in *practice*, rather than theory.

working-class black women, working-class men, and so on?[119] Or will feminism continue to place the oppression of women and the reproduction of labour power at the centre, focusing primarily on social reproduction rather than linking social reproduction struggles to class struggles?

The authors of the different perspectives on SRT, briefly presented earlier in this chapter, agree on conceptualising struggles for the conditions of reproduction as forms of class struggle outside the workplace. Objectively, they are; subjectively, they tend to be fought under identity banners that divide the working class. Their success, important to those who may benefit from them, leaves the structures of capitalism intact and does not further working-class power and self-understanding. According to Ferguson, for example, 'if social relations are internally related, a change in one alters all the others ... there is no compelling reason to prioritize so-called economic or work-place based struggles in the fight for a better society. *Any* struggle within the realm of social reproduction – be it anti-racist, feminist, anti-colonial, or be it over education, healthcare, transportation – that promotes human need over capital's interests can chip away at the capitalist social formation'.[120] In the United States, in the aftermath of the 2016 election, we are now witnessing the effects of prioritising all struggles *except* class struggles at the workplace, e.g. working-class struggles for employment, job training, better wages and less toxic working conditions. Advancements in civil rights, success in struggles against racial and other forms of discrimination, facilitating access of women and minorities to higher education and higher status occupations, struggles that helped acquire skills for better paying jobs, thus enhancing access to better conditions of reproduction and satisfaction of 'human needs' left invisible, unrecognised, the needs of working-class men, women and their families left behind by processes of de-industrialisation and outsourcing that started about a decade after the social movements of the 1960s. Such successes did not chip away at capitalism, and the forms of collective and political consciousness that spilled over from various theoretical analyses of oppression into the media and political discourse excluded any recognition of the working class, the unemployment and under-employment affecting blue-collar workers, their downward mobility, and so on.[121]

---

119   Words cannot change material conditions but could help create awareness of the one commonality underlying all the identity divisions and social antagonisms within capitalist social formations; i.e. class location, to which common class interests are attached.

120   Ferguson 2016, p. 57, emphasis in the text.

121   For a critical examination of the limitations of identity politics in the US and their significance within the 2016 presidential election, see Lilla 2016.

The topics covered by *capitalist social reproduction* and SRTs are similar: the differences are theoretical and, consequently, political. The issue, at this point, is not whether one or the other is right or wrong, but what these perspectives tell us about the future of feminism. Will it become a working-class women's feminism, in solidarity with all workers regardless of gender and other differences, or a social reproduction feminism, primarily concerned with the female portion of the working class? I have no answer to those questions. As the material conditions change, theories change.

PART 3

Whither Feminism?

..

CHAPTER 14

Connecting Marx and Feminism in the Era of Globalisation: a Preliminary Investigation

'Connecting Marx and Feminism in the Era of Globalization: A Preliminary Investigation', in *Socialism and Democracy*, Vol. 18, No. 1 (January–June 2004): 85–106.

The purpose of this chapter is to explore the relevance of some of Marx's methodological insights for thinking about feminist issues and politics in the context of globalisation. In the short space available here, I want to set down some general observations.

Since the fall of the Soviet Union and the dismantling of the socialist bloc, 'globalisation' has become the lens through which everything has to be experienced, examined, and understood. Against the view that everything we knew or thought we knew – including Marx and feminism – has to be re-theorised through the lens of globalisation, I will argue instead that it is through the lens of Marx's work and the work of those who followed in his footsteps that we can fully grasp the nature of globalisation. Further, it is through the lens of Marxist-feminism that we can fully comprehend not only the effects of globalisation on women, but also the material conditions determining the ideological forms in which women understand their changing conditions of existence. Finally, to go beyond those ideological forms, I will argue, a new kind of feminism is needed, one which is fully aware of its ideological assumptions and of its historical specificity and conditions of possibility and, consequently, of the capitalist limits of gender politics.

To sketch out this argument, I will discuss the characteristics of globalisation and its effects on women. I will present a Marxist critique of the concept of globalisation. I will outline the theoretical and ideological polarisations within feminist thought which have emerged in the context of globalisation. And I will present an alternative way of thinking about Marx, feminism and globalisation which, I will argue, transcends these polarities in feminist thought and opens the way to a different theoretical and political understanding of the political options facing women in the context of globalisation.

1   **Working Assumptions**

First, what is globalisation? Globalisation is a de-politicised, euphemistic way
to refer to the spread of capitalism over the globe. It is a fetishised way of talk-
ing about the effects of capitalist development without having to talk about
capitalism itself. Using the term globalisation means that one does not have to
acknowledge the capitalist material basis of the phenomena lumped together
under the globalisation label.[1] Trendy and ubiquitous, globalisation is, as its
market value confirms, an inherently conservative way of thinking about and
analysing current processes of social, economic, political and cultural change.
The intensity, speed and dramatic effects of the economic and ideological
victories of capitalism in poor, debtor countries including Eastern Europe,
strengthen the notion that there are no alternatives to neoliberal economic
policies and the penetration of capitalist relations and ideologies into every
corner of the globe. The globalisation discourse is itself a powerful ideology
that obscures the capitalist nature of these processes and their effects and,
therefore, the roots, in the capitalist mode of production, of the deepening
inequality and decline in living standards that afflict the majority of the world's
population, particularly the female population, since the fall of the Berlin Wall
in 1989.[2]
     Second, what is feminism? I argue that the women's movement is a response
to the development of capitalism in the advanced industrial economies. In
the advanced capitalist countries, capitalism has had contradictory effects on
women. It contributed to undermining traditional forms of gender inequality
while, at the same time creating new forms which, paradoxically, contributed in
the long-run to increased gender inequity. The capitalist economy has opened
up new employment and educational opportunities for working women, especially for middle and upper middle class women. These opportunities, in turn,
contribute to their ability to envision and struggle for self-determination. In the
short-term, there is an intensification of inequality, but in the long-term, propertyless working women's opportunity structures are changed for the better.
     It is important to acknowledge that there are differences in the effects and
timing of these processes, differences linked to countries' specific characteristics, histories, levels of capitalist penetration and development, and modes
of insertion in the world economy. Nevertheless, it would be possible to argue

1   Gimenez 2002, pp. 85–7.
2   For a critical assessment of globalisation, see Mander and Goldsmith 1996; Rowbotham and
    Linkogle 2001; and Stiglitz 2002.

that, as capitalism developed, working women were able to leave farm work, domestic service, and home-based strategies of economic survival (e.g. taking in boarders, laundry, sewing, or producing goods for local markets) to find employment in factories, offices, department stores, schools, and eventually, professions and businesses. In the more advanced capitalist countries, like the United States, the contradictory demands of family and waged or salaried work awakened women's resistance and contributed to the rise of the Women's Liberation Movement in the 1960s.

One of the main political and theoretical issues was domestic labour, a topic that led to an abundant and interesting literature as well to the rise of ideologies extolling the need for an egalitarian domestic division of labour. As I argued in a previous work,[3] had most working women in the US and other wealthy countries had access to full-time domestic servants, the contentious issue of the domestic division of labour would not have arisen. In Argentina, a country where capitalism had not yet created opportunities for most working-class women, during the 1950s and 1960s domestic service was the main alternative for poor women, particularly the young and unmarried, and most middle-class households employed maids, cooks, and nannies, on an hourly or, as was often the case, on a live-in basis. As waged labour opportunities increased in Argentina, domestic labour became more scarce, expensive, and available mainly to the very wealthy. Both the US and Argentina were and continue to be characterised by gender inequality; but gender inequality assumed different forms and triggered different forms of consciousness among women.

In the US, women's struggles eventually attained legal, political and ideological changes that furthered women's incorporation in the labour force, in education, and as income-earners. In Argentina, capitalist development eventually opened up opportunities for working-class women, offering them a better alternative to domestic service. The Argentine experience, however, which replicated changes that took place in the US in the late nineteenth and early twentieth centuries, is not typical of every poor country but is useful to highlight the differences in timing and other conditions that characterise the changing effects of capitalist development on the status of women.

Furthermore, these processes are uneven; they contribute to the liberation and emancipatory objectives of the more privileged women while strengthening the oppression of working-class women. For example, in the US (and, very likely, in other wealthy countries) the media extols the increasing number of businesses (generally small, however) owned by women and the presence of a

---

tiny number of women in the yearly lists of the wealthiest individuals. And the proportion of women in executive, administrative and managerial positions, as well as in professions previously considered 'male' (e.g. medicine, law, architecture), has indeed grown since the 1970s; today over 50 percent of college students are women. Affirmative action and Civil Rights legislation have opened doors to women and have empowered them to fight for fair wages and better working conditions.

But despite considerable advances in women's education, employment and income, most women still work in sex-segregated occupations and occupy the lower levels in the occupational hierarchies. Working women are still more likely to be nurses, dieticians and elementary school teachers than pilots, engineers or dentists.[4] Changes are, consequently, uneven, and just as the opportunities and quality of life of educated and relatively privileged working women improve, they have worsened for the vast majority who remain trapped in low paying, sex-segregated jobs. There is no better indicator of the deepening class and socio-economic status differences among women than the growth in the number of corporations like Merry Maids, which provide domestic servants for upper and upper middle class women and their families.[5]

These advances in the status of more privileged women characterised the experience of the advanced capitalist countries, where capitalist development entailed changes not just at the level of production (i.e. proletarianisation and commodification) but also in property laws, the division of labour, urbanisation, education, health, demographic processes (i.e. declining fertility and mortality, and lower family size), mass education and employment, as countries followed the path of Britain over two centuries of industrialisation. Most importantly, the contradictions in capitalist development led to major political mobilisations and challenges to the status quo by organised labour and other social movements. Crucial among these was the rise of the women's liberation movements of the late 1960s and the flourishing of academic feminism in its wake.

Once the movements died, academic feminism became the dominant venue for feminist activity, as theorising and research became functional alternatives to feminist activism, and feminist politics, having lost its radical and socialist concerns, continued in a largely reformist, liberal path, in lobbying groups, professional caucuses, and multiple institutional and localised settings. These changes were conducive to the emergence of a female 'aristocracy', as different

---

4   Blau, Ferber and Wingler 1998, Chapters 6 and 7.
5   For a trenchant analysis of this phenomenon, see Ehrenreich 2000, pp. 59–70.

in its life chances from women in the rest of the world (except for the women in the bourgeoisie of the poorer countries) as the earlier 'labour aristocracies' were from the majority of the working class.

Third, I argue that the emergence of a female aristocracy derives from the exploitation of the third world. The rise of a rich and powerful class of working women in the advanced capitalist countries was made possible because of the exploitative relationship between the imperialist countries and their colonies and neo-colonies. Because of the systemic nature of capitalist development, where the wealth of the few is predicated on the exploitation and poverty of the many, economic inequality within and between nations is unavoidable. At best, some countries 'in between' (e.g. the so-called 'Asian tigers') can improve while most countries stay the same or lose ground (e.g. Argentina, Russia, or Brazil), so that the world's 'stratification profile' tends to remain relatively unchanged. In other words, structured inequality at the world level of analysis remains relatively unchanged, even though some nation states may move up or down the ladder, just as wealth and income distribution in the core or advanced capitalist countries are not substantially altered despite the fact that in any given year a variable proportion of the population experiences upward and downward mobility.

By stratification profile I mean the structural distribution of wealth and income. The US stratification profile, historically, remained relatively unchanged until the Reagan years, when the gap between the wealthy and the rest of the population began to intensify, a process accelerated under Bush and his tax cuts approved in 2002–03.[6] However, at the same time, sociologists could document some degree of individual and structural mobility. One could point to the decline of the industrial sector and the rise of the white-collar, service, and information technology sectors of the economy, which means that more people work outside industry not just because of their 'achievement motivation', but also because of the decline in the demand for skilled blue-collar labour. And, of course, once in a while, there were individuals who rose from the middle and even the lower strata of the working class to the capitalist class (e.g. Bill Gates, Sam Walton, Oprah) while others fell from top capitalist to lesser capitalist, or from the upper middle to the middle, in addition to the many who experienced disastrous downward mobility because of de-industrialisation and downsizing.[7] But the overall picture of the US stratification profile is one of secular stability.

---

6   Phillips 1990.
7   See, for example, Newman 1988 and 1993.

I am making the same argument about the world stratification profile. The rise of some countries (e.g. Japan, South Korea) and the fall of others (e.g. Russia, Argentina, which was the 10th-ranking economy at the beginning of the twentieth century)[8] does not substantially alter the proportion of the world's wealth controlled by the core countries. Giovanni Arrighi makes this argument in his article, 'World Income Inequalities and the Future of Socialism'.[9] In other words, the upward or downward mobility of individuals or of countries leaves the macro-level distribution of wealth and power unchanged. It is a zero-sum game. What is historically possible for some individuals and for some nation states is not possible for all the individuals or all the nation states at the same time; so, while some go up, others go down and the overall division of classes or between core, periphery and semi-periphery remains, for all practical purposes, the same.

Today, the structural adjustments imposed by the International Monetary Fund and the World Bank on debtor countries, which require the implementation of neoliberal economic policies (including the privatisation of formerly public sectors of the economy, deep cuts to state expenditures, the dismantling of social provisions, and the so-called flexibilisation of labour contracts), have begun to turn the economic clock back in many areas of the world. Unemployment and the growth of the informal economic sector, the feminisation of poverty, male and more recently female out-migration, and deepening income and wealth inequality are some of the effects of economic policies designed to service the foreign debt rather than to satisfy people's basic needs. For the powerful and affluent, globalisation may have signalled 'the end of history'. However, for the vast majority of the world's population living in the poor, debtor countries of Africa, Latin America, Asia and Eastern Europe, it has meant 'the revenge of history', as the dismantling of state-sponsored industrialisation and adoption of the neoliberal gospel of privatisation and free markets has undermined the power of organised labour and destroyed both internal markets and national economies. (I prefer to stress the realities of the world situation by referring to poor and debtor countries, instead of using ideological or geographical metaphors such as the South or the Third World).

Fourth, I want to argue that in understanding feminism, we need to distinguish between two levels of analysis. The first is at the level of the mode of

---

8   See http://www.economist.com/news/briefing/21596582-one-hundred-years-ago-argentina
     -was-future-what-went-wrong-century-decline.
9   Arrighi 1991.

production, while the second is at the level of social formation. One of Marx's methodological injunctions is that we must differentiate between conflictual, objective macro-level processes of structural change, and the ideological ways in which people become conscious of those conflicts and fight them out.[10] At the level of analysis of the mode of production as such, it is possible theoretically to identify the capitalist macro-level processes of surplus extraction which operate both in the world as a whole and within nation states. At the level of analysis of social formations, however, the political, social, cultural and ideological contexts within which these processes unfold are extremely complex and diverse. This makes it difficult, if not impossible, to predict, even within nation states, the empirical effects of macro-level structural changes on social and political relations and forms of consciousness.

It is certainly the case that the global media and culture industries, together with the worldwide distribution and consumption of Western goods, exert a homogenising effect on other cultures. I would argue, however, that the effect is superficial. The consumption of Western-style food, clothing and entertainment cannot substantially alter the role of nation states, and of national and local cultures, in the production and reproduction of people's earliest identities and forms of consciousness.

It may be argued that the effects of colonial and neo-colonial rule compromise the presumed integrity of national and local cultures. This may be so from the standpoint of the foreign observer. But from the standpoint of the persons raised in those contexts, in the absence of a theoretically grounded critical examination of identities and culture, who they are and how they live – and the ideologies that guide their lives – are the 'real thing'. The weight of these social and ideological forces is evident in the way immigrants everywhere engage in the struggle to recreate some aspects of their homelands. That this is a losing battle, that eventually they will develop 'hybrid' identities reflecting both their actual experiences as well as their 'imagined communities' of origin, is beside the point. The crucial issue is the persistence, in immigrant communities, (albeit intermingled with new patterns) of customs, traditions, kinship patterns, gender roles and expectations that shape individuals' identities and abilities to envision the possibility of change. At the same time, however, it is evident that the expansion of Western capitalism undermined the manifold traditional social and economic networks within which most people lived their lives and, consequently, the material conditions for the impact of traditional

---

10   See Marx 1970, p. 21.

cultural, religious, ideological and moral constraints on people's behaviour. It is in the context of this complex unity of stability and change that questions about Marx, feminism, and globalisation must be raised.

2   Western Individualism, Feminism, and the Critique by Postmodernists and Third World Feminists

The rise of the abstract individual, the bearer of economic, political, civil and human rights, is both a prerequisite for the development of capitalism and a continuing capitalist structural effect that contributes to its ongoing reproduction. Feminism is one of the important expressions of Western individualism. The possibility of thinking of women 'as women', and of women's problems, rights, and needs as abstracted from the other social relations within which women's lives are unavoidably embedded, required material conditions that arose only in the context of advanced capitalism.

Feminist ideologies – whether liberal, radical, socialist or Marxist – rest upon the conceptual bedrock of an abstract, transnational notion of women. This notion is open to criticisms similar to those levied against the abstract individual political subjects or citizens who dwell in the terrain of Western formal democracy. The Beijing Declaration and Platform for Action of the 4th United Nations-sponsored World Conference on Women in 1995 epitomises this theoretical and political standpoint, as captured in the slogan: 'Women's rights are human rights'. The explicit inclusion of women and girls within the scope of international human rights documents and agreements such as the UN Universal Declaration of Human Rights of 1948 is in itself an important step in feminist struggles. This commitment to the full panoply of human rights for women as human beings – including the right to work, own property, obtain credit, education, and job training; to political participation, to freedom of thought and religion; to health, sexual expression, and reproductive self-determination – raises social awareness about the magnitude of the problems facing most women in the world today, and about the many barriers that stand in the way of achieving even modest improvements in working women's lives.

Not all of these rights, which capture the tentative achievements of Western women, are welcomed by women in the rest of the world, for they challenge deeply held cultural and religious beliefs. Depending on the context, they can be seen as eroding desirable kinship and social networks. An important debate about the deficiencies of the 'women's rights are human rights' model has been conducted within academic feminism for the past three decades. Postmodern feminist theorists as well as non-Western feminists argue that universalistic notions of women's rights are unavoidably suspect, for they rest on an essentialist[11] understanding of women and their needs.[12] In addition, they express the views and the experiences of privileged Western women, thus ignoring the qualitative (i.e. substantive, not superficial) differences (of class, race, ethnicity, and national origin) between women within and among nation states.

Women differ greatly in terms of their historically specific identities, problems, and needs. Because of the localised, narrow familial and community contexts that shape their experiences, they are necessarily thrown into different political struggles, fought with different outcomes in mind, outcomes with which Western feminists might not necessarily agree. For example, feminists in Muslim cultures might consider using the veil as an act of resistance to Western imperialism, or a practice that allows women to leave their homes, preserving their modest deportment in the light of traditional and religious demands, while being able to move freely in the process of acquiring skills and education or participating in the labour force. Similarly, for Western feminists, female genital mutilation is a heinous expression of patriarchal domination and a violation of women's human rights. Some African feminists, on the other hand, view such criticisms as reflecting 'the total lack of consideration of the particular context in which African women are struggling ... it is essentially up to ... African women to decide to mobilize about certain aspects of their reality – those which seem most urgently in need of change, and to decide how that struggle could be waged'.[13] Non-Western feminists reject, therefore, what they perceive as an imperialist, ethnocentric agenda that essentialises non-Western women as powerless victims, oppressed by a universal and ubiquitous patriarchy. Such an agenda obscures the actual contexts within non-Western feminists live and the historical realities that shape their political priorities, self- understanding and actual possibilities.[14]

Western postmodern feminists identify essentialism as the central flaw in the liberal feminist concern to provide women everywhere with women's

---

11   Essentialism is a form of conceptualising women as if they shared a common universal nature; it postulates an ahistorical, universal commonality among women that transcends historical and cross-cultural differences. Essentialist views about women can be based on women's biology (e.g. their reproductive capacity), psychology (e.g. their inherently nurturant traits), or historical experiences, when those experiences are universalised (e.g. Western feminists' assumptions that domestic labour is a universal form of oppression suffered by all women). See, for example, Brooks 1997, pp. 20–1.

12   For discussions of essentialism and its implications, see Alcoff 1989, pp. 295–326; and Ramazanoglu 1989.

13   Bilotti, http://www.medmedia.it/review/numero3/en/art2.htm.

14   Ramazanoglu 1989, Part Two; Mohanty, Russo and Torres 1991.

rights, and to ensure that globalisation does not leave women behind. In contrast, non-Western feminists focus on the powerful impact of nationalism, culture, religion and kinship in structuring women's lives. These are forms of consciousness and responsibilities which render the feminist agenda not only unworkable but unacceptable for many women. Aihwa Ong,[15] for example, points out how in Asian countries, where colonial and postcolonial struggles have been fought in terms of people's collective interests, it is very difficult, and perhaps even antithetical to women's self-understanding, to postulate individual rights as independent from and even superior to the interests of the state. In this context of national liberation struggles, women's individual rights are subordinate to the state's political and economic requirements to further the kind of economic development that would ensure the well-being of the population as a whole. State ideologies about citizens' duties are not the only ideologies legitimating inequality. Communal, religious and kinship norms and expectations narrow the opportunities of women legitimate the appropriation of their wages and the subordination of their needs to those of the collectivity within which they live. It is within these contexts that women have to develop their own strategies towards attaining feminist objectives, strategies that acknowledge and support their loyalty to the various ideologies and networks of relations within which they must construct their lives. Such women require a vision of equality that does not entail the total rejection of their self-understanding and of their social and religious responsibilities.

There is, then, a strong polarity of views. On the one hand, we have the universalistic, liberal feminist goals expressed in documents produced by the United Nations and by innumerable NGOs all over the world. On the other, we have the postmodern and non-Western feminist critique of these goals, rejected as essentialist, and the prioritising of cultural, religious and national differences over any universalised notion of women's rights. I want to argue that this polarisation of views expresses, at the level of ideology, the uneven material development of the capitalist world. These views are the expression, at the level of ideologies and forms of consciousness, of the enormous gap between the material conditions that shape the experiences and political consciousness of relatively privileged Western and Western-educated women on the one hand, and the vast majority of the globe's female population on the other.

Underlying both sides of this polarisation there is an important assumption held in common. For liberal feminists, it is assumed that the goals of liberal feminism, as stated in the Beijing Declaration and countless other documents,

---

15   Ong 1996.

are difficult to attain, but will eventually be reached through long and protracted political struggles. Non-Western feminists make a similar assumption. They believe that localised, alternative visions of female political, economic and social integration, which incorporate Western universalist ideals, albeit in modified forms, are capable of being realised. Postmodern feminists, on the other hand, to the extent that they write about politics, and consistently with their anti-essentialist theoretical standpoint, view the political arena as fragmented in a multiplicity of local struggles concerned with ungeneralisable goals.

3   **The Debates within Feminism Echo the Debates over Modernisation Theory: Both Lead to a Dead End**

These two paths to feminist liberation are reminiscent of the debates around modernisation theory from the 1950s to the 1970s. Like the modernisation theories of the 1950s and early '60s, including those of W.W. Rostow and many others,[16] which postulated processes of technological and cultural diffusionism, liberal feminist thinking assumes the possibility of what might be called the 'modernisation of women'. They envision the attainment, by women from poorer countries, of opportunities and rights similar to those enjoyed by relatively privileged women in the advanced capitalist countries. Similarly, like non-Western critics of modernisation theory,[17] non-Western feminists emphasise what amounts to a multiplicity of localised roads to feminist modernisation, roads that modify and at the same time preserve national, religious, and cultural differences.[18]

Both sides in this debate assume that the experience of the advanced capitalist countries – be it in attaining 'modernisation' or economic development, or in advances in the economic and political status of women correlated with modernisation – can be replicated. They differ in the extent to which they believe that every country has to follow the same path to economic development (i.e. capitalist industrialisation), rather than a populist 'third way', à la Juan Perón, or a socialist or communist way, like Cuba or the former Soviet Union. However, the historical record of the last 50 years has shown the failure both of modernisation theory and of national development projects, whether from the right, the centre or the left. The attainment of national economic

---

16   See, for example, Levy 1966; Rostow 1991; and Inkeles 1974.
17   See, for example, Amin 1976; and Cardoso and Faletto 1979.
18   Ramazanoglu 1989, Part Three.

development or 'capitalism in one country' (i.e. advanced economic development or, in the world-systems framework, 'core country' status) is as impossible as the attainment of 'socialism in one country', for capitalism from its inception has been a world system.[19] As Wallerstein has persuasively argued,[20] the developmentalist goal underlying bourgeois nationalist, populist, socialist and communist development strategies in Latin America, Africa, Asia and Eastern Europe has ended in failure.[21] Despite the billions of dollars loaned to non-socialist countries, the objectives of the Alliance for Progress in Latin America, and the short-term successes of state-sponsored development strategies from the left (e.g. the USSR and the socialist bloc) and the right (e.g. Argentina under Juan Perón), the so-called 'developing nations' were unable to attain sustained levels of economic growth conducive to the growth of their middle strata and attainment of political as well as cultural 'modernisation'. 'Developed' or 'core state status', whether under the aegis of capitalist, socialist or communist ideologies and development strategies, remained unattainable to most countries, with the exception of the few, like the so-called 'Asian Tigers' who attained semi-periphery status. Russia, the first 'underdeveloped country',[22] failed as well despite its initial successes and attainment of 'superpower status', like the far less 'developed' countries of Latin America, the USSR was divided between its small, industrialised 'modern' sector and its vast, poor and undeveloped hinterlands and was unable to withstand the effects of accelerating technological and economic changes in the world system. Despite its size and power, the USSR, like the rest of the underdeveloped world, was unable to escape the 'laws of motion' of the capitalist world system, which, while it allows individual

---

19   While Bolshevik theory postulated that the success of the Russian Revolution depended on the spread of revolution throughout Europe and beyond, Stalinist theory introduced the notion of socialism in one country in 1924, after Lenin's death. Modernisation theory and the development projects of the 1950s and 1960s assumed that it was possible for single countries to attain 'capitalism in one country', irrespective of the place of that country within the world economy. If the systemic nature of capitalism as the dominant mode of production in the world is acknowledged, it becomes clear that the extent to which individual nation states can 'develop' and 'modernise', thus achieving upward mobility within the capitalist world system, is circumscribed by complex political and economic networks beyond the control of a single nation state.

20   Wallerstein 1995; see especially 'The Concept of National Development, 1917–1989: Elegy or Requiem?'

21   It would beyond the scope of this chapter to present and assess the merits of the different arguments scholars have advanced to explain the failure of export substitution development strategies in the poor and relatively poor countries, and the fall of the Soviet Union and its satellites.

22   Shanin 1985.

countries to experience upward mobility, simultaneously pushes others down so that the world stratification profile remains roughly unchanged.

Likewise, the attainment in practice of the full range of human rights or of women's rights in every country is, to a large degree, beyond reach as long as such rights presuppose a relatively advanced degree of capitalist economic, political and legal development. States may copy Western forms of political organisation and foundational documents (such as constitutions). They may go as far as passing legislation aimed at breaking down legal, economic, political and educational barriers to women's full participation and self-determination. But the actual implementation and practice of such reforms presuppose material conditions unattainable by each and every country at the same time. There are both systemic and ecological limits to the attainment, by all countries at the same time, of the status of 'advanced capitalist country'. By systemic I mean rooted in the operation of capitalism as a world system.[23] By ecological I mean the contradiction between the relentless capitalist pursuit of economic growth and the maintenance of environmental sustainability. These same limits are also the limits to the universal emancipation of women, whether we follow the terms of liberal feminism on the one hand or those of postmodern and Third World feminism on the other.

4   Alternative Concept of Universality Rooted in Women's Material Conditions

From a Marxist standpoint, examining these issues at the highest level of abstraction (i.e. the mode of production)[24] means that the alternative to the

---

23   Wallerstein 1974.

24   In *Capital*, Marx presents, at the highest level of abstraction, his theory of how the capitalist mode of production functions, and explains its structure, processes, tendencies and contradictions as if capitalism existed in a pure state, unaffected by nature and history. But in the real world, we do not observe the capitalist mode of production as such; at a lower level of abstraction we observe what Wallerstein calls 'historical capitalism', or what Marxist theorists like Poulantzas call social formations. The key theoretical distinction between the level of analysis of the mode of production and the level of social formations is expressed by Marx as follows: 'The specific economic form, in which unpaid surplus labour is pumped out of direct producers, determine the relationship of rulers and ruled, as it grows directly out of production itself and, in turn, reacts upon it as a determining element. Upon this, however, is founded the entire economic formation of the economic community which grows up out of the production relations themselves, thereby simultaneously its specific political form. It is always the direct relationship of the owners of the conditions of production to the direct producers ... which reveals the innermost secret, the

problems inherent in the transhistorical, universalist notions underlying Western feminism is not the uncritical 'privileging' of the multiplicity of contexts that produce 'diversity' among women, yielding localised struggles with limited and sometimes non-transferable objectives. By non-transferable objectives, I mean the following. On a local level, women, depending on where they live, organise to get things which women in other parts of the world already have (e.g. access to contraceptives) or which would not be meaningful or acceptable to all women everywhere (e.g. the right not to wear a veil; the right to organise as sex workers; the right to keep their income for themselves or to travel without their father's or any other male relative's approval). By non-transferable I don't mean undesirable; I mean either culturally specific, or redundant, in the sense that some battles have already been won in some places while not even attempted in others.

Rather, the alternative is to acknowledge that there is a different kind of universality, rooted in the material conditions that shape the lives of most women on the planet: their location in the organisations of production and reproduction. The vast majority of the world's women work for their economic survival and the survival of their families; most women also participate in the structures where reproduction, biological and social, daily and generational, takes place continuously. I am not arguing that there is an essential unity among women because production and reproduction are activities explainable in terms of their nature. I want to call attention to the fact that most women, regardless of differences associated with nationality, religion, culture, race, and so forth, are working women, engaged in tasks of reproduction and production which, while they vary in their form of organisation between and, sometimes, within countries, are at the same time subject to the effects of the ups and downs of the capitalist national and world economy. For many complex and interrelated

---

hidden basis of the entire social structure, and with it the political form of the relation of sovereignty and dependence, in short, the corresponding specific form of the state. This does not prevent the same economic basis – the same from the standpoint of its main conditions – due to innumerable different, empirical circumstances, natural environments, racial relations, external historical influence, etc. from showing infinite variations and gradations in appearance, which can be ascertained only by analysis of the empirically given circumstances' (Marx 1974, pp. 791–2). Consequently, to theorise at the level of the mode of production and reproduction means to identify structures, processes and contradictions common to all the social formations (e.g. regions, nation states) where the capitalist mode of production is dominant which, in turn, affect people in similar ways. Arguments made at the level of the mode of production, however, must be qualified by the 'innumerable differences, empirical circumstances ...' etc. characteristic of the social formation under consideration.

economic, demographic, political, and ideological reasons, the vast majority of the world's working population is female; women are the poorest of the world's poor. Seventy percent of the 1.3 billion people who live in absolute poverty are women. Women work two-thirds of the world's working hours, produce half of the world's food and yet earn only 10 percent of the world's income and own less than 1 percent of the world's property.[25] Finally, most of the work entailed in the physical and social, daily and generational reproduction of the labouring, propertyless population is done by women. Their common location in the relations of production and reproduction is a universal, yet historical, material base for their potential mobilisation and political organisation. This refers not to women in the abstract, but to working women who, while divided by their historically specific backgrounds, nevertheless share a common objective interest, though not always formulated or understood under 'feminist' ideological principles, based on their working conditions, their earning power, and their concern for the material well-being of themselves and their families.

Theoretically, at the level of analysis of the mode of production, working women's economic interests are objectively similar to those of working men. A feminism that speaks for the interests of working women, rather than women as such, must forcefully acknowledge the self-defeating nature of feminist ideologies and political struggles that place the interests of individual women first. Such ideologies overlook the reality that women, like men, are 'ensembles of social relations', and that their well-being therefore matters to others besides themselves.

At this high level of abstraction, the existence of objective material interests that transcend gender stems from the common class location of propertyless men and women. But at the level of social formations and in the context of everyday social interactions, such common interests are obscured by conflictual, oppressive relations between men and women, rooted in the historical articulation between production and reproduction. These relations affect their relative power and access to key economic, political, social and cultural resources. These relations are contradictory, a unity of cooperation and oppression, and they are as powerful as class relations in shaping working men's and women's life chances, consciousness and identity. The concrete, observable effects of these relations, on the other hand, cannot be deduced a priori from the interests that might theoretically be imputed to them on the basis of their roots in the capitalist organisation of production and reproduction; such

---

25   National Council of Women's Organizations, Facts on Women, http://www
      .womensorganizations.org/facts/facts_11.htm.

effects will be shaped by the historically specific conditions in which people live, namely the political, legal, ideological, and cultural characteristics of the historical context (e.g. locality, region, nation state) under consideration.

I mentioned earlier the need to follow Marx's methodological injunction to differentiate between macro-level processes of structural change and the ideological ways that people become aware of the conflicts caused by such changes and engage in political struggles. If we look at the ways women have been mobilising and organising politically after the women's liberation movements of the 1970s faded, we observe that they do so – in the advanced capitalist countries as well as in the rest of the world – around matters that directly affect their lives as working women, as mothers, and as persons responsible for the well-being of others. They mobilise around issues that affect the physical and economic survival of themselves and their families and, in the process, they struggle for the civil, economic and political rights necessary for attaining those goals. Women involved in grassroots struggles do not deploy individualistic identities. Their spontaneous, common sense understanding of themselves is thoroughly relational and shaped by their location in the relations of reproduction and production.

It is not wealthy, capitalist women who mobilise and organise to struggle for small loans, the right to an education, job training, access to birth control, healthcare, jobs, and better wages. It is propertyless, poor, working-class women who overwhelmingly do so. However, they act often under the leadership of educated women whose aspirations for upward mobility and economic independence are thwarted by the dominant kinship, social and political expectations. Historically, women have not mobilised exclusively under specifically feminist banners, just as class struggles have often been waged under a variety of ideological legitimations. Grassroots women's movements organised around livelihood issues are not new, but have now proliferated all over the world in the wake of the devastation ushered in by globalisation. As structural adjustments erode the availability of waged labour, men and women have had to rely on survival strategies of their own, such as migration and the production of goods and services, for sale and barter, within the growing informal sector of their countries' economies.

From the standpoint of liberal Western feminism, grassroots movements may be celebrated as examples of women's resilience and ingenuity, viewed as a stage in the process of development of feminist consciousness, or, depending on their ideological legitimations, seen as examples of how local customs, cultures, and patriarchal relations keep women from developing a 'true' feminist consciousness. From the standpoint of postmodern feminism, such movements are not just examples of the only kind of politics possible after the demise of metanarratives, but proof that the Enlightenment and Marxist metanarratives have utterly failed.

From the standpoint of Marxist theory, however, these movements are examples of the ways women become conscious of the material processes that tear their lives apart, and do their best to fight for their survival and the survival of their communities. They embody a feminism which expresses itself through struggles centred round issues that include, but transcend, gender. The problems these women face are rooted, not in their identities, but in their common location in the structures of oppression which shape their lives. These structures are a complex unity of universal and particular elements: the universal is capitalism; the particular is the historically specific constellation of kinship, racial, ethnic, and religious inequalities that characterise the social formations where these movements emerge.

Rather than postulating the abstract trilogy of race, gender and class, and/or abstract interlockings of oppressions including and going beyond the standard reference to the trilogy[26] routinely invoked in the literature these days, Marxist theory directs our attention to two areas: (1) the material conditions that affect women's experiences and problems; and (2) the diverse single or combined forms[27] (e.g. gender, ethnic, national origin, racial, or cultural) in which women become conscious of their collective needs and struggle to attain their goals. These forms of consciousness can range from sophisticated theoretical analyses to spontaneous common sense understanding of their responsibilities as

---

26   The race, gender and class social perspective, which emerged in the early 1990s, has acquired enormous visibility as demonstrated by the proliferation of journal articles and books with 'race, gender and class' in their titles, and the creation of a large and growing section within the American Sociological Association and a journal, *Race, Gender & Class*, originally called *Race, Sex & Class*. This perspective emerged as a reaction to feminist theories that neglected racial, ethnic and class differences among women, and as a corrective to Marxism's alleged shortcomings. The routine invocation of this trilogy through the use of a variety of descriptive metaphors (e.g. race, gender and class form a 'matrix' of oppression; they are 'interacting', 'interweaving', or 'interlocking') is insufficient to advance our understanding of the nature of the relations this perspective considers to be fundamental. For examples of this literature, see Collins 1993; Belkhir 1994; Andersen and Collins 1995; and Rothenberg 2000. For critical assessments of the trilogy, see Eagleton 1996 and Gimenez 2001.

27   For example, whether women of Mexican ancestry will self-identify in the US as Mexican-American (an ethnic marker), as Mexican (in the sense of national origin, likely to be chosen by newly arrived immigrants), as Mexican-American women, as Hispanic women or as Latinas depends on their social class, citizenship status, education, region of the country where they live, the visibility of women's organisations and activism where they live, and the effects of the US policies of racial and ethnic classification prevalent at the time, among other factors.

wives and mothers. All of them are the ideological ways in which women construct their identities, become aware of their needs, and envision their goals. These diverse forms of consciousness should not be construed as the only level of analysis within which these phenomena should be theorised. It is important to link these forms of consciousness to their historical conditions of possibility; i.e. to the processes of social change that were conducive to their political mobilisation and organisation.

Once feminist theory acknowledged the historical heterogeneity of real women and exploded into a myriad of feminisms of difference, the feminist political subject became extraordinarily elusive, fragmented along every conceivable axis of difference.[28] Marxist theory illuminates the underlying material conditions, common to all propertyless women, which are key to understanding the limits of theories and politics which ignore the capitalist basis of women's lives. Women's struggles against capitalism, whether self-consciously anti-capitalist and anti-globalisation or cloaked in different forms of ideological legitimation, are object lessons on the relevance of Marx's profound insight: that we are an ensemble of social relations and it is as such that we do everything we do, including struggling for economic survival and social and political rights. Underlying the historical and cross-cultural variability in the ideologies and identities deployed in women's resistance to globalisation is their common location in the modes of production and reproduction.

Conclusion

Feminism in the era of globalisation has to be a Marxist feminism, a feminism that, while supporting struggles for rights and opportunities that matter to all women, courageously acknowledges that all women do not share the same class interests. Such a feminism must see that most of the world's women are working women, whether or not they are proletarianised, and that it is on these grounds that a new kind of feminist theorising and politics could emerge. This is how I envision the relation between Marx and what I call a working women's feminism in the era of globalisation. Marxist theory illuminates the common location of most women in the mode of production, as the most oppressed and exploited members of the world's working classes. At the same time, it illuminates the structures of power and domination and hierarchical relations

---

28   Ramazanoglu 1989, Parts Two and Three; Alcoff 1989; DiStefano 1999, pp. 37–45; Brooks 1997, pp. 92–113.

that underlie the cultural, religious, ideological, national, and ethnic differences among women. More importantly, Marxist theory indicates the limits of struggles for women's rights in a context where the practice of those rights might be forever deferred, given the systemic barriers to the attainment of substantive changes in the standard of living and quality of life for most of the world's population, male and female. While acknowledging the importance of those economic, social and political rights, it shows the need to remain aware that success in the struggles for those rights is not the point of arrival, but the point of departure, a first step in the struggle for systemic change. Women's struggles, which stress the importance of subordinating profits to the satisfaction of people's material and spiritual needs, point the way to the objectives any sustainable alternative to capitalism must fulfil in order to foster people's ability to live up to their potential.

CHAPTER 15

Global Capitalism and Women: from Feminist Politics to Working-Class Women's Politics

In *Globalization and Third World Women: Exploitation, Coping and Resistance*, edited by Ligaya Lindio-McGovern and Isidor Wallimann, Farnham: Ashgate, 2009, pp. 35–48.[1]

Introduction

As capitalism changes the economic, social and political terrain in which the world's working populations struggle to survive, it is more important than ever to examine how these processes are changing women's lives and women's politics. Those processes cannot be properly understood if one takes, as a point of departure, the ideological way in which they have been politically constructed. I have replaced the widely used but misleading term, 'globalisation', with global capitalism to stress the need to understand theoretically and politically the nature of the current processes of change that have united the world under the rule of unfettered capitalism. The world is not undergoing today a benign process of unification under the auspices of anonymous market and social forces. The fall of the Iron Curtain and the Berlin Wall meant the end of political barriers to the emergence, in actuality, of the capitalist world market which Marx and Engels had foreseen in the Manifesto.[2] It is in the context of these processes of accelerated economic and cultural transformation, that changes in the conditions facing working women must be examined. Marxist-feminist theory can contribute by illuminating the capitalist processes altering the lives of all women, particularly working women today.

There is an abundant literature about how global capitalism victimises most working women while creating, at the same time, favourable conditions for the rise of women's resistance. All over the world there are numerous instances of women's grassroots efforts to struggle around a variety of issues such as education, reproductive rights, healthcare, and economic survival.[3] Global capital-

---

1 I have discussed some of these ideas in Gimenez 2004.
2 McCarney 1991, pp. 19–38.
3 See, for example, Rowbotham and Linkogle 2001; Naples and Desai 2002.

ism, however, has other contradictory and important effects on women which need to be theorised to inform future research into the possibilities and limits for the political mobilisation and organisation of women in the US. This is why, in this chapter, I focus on neither women's victimisation nor women's agency, but rather the structural and ideological consequences of global capitalism on working women. More specifically, I focus on the effects of changes in the social relations in the context of which social classes and strata within classes are reproduced. These changes, I will argue, deepen the class divisions among women and are likely to have profound and contradictory effects on women's experiences, consciousness, and the future viability of feminism as a political ideology capable of energising and mobilising women in the United States.[4]

Inequality, Reproduction, and Women's Opportunities under Global Capitalism

One of the most salient and well-known effects of global capitalism is the increase in economic and political inequality within and between nation states. The uncontrolled circulation of capital, legitimated by neoliberal ideologies that celebrate the intrinsic goodness of free markets and deny the necessity of state intervention to ameliorate the negative consequences of economic change have intensified class differences and increased the power and wealth of the capitalist classes. In the poorer countries, the dominant political classes uncritically accepted the neoliberal economic gospel; they implemented structural adjustment policies imposed by the World Bank and the IMF; they privatised national industries, natural resources, utilities and social services, imposing the so-called 'flexibilisation' of labour contracts, a measure that put an

---

4 My analysis rests upon the Marxist notion of class, understood as a relationship between capitalists and workers, mediated by their relationship to the means of production. At the level of analysis of the mode of production, there are two main classes: owners of the means of production and non-owners, the vast majority of the people who must sell their labour to survive. At the level of social formations (e.g. regions, nation states), each class is stratified according to the social and technical division of labour and divided in terms of socio-economic statuses (SES) based on income, occupation and educational differences. Most of the discussion in this chapter proceeds at the level of social formations, where working women are divided by class (e.g. capitalist women working in business or bureaucracies do not share the same interest as women who are factory or office workers), and by socio-economic status (i.e. differences in education, income and occupation which produce antagonisms among women who, in terms of their relationship to the means of production, share the same class position).

end to working-class gains in job stability and pay. Unavoidably, such policies intensified income and wealth inequalities.

The wealthier capitalist countries are not exempt from this process of concentration of wealth and income in the hands of the very few: in the United States, for example, in 2001, 33.4 percent of all privately-held wealth was in the hands of the top 1 percent of households, while 51 percent was in the hands of managers, professionals and small businesses altogether comprising 19 percent of households. This means that 20 percent of households owned 84 percent of the wealth, leaving 16 percent for the bottom 80 percent of households.[5]

The circulation or mobility of capital, which deepens inequality everywhere, is mirrored by the circulation of labour. Migration is not a new economic survival strategy, but the intensification in the circulation of capital and the economic upheavals it produces have, at the same time, increased intra-national and international migration flows. Migrants traveling back and forth between their place of work and country of origin, add to the increasing numbers of people circulating around the globe for personal and political reasons.

It is individuals from the top (e.g. CEOs, top executives, professionals, etc.) and the bottom (e.g. low skill, manual workers) layers of the social classes that circulate the most. The most negatively affected are the working classes, especially working women and their families. We must keep in mind that the well-being of most women is tied to the economic fate of the men of their class. As male wages decline, as male unemployment grows and profit-seeking employers replace male with female labour, women's responsibility for the economic survival of their families expands. In poor countries, women's economic strategies include now, more than ever, migration within and across national borders, for globalisation has resulted in the immiseration of working-class women[6] and the feminisation of the proletariat. The 'feminisation of migration' hints at the enormity of the changes in family organisation and women's roles and expectations taking place today both in wealthy and poor countries because 'in both developing and developed regions, the stable, organized, and mostly male labour force has become increasingly "flexible" and "feminized." Keeping the cost of labour low has encouraged the growth of demand for female labour, while declining household budgets have led to an increase in the supply of job-seeking women'.[7]

Overall, in the 1990s, 50 percent of the world's migrants, about 60 million, are believed to be women; over half of all Filipino immigrants to all coun-

5   Domhoff, 'Wealth, Income and Power', http://sociology.ucsc.edu/whorulesamerica/power.
6   Aguilar 2004, p. 406.
7   Moghadam 1999, pp. 370–1.

tries were women; women comprise about half of all migrants leaving Mexico, India, Korea, Malaysia and African countries, and over half of the migrants arriving to the United States, Canada, Sweden, the United Kingdom and Israel throughout the 1990s.[8] Western and Asian wealthy countries are the chosen destination of millions of women who are unable to find employment in their countries of origin. This unprecedented mobilisation of women across vast distances and national borders reflects the deteriorating conditions facing most male workers in their countries of origin. The switch to export led economic development in the developing countries, together with the effects of structural adjustments imposed by the IMF and the World Bank undermined the power of organised, mainly male labour and resulted in a more flexible, feminised labour force, together with growth in the informal sector, temporary employment and self-employment.[9] Undoubtedly, population growth must be viewed as a contributing factor to poverty and migration but demographic factors must be considered with caution. Contrary to the neo-Malthusian belief that poverty would decrease and wages would rise if the working class were to control its natural increase, it must be kept in mind that 'the demand for labour is not identical with increase of capital' and 'the supply of labour is, to a certain extent, independent of the supply of labourers'.[10] Capital accumulation, which rests upon unceasing changes in the forces of production, as it absorbs some kinds of labour declare others obsolete thus unceasingly producing and reproducing a reserve army of labour or surplus population, some of whose members might choose migration as a survival strategy. This analysis presupposes Marx's distinction between 'labour power' (the capacity to work) and the owners of labour power, the workers themselves; the demand for labour and the level of wages are not determined by the size of the workforce (except under exceptional conditions and temporary conditions) but by economic and political criteria.[11] At any given time, therefore, growth of the surplus population tends to outpace economic growth and increases in the demand for labour, a phenomenon usually understood in ideological, solely demographic, Malthusian terms, a perspective that naturalises the historical effects of the laws of capital accumulation.[12]

The relative decline in economic opportunities for male workers is not exclusive to the poorer countries. In the United States, for example, declining

---

8   Ehrenreich and Hochschild 2002, pp. 5–6.
9   Moghadam 1999, p. 370.
10   Marx 1974, p. 640.
11   See Chapter 6.
12   Marx 1974, pp. 612–712; Gimenez 1998, pp. 461–5.

male earnings, downsizing, de-industrialisation, outsourcing, growth in temporary and contingent work, etc., have pushed countless working women to the labour force. In the US today, the proportion of married couples, with or without children, where men are the sole breadwinners has declined steadily for the last 65 years. In 1940, men were the sole breadwinner in 94 percent of married couples with children under 17. In 2000, men are the sole breadwinner in only 29 percent of these families. Two-pay-check and two-career families are now the norm and women's earnings are keeping millions of families above the poverty level.

This does not mean, however, that there have been no improvements in the status of women in the United States. In the 1960s, civil rights, anti-war and other social movements, including the women's liberation movement changed the political landscape and opened real opportunities for women and racial/ethnic minorities. These processes of change, however, have had contradictory results; they contributed to the liberation and emancipatory objectives of the more privileged women, while strengthening the oppression of working-class women. Today, there are more businesses owned by women, and the proportion of women in executive, managerial and professional occupations has grown since the 1970s. However, despite considerable advances in women's education, employment and income, most women work still in sex-segregated occupations and can be found in the lower levels in the occupational hierarchies.

It is here that we find the confluence between two apparently independent processes of global capitalism:

1. Processes that generate male and female unemployment and poverty in poor countries, pushing millions of working women to migrate and seek employment in the United States and other wealthy countries.
2. Changes in the US economy that eliminated millions of well paid, blue-collar jobs and pushed millions of women into the labour force, thus substantially increasing the demand for service workers willing to do the domestic work that middle-class working women cannot do and more privileged women will not do.

The combined effects of stagnating male wages, increase in women's employment and increase in the number of immigrant women willing to do service work, regardless of their skills and education, is altering the organisation of domestic labour or, from the standpoint of Marxist-feminist theory, the domestic social relations of reproduction. In the long-run, this reorganisation is likely to have contradictory ideological effects. Among the more privileged, upper strata of working women, it has the potential to undermine their support for feminism and feminist politics. Among middle and working-class women, there is the possibility of greater openness to women's politics. Last, but not least, among the domestic workers themselves, immigrant and native, white and non-white, it creates the conditions potentially favourable for political mobilisation and unionisation.

I define the domestic relations of reproduction as the relations between the agents of reproduction (e.g. the relations between married or cohabiting men and women and their children; the relations between couples and their paid domestic workers, etc.) mediated by their relationship to the conditions of reproduction (e.g. the house, its contents and grounds; the money and other resources necessary to provide for household needs; household tools, implements, appliances, etc.). The degree of women's economic dependence on their husbands' or partners' income; the extent of their own economic resources and contributions to the household; the use of domestic workers and the quantity and quality of domestic labour they can purchase affect their relative power, and the quality of the domestic relations of reproduction. This terminology might appear cumbersome; wouldn't it be easier to refer to the effects of the increased availability and affordability of domestic workers as changes in the domestic division of labour within the family? Family, however, is an ideologically loaded concept that obscures the nature of the social processes that go on within it. Ideologies about romance, motherhood, gender, family roles, social norms and expectations about husbands and wives, parents and children shape the common sense understanding of family and family life. These ideologies surrounding the family exclude from consideration what the domestic social relations of reproduction actually accomplish. Whatever the family structure, size, sexual preferences of the adult members, class location, and location in the racial and ethnic structures may be, the social relations of reproduction reproduce social classes and strata within classes. Instead of asking whether or not working women, native born or immigrants, are appropriately fulfilling their gender and care taking roles, it is important to ask, how are social classes reproduced? How are the physical and psychological energies of workers of all kinds, and managers, and capitalists and small business owners, etc., replenished every day? How are the new generations of members of these classes reproduced so that when they grow old and die there are others who will take their place? In what context are gender, racial and ethnic identities formed? Asking such questions leads us to focus on the social relations within which classes and strata within classes are reproduced and to wonder about the ideological impact, on the present and future generations, of changes in the social relations of reproduction.

A focus on families and family roles leads social scientists to view the results of transnational migration as the creation of 'care deficits'. A 'care deficit' is created in the wealthy countries, as more women seek and find full time employment and cannot care for their homes and families. Simultaneously, a 'care deficit' is created in the poor countries, because women who migrate leave uncared for children and elderly parents at home in order to give strangers' children and homes, thousands of miles away, the love and care they should have been bestowing upon their own families. In an important and informative article, for example, Professor Salazar-Parreñas[13] writes that there is a care crisis in the Philippines, where the children of migrant women experience a variety of problems. The women themselves are vilified by the media and the government for not fulfilling their nurturant role, though between 43 and 54 percent of the Filipino population is supported by migrant women's monthly remittances to their families. This article is important because it highlights the contradiction between the new experiences that global capitalism is imposing upon migrant women, and the persistence of traditional expectations about women's family roles. This situation is likely to remain unchanged, in the Philippines and other countries which are also source of large outflows of migrant women, because the efficacy, strength or persistence of traditional values or ideologies depends on whether or not people continue to live according to those values.

In poor countries, neoliberal economic policies have succeeded in excluding the majority of the population from benefitting from economic growth. Most people continue to struggle for a living under conditions that remain relatively unchanged, in which the traditional ideologies continue to make sense. At the same time, as national job markets shrink, overseas opportunities open for employment in service jobs traditionally reserved for women. Working-class women are forced to transcend the limitations of gender ideologies and family expectations in order to find employment wherever it may be available. The contradictory effects of global capitalism both sustain the strength of traditional ideologies among those left behind, while at the same time undermining them, by forcing masses of people, mostly women, to violate their injunctions in order to support their families.

This analysis of care deficits in the family, heightened demand for domestic workers and service workers in wealthy countries, and government insensibility to the conflicting demands that tear migrant women's lives apart is important but insufficient to understand the implications of current processes of change. It describes the visible effects of underlying changes in the capitalist organisation of social reproduction.

---

13   Salazar-Parreñas, 2003.

The Gendered Social Reproduction of Class and Potentials for Struggle and Resistance

Under capitalism, the process of working-class reproduction in all its aspects is left mainly to the ingenuity of the workers themselves; it is private and the extent to which the state takes some responsibility depends on the outcome of class struggles and political compromises. Employed wage and salary workers are able to create relatively stable living conditions for themselves and their children, the future members of their class. Those who cannot find work or find work at poverty or near poverty wages, reproduce the future members of the poverty population which in the US, in 2006, numbered 36.5 million, including 12.8 million children under age 18.[14]

The conflict between domestic and paid labour demands place most working people, particularly working women, in a very difficult position. Global capitalism intensifies this conflict by creating the conditions that push an ever-increasing proportion of women to the labour force, whether in their own countries or elsewhere. By 2004, 59.2 percent of American women were in the labour force (a light decline from 60 percent in 1999); 71 percent of mothers with children under 18 are in the labour force and 35 percent of working wives contribute 35 percent of the family income.[15] At the same time, global capitalism provides also a solution, through the growth in the numbers of legal and undocumented immigrant women, open to exploitation in low paid service occupations in the public sector and low-paid domestic work such as nannies, maids, baby sitters, cooks, etc.

In the Philippines, Mexico and the many other countries that have become exporters of female labour, underlying the 'care deficit' is a crisis in the reproduction of the working classes. While their social reproduction was never secure, migration, especially the migration of women, forces the relatives left behind to care for children and the elderly, developing survival strategies that could potentially result in collective solutions at the grassroots level. This situation calls for state intervention through welfare policies providing support to unemployed or underemployed fathers left in charge of their children and/or to the relatives or elderly parents who step in to care for children whose mothers work abroad.

---

14   US Bureau of the Census, Poverty: 2006 Highlights, http://www.census.gov.hhes/www/
      poverty/poverty06/povo6hi.html. Last retrieved in 2006.
15   Women in the Labor Force: A Databook [Highlights]. *US Department of Labor, Bureau of
      Labor Statistics*, http://www.bls.gov/cps/wlf-databook2005.html. Last retrieved in 2006.

State priorities in poor countries, however, are biased against the interests of those too poor and too powerless to challenge, politically, the status quo. It is left to the ingenuity of the people left in care of their children and the elderly to devise strategies for care and survival, strategies which have the potential to create community based or collective solutions. Fundamental to activate this potential would be a change in the way the situation is framed in public discourse. A discourse that frames the issue as one of 'care deficit' reproduces the traditional nurturant female role and does not transcend the privatised nature of social reproduction under capitalism. An alternative discourse could highlight the importance of household or domestic labour as the labour that reproduces the working classes; instead of criticising migrant women, it would explore possible alternative social relations of reproduction designed to ensure the health and education of future generations of workers. Such a discourse could, hypothetically, lead to a different and positive appreciation of the sacrifices migrant women make and could contribute to the reorganisation of the relations of reproduction in ways that could trigger processes of grassroots organisation and self-reliance.

If the tasks required for reproducing the present and future generations of workers are ideologically delinked from gender expectations and, instead, are understood as forms of socially necessary labour of crucial importance for the well-being of the working classes and the nation as a whole, this change in articulating their significance could help alleviate ideological and social pressures on migrant women, thus opening the way for the exploration of community or collective solutions. Changes in dominant ideologies or discourses are not easy and cannot be achieved overnight – but women's organisations in the US and in the countries that export female labour, like the Philippines, could begin the hard work of de-gendering the social relations of reproduction, and legitimating collective forms of social reproduction in which men and women, kin and non-kin members of the community would be engaged.

In wealthy countries, like the US, that people resolve the conflict between family and work by substituting their own labour with the labour of others, or by lowering household cleanliness standards and eating out is not a new phenomenon. What is new is the growth in the supply of household workers who sell their labour either on an individual basis or through corporations such as the Merry Maids. Global capitalism is democratising the use of domestic servants in the US.[16] Formerly a privilege of the wealthy, who have always had an array of household workers (butlers, housekeepers, governesses, nannies,

---

16   Ehrenreich 2000, pp. 59–70.

maids, cooks, gardeners and chauffeurs), the use of domestic workers is spreading from the wealthy and the upper middle classes to the rest of the population, especially in the main urban centre where immigrants tend to flock. The spread of the use of domestic workers is altering, in the context of middle-class households, the nature of domestic relations of reproduction between men and women. The issue of domestic labour and the conflict between men and women, parents and children, about who does what, when, and where; and the conflict between paid work and domestic work were a cornerstone of feminist theorising in the late 1970s and 1980s and continue to be one of the contributing determinants of gender inequality. I will not claim that, by shifting most of these tasks to the labour of paid workers, those conflicts are fully resolved. All that the use of domestic workers accomplishes is to minimise marital or partner conflict while maintaining the privatised nature of social reproduction under capitalism unchanged. My concern is different and has to do with the ideological and reproductive effects of this massive reorganisation of the mode of reproduction upon the women who hire domestic workers, upon their children, especially the daughters, and upon the women, mostly immigrant, who work as domestic workers.

Social Reproduction and Feminist Ideology and Policies

What is the potential ideological effects, on women who hire domestic workers, of the experience of largely doing away with all or most of the demands of household work? This experience has the potential to change women's self-understanding, identity, awareness of possibilities, and relative openness to feminist politics. My hypothesis is that women who, as children, grew up in a household where domestic labour was done by paid workers, while their mothers were full-time workers focused mainly on the social aspects of reproduction (e.g. child socialisation, play, education, etc.) are likely to find it difficult to empathise with or understand fully the inequalities that continue to shape most women's lives. Combining family and work responsibilities is likely to seem easy to young women raised in such a home environment, where having domestic workers is taken for granted as a part of everyday life. The argument I want to make, therefore, is that global capitalism has the potential to undermine – among a substantial proportion of US working women – the ability to mobilise politically as women, by undermining the experiential grounds for their receptivity to feminist ideology and politics, especially those forms of feminism that stress not just women's inequality in the world of work, but women's inequality and oppression in their own homes.

Feminist ideology in the United States reflected special historical conditions which made it unavoidable for women to select gender as their primary identity rather than class, work, race, ethnicity, nationality or other potential identities. The very success of the American economy in providing paid employment for working-class women, reduced the supply and increased the cost of household help, especially the live-in kind. After the Second World War, the employment of domestic workers ceased to be the badge of middle-class status but remained, primarily, the customary privilege of the capitalist and the upper-middle classes. Middle-class, educated American women thus experienced the kind of domestic oppression that their counterparts in poor countries seldom knew, for in poor countries there is an oversupply of poor girls and young women for whom domestic service is the first step out of the farm or out of poverty and into the world of work. This experience of domestic oppression was one of the forces that fuelled the late 1960s women's movement and the development of socialist and Marxist-feminist theories.[17] As global capitalism increases the supply of domestic workers, thus lowering their cost, the use of domestic workers for childcare, cooking, housecleaning, elder care, and so forth, is likely to increase. This practice, it can be plausibly argued, is likely to weaken and perhaps eliminate, particularly among women who hire full-time domestic workers, the experiences of domestic inequality and oppression necessary for women's self-perception in terms of their gender, and for their support for feminist ideologies and politics.

Full-time work is also likely to have important ideological effects. Women's employment, which has increased to the point that almost 60 percent of women are in the labour force by changing women's experiences and self-understanding, has the potential to open up the possibility that women may begin to see themselves primarily as working women, whose issues have to do not only, or necessarily, with their gender but with their location in the occupational and class structures as female workers. This could be considered a welcome potential change, conducive to the emergence of a working women's feminism.

So far, this discussion has been centred round the middle and upper-middle strata. However, most women workers are part of working class, dual paycheck, not dual career families, and the main reason why they work is likely to be economic necessity. These households are not likely to use domestic servants like the more affluent dual career or single earner households. Their way of coping with the conflicting demands of household work and waged work is

17   Gimenez 1990, pp. 25–45.

likely to be declining health (because of the consumption of fast foods) and quality of life. Working-class women's employment and income increase their power in the home but do not undermine the economic importance of marriage or a stable partnership. And what about the potential ideological effects, among immigrant women, of doing domestic work or low-paid service work in a place so distant from their homes and culturally so different? All immigrant women, whether students or workers, are caught between competing loyalties to their homeland and families on the one hand, and to themselves on the other, for their decision to immigrate is also a decision to change and develop in ways unforeseen in their childhood. What can feminism offer to them?

In the US today, immigrant women workers and students face two main feminist alternatives: 1) universalistic feminist goals expressed in documents produced by the United Nations and innumerable NGOs all over the world; and 2) the postmodern and non-western feminist critique of those goals, which give priority to cultural, religious, and national differences and identities.[18] Western feminists can stress the importance of individual rights and individual self-determination because they do not live within tightly knit communities and extended kinship networks in which kin ties are also economic ties. And postmodern western feminists celebrate the fluidity of identities and the primacy of culture, race and ethnicity over class, because they do not experience the constraints many cultures impose upon women, and because their secure economic positions renders class theoretically invisible.

Neither ideological path offers a politically acceptable alternative to immigrant women workers and students. To self-identify as women, in pursuit of equal economic, political and civil rights, is important individually, but insufficient to attain collective improvements in their location, as a group, in the economic and racial/ethnic stratification of this country. To self-identify in terms of racial/ethnic or cultural identities can be both empowering and, at the same time, self-defeating. Why? Because acceptance of the racial, ethnic minority label means that their work-related grievances can be heard only if framed in the context of civil rights violations, not in the context of violations of their rights as working women. Self-identification as women leads to the same

---

18 This polarisation of views reflects, at the level of ideology, the uneven material development of global capitalism and the enormous gap between the material conditions that shape the experiences and political consciousness of relatively privileged western and western-educated women on the one hand, and the vast majority of the world's female population on the other.

paradoxical situation: woman and/or minority woman are identities accept-able within the dominant political discourse; working-class and working-class women do not fit, particularly if women do not have a union to back their claims.

Marxist-feminist theory offers an alternative perspective that both preserves and transcends this polarity, an alternative based on the universality rooted in the material conditions that shape the lives of most women on the planet: their location in the organisations of production and reproduction. The vast majority of the world's women work for their economic subsistence and the economic survival of their families. Their work reproduces the world's working classes. Most women, regardless of differences associated with culture, religion, nationality, race, etc., are working women who are subject to the ups and downs of the capitalist national and world economies. Their common location in the relations of production and reproduction is a universal, yet historical, material base, for their potential mobilisation and political organisation not as women and not as workers, but as working women.

Conclusion

As global capitalism alters the employment opportunities of the world's work-ing classes, it simultaneously changes the organisation of social reproduction; i.e. the network of social relations within which present and future members of different social classes are physically and socially reproduced, daily and genera-tionally. In poor countries, the effects of these processes fall most heavily upon the rural and urban working populations. The relative decline in employment opportunities for working-class men has led to the 'feminisation' of interna-tional migration and the rise of a 'care deficit', which leaves the care of children and the elderly in the hands of fathers and relatives. Working-class relations of reproduction are thus changed in ways that could potentially increase state involvement and awareness of the need to assume responsibility for the future generations of workers. However, given the capitalist trend to substitute living labour with dead labour objectified in machinery and technology, it is unlikely that states, usually eager to foster investments, will respond in ways favourable to the reproduction of a healthy, educated and skilled working class. It is up to women's organisations to challenge the gendered ideological understanding of the effects of female migration, and to posit instead, the valorisation of repro-ductive labour, delinked from gender expectations and politically constructed as a valuable socially necessary labour which should be a social, rather than private responsibility.

In wealthy countries, the increased availability and use of domestic workers by a broad strata of the working population is likely to lessen present and future generations of relatively privileged working women's receptivity to feminist politics beyond claims for individual rights that transcend class divisions such as, for example, reproductive rights and equal employment and educational opportunities. Global capitalism, then, deepens class, socio-economic and racial/ethnic inequality among women but, as it increases women's employment, it also opens the possibility for the emergence of a different form of women's political consciousness which, at this time, I call 'working women's feminism'. Capitalism, I argue, has the potential of producing contradictory ideological effects, dividing women's interests, undermining feminist concerns with women's oppression 'as women' while opening, at the same time, the possibility for the emergence of a new feminism, one that acknowledges and seeks to transcend the real antagonisms among working women, whether native-born or immigrant.

As the paid labour of household workers changes the domestic division of labour and the constraints more privileged working women face in their daily lives, their work and home experiences change qualitatively, thus modifying their self-perception as well as their children's views about gender roles. As women's experience of oppression moves from the home to the workplace, there is the potential for the rise of a new feminism which, like the old, will continue to be predicated upon the contradictions inherent in capitalist societies, now intensified by the effects of global capitalism. However, this might be an excessively optimistic scenario; as more American women live lives relatively unconstrained by household responsibilities, this might altogether undermine their openness to feminist ideologies and politics, except those that are unlikely to challenge their class and job privileges.

I have identified the changing contexts where women work and live and have presented some considerations about the potential effects of these changes upon women's consciousness. But structural changes do not generate ideologies automatically; it is important that women concerned with the need for a new women's movement may start dialogues between working women, immigrants and native-born, white and non-white. These dialogues should challenge the dominant cultural and political discourses because they endorse identity politics, de-legitimating class as a key dimension of everyone's life, and do not acknowledge the individual and social significance of work, including the socially necessary private and social reproduction work done by tens of thousands of workers, mostly immigrant women of colour, engaged in cleaning and service work. Such dialogues should make visible working women's class location, identifying shared interests as workers while acknowledging also, in a straightforward manner, the class interests that divide them. Working-class feminism may seem Utopian today. But identity politics have structural limits that need to be acknowledged. Legislation against gender, racial and immigrant discrimination and in support of equal opportunity does not change the material realities of job scarcity, working-class exploitation, and racial/ethnic oppression. Capital's mobility and capacity to close plants, downsize and outsource with impunity has undermined the class power of working men and women. But working women employed in service occupations, for example, both in domestic and public settings, are engaged in socially necessary labour, a labour that cannot be outsourced or downsized without dire social consequences. Objectively, this gives them some leverage, but objective conditions are not sufficient; social movements spring to life as society changes and alters the outlook of many people at the same time. In the meantime, women activists can raise awareness of the social significance of the work women do and of the importance of recognising that gender and racial/ethnic identities are, within the context of American politics, the ideological ways in which consciousness of exploitation and oppression start. Consciousness-raising may seem somewhat old-fashioned today, but society has changed in ways that perhaps make it imperative to start all over again, this time with a broader comprehension of the macro-level, global processes that affect working women's lives.

CHAPTER 16

Capitalism and the Oppression of Women: Marx Revisited

'Capitalism and the Oppression of Women: Marx Revisited', in *Science & Society*, Vol. 69, No. 1 (January 2005): 11–32.

Since the end of the Soviet Union and the socialist bloc, capitalism has intensified its grasp over the entire world, unleashing processes of economic change that intensify and render increasingly visible the links between the fate of people in the advanced capitalist countries and the rest of the world's population. In this historical context, a return to an examination of the relevance of Marx for feminism makes sense – despite the now fashionable academic belief in its irrelevance – because, as long as capitalism remains the dominant mode of production, it is impossible fully to understand the forces that oppress women and shape the relations between men and women without grounding the analysis in Marx's work.

Like the social sciences, second wave feminist thought developed largely in a dialog with Marx; not with the real Marx, however, but with a 'straw Marx' whose work is riddled with failures (e.g. failure to theorise childbirth, women's labour, the oppression of women), determinisms and reductionisms (e.g. class reductionism, economic determinism, vulgar materialism), disregard for 'agency', 'sex blind categories', and 'misogyny'.[1] If Marx's work (and the Marxist tradition, by implication) were indeed substantively afflicted by all the shortcomings that social scientists and feminists attribute to it, it would have been long forgotten. But Marx's intellectual power and vitality remain undiminished, as demonstrated by the extent to which even scholars who reject

---

1 See, for example, Eisenstein 1979; Hartmann 1981, pp. 1–41; O'Brien 1981. Vogel's point, that socialist feminists 'have worked with a conception of marxism that is itself inadequate and largely economistic' (Vogel 1981, p. 197) is relevant to earlier and more recent feminist critiques of Marx and Marxist thought. See also Benhabib and Cornell 1987, pp. 1–5; Nicholson 1987, pp. 16–30; DiStefano 1991, pp. 146–63. With the exception of Nicholson and DiStefano, most feminist writings since the late 1960s offer unsupported assertions about standardised flaws (class reductionism, economic determinism, etc.) in Marx and in Marxist theory in general. This practice indicates that many feminist writers and their editors share a set of taken-for-granted stereotypical beliefs about Marx and Marxism such that editors do not insist on citations to support the standard criticisms.

it must grapple with his work, so much so that their theories are shaped by the very process of negating it. For example, early feminist rejection of Marx's 'economic determinism' led to the production of ahistorical theories of patriarchy that sought the origins of male domination outside modes of production.[2] More recent feminist theories (grounded in the poststructuralist rejection of Marxism) have, paradoxically, turned to discourse determinism in their efforts to reject Marx's alleged 'economic determinism' and 'class reductionism'.[3] The deconstruction of 'women' as a category of analysis, the focus on 'discursively constructed' genders, sexualities, bodies, and manifold differences among women seem to have severed the links between Marx's work, feminist theory and women's liberation. As Epstein argues, 'feminist theory has come to mean feminist post-structuralism' and this entails the adoption of principles (e.g. anti-essentialism, social constructionism, the reduction of social reality to discourse, relativism, the rejection of macro-level theories, the so-called 'metanarratives') antithetical to the development of social analyses and political strategies useful for all social movements, including women's liberation.[4] The very idea of women's oppression and struggles for liberation presupposes the material reality of their plight and the validity of their claims, notions outside the purview of theories for which everything is relative and discursively constructed.

Equally important as a barrier to the development of Marxist feminism is the belief, widespread among Marxist scholars, students, and academics in general, that while Marx's work might be important for the study of political economy, the state, ideology, social class and other aspects of capitalist societies, it has little to contribute to feminism, beyond the awareness that it is important to examine the ways capitalism, in addition to patriarchy, or to systems of male dominance, contributes to the oppression of women.

It is not my goal, however, to engage in a critique of feminist poststructuralism, the feminist literature about/against Marx, or the views of those who,

---

2   Chapter 2, in this volume, offers an earlier examination of the problems inherent in earlier feminist theories, including patriarchy. For a critical assessment of ahistorical theories of patriarchy, see Barrett 1980; McDonough and Harrison 1978, pp. 11–41; Beechey 1987, pp. 95–116. Attempts to historicise patriarchy (e.g. McDonough and Harrison 1978, pp. 11–41; Hartmann 1976, pp. 137–69) result in the study of its changing forms while patriarchy itself remains constant. For a critique of theories of patriarchy as an ahistorical and tautological attempt to account for the ubiquitous nature of gender inequality, see Middleton 1988, pp. 41–5.

3   The poststructuralist reduction of social reality to discourse or text has been critiqued as discourse determinism or reductionism by, for example, Alcoff 1989 and Ebert 1995. For a critical understanding of discourse that links it to the workings of capitalism, see Hennessy 1993.

4   Epstein 1995, p. 83; see also DiStefano 1989, pp. 75–6.

though knowledgeable about Marx's work, have a relatively narrow view of its theoretical scope. Instead, I will present my understanding of the usefulness of some aspects of Marx's work that are theoretically and politically important for feminists.[5]

Marx's Method and Its Relevance for Understanding How Capitalism Oppresses Women

Although Marx did not write specifically and at length about the oppression of women, his work is a source of methodological and theoretical insights necessary to grapple with the oppression of women under capitalism, and with the limitations capitalism poses to feminist politics.

Any consideration of the oppression of women brings to mind a variety of psychological, economic, social and political phenomena affecting women's lives, ranging from rape, incest, domestic violence and sexual harassment, to social stereotyping, low-paid and gender-segregated employment, discrimination in educational and occupational institutions, the sexual division of labour, domestic labour and the contradiction between domestic and work demands, reproductive issues and the struggle for reproductive self-determination, the under-representation of women in political offices and public leadership roles and, unavoidably, patriarchy.

In its various formulations, patriarchy posits men's traits and/or intentions as the cause of women's oppression. This way of thinking diverts attention from theorising the social relations that place women in a disadvantageous position in every sphere of life and channels it towards men as the cause of women's oppression. But men do not have a privileged position in history such that, independent of social determinations, they have the foresight and power consciously to shape the social organisation in their favour. Men, like women, are social beings whose characteristics reflect the social formation within which they emerge as social agents.

---

5   My work, influenced by my training as a sociologist and by Althusser's and Godelier's work (Althusser 1970; Althusser and Balibar 1970; Godelier 1972; 1973, pp. 334–68), shares their interest in Marx's methodology. Like Vogel, I give importance to the organisation of reproduction as one of the foundations of the oppression of women, but my writings have been more self-consciously methodological. I have explored the relevance of Marx's method, as developed by Marx and elaborated by Althusser and Godelier, to identify the non-observable structures and social relations underlying the visible patterns of interaction between men and women that place the latter in a subordinate position.

Marx cautions against projecting into the past or into a universal human nature the attributes people exhibit in the present; e.g. the individual for whom it is natural to engage in market competition and utility maximisation is the product of bourgeois society, of a particular historical epoch.[6] Likewise, we have to examine the historical conditions that produce and reproduce current unequal social relations and forms of consciousness among men and women[7] resulting in the various phenomena listed above, and this entails examination of their capitalist conditions of possibility. To do so from within Marx's theoretical and methodological standpoint requires an understanding of the relevance, for the analysis of the oppression of women, of Marx's dialectical and materialist ontology and methodology as well as of the basic premises of historical materialism. What follows is my interpretation of some of Marx's texts on methodology, political rights, historical materialism and capitalism to show their relevance for both Marxist and feminist theory and politics.

To grasp the capitalist determinants of the oppression of women it is indispensable to follow Marx's methodology,[8] i.e. his dialectical understanding of abstraction, his critique of the search for origins in isolation from and prior to the analysis of the historically specific structures and relations underlying the phenomena under consideration, his conception of history and the dialectics of the general and the particular. I believe that Marx's most important potential contributions to feminist theory and politics reside precisely in the aspect of his work that most feminists ignored: his methodology. Exclusive focus on what he said and did not say about women has precluded feminist theorists from exploring the potential of his methodological insights to deepen our understanding of the phenomena called 'the oppression of women' or, in earlier times, the 'woman question'.

In his only explicitly methodological statement,[9] Marx argues that those aspects of social reality that seem to us the most concrete and obvious, the starting point of our investigations are, however, the least informative because they presuppose multiple historical conditions of possibility that cannot be

---

6 Marx 1970, p. 189.

7 I am aware of the problematic implications of using men and women as categories of analysis. But to consider that one's only theoretical options are essentialism and its negation, the fragmented and decentred postmodern subject, is to remain mired in undialectical thinking. I view 'men' and 'women' as universal concretes, as the unity of the universal material aspects of the human species (i.e. the ways in which humans are conditioned by their biology and the natural environment), and the historically specific ensemble of social relations within which people live their lives and organise production and reproduction.

8 See, for example, Marx 1970, pp. 20–1 and 188–214.

9 Marx 1970, pp. 205–14.

grasped without further theoretical and historical analysis.[10] We attain knowledge when we advance from those 'imaginary concrete concepts' (e.g. women, men, family, childcare, etc.) to 'increasingly simple concepts' or abstractions, meaning partial, one-sided aspects of complex phenomena such as domestic labour, sexual division of labour, and gender. Then, after theoretical and empirical investigation of the historical social relations or conditions of possibility of these abstractions, we return to the phenomena that concerned us, now understood as 'a totality comprising many determinations and relations'. The concept is now a 'real concrete' because it is 'a synthesis of many definitions, thus representing the unity of diverse aspects'.[11]

Marx's dialectical ontology posits that every abstraction or category of analysis captures only a moment or aspect of a complex totality; things are what they are because of their relationships with other things, which are not always visible to immediate perception but can be identified if, instead of taking for granted the empirically observable in itself, as all there is, we inquire instead about its conditions of possibility and change. This methodological stance entails a distinction between the observable and the unobservable aspects of social reality and directs us to the search for the underlying conditions and social relations that render possible that which we are able to observe; 'all science would be superfluous if the outward appearance and the essence of things directly coincided'.[12]

For example, we become aware of the inequality between men and women through its observable forms: unequal pay, unequal education and opportunities, domestic violence, women's main responsibility for children and domestic work, etc. Feminists, working mainly with the theoretical tools of the social sciences, produced 'simple abstractions'; e.g. sexual division of labour, sexual stratification, gender, gender stratification, patriarchy, sex/gender system, the exchange of women, etc. The feminist question, 'Why are women oppressed "as women"?' – women being an abstraction that not only ignores the heterogeneity of the population it describes, but also fails to interrogate the conditions under which females would self-identify as such rather than in terms of class, national origin or other possible identities – together with the political rejection of Marxism's alleged class reductionism and economism, produced ahistorical answers: e.g. biological inequality in procreation;[13] men's exchange of

---

10   Ibid., p. 205.
11   Ibid, pp. 205–6.
12   Marx 1968, p. 817.
13   Firestone 1971.

women;[14] men's decision to control reproduction in order to oppress women;[15] mothering;[16] and patriarchy or men's desire to control and benefit from women's domestic services.[17]

Marx's methodological insights suggest that we need to look at the inequality between men and women in their historical context. In the Marxist sense, this does not mean a search for origins or a chronological account of changes in, for example, the sexual division of labour, sexual or gender stratification, ideological or discursive constructions of gender, etc. To place a phenomenon and the categories with which we attempt to characterise it in their historical context means, first, to elucidate its conditions of possibility and support within a given mode of production (e.g. capitalism) and, second, to investigate the historical processes leading to its capitalist form. Marx states:

> It would be inexpedient and wrong ... to present the economic categories successively in the order in which they have played the dominant role in history. On the contrary, their order of succession is determined by their mutual relation in modern bourgeois society and this is quite the reverse of what appears to be natural to them or in accordance with the sequence of historical development. The point at issue is ... their position within modern bourgeois society.[18]

Marx acknowledges that all modes of production have common features, the basis for general categories of analysis that social scientists identify through historical and cross-cultural comparisons. However, these general concepts (e.g. sexual division of labour, sexual inequality, etc.) are themselves 'a multifarious compound comprising divergent categories ... The most modern periods and the most ancient periods will have [certain] categories in common', a commonality that follows 'from the very fact that the subject, mankind, and the object, nature, are the same'; but what matters, what constitutes the development of these categories is 'precisely their divergence from those general and common features ... their essential differences'.[19]

---

14   Rubin 1975, pp. 157–210.
15   Einsenstein 1979.
16   Chodorow 1978.
17   Hartmann 1981.
18   Marx 1970, p. 213.
19   Marx 1970, p. 190.

Production and Reproduction as Historically Specific Phenomena

For Marx, simple abstractions or general categories yield only partial and mis-leading knowledge, misleading because they universalise that which is histor-ically specific to a given mode of production. He gives the example of capital; if the specific relations of production and the specific form of surplus appropri-ation are omitted, any accumulation of wealth can be viewed as capital which, then, appears as 'a universal and eternal relation given by nature'.[20] In the case of the reproduction of human beings, if the historically specific social relations within which biological, physical and social reproduction occur are omitted, it appears as if human reproduction (and the relations between men and women, parents and children it entails) is an unchanging societal universal so powerful, in the eyes of some feminists, that equality between the sexes might require the use of technology to abolish biological reproduction.[21]

More precise knowledge, Marx argues, is produced through recognition of the historical specificity of the phenomena we intend to understand with the use of general categories.[22] There is *no production in general* and, likewise, *no human reproduction in general*; instead, there is capitalist or feudal or sub-sistence production (or reproduction), and so forth. Also, there is *no general production or general reproduction*; production and reproduction are always *particular*, e.g. industrial production, reproduction of specific social classes, etc.

True, Marx did not write at length about the inequality between men and women; nevertheless, his views on the logic of inquiry are important to help us theorise the capitalist structures, processes and contradictions that underlie the observable phenomena called the oppression of women or gender inequal-ity. Marx historicises competitive market relations and their corresponding political and legal frameworks by identifying the capitalist coercive (i.e. inde-pendent of people's will), unequal and exploitative relations of production underlying the sphere of 'Freedom, Equality, Property and Bentham'.[23] Like-wise, it is possible to historicise the observable market, social stratification and household forms of inequality between men and women (e.g. sex-segregated employment, the sexual division of labour within and outside households) by identifying their conditions of possibility in underlying historically spe-cific (capitalist) relations among men and women, as producers and reprodu-

---

20   Ibid.
21   Firestone 1971.
22   Marx 1970, p. 191.
23   Marx 1967, p. 176.

cers. These capitalist social relations of reproduction are not intersubjective relations; they are relations between men and women mediated by their relations to the conditions of production and reproduction.[24] Just as the relations between social classes are mediated by people's relationship to the means of production (the material basis of the power the owners of the means of production exert over the non-owners), so the relationships between men and women under capitalism are mediated by their differential access to the conditions necessary for their physical and social reproduction, daily and generationally.

The fundamental principle underlying this analysis is that, in the social formations where capitalism is the dominant mode of production, the functioning of the mode of production determines the social organisation – establishes historical limits for its variability – and the economic foundations of human reproduction or mode of reproduction.[25] The mode of reproduction, in the context of this analysis, is the historically specific combination of labour, and the conditions and means of reproduction (the material basis – biological and economic – for the performance of reproductive tasks) in the context of relations among the agents of reproduction.

There is no historically specific name for the mode of reproduction, except the common sense, ahistorical concept of 'family', which denotes its most widespread observable forms. Though awkward, in light of the ease with which it is possible to think about family and domestic relations, the concepts of mode of reproduction and agents of reproduction are important because they shift attention from 'the family' and different or 'deviant' (depending on the observer's values) family forms to a different object of theorising and research: the transhistorical, necessary process of human physical and social reproduction and the capitalist underpinnings of its observable forms within societies where the capitalist mode of production is dominant; e.g. nuclear families, single-parent households, orphanages, etc.

---

24 Mediation, as a mode of determination, refers to the way the relationship between two variables is shaped by the relationship between each one and a third variable. For example, the relationship between capitalists and workers is the effect of their respective relations (ownership and non-ownership) to the means of production. Among people who need to work for a living, on the average, men earn higher wages or salaries than women; this places women, especially single women and single mothers, in a dependent, subordinate position. For further discussion of this mode of determination, see Wright 1978, p. 23.

25 For other Marxist-feminist analyses of the role of reproduction in the oppression of women, see Vogel 1983; Brenner and Ramas 1984. Engels 1972 argued that production is always twofold, for it entails the production of things and, at the same time, the production of human life; his work established the theoretical foundations for Marxist feminism.

While the vast majority of households start as heterosexual unions, whether or not the actual organisation of reproduction takes the form of a nuclear family (parents and children only) or includes other biologically related and/or unrelated members, varies according to social class, marital status, socio-economic status, sexual preference, employment, culture, race, ethnicity, the relative powers of classes reflected in state welfare and family policies, and so forth.

Furthermore, changes in the 'forces of reproduction' (i.e. changes in reproductive technologies) have been instrumental in creating conditions for novel forms of separation between social relations of reproduction and procreation, so that at this time we are confronting the emergence of new agents of procreation (i.e. agents involved only in the process of physical reproduction) related only through market exchanges which entail the buying and selling of the biological elements of generational physical reproduction.[26]

Production, Reproduction and the Oppression of Women

The notion that under capitalism the mode of production determines the mode of reproduction and, consequently, observable unequal relations between men and women is not a form of 'economism' or 'class reductionism', but rather the recognition of the complex network of macro-level effects on male-female relationships, of a mode of production driven by capital accumulation rather than by the goal of satisfying people's needs. To argue otherwise, postulating the 'mutual interaction' between the organisation of production and the organisation of reproduction, or giving causal primacy to the latter, is to overlook the theoretical significance of the overwhelming evidence documenting the capitalist subordination of reproduction to production.

Production determines reproduction because it establishes its material conditions of possibility within relatively narrow structural limits; this implies that some forms of the mode of reproduction are structurally excluded, while some possible forms are more likely than others. For example, while it is logically possible for sets of households to pool resources, live together and raise children collectively, it is difficult, if not impossible, to sustain such alternative forms within a mode of social and legal organisation that rests on private property and individual responsibility. Communal or collective living arrangements are, consequently, fated to be the exception rather than the rule, and do not

---

26   For further elaboration of these issues, see Chapter 7.

substantially challenge the social order because people, while willing to share cooking and childcare, are unlikely to go as far as to share their economic assets.

Production subordinates reproduction to itself because, whether or not individuals have access to the necessary conditions for reproduction (employment with a wage or salary sufficient to support parents and children) shapes their reproductive strategies and their outcome. The consequences of these relations of determination and subordination, which make reproduction contingent on the vagaries of the accumulation process, are the creation of intractable problems and enormous suffering among a large proportion of the population. For example, among the poor, sex and procreation go on, but the reproduction of labour power (which entails the reproduction of social and work skills) is not funded or funded only to a minimum extent. Hence the growth, in all capitalist societies, in the proportion of families headed by women and of populations excluded from present and future labour force participation. The subordination of reproduction to production means that the satisfaction of people's needs and the needs of future generations of workers are dependent on the ups and downs of the business cycle and business decisions aimed at profit maximisation. The emergence of the welfare state in its various forms: poverty, unemployment, class differences in fertility, mortality and morbidity; the never-ending struggles around wages, etc. These are some of the ways in which the subordination of reproduction to profit-making is manifested.

Production determines reproduction through the narrowing of the choices open to propertyless men and women (those who do not own means of production and must sell their labour for wages or salaries); they are able to sustain themselves and establish stable relations of reproduction to the extent they have access to the material conditions necessary to sustain life, something that depends, ultimately, on complex processes beyond the control of individuals. The combined effects of proletarianisation, universalisation of commodity production, and chronic unemployment and underemployment compel men and women to sell their labour to earn the money necessary to purchase those basic necessities. Employment is chronically scarce and changes in the forces of production result in a social and technical division of labour characterised by a complex gradation of skills and remunerations. It is therefore *structurally impossible* for capitalism to provide full employment and to pay all workers, regardless of gender (or any other socially relevant attribute), a wage sufficient to support themselves and their families. Male and female workers are forced to compete with each other for scarce jobs, a competition tempered by the development of sex-segregated labour markets but intensified when women's political struggles result in policies that further women's access to educational and occupational opportunities traditionally reserved for men.

Competition among workers is also intensified by constant changes in the division of labour, which segment the labour force and periodically render workers' skills obsolete, and by ideological legitimations evolved around racial, ethnic, gender, national origin and other politically constructed differences.

While the subordination of reproduction to production is a feature of the capitalist mode of production and is therefore common to all capitalist societies, its observable manifestations will vary according to their historical and environmental conditions and location within the world capitalist economy. For example, the proliferation of shanty towns in less-developed nations has its counterpart in the housing projects that warehouse the poor in the wealthier nations; underlying the so-called 'feminisation of poverty' are capitalist relations of production that systematically deny access to well-paid employment to a substantial proportion of the propertyless population, male and female, so that their ability to reproduce themselves and the future generation is seriously impaired and their subordination is self-perpetuating. From this standpoint, the poverty of women is one aspect of a broader phenomenon: the exclusion of a growing proportion of the propertyless population, male and female, from access to the minimum conditions necessary for their reproduction.

At the level of observable market relations, men and women workers are objectively placed in competitive relations, somewhat ameliorated in the more sex-segregated sectors of the labour market, which are spontaneously understood and fought through a variety of ideologies, including ideologies about gender. But male and female relationships are not exclusively social or historical; biologically, and as long as the 'forces of reproduction' remain largely unchanged for the vast majority of people, men and women are placed in complementary sexual and procreative relations. This is the material basis for the fact that they do not confront each other purely as competitors in the market, but also as potential sexual partners and potential parents – i.e. as potential agents of reproduction. Other divisions among workers can be overcome through labour unions and other organisations. The family, which is the site where the labour force is reproduced daily and generationally, is the main institution bringing sexual partners and parents and children together. Given the structurally produced poverty and exclusion from employment and from a living wage of a large and fluctuating population, at any given time a substantial proportion of propertyless people can satisfy their material needs through claims upon the resources of salaried and waged workers, or with the help of charities and state subsidies. At the present time, it is through marriage and kinship relations that many people who are unable to work (for whatever reasons, including the effects of capitalist restructuring, downsizing, etc.) or unable to support themselves despite working full-time, can have access to the resources necessary to satisfy their needs. This is why the family wage, usually criticised as a prime example of male workers' interest in appropriating women's labour for themselves, should be also dialectically understood as a working-class survival strategy which made a great deal of sense in the conditions affecting the working class in the nineteenth century,[27] while today it remains as a relatively unattainable ideal basis for a higher standard of living for workers, although it has never been available to the majority of workers at any given time.

Within the constraints imposed by capital accumulation, then, male workers have one major source of economic survival – waged or salaried labour – whereas female workers have, in addition to paid work, unpaid domestic work. Changes in capital accumulation set the conditions for family formation among the propertyless and, at the same time, continuously undermine it, so that a stable union becomes increasingly unattainable or unstable for the more vulnerable sectors of the working class. But 'family' in its various current forms is only, to use Marx's terminology, an 'imaginary concrete'; the 'real concrete' or 'totality comprising many determinations and relations' is the capitalist organisation of social reproduction and the resulting changing networks of social relations within which social reproduction becomes possible at a given time for different strata within the propertyless population.

Marx's logic of inquiry thus results in the identification of a structural foundation (one that is not reducible to individual-level explanations) for the capitalist mode of reproduction among the propertyless which, though it is one that on the surface appears to be simply the timeless, pseudo-universal 'family', has structural conditions of possibility specific to the capitalist mode of production. The capitalist structural constraints affecting how propertyless men and women can make a living and the likelihood they will be able to form stable unions are the material basis for the structured inequality between men and women. Gender inequality thus conceptualised, as a structural characteristic of capitalist social formations, is irreducible to microfoundations; i.e. it cannot be solely or primarily explained on the basis of either men's or women's intentions, biology, psycho-sexual development, etc. because it is the structural effect of a complex network of macro-level processes through which production and reproduction are inextricably connected. This network sets limits to the opportunity structures of propertyless men and women, allocating women primarily to the sphere of domestic/reproductive labour and only secondarily to paid (waged or salaried) labour, thus establishing the objective basis for differences in their relative economic, social and political power. However, ana-

---

27   See, for example, Humphreys 1977.

lysis of concrete or specific instances of gender inequality within households, enterprises, bureaucracies, etc. is not only amenable to study at the level of microfoundations, but requires this. We cannot fully explain oppressive practices in a given institution without taking into account the agency of the major social actors; these actors' intentions, attitudes, beliefs, and practices have to be explained in terms of the structural conditions that made them possible.

The subordination of reproduction to production not only structures gender inequality as a macro-level aspect of capitalist social formations; in doing so it also affects people's existence and practices and, therefore, their consciousness. These relations establish the conditions for the effectivity of pre-capitalist and capitalist ideologies and practices about gender, sexuality, etc., as well as for the emergence of new ones. To make the point differently, the presence of pre-capitalist elements in the culture and ideology of any given social formation is not an indicator of the pervasiveness of gender inequality as a transhistorical phenomenon, nor a simple instance of pre-capitalist 'survivals'. Rather, it is evidence of the existence of capitalist material conditions that allow for the effectivity of behaviour guided by such cultural and ideological elements. When those material conditions change, people's behaviour as well as their allegiance to traditional views on gender, sexuality, family size, etc., also change. As social change is always uneven, and some sectors of the population are more affected than others, ideological struggles and divisions within social movements are the unavoidable result, as exemplified by past and current divisions among women and among feminist theorists, and the ambivalence many women feel towards feminism today.

For the sake of brevity, I have explored these determining effects among the propertyless. Among the owners of capital, the intergenerational transmission of capital is ensured through ideological, legal and political conditions which, while reflecting the requirements for the intergenerational reproduction of the capitalist class, apply to all social classes, as if 'the family' were a classless phenomenon and its conditions of possibility were the same for everyone. The constraints and opportunities shaping the relations between male and female owners of capital and the forms of oppression faced by wealthy women are different, in some respects, from those affecting propertyless women, but I have chosen to focus on the latter because most women (and most men as well) are propertyless. It was their experiences and grievances that gave rise to the Women's Movement in the 1960s and will give rise to class politics enriched by feminist politics in the future.

Conclusion: Marx and Feminism Today

In this chapter, I have explored the relevance of Marx's methodology for deepening our understanding of the structural basis for the inequality between women and men under capitalism. This is a preliminary analysis, limited to mapping out those structural conditions at the level of the mode of production, establishing the grounds for empirical analyses of their effects in historically specific contexts. I have argued that Marx's methodology leads to a conceptualisation of the oppression of women as the visible or observable effect (e.g. in the labour market, socio-economic stratification, domestic division of labour, etc.) of underlying structured relations between men and women which are, in turn, an effect of the ways in which capitalist accumulation determines the organisation of reproduction among the propertyless, making it contingent on the ability of people to sell their labour.

Does this conceptualisation matter? Isn't it a form of 'economism' or 'class reductionism'? I do not think so. To argue that women and men are not equal because the subordination of reproduction to capital accumulation makes that inequality unavoidable is to ground the oppression of women in capitalist societies in the core processes and features of the capitalist mode of production itself. The implications for feminist theory and politics are important.

Theoretically, a focus on underlying relations between men and women leads to the replacement of a men vs. women mode of thinking with a more complex and dialectical framework according to which sexist ideologies, 'discourses', the beliefs, attitudes and practices of individuals, male and female, have structural conditions of emergence and effectivity that are not reducible to individuals' intentions and characteristics. Relations, as objects of inquiry, can be grasped only through their effects. We do not see class relations, but we see and experience their effects when, for example, downsizing leaves thousands unemployed or when, despite growth in labour productivity and profits, workers' real wages decline. Likewise, we do not see the relations between propertyless men and women based on their unequal access to the conditions of reproduction and the means of exchange, but we do see their effects in women's relative lack of power at work and in the home. It may be argued that it is superfluous to conceptualise these underlying relations, and that it is enough to document wage/salary differentials, differences in socialisation, ideologies, social constructions of gender that belittle women, male prejudices, discriminatory practices, etc. These are important phenomena which, however, must themselves be explained if we are to avoid falling into tautology (i.e. explaining male domination on the basis of the phenomena used to infer its existence), while struggling for changes likely to be ineffective in the long-run, no matter how significant they might be in the short-run. The alternative to explanations of the oppression of women grounded in their historically specific material conditions of existence (the capitalist processes that place propertyless men and women in unequal relations to the conditions necessary for production and reproduction) are ahistorical theories based on societal requirements or on individuals' attributes (biology, psychology, psycho-sexual development, etc.) which, in terms of Marx's logic of inquiry, are at best descriptive, partial and therefore misleading accounts of the observable phenomena we call the oppression of women.

In light of the preceding remarks, the Marxist-feminist analysis I offer in this chapter is not 'reductionist' but historical in the Marxist sense; it postulates that just as the production of things is organised in qualitatively different ways or modes of production, so the reproduction of life and concomitant social relations are also structured in qualitatively different ways. Although at the level of observable phenomena there appears to be such a degree of continuity to warrant the conclusion that gender differences and gender inequality are a transhistorical phenomenon rooted in transhistorical societal or individual causes, Marx's methodology leads to the identification of underlying historically different structural conditions of possibility under capitalism, conditions that remain unchanged despite changes at the level of observable phenomena such as, for example, greater male involvement in housework and childcare, increases in women's income, women's access to male-dominated jobs, professions, careers, political office, etc. This approach transcends the issue of whether class or gender is 'primary', or whether they 'interact', by postulating that at any given time people, as ensembles of social relations, act in ways that reflect the interconnections of the historically specific structures that shape their lives, among which production and reproduction are paramount. Capitalist production entails class divisions and contradictions between the interests of capitalist women and propertyless women; among the latter, socio-economic status differences create antagonisms between, for example, 'middle-class' and working-class women. Reproduction, on the other hand, entails important commonalities of experience, most of which cut across classes, establishing a material base for women's solidarity and shared interests (sexuality, childcare, reproductive rights, domestic responsibilities, problems and joys, etc.). There are, however, important class and socio-economic status differences in women's experiences of biological reproduction, reflected in their attitudes towards abortion, desired family size, etc. as well as differences in the organisation of social reproduction: the use of paid domestic workers, not only by capitalist women but also by women affluent enough to afford them, highlights how oppression is not something that only men can inflict upon women. The real advances upper-middle-class professional and business women (those earning six-figure salaries) have made in the last 30 years presupposes the existence of a servant stratum, drawn from the less skilled layers of the working class, including a large proportion of women from racial and ethnic minorities, often undocumented immigrants.

While the nature and number of divisions among women varies at the level of social formations, class divisions are common to all capitalist social formations, and all social groups (e.g. immigrant populations, races, ethnicities, etc.) are themselves divided by class. In light of recent feminist theory's 'retreat from class' and from Marx, it must be borne in mind that regardless of what theorists may think of class as a category of analysis, class as a mechanism of surplus extraction and as a social relation that constrains people's opportunities for survival and self-realisation continues to affect women's (and men's) lives: 'Without understanding the significance of class positioning ... women's movements through social space, through education, families, labour markets and in particular, in the production of their subjectivity, could not be understood'.[28]

Politically, the existence of class divisions establishes limits to qualitative changes in the situation of women under capitalism. Feminist struggles for women's rights, though important for the attainment of substantial improvements in the opportunities and quality of life of many individual women, do not and cannot substantially alter the status of all women. Women's success in their struggle for economic, political and civil rights does not alter the material conditions that created the problems that motivated those struggles; it only implies full membership in capitalist society. This is indeed important, for most women, like most men, must work to support themselves and their families. The abolition of gender barriers to education, employment, career advancement, political participation, etc. is a necessary and key aspect of the struggle against the oppression of women. But, as Marx argued, political emancipation and the attainment of political and civil rights are inherently limited achievements because, though the state may abolish distinctions that act as barriers to full political participation by all citizens, it does not abolish the social relations that are the basis for those distinctions and are presupposed by the very existence and characteristics of the state:

> The political annulment of private property has not only not abolished private property, it actually presupposes it. The state does away with dif-

---

28   Skeggs 1997, p. 6.

ference in birth, class, education, and profession in its own manner when it declares birth, class, education, and profession to be unpolitical differences, when it summons every member of the people to an equal participation in popular sovereignty ... Nevertheless the state still allows private property, education ... to have an effect in their own manner ... and makes their particular nature felt. Far from abolishing these factual differences, its existence rests on them as a presupposition.[29]

Today we can add gender, race, ethnicity, immigrant status and other distinctions to those aspects of people's lives used to exclude them from full economic and political participation. Contemporary legislation designed to abolish male (and other forms of) privilege will not put an end to these forms of inequality. The most propertyless women can expect, under capitalist conditions, is a stratification profile that mirrors that of men. Women would then cease to be disproportionately poor. While this would be an enormous improvement in the status of women, it is unlikely to happen. Given the flexibilisation of labour contracts, the unhampered mobility of capital, and changes in the forces of production which increase productivity with decreasing labour inputs, women's and other oppressed groups' struggle for equality within the structural limits of capitalist society are likely to be protracted, with no happy ending in sight, as long as the capitalist mode of production prevails.

There are limits to political gains also. Women's attainment of proportional representation in political office and leadership positions would not substantially change the conditions affecting the lives of most women (though it could benefit the most skilled, educated and economically privileged), just as the over-representation of men in political positions and leadership roles does not alter the vast political, class, and socio-economic inequalities among men. In fact, economic inequalities among men have deepened in the last 20 years; in the United States, for example, the observed narrowing of the income gap between male and female earnings owes its existence not just to higher real wages for women but to declines in real male wages.[30]

This admittedly sketchy account of some of the implications of Marx's work for feminism indicates that as long as capitalism rules, propertyless women will remain oppressed because most men's and women's ability to satisfy their needs, reproducing themselves daily and generationally, will remain subordinate to the changing needs of capital accumulation. To the extent feminist

29   Marx 1994, p. 7.
30   Mishel, Bernstein and Schmitt 2001, pp. 127–9.

theory and politics reject as 'reductionist' any grounding of the oppression of women in capitalist material conditions of existence, they could become increasingly irrelevant for the lives of most women, except academics and the relatively affluent. As the world capitalist economy grows in strength and the unprecedented mobility of capital can overnight devastate national and regional economies, the vulnerability of workers increases exponentially. In this context, there is bound to be a resurgence of labour organising within and across national boundaries. Feminism cannot afford to be absent from the process, but this would require the recognition of the relevance of Marx's work for the emancipation of women and acknowledgment of the significance of class divisions among women, thus raising the issue whether feminist theory can ignore class and remain politically relevant for the vast majority of women. This acknowledgement of the importance of Marx for the cause of women would therefore entail not only the development of new scholarship researching and documenting the relationship between the capitalist structures that oppress women and issues of gender formation, consciousness, sexuality, reproduction, etc., but also the rediscovery and acknowledgement of the heritage of Marxist, socialist and materialist feminist theory from the 1970s and early 1980s.[31] More importantly, it would hopefully result in the strengthening and greater visibility of a feminism that transcends the fragmentation of voices and identities to concern itself with the plight of working women. Underlying the unquestionable and important historical, cultural and politically constructed differences among women there is the fundamental fact that the overwhelming majority of women, in the United States and elsewhere, are propertyless and have to work for a living, facing similar forms of exploitation and oppression and similar constraints on their life choices.

This preliminary analysis has shown how it is possible to use the methodological and theoretical tools available in Marx's work to theorise the capitalist foundations of women's oppression, and the possibilities today open to feminist politics. History is repeating itself; as in the early nineteenth century, male workers' wages and employment opportunities are declining as the proletarianisation of women and children intensifies. In this context, it is through the contributions of Marxist feminism that both Marxism and feminism can be revitalised to meet the challenges of our time.

---

31   Two relatively recent collections do bring to the attention of students and younger feminists important Marxist-feminist contributions overlooked by third wave feminism: Vogel 1995; Hennessy and Ingraham 1997.

Bibliography

Adelman, Irma and C.T. Morris 1973, *Economic Growth and Social Equity in Developing Countries*, Stanford, CA: Stanford University Press.

Aguilar, Delia D. 2015, 'Intersectionality', in *Marxism and Feminism*, edited by Shahrzad Mojab, London: Zed Books.

Aguilar, Delia D. and Anne E. Lacsamana (eds) 2004, *Women and Globalisation*, Amherst, NY: Prometheus Books.

Alcoff, Linda 1989, 'Cultural Feminism versus Poststructuralism: The Identity Crisis in Feminist Theory', in *Feminist Theory in Practice and Process*, edited by Micheline Malson et al., Chicago: University of Chicago Press.

Alliance Against Women's Oppression (AAWO) 1983, 'Poverty: Not for Women Only – A Critique of the Feminisation of Poverty', AAWO Discussion Paper No. 3, September.

Althusser, Louis 1970, *For Marx*, New York: Vintage Books.

Althusser, Louis 1971, 'Ideology and Ideological State Apparatuses', in *Lenin and Philosophy and Other Essays*, New York: Monthly Review Press.

Althusser, Louis 1976, *Essays in Self-Criticism*, London: NLB.

Althusser, Louis 2014, *On The Reproduction of Capitalism*, London: Verso

Althusser, Louis and Etienne Balibar, 1970, *Reading Capital*, New York: Pantheon Books.

Amin, Samir 1976, *Unequal Development*, New York: Monthly Review Press.

Andersen, Margaret L. and Patricia H. Collins (eds) 1995, *Race, Class and Gender: An Anthology*, second edition, Belmont, CA: Wadsworth Publishing Company.

Archer, Margaret S. 1995, *Realist Social Theory: The Morphogenetic Approach*, Cambridge: Cambridge University Press.

Arditti, Rita, R. Duelli-Klein and Shelley Minden (eds), *Test Tube Women: What Future for Motherhood?* London: Pandora Press.

Arrighi, Giovanni 1991, 'World Income Inequalities and the Future of Socialism', *New Left Review* I/189 (September–October): 39–65.

Arruzza, Cinzia 2013, *Dangerous Liaisons: The Marriages and Divorces of Marxism and Feminism*, Pontypool: Merlin Press.

Arruzza, Cinzia 2016, 'Functionalist, Determinist, Reductionist: Social Reproduction Feminism and Its Critics', in *Science & Society*, 80, 1 (January): 9–30.

Autor, David and Melanie Wasserman 2013, 'Wayward Sons: The Emerging Gender Gap in Labour Markets and Education', available from: http://economics.mit.edu/files/8754

Babay, Emily 2013, 'Census: Big Decline in Nuclear Family', available from: http://www.philly.com/philly/news/How_American_families_are_changing.html

Baldwin, Wendy H. and C. Winquist Nord 1984, 'Delayed Childbearing in the US: Facts and Fictions', *Population Bulletin*, 39, 4 (November), Washington DC: Population Reference Bureau.

Barnett, M.B., R. Brewer and M. Bahati Kuumba 1999, 'New Directions in Race, Gender & Class Studies: African American Experiences', in *Race, Sex & Class*, 6, 2: 7–28.

Barrett, Michele 1980, *Women's Oppression Today*, London: Verso.

Barrett, Michele and Mary McIntosh 1982, *The Anti-Social Family*, London: Verso.

Bartholet, Elizabeth 1992, 'In Vitro Fertilization: The Construction of Infertility and of Parenting', in *Issues in Reproductive Technology: An Anthology*, edited by Helen B. Holmes, New York: Garland Publishing Inc.

Becker, Gary S. 1960, 'An Economic Analysis of Fertility', in National Bureau of Economic Research, *Demographic Change in Developed Countries*, Princeton, NJ: Princeton University Press.

Beechey, Veronica 1987, 'On Patriarchy', in *Unequal Work*, London: Verso.

Belkhir 1993, 'Editor's Introduction: Integrating Race, Sex & Class in Our Disciplines', *Race, Sex & Class*, 1, 1: 3–11.

Belkhir 1994, 'The "Failure" and Revival of Marxism in Race, Gender & Class Issues', *Race, Sex & Class*, 2, 1: 79–107.

Benhabib, Seyla and Drucilla Cornell (eds) 1987, 'Introduction: Beyond the Politics of Gender', in *Feminism as Critique*, Minneapolis, MN: University of Minnesota Press.

Bennet, Jessica 2014, 'Company-Paid Egg Freezing Will Be the Great Equalizer', *TIME*, available from: http://time.com/3509930/company-paid-egg-freezing-will-be -the-great-equalizer/

Benston, Margaret 1969, 'The Political Economy of Women's Liberation', *Monthly Review*, 21, 9: 13–27.

Berberoglu, Berch 1994, 'Class, Race & Gender: The Triangle of Oppression', *Race, Sex & Class*, 2, 1: 69–77.

Berman, Daniel M. 1978, *Death on the Job: Occupational Health and Safety Struggles in the United States*, New York: Monthly Review Press.

Bezanson, Kate and Meg Luxton 2006, *Social Reproduction: Feminist Political Economy Challenges Neo-Liberalism*, Montreal: McGill-Queen's University Press.

Bhattacharya, Tithi 2013, 'What is Social Reproduction Theory?', in *SocialistWorker.org*, available from: https://socialistworker.org/2013/09/10/what-is-social-reproduction -theory

Bhattacharya, Tithi 2015, 'How Not to Skip Class: Social Reproduction of Labour And The Global Working Class', *Viewpoint*, available from: https://viewpointmag.com/ 2015/10/31/how-not-to-skip-class-social-reproduction-of-labor-and-the-global -working-class/

Bianchi, S.M. 1999, 'Feminization and Juvenilisation of Poverty: Trends, Relative Risks, Causes, and Consequences', *Annual Review of Sociology*, 25: 307–33.

Bilge, Sirma 2010, 'Recent Feminist Outlooks on Intersectionality', *Diogenes*, 225: 58–78.

Bilge, Sirma 2013, 'Intersectionality Undone: Saving Intersectionality from Feminist Intersectionality Studies', *Du Bois Review*, 10, 2: 405–24.

Birke, Lynda, Susan Himmelweit and Gail Vines 1990, *Tomorrow's Child: Reproductive Technologies in the 1990s*, London: Virago.

Blake, Judith 1965, 'Demographic Science and the Redirection of Population Policy', *Journal of Chronic Diseases*, 18: 1181–2000.

Blake, Judith 1968, 'Are Babies Consumer Durables?', *Population Studies*, 22: 5–25.

Blake, Judith 1974, 'Coercive Pronatalism and American Population Policy', in *Pronatalism: The Myth of Mom and Apple Pie*, edited by Ellen Peck and J. Senderowitz, New York: T.Y. Crowell.

Blau, Peter M. and O.C. Duncan 1968, *The American Occupational Structure*, New York: Wiley.

Blau, Francine D. and Anne E. Wingler 1998, *The Economics of Women, Men, and Work*, third edition, Upper Saddle River, NJ: Prentice Hall.

Bluestone, Barry and Bennett Harrison 1982, *The Deindustrialization of America*, New York: Basic Books.

Bluestone, Barry and Bennett Harrison 1986, 'Most Jobs in the US Low Paying', in *Boulder Daily Camera*, 10 December.

Boehm, Michael 2014, 'Job Polarisation and the Decline of Middle Class Workers' wages', available from: http://www.voxeu.org/article/job-polarisation-and-decline-middle-class-workers-wages

Boserup, Ester 1970, *Women's Role in Economic Development*, New York: St. Martin's Press.

Braverman, Harry 1974, *Labour and Monopoly Capital: The Degradation of Work in the Twentieth Century*, New York: Monthly Review Press.

Braudel, Fernand 1982, *Civilization and Capitalism, the 15th–18th Century: The Wheels of Commerce*, Berkeley, CA: University of California Press.

Brenner, Johanna 2000, *Women and the Politics of Class*, New York: Monthly Review Press.

Brenner, Johanna and Barbara Laslett 1991, 'Gender, Social Reproduction and Women's Self-Organization', *Gender & Society*, 5, 3 (September): 311–33.

Brenner, Johanna and Maria Ramas 1984, 'Rethinking Women's Oppression', *New Left Review*, 144: 33–71.

Brenner, Johanna and Bill Resnik 1987, 'Baby M, Family Love and the Market in Women', *Against the Current*, 5: 3–6.

Bridenthal, Renate 1976, 'The Dialectics of Production and Reproduction in History', *Radical America*, 10, 2 (March–April): 3–11.

Brooks, Ann 1997, *Postfeminisms: Feminism, Cultural Theory and Cultural Forms*, New York: Routledge.

Brophy, Brigid 1971, 'Women are Prisoners of their Sex', in *The New Feminism in Twentieth Century America*, edited by June Sochen, Lexington, MA: D.C. Heath & Co.

Brown, Heather 2013, *Marx on Gender and the Family: A Critical Study*, Chicago, IL: Haymarket Press.

Brown, Judith B. 1969, 'Female Liberation First, and Now', in *Masculine/Feminine: Readings in Sexual Mythology and the Liberation of Women*, edited by Betty Roszak and T. Roszak, New York: Harper & Row.

Brown, Larry J. 1987, 'Hunger in the US', *Scientific American*, 256, 2: 37–41.

Browner, C.H. and N.A. Press 1996, 'The Production of Authoritative Knowledge in American Prenatal Care', *Medical Anthropology Quarterly*, 10, 2: 141–56.

Bureau of Labor Statistics Report 2014, 'Women in the Labour Force', available from: http://www.bls.gov/opub/reports/cps/women-in-the-labor-force-a-databook-2014 .pdf. Last retrieved in 2014.

Burnham, Linda and Miriam Louie 1985, 'The Impossible Marriage: A Marxist Critique of Socialist Feminism', *Line of March*, 17 (Spring): 1–128.

Burns, Scott 1977, *The Household Economy*, Boston, MA: Beacon Press.

Burris, Val 1982, 'The Dialectics of Women's Oppression: Notes on the Relation Between Capitalism and Patriarchy', *Berkeley Journal Of Sociology*, XXVII: 51–74.

Buss, Terry and F.S. Redburn with J. Waldron 1983, *Mass Unemployment: Plant Closings and Community Mental Health*, Beverly Hills, CA: Sage Publications.

Cammack, Paul 2015, 'Production and Social Reproduction in the Contemporary World Market: The Social Production Complex', paper presented at the 9th Pan-European Conference on International Relations, Giardini-Naxos, Sicily, 23–26 September.

Carasthatis, Anna 2008, 'The Invisibility of Privilege: A Critique of Intersectional Models of Identity', *Les Ateliers de L'Ethic*, 3, 2 (Autumn): 23–38.

Carbin, Maria and Sara Edenheim 2013, 'The Intersectional Turn in Feminist Theory: A Dream of a Common Language', *European Journal of European Studies*, 20, 3: 233–48.

Carbone, June and Naomi Cahn 2014, *Marriage Markets: How Inequality is Remaking the American Family*, Oxford: Oxford University Press.

Cardoso, Fernando Henrique and Enzo Faletto 1979, *Dependency and Development in Latin America*, Berkeley, CA: University of California Press.

Case, Anne and Angus Deaton 2015, 'Rising Morbidity and Mortality in Midlife Among White Non-Hispanic Americans in the 21st Century', *Proceedings of the National Academy of Sciences*, 112: 49, available from: http://www.pnas.org/content/112/49/ 15078

Castles, Stephen and G. Kosack, 'The Functions of Labour Immigration in Western European Capitalism', *New Left Review*, 73 (May–June): 3–21.

Castro, Josue de 1967, *The Black Book of Hunger*, Boston, MA: Beacon Press.

Center for the Study of Social Policy 1986, 'The Flip Side of Black Families Headed by Women: The Economic Status of Black Men', in *The Black Family*, edited by R. Staples, Belmont, CA: Wadsworth.

Cerullo, Margaret, Judith Stacey and Wini Breines 1977–78, 'Alice Rossi's Sociobiology and Anti-Feminist Backlash', *Berkeley Journal of Sociology*, 22: 167–77.

Chavkin, Wendy (ed.) 1984, *Double Exposure: Women's Health Hazards on the Job and at Home*, New York: Monthly Review.

Cherlin, Andrew J. 2011, 'Between Poor and Prosperous: Do the Family Patterns of Moderately Educated Americans Deserve a Closer Look?', in *Social Class and Changing Families in an Unequal America*, edited by Marcia J. Carlson and Paula England, Stanford, CA: Stanford University Press.

Cherlin, Andrew J. 2014a, *Labor's Love Lost: The Rise and Fall of the Working-Class Family in America*, New York: Russell Sage Foundation.

Cherlin, Andrew J. 2014b, 'The Real Reason Richer People Marry', *New York Times*, available from: http://www.nytimes.com/2014/12/07/opinion/sunday/the-real-reason-richer-people-marry.html

Cherlin, Andrew J. 2016, 'The Downwardly Mobile for Trump', available from: http://www.nytimes.com/2016/08/25/opinion/campaign-stops/the-downwardly-mobile-for-trump.html?_r=0

Chinchilla, Norma 1980, 'Ideologies of Feminism: Liberal, Radical, Marxist', in *Social Sciences Research Reports*, 61 (February), School of Social Sciences, University of California, Irvine.

Cho, Sumi, Kimberlé W. Crenshaw and Leslie McCall 2013, 'Toward a Field of Intersectionality Studies: Theory, Applications, and Praxis', *Signs*, 38, 4 (Summer): 785–810.

Chodorow, Nancy 1977–78, 'Considerations on a Biosocial Perspective on Parenting', *Berkeley Journal of* Sociology, 22: 179–97.

Chodorow, Nancy 1978, *The Reproduction of Mothering*, Berkeley, CA: University of California Press.

Chozik, Amy 2015, 'Middle-Class Disappearing, at Least from Vocabulary of Possible 2016 Contenders', available from: http://www.nytimes.com/2015/05/12/us/politics/as-middle-class-fades-so-does-use-of-term-on-campaign-trail.html

Cisler, Lucinda 1970, 'Unfinished Business: Birth Control and Women's Liberation', in *Sisterhood is Powerful*, edited by Robin Morgan, New York: Vintage Books.

Collins, Patricia H. 1993, 'Toward a New Vision: Race, Class and Gender as Categories of Analysis and Connection', *Race, Sex & Class*, 1, 1: 25–45.

Collins, Patricia H. 1997, 'On West and Fenstermaker's "Doing Difference"', in *Women, Men and Gender*, edited by M. Roth Walsh, New Haven, CT: Yale University Press.

Collins, Patricia H. and Sirma Bilge 2016, *Intersectionality*, Cambridge: Polity Press.

Collins, Randall 1971, 'A Conflict Theory of Social Stratification', *Social Problems*, 19 (Summer): 3–21.

Congressional Quarterly 1983, 'Problems of the Unemployed', in *Employment in America*, Washington, DC: CQ Press.

Coontz, Stephanie 2014a, 'How Can We Help Men? By Helping Women', available from: http://www.nytimes.com/2014/01/12/opinion/sunday/how-can-we-help-men -by-helping-women.html

Coontz, Stephanie 2014b, 'The New Instability', available from: http://www.nytimes .com/2014/07/27/opinion/sunday/the-new-instability.html

Corea, Gena 1985, *The Mother Machine*, New York: Harper & Row.

Corea, Gena 1987, 'Prologue', in *The Myth of Reproductive and Genetic Progress*, edited by Patricia Spallone and D.L. Steinberg, Elmsford, NY: Pergamon Press.

Corea, Gena et al. 1987, *Man-Made Women: How New Reproductive Technologies Affect Women*, Indiana: Indiana University Press.

Coulson, Margaret et al. 1975, 'The Housewife and Her Labour Under Capitalism: A Critique', *New Left Review*, 89 (January–February): 59–71.

Cowan, Ruth Schwartz 1983, *More Work for Mother*, New York: Basic Books.

Crenshaw, Kimberlé W. 2011, 'Demarginalising the Intersection of Race and Sex: A Black Feminist Critique of Anti-discrimination Doctrine, Feminist Theory, and Anti-Racist Politics', in *Framing Intersectionality: Debates on a Multi-Faceted Concept in Gender Studies*, edited by Helma Lutz, Maria Teresa Herrera Vivar and Linda Supik, Farnham: Ashgate.

Crowe, Cristine 1990, 'Whose Mind Over Whose Matter? Women In Vitro Fertilization and the Development of Scientific Knowledge', in *The New Reproductive Technologies*, edited by Maureen McNeil et al., New York: St. Martin's Press.

Dahrendorf, Ralf 1959, *Class and Class Conflict in Industrial Society*, Stanford, CA: Stanford University Press.

Darnovsky, Marcy 2014, 'Genetically Modified Babies', available from: http://www .nytimes.com/2014/02/24/opinion/genetically-modified-babies.html

Davis, Kingsley and Judith Blake 1956, 'Social Structure and Fertility: An Analytical Framework', *Economic Development and Cultural Change*, 4: 211–35.

Deckard, Barbara 1975, *The Women's Movement*, New York: Harper & Row.

Delphy, Christine 1977, *The Main Enemy: A Materialist Analysis of Women's Oppression*, London: Women's Research and Resources Centre Publications.

Delphy, Christine 1980, 'A Materialist Feminism is Possible', *Feminist Review*, 4: 87.

Demerath, N.J. and Richard A. Peterson 1967, *System, Change and Conflict*, New York: The Free Press.

Dickinson, James and Bob Russell (eds) 1986, 'Introduction: The Structure of Reproduction in Capitalist Society', in *Family, Economy and State: The Social Reproduction Process Under Capitalism*, New York: St. Martin's Press.

Dill, Bonnie Thornton 1987, 'Race, Class and Gender: Prospects for an All-Inclusive Sisterhood', in *From Different Shores: Perspectives on Race and Ethnicity in America*, edited by R. Takaki, Oxford: Oxford University Press.

DiStefano, Christine 1989, 'Dilemmas of Difference: Feminism, Modernity, and Post-modernism', in *Feminism/Postmodernism*, edited by Linda Nicholson, New York: Routledge.

DiStefano, Christine 1991, 'Masculine Marx', in *Feminism/Postmodernism*, edited by Linda Nicholson, New York: Routledge.

Dixon, Marlene 1969, 'The Rise of Women's Liberation', in *Masculine/Feminine in Sexual Mythology and the Liberation of Women*, edited by Betty Roszak and T. Roszak, New York: Harper & Row.

Dixon, Marlene 1972, 'Why Women's Liberation?', in *Female Liberation*, edited by Roberta Salper, New York: A. Knopf.

Dixon, Marlene 1975, 'Women's Liberation: Opening Chapter Two', *Canadian Dimension*, 10, 8: 56–58.

Dixon, Marlene 1979, *Women in Class Struggle*, San Francisco: Synthesis Publications.

Dobbins, Peggy Powell 1977, 'Towards a Theory of the Women's Liberation Movement and Women's Wage Labor', *The Insurgent Sociologist*, 7, 3: 53–68.

Domhoff, William G. 2001, 'Wealth, Income and Power', in *Who Rules America?*, available from: http://www2.ucsc.edu/whorulesamerica/power/wealth.html

Doudna, Jennifer 2015, 'Jennifer Doudna, A Pioneer Who Helped Simplify Genome Editing', available from: http://www.nytimes.com/2015/05/12/science/jennifer-doudna-crispr-cas9-genetic-engineering.html

Dunbar, Roxanne 1971, 'Female Liberation as the Basis for Social Revolution', in *The New Feminism in Twentieth Century America*, edited by June Sochen, Lexington, MA: D.C. Heath & Co.

Dyck, Arthur J. 1971, 'Population Policies and Ethical Acceptability', in *The American Population Debate*, edited by D. Callahan, New York: Doubleday Anchor Books.

Eagleton, Terry 1996, *The Illusions of Postmodernism*. London: Blackwell.

Easterlin, Richard A. 1969, 'Towards a theory of Fertility', in *Fertility and Family Planning*, edited by S.J. Behrman et al., Ann Arbor, MI: University of Michigan Press.

Easterlin, Richard A. 1975, 'An Economic Framework for Fertility Analysis', *Studies in Family Planning*, 6, 3: 54–63.

Ebert, Teresa L. 1995, '(Untimely) Critiques for a "Red Feminism"', *Post-ality: Marxism and Postmodernism*, edited by Mas'ud Zavarzadeh, Teresa L. Ebert and Donald Morton, Washington, DC: Maisonneuve Press.

Ebert, Teresa L. 1996, *Ludic Feminism and After: Postmodernism, Desire, and Labour in Late Capitalism*, Ann Arbor, MI: University of Michigan Press.

Ebert, Teresa L. and Mas'ud Zavarzadeh 2008, *Class in Culture*, Boulder, CO: Paradigm Publishers.

Edholm, Felicity, Olivia Harris and Kate Young. 1977, 'Conceptualizing Women', in *Critique of Anthropology*, Vol. 3, 9 & 10: 101–130.

Edin, Kahtryin, Timothy Nelson and Joanna Miranda Reed, 'Daddy, Baby; Momma, Maybe. Low Income Urban Fathers and the "Package Deal" of Family Life', in *Social Class and Changing Families in Unequal America*, edited by Marcia J. Carlson and Paula England, Stanford, CA: Stanford University Press.

Ehrenreich, Barbara 2000, 'Maid to Order: The Politics of Other Women's Work', *Harper's*, April: 59–70.

Ehrenreich, Barbara and Arlie R. Hochschild (eds) 2001, *Global Woman: Nannies, Maids and Sex Workers in the New Economy*, New York: Henry Holt and Co.

Einsenstein, Hester 2010, *Feminism Seduced: How Global Elites Use Women's Labour and Ideas to Exploit the World*, Boulder, CO: Paradigm Publishers.

Einsenstein, Zillah 1979, 'Developing a Theory of Capitalist Patriarchy and Socialist Feminism', in *Capitalist Patriarchy and the Case for Socialist Feminism*, edited by Zillah Einsenstein, New York: Monthly Review Press.

Engels, Frederick 1940 [1872–82], *Dialectics of Nature*, New York: International Publishers.

Engels, Frederick 1959, 'Letters on Historical Materialism', in *Marx and Engels: Basic Writings in Politics and Philosophy*, edited by L.S. Feuer, New York: Doubleday.

Engels, Frederick 1972 [1884], *The Origin of the Family, Private Property and the State*, New York: International Publishers

Epstein, Barbara 1995, 'Why Poststructuralism is a Dead End for Progressive Thought', *Socialist Review*, 5, 2: 83–119.

'Even Young Men Feel the Pinch' 1987, *Dollars & Sense*, 131 (November): 10–11.

Farquar, Dion 1996, *The Other Machine: Discourse and Reproductive Technologies*, London: Routledge.

Ferguson, Susan 2016, 'Intersectionality and Social Reproduction Feminisms', *Historical Materialism*, 24, 2: 38–60.

Ferguson, Susan and David McNally 2014, 'Precarious Migrants: Gender, Race and the Social Reproduction of a Global Working Class', in *Transforming Classes – Socialist Register 2015*, edited by Leo Panitch and Greg Albo, New York: Monthly Review Press.

Ferguson, Susan and David McNally 2015, 'Social Reproduction Beyond Intersectionality: An Interview', *Viewpoint*, 31 October, available from: https://viewpointmag.com/2015/11/02/issue-5-social-reproduction/

Ferguson, Susan et al. 2016, 'Introduction', *Historical Materialism*, 24, 2: 25–37.

Firestone, Shulamith 1971, *The Dialectic of Sex: The Case for Feminist Revolution*, New York: Bantam Books.

Floyd, Kevin 2016, 'Automatic Subjects: Gendered Labour and Abstract Life', *Historical Materialism*, 24, 2: 61–86.

Folbre, Nancy 1976, 'Economics and Population Control', *Science for the People*, 8 (November–December): 10–14 and 22–3.

Folbre, Nancy 1977, 'Population Growth and Capitalist Development in Zongolica, Veracruz', *Latin American Perspectives*, 4, 4 (Fall): 41–55.

Franklin, Sarah 1990, 'Deconstructing "Desperateness": The Social Construction of Infertility in Popular Representations of New Reproductive Technologies', in *The New Reproductive Technologies*, edited by Maureen McNeil et al., New York: St. Martin's Press.

Franklin, Sarah 1992, 'Making Sense of Missed Conceptions: Anthropological Perspectives on Unexplained Fertility', in *Changing Human Reproduction: Social Science Perspectives*, edited by Meg Stacy, London: Sage.

Franklin, Sarah 1995, 'Postmodern Procreation: A Cultural Account of Assisted Reproduction', in *Conceiving the New World Order: The Global Politics of Reproduction*, edited by Faye D. Ginsburg and R. Rapp, Berkeley, CA: University of California Press.

Freeman, Jo 1972, 'The Women's Liberation Movement, its Origins, Structures, and Ideas', in *Family, Marriage, and the Struggle of the Sexes*, edited by Hans Peter Dreitzel, New York: Macmillan Co.

Friedan, Betty 1963, *The Feminine Mystique*, New York: W.W. Norton & Co.

Gardiner, Jean 1975, 'Women's Domestic Labour', *New Left Review*, 89 (January–February): 47–58.

Geras, Norman 1972, 'Louis Althusser: An Assessment', *New Left Review*, 71: 80–6.

Gimenez, Martha E. 1973a, 'Befolkningsproblemet – Marx kontra Malthus', in *Den Ny Verden*, Tidsskrift for Urlandproblemer, 8 Argang, 73–88.

Gimenez, Martha E. 1973b, *Population Structure and Processes within the Capitalist Mode of Production*, unpublished PhD dissertation, University of California, Los Angeles.

Gimenez, Martha E. 1975, 'Marxism and Feminism', *Frontiers: A Journal of Women Studies*, 1, 1: 61–80.

Gimenez, Martha E. 1978, 'Structuralist Marxism and the "Woman Question"', *Science & Society*, 42, 3: 301–23.

Gimenez, Martha E. 1982, 'The Oppression of Women: A Structuralist Marxist View', in *Structural Sociology*, edited by Ino Rossi, New York: Columbia University Press.

Gimenez, Martha E. 1987, 'The Feminization of Poverty: Myth or Reality?', *The Insurgent Sociologist*, 14, 1 (Fall): 5–30.

Gimenez, Martha E. 1990, 'The Dialectics of Waged and Unwaged Work', in *Work Without Wages*, edited by Jane L. Collins and Martha E. Gimenez, New York: State University of New York Press.

Gimenez, Martha E. 1990, 'The Feminization of Poverty: Myth or Reality? (expanded and updated)', *Social Justice*, 17, 3 (Fall): 43–69.

Gimenez, Martha E. 1991, 'The Mode of Reproduction in Transition: A Marxist Feminist

Analysis of the Effects of Reproductive Technologies', *Gender & Society*, 5 (Spring): 334–50.

Gimenez, Martha E. 1995, 'Sociologist by Default: Reflections on Past Choices and Future Goals', in *Individual Voices, Collective Visions*, edited by Ann Goetting and Sarah Fenstermaker, Philadelphia, Temple University Press.

Gimenez, Martha E. 1999, 'For Structure: A Critique of Ontological Individualism', *Alethia*, 2, 2 (October): 19–25.

Gimenez, Martha E. 2001a, 'Marxism and Class, Gender and Race: Rethinking the Trilogy', *Race, Gender & Class*, 8, 2: 23–33.

Gimenez, Martha E. 2001b, 'Die Heraufkunft der kapitalistischen Fortpflanzungsweise-Umbruche der Reproduktion im 21. Jahrhundert', [The Nascent Capitalist Mode of Procreation: Reproductive Changes in the 21st Century], *Das Argument, Zeitschrift für Philosophie und Sozialwissenschaften*, 242 Jahrgang Heft 4/5: 657–70.

Gimenez, Martha E. 2002, 'The Global Fetish', *Latin American Perspectives*, 29, 6 (November): 85–7.

Gimenez, Martha E. 2004, 'Connecting Marx and Feminism in the Era of Globalization', *Socialism and Democracy*, 18, 1: 85–105.

Gimenez, Martha E. 2005, 'Capitalism and the Oppression of Women: Marx Revisited', *Science & Society*, 69, 1 (January): 11–32.

Gimenez, Martha E. 2006, 'Loving Alienation: The Contradictions of Domestic Work', in *The Evolution of Alienation: Trauma, Promise, and the* Millennium, edited by Lauren Langman and Devorah Kalekin-Fishman, Lanham, MD: Rowman & Littlefield.

Gimenez, Martha E. 2007, 'Self-Sourcing: How Corporations Get Us To Work Without Pay!' *Monthly Review*, 59, 7 (December): 37–41.

Gimenez, Martha E. 2009, 'Global Capitalism and Women: From Feminist Politics to Working Class Women Politics', in *Globalization and Third World Women: Exploitation, Coping and Resistance*, edited by Ligaya Lindio-McGovern and Isidor Walliman, Farnham: Ashgate.

Ginsburg, Faye D. and Rayna Rapp (eds) 1995, *Conceiving the New World Order: The Global Politics of Reproduction*, Berkeley, CA: University of California Press.

Glazer, Nona 1984, 'Servants to Capital', *Review of Radical Political Economics*, 16, 1: 61–87.

Glen, Kristin Booth 1978, 'Abortion in the Courts: A Laywoman's Historical Guide to the New Disaster Area', *Feminist Studies*, 4, 1: 1–26.

Glucksmann, Andre 1972, 'The Althusserian Theatre', *New Left Review*, 72: 68–92.

Godelier, Maurice 1970, 'Structure and Contradiction in *Das Kapital*', in *Introduction to Structuralism*, edited by Michael Lane, Boston, MA: Basic Books.

Godelier, Maurice 1972, *Rationality and Irrationality in Economics*, New York: Monthly Review Press.

Godelier, Maurice 1978, *Perspectives in Marxist Anthropology*, New York: Cambridge University Press.

Godelier, Maurice 1982, 'The Problem of the "Reproduction" of Socioeconomic Systems', in *Structural Sociology*, edited by Ino Rossi, New York: Columbia University Press.

Goldscheider, Calvin 1971, *Population, Modernization and the Social Structure*, Boston, MA: Little Brown and Company.

Goode, W.J. 1963, *World Revolution and Family Patterns*, New York: The Free Press of Glencoe.

Gordon, Linda 1970, 'Functions of the Family', in *Voices From Women's Liberation*, edited by Leslie B. Tanner, New York: Signet Books.

Gordon, Linda 1976, *Woman's Body, Woman's Right*, New York: Grossman Publishers.

Gorelick, Sherry 1996, 'Contradictions of Feminist Methodology', in *Race, Class and Gender: Common Bonds, Different Voices*, edited by E. Ngan-Ling Chow, D. Wilkinson and M. Baca Zinn, London: Sage.

Greenfield, S.M. 1969, 'Love and Marriage in Modern America: A Functional Analysis', in *Marriage and the Family*, edited by H.K. Hadden and M.L. Borgatta, Itasca, IL: Peacock Publishers.

Greenhouse, Steven 2013, 'Our Economic Pickle', available from: http://www.nytimes.com/2013/01/13/sunday-review/americas-productivity-climbs-but-wages-stagnate.html?_r=0

Groat, Theodore H. and Arthur G. Neal 1973, 'Social Class and Alienation Correlates of Protestant Fertility', *Journal of Marriage and the Family*, 35: 83–8.

Groat, Theodore H. and Arthur G. Neal 1975, 'A Social Psychological Approach to Family Formation', in *Population Studies: Selected Essays and Research*, edited by Kenneth C.W. Kammeyer, Chicago: Rand McNally.

Grzanka, Patrick R. (ed.) 2014, *Intersectionality: A Foundations and Frontiers Reader*, Boulder, CO: Westview Press.

Gunnarsson, Lena 2011, 'A Defense of the Category "Women"', *Feminist Theory*, 12, 1: 23–37.

Gunnarsson, Lena 2013, 'The Naturalistic Turn in Feminist Theory: A Marxist-Realist Contribution', *Feminist Theory*, 14, 1: 3–19.

Haimes, Erica 1992, 'Gamete Donation and the Social Management of Genetic Origins', in *Changing Human Reproduction*, edited by Meg Stacy, London: Sage.

Hamilton, Roberta and Michele Barrett (eds) 1986, *The Politics of Diversity*, London: Verso.

Harnecker, Marta 1971, *Los Conceptos Fundamentales del Materialismo Historico*, Mexico: Siglo XXI.

Harrington, Michael 1984, *The American Poverty*, New York: Penguin.

Hartmann, Heidi 1976, 'Capitalism, Patriarchy, and Job Segregation by Sex', *Signs*, 1, 3: 137–69.

Hartmann, Heidi 1981, 'The Unhappy Marriage of Marxism and Feminism', in *Women and Revolution*, edited by Lydia Sargent, Boston, MA: South End Press.

Harvey, David 2014, *Seventeen Contradictions and the End of Capitalism*, Oxford: Oxford University Press.

Heller, Nathan 2016, 'The New Activism of Liberal Arts Colleges', *The New Yorker*, 30, May 30, available from: http://www.newyorker.com/magazine/2016/05/30/the-new-activism-of-liberal-arts-colleges

Hennessy, Rosemary 1993, *Materialist Feminism and the Politics of Discourse*, New York: Routledge.

Hennessy Rosemary and Chrys Ingraham (eds) 1997, *Materialist Feminism: A Reader in Class, Difference, and Women's Lives*, New York: Routledge.

Holland, Joshua 2014, 'Study Show the Madness of States Refusing to Expand Medicaid', available from: http://billmoyers.com/2014/08/14/study-shows-the-madness-of-states-refusing-to-expand-medicaid/

Holmes, Helen Bequaert (ed.) 1992, *Issues in Reproductive Technology: An Anthology*, New York: Garland Publishing Inc.

Holmstrom, Lynda L. 1972, *The Two-Career Family*, Cambridge, MA: Schenkman.

Holter, Harriet 1873, *Sex Roles and Social Structure*, Oslo: Universitetsforlaget.

Horton, John 1966, 'Order and Conflict Theories of Social Problems as Competing Ideologies', *American Journal of Sociology*, 71, 6: 701–21.

Humphries, Jane 1977, 'Class Struggle and the Persistence of the Working-Class Family', *Cambridge Journal of Economics*, 1, 3: 241–58.

Humphries, Jane 1987, 'The Origin of the Family: Born Out of Scarcity Not Wealth', in *Engels Revisited: New Feminist Essays*, London: Tavistock.

Huxley, Aldous 1969, *Brave New World*, New York: Harper & Row.

Inkeles, Alex 1974, *Becoming Modern*, Cambridge, MA: Harvard University Press.

Intercom 1976, 'Development Argument Wanes', *Intercom: The International Newsletter on Population*, 4 (December): 11–12.

Israel, Joachim 1971, *Alienation from Marx to Modern Sociology: A Macro-sociological Analysis*, Boston, MA: Allyn & Bacon.

Jacobi, Russell 1973, 'The Politics of Subjectivity', *New Left Review*, 79: 37–49.

Johnston, Josephine and Miriam Zoll 2014, 'Is Freezing Your Eggs Dangerous? A Primer', *New Republic*, available from: https://newrepublic.com/article/120077/dangers-and-realities-egg-freezing

Jones, Katherine Castiello, Joya Misra and K. McCurley 2013, 'Intersectionality in Sociology', available from: http://www.socwomen.org/wp-content/uploads/swsfactsheet_intersectionality.pdf. Last retrieved in 2014.

Kandal, Terry 1995, 'Gender, Race and Ethnicity: Let's not Forget Class', *Race, Gender & Class*, 2, 2: 139–62.

Kotkin, Joel 2014, 'The US Middle Class is Turning Proletarian', available from: http://

www.forbes.com/sites/joelkotkin/2014/02/16/the-u-s-middle-class-is-turning
-proletarian/

Krugman, Paul 2012, 'Where the Productivity Went', available from: http://krugman
.blogs.nytimes.com/2012/04/28/where-the-productivity-went/

Kuhn, Annette and Ann Marie Wolpe 1978, *Feminism and Materialism: Women and Modes of Production*, London: Routledge.

Laborie, Francoise 1987, 'Looking for Mothers, You Only Find Fetuses', *Made to Order: The Myth of Reproductive and Genetic Progress*, edited by P. Spallone and D.L. Steinberg, Oxford: Pergamon Press.

Landry, Donna and Gerald Maclean 1993, *Materialist Feminisms*, Oxford: Blackwell.

Larguia, Isabel and J. Dumoulin 1972, 'Toward a Science of Women's Liberation', *NACLA's Latin America and Empire Report*, 6 (December): 3–20.

Levy Jr., Marion J. 1966, *Modernization and the Structure of Societies*, Princeton: Princeton University Press.

Lilla, Mark 2016, 'The End of Identity Liberalism', *New York Times*, available from: http://www.nytimes.com/2016/11/20/opinion/sunday/the-end-of-identity-liberalism.html?_r=0

Lukács, Georg 1971, *History and Class Consciousness*, Cambridge, MA: The MIT Press.

Lundberg, Ferdinand 1969, *The Rich and the Super-Rich*, New York: Bantam Books.

Lutz, Helma, Maria Teresa Herrera Vivar and Linda Supik (eds) 2011, *Framing Intersectionality: Debates on a Multi-Faceted Concept in Gender Studies*, Farnham: Ashgate.

Luxton, Meg 2006, 'Feminist Political Economy in Canada and the Politics of Social Reproduction', in *Social Reproduction: Feminist Political Economy Challenges Neo-Liberalism*, edited by Kate Bezanson and Meg Luxton, Montreal: McGill-Queen University Press.

Luxton, Meg 2017, 'The Production of Life Itself: Gender, Social Reproduction and International Political Economy', in *Handbook of International Political Economy of Gender*, edited by Adrienne Roberts and Juanita Elias, Cheltenham: Edward Elgar Publishing.

MacLean, Judy 1976, 'N.O.W.', *Socialist Revolution*, 29: 39–50.

Malthus, Thomas R. 1933 [1798], *An Essay on The Principle of Population*, New York: E.P. Dutton & Co. Inc.

Mamdani, Mahmood 1972, *The Myth of Population Control: Family, Caste and Class in an Indian Village*, New York: Monthly Review Press.

Mamdani, Mahmood 1974, 'The Ideology of Population Control', *Concerned Demography: Emergent Population Alternatives*, 4 (Winter): 13–22.

Mandel, Ernest 1971, *The Formation of the Economic Thought of Karl Marx*, New York: Monthly Review Press.

Mander, Jerry and Edward Goldsmith 1996, *The Case Against the Global Economy: And For a Turn Toward the Local*, San Francisco: Sierra Club Books.

Marcuse, Herbert 1962, *Eros and Civilization*, New York: Vintage Books.

Marcuse, Herbert 1964, *One Dimensional Man*, Boston, MA: Beacon Press.

Marcuse, Herbert 1971, *An Essay on Liberation*, Boston, MA: Beacon Press.

Mass, Bonnie 1972, *The Political Economy of Population Control in Latin America*, Montreal: Editions Latin America.

Mass, Bonnie 1977, 'Puerto Rico: A Case Study Of Population Control', *Latin American Perspectives*, 4, 4 (Fall): 66–82.

Marx, Karl 1964 [1844], 'Alienated Labor', in *Karl Marx: Early Writings*, edited by T.B. Bottomore, New York: McGraw Hill Book Co.

Marx, Karl 1968 [1894], *Capital*, Volume 3, New York: International Publishers.

Marx, Karl 1969 [1852], *The Eighteenth Brumaire of Louis Bonaparte*, New York: International Publishers.

Marx, Karl 1970a [1859], *A Contribution to the Critique of Political Economy*, New York: International Publishers.

Marx, Karl 1970b [1875], *Critique of the Gotha Programme*, New York: International Publishers.

Marx, Karl 1972 [1857], *Grundrisse*, edited by David McLellan, New York: Harper & Row.

Marx, Karl 1974 [1867], *Capital*, Volume 1, New York: International Publishers.

Marx, Karl 1976 [1845], 'Theses on Feuerbach', in *Karl Marx and Frederick Engels Collected Works*, Volume 5, New York: International Publishers.

Marx, Karl 1977 [1844], 'Alienated Labor', in *Karl Marx: Selected Writings*, edited by David McLellan, London: Oxford University Press.

Marx, Karl 1994 [1844], 'On The Jewish Question', in *Karl Marx Selected Writings*, edited by Lawrence H. Simon, Indianapolis: Hackett Publishing Company, Inc.

Marx, Karl and Friedrich Engels 1947 [1845–46], *The German Ideology*, New York: International Publishers.

Marx, Karl and Friedrich Engels 1976 [1845–46], 'The German Ideology', in *Collected Works*, Volume 5, New York: International Publishers.

Marx, Karl and Friedrich Engels 1994 [1845], 'The German Ideology', in *Karl Marx Selected Writings*, edited by Lawrence H. Simon, Indianapolis: Hackett Publishing Company, Inc.

Marx, Karl and Friedrich Engels 1994 [1847–48], 'The Communist Manifesto', in *Karl Marx Selected Writings*, edited by Lawrence H. Simon, Indianapolis: Hackett Publishing company, Inc.

McAfee, Kathy and Myrna Wook 1971, 'Bread and Roses', in *From Feminism to Liberation*, edited by Edith Hoshino Alback, Cambridge, MA: Schenckman Publishing Co.

McCarney, J. 1991, 'The True Realm of Freedom: Marxist Philosophy After Communism', *New Left Review*, 189 (September–October): 19–38.

McDonough, Roisin and Rachel Harrison 1978, 'Patriarchy and Relations of Production', in *Feminism and Materialism*, edited by Annette Kuhn and AnneMarie Wolpe, London: Routledge and Kegan Paul.

McKibbin, Gemma, Rachel Duncan, Bridget Hamilton, Cathy Humphreys and Connie Kellett 2015, 'The Intersectional Turn in Feminist Theory: A Response to Carbin and Edenheim (2013)', *European Journal of Women's Studies*, 22, 1: 99–103.

McLanahan, Sara 2011, 'Family Instability and Complexity after a Non-Marital Birth: Outcomes for Children in Fragile Families', in *Social Class and Changing Families in an Unequal America*, edited by Marcia J. Carlson and Paula England, Stanford, CA: Stanford University Press.

McNeil, Maureen, Ian Varcoe and Steven Yearly (eds) 1990, *The New Reproductive Technologies*, New York: St. Martin's Press.

Meek, Ronald L. 1971, *Marx and Engels on the Population Bomb*, Berkeley, CA: Ramparts Press, Inc.

Melotti, Umberto 1969, *Sociologia del Hambre*, Mexico D.F.: Fondo de Cultura Economica.

Mészáros, István 1970, *Marx's Theory of Alienation*, New York: Harper & Row.

Middleton, Chris 1988, 'The Familiar Fate of the Famulae: Gender Divisions in the History of Wage Labour', in *On Work: Historical, Comparative and Theoretical Approaches*, edited by Ray Pahl, London: Basil Blackwell.

Millet, Kate 1971, *Sexual Politics*, New York: Avon Books.

Mills, Charles W. 1985, 'Marxism and Naturalistic Mystification', *Science & Society*, 49, 4 (Winter): 472–83.

Mishel, Lawrence, Jared Bernstein and John Schmitt 2001, *The State of Working America 2000/2001*, Ithaca, NY: Cornell University Press.

Mitchell, Juliet 1969, 'Women: The Longest Revolution', *New Left Review*, 40: 19–26.

Mitchell, Juliet 1971, *Woman's Estate*, New York: Pantheon Books.

Moen, Elizabeth W. 1979, 'What Does "Control Over Our Bodies" Really Mean?', *International Journal of Women's Studies*, 2, 2: 129–43.

Moghadam, Valentine M. 1999, 'Gender and Globalisation: Female Labor and Women's Mobilisation', *Journal of World-Systems Research*, 5, 2 (Summer): 367–88.

Mohanty, Chandra T., Ann Russo and Lourdes Torres, *Third World Women and the Politics of Feminism*, Indiana: Indiana University Press.

Moi, Toril and Janice Radway 1994, 'Editor's Note', special issue of *South Atlantic Quarterly*, 93: 4.

Molyneux, Maxine 1979, 'Beyond the Domestic Labour Debate', *New Left Review*, 116 (July–August): 3–27.

Moran, Theodore H. and Lindsey Oldenski 2014, 'The US Manufacturing Base: Four Signs of Strength', Policy Brief, Peterson Institute for International Economics, available from: https://www.piie.com/publications/pb/pb14-18.pdf

Morgan, Robin (ed.) 1970, *Sisterhood is Powerful*, New York: Vintage Books.

Morton, Peggy 1972, 'Women's Work is Never Done', in *Women Unite*, Toronto: Canadian Women Educational Press.

Naples, Nancy A. and Manisha Desai (eds) 2002, *Women's Activism and Globalisation: Linking Local Struggles and Transnational Politics*, New York: Routledge.

National Research Council 2008, 'Labor Market Trends: A Loss of Middle Class Jobs?', in *Research on Future Skill Demands*, Washington, DC: The National Academies Press, available from: http://www.nap.edu/openbook.php?record_id=12066&page=R1

National Women's Law Centre 2014, 'Insecure and Unequal: Poverty and Income Among Women and Families 2000–2013', available from: http://www.nwlc.org/sites/default/files/pdfs/final_2014_nwlc_poverty_report.pdf

Navarro, Vicente 1989, 'Race or Class or Race and Class', *International Journal of Health Services*, 18: 311–14.

Navarro, Vicente 1990, 'Race *or* Class or Race *and* Class: Growing Mortality Differentials in the United States', *International Journal of Health Services*, 21: 229–35.

Nelson, Hilde L. 1992, 'Scrutinizing Surrogacy', in *Issues in Reproductive Technology: An Anthology*, edited by Helen B. Holmes, New York: Garland Publishing Inc.

Newman, Katherine S. 1988, *Falling From Grace: The Experience of Downward Mobility in the Middle Class*, New York: Free Press.

Newman, Katherine S. 1993, *Declining Fortunes: The Withering of the American Dream*, New York: Basic Books.

Nicholson, Linda J. 1987, 'Feminism and Marx: Integrating Kinship with the Economic', in *Feminism as Critique*, edited by Seyla Benhabib and Drucilla Cornell, Minneapolis, MN: University of Minnesota Press.

Nurse, Keith 2003, 'The Masculinization of Poverty: Gender and Global Restructuring', IIIS Discussion Paper No. 20, available from: http://www.academia.edu/3436183/The_Masculinization_of_Poverty_Gender_and_Global_Restructing

O'Brien, Mary 1981, *The Politics of Reproduction*, London: Routledge and Kegan Paul.

O'Connell, Martin and D.E. Bloom 1987, 'Juggling Jobs and Babies: America's Childcare Challenge', Occasional Paper No. 12, February, Washington, DC: Population Reference Bureau.

O'Hare, William 1985, 'Poverty in America: Trends and New Patterns', *Population Bulletin*, 40, 3, Washington, DC: Population Reference Bureau.

Ollman, Bertell 1971, *Alienation: Marx's Concept of Man in Capitalist Society*, New York: Cambridge University Press.

Ong, Aihwa 1996, 'Strategic Sisterhood or Sisters in Solidarity? Questions of Communitarianism and Citizenship in Asia', *Indiana Journal of Global Legal Studies*, 4, 1 (Fall): 107–35.

Oppenheimer, Martin, Martin J. Murray and Rhonda F. Levine (eds) 1991, *Radical Sociologists and the Movement: Experiences, Lessons, and Legacies*, Philadelphia: Temple University Press.

Ortner, Sherry B. 1974, 'Is Female to Male as Nature is to Culture?', in *Women, Culture and Society*, edited by M.Z. Rosaldo and L. Lamphere, Stanford, CA: Stanford University Press.

Ossowski, Stanislaw 1963, *Class Structure in the Social Consciousness*, New York: The Free Press of Glencoe.

Patton, H.M. and J.W. Patton 1984, *The Displaced Worker and Community Response: Case Study of Portsmouth, Scioto County, Ohio*, Lexington, KY: State Research Associates.

Pearce, Diana 1978, 'The Feminisation of Poverty: Women, Work and Welfare', *The Urban and Social Change Review*, 11, 1/2: 28–36.

Peck, Ellen and Judith Senderowitz (eds) 1974, *Pronatalism: The Myth of Mom and Apple Pie*, New York: Thomas Y. Crowell Company.

Petchesky, Rosalind Pollack 1980, 'Reproductive Freedom: Beyond "A Woman's Right to Choose"', *Signs: Journal of Women in Culture and Society*, 5, 41: 661–85.

Petchesky, Rosalind Pollack 1987, 'Foetal Images: The Power of Visual Culture in the Politics of Reproduction', in *Reproductive Technologies: Gender, Motherhood and Medicine*, edited by Michelle Stanworth, Minneapolis, MN: University of Minnesota Press.

Phillips, Kevin 1990, *The Politics of Rich and Poor: Wealth and the American Electorate in the Reagan Aftermath*, New York: Random House.

Piven, Frances F. and R.A. Cloward 1985, *The New Class War: Reagan's Attack on the Welfare State and its Consequences*, New York: Pantheon.

Preston, Jennifer 2013, 'UK Law Approaches Surrogacy – Which Way Forward?', available from: https://bucks.ac.uk/whoswho/school_of_applied_management_and_law/law/blog/UK_law_approaches_to_surrogacy/. Last retrieved in 2014.

Puar, Jasbir K. 2014, 'From Intersections to Assemblages', in *Intersectionality: A Foundations and Frontiers Reader*, edited by Patrick R. Grzanka, Boulder, CO: Westview Press.

Purdy, Laura M. 1989, 'Surrogate Mothering: Exploitation or Empowerment?', *Bioethics* 3, 1: 40–4.

Purdy, Laura M. 1992, 'Another Look at Contract Pregnancy', in *Issues in Reproductive Technology: An Anthology*, edited by Helen B. Holmes, New York: Garland Publishing Inc.

Radin, Margaret Jane 1996, *Contested Commodities*, Cambridge, MA: Harvard University Press.

Rainie, Lee and Lanna Anderson 2017, 'The Future of Jobs and Job Training', Pew Research Center, http://www.pewinternet.org/2017/05/03/the-future-of-jobs-and-jobs-training/

Ramazanoglu, Caroline 1989, *Feminism and the Contradictions of Oppression*, New York: Routledge.

Ranciere, Jacques 1974, 'On the Theory of Ideology (The Politics of Althusser)', *Radical Philosophy*, 7 (Spring): 2–15.

Rapp, Raya 1984, 'XYLO: A True Story', in *Test Tube Women: What Future for Motherhood?*, edited by Rita Arditti et al., London: Pandora Press.

Raymond, Janice G. 1987, 'Fetalists and Feminists: They Are Not The Same', *Made to Order: The Myth of Reproductive and Genetic Progress*, edited by P. Spallone and D.L. Steinberg, Oxford: Pergamon Press.

Raymond, Janice G. 1993, *Women as Wombs: Reproductive Technologies and the Battle over Women's Freedom*, New York: Harper Collins.

Raymond, Janice G. 2013, *Not a Choice, Not a Job: Exposing the Myths about Prostitution and the Global Sex Trade*, Dulles, VA: Potomac Books.

Reich, Michael 1978, 'The Development of the Wage Force', in *The Capitalist System*, second edition, edited by R.C. Edwards et al., Englewood Cliffs, NJ: Prentice Hall.

Reiss, Ira L. 1967, 'The Universality of the Family: A Conceptual Analysis', *Journal of Marriage and the Family*, 27, 4: 443–52.

Robles, Frances 2015, 'State Legislatures Put Up Flurry of Roadblocks to Abortion', available from: http://www.nytimes.com/2015/05/09/us/politics/state-legislatures-put -up-flurry-of-roadblocks-to-abortion.html?_r=0

Rodgers Jr., Harrell R. 1986, *Poor Women, Poor Families*, New York: M.E. Sharpe.

Rollins, Judith 1985, *Between Women: Domestics and their Employers*, Philadelphia, PA: Temple University Press.

Rosaldo, M.Z. 1980, 'The Use and Abuse of Anthropology: Reflections on Feminism and Crosscultural Understanding', *Signs*, 5 (Spring): 389–417.

Rose, Stephen J. 1986, *The American Profile Poster*, New York: Pantheon.

Rose, Stephen J. 1992, *Social Stratification in the United States: The American Profile Poster Revised and Expanded*, New York: The New Press.

Rosenblum, Emma 2014, 'Later, Baby', *Bloomberg Business Week*, 21–27 April: 44–9.

Ross, Heather and Isabel V. Sawhill 1975, *Time of Transition: The Growth of Families Headed by Women*, Washington, DC: The Urban Institute.

Rossi, Alice 1969, 'Sex Equality: The Beginning of Ideology', in *Masculine/Feminine: Readings in Sexual Mythology and the Liberation of Women*, edited by B. Roszak and T. Roszak, New York: Harper & Row.

Rossi, Alice 1977, 'A Biosocial Perspective on Parenting', *Daedalus: Special Issue on the Family*, 106, 2: 1–31.

Rostow, W.W. 1991, *The Stages of Economic Growth*, third edition, Cambridge: Cambridge University Press.

Roszak, Betty and Theodore Roszak (eds) 1969, *Masculine/Feminine: Readings in Sexual Mythology and the Liberation of Women*, New York: Harper & Row.

Rothenberg, Paula S. (ed.) 2000, *Race, Class, and Gender in the United States: An Integrated Study*, fifth edition, New York: Worth Publishers.

Rothman, Barbara Katz 1984, 'The Meaning of Choice in Reproductive Technology', in *Test Tube Women: What Future for Motherhood?*, edited by Rita Arditti et al., London: Pandora Press.

Rothman, Barbara Katz 1987a, *The Tentative Pregnancy: Prenatal Diagnosis and the Future of Motherhood*, New York: Penguin Books.

Rothman, Barbara Katz 1987b, 'Comment on Harrison: The Commodification of Motherhood', *Gender & Society*, 3: 312–16.

Rowbotham, Sheila 1974, *Woman's Consciousness, Man's World*, London: Penguin Books.

Rowbotham, Sheila and Stephanie Linkogle 2001, *Women Resist Globalisation: Mobilising for Livelihood and Rights*, London: Zed Books.

Rubin, Gayle 1975, 'The Traffic in Women: Notes on "The Political Economy" of Sex', in *Toward an Anthropology of Women*, edited by Rayna R. Rayter, New York: Monthly Review Press.

Ryan, Mary P. 1976, *Womanhood in America*, New York: New Viewpoints.

Salazar-Parreñas, Rhacel 2003, 'The Care Crisis in the Philippines: Children and Transnational Families in the New Global Economy', in *Global Woman*, edited by B. Ehrenreich and A.R. Hochschild, New York: Henry Holt and Company.

Salper, Roberta (ed.) 1972, *Female Liberation*, New York: A. Knopf

Saraceno, Jon 2015, 'Last Chance Babies: Sure They Do it – But *Should* They?', *AARP* Bulletin, 56, 1: 22–4.

Saul, Stephanie 2009, 'Building a Baby, with Few Ground Rules', *New York Times*, available from: http://www.nytimes.com/2009/12/13/us/13surrogacy.html?pagewanted=all&_r=0

Sawhill, Isabel V. 2014, *Generation Unbound: Drifting into Sex and Parenthood without Marriage*, Washington, DC: Brookings Institution Press.

Sayers, Janet 1982, *Biological Politics: Feminist and Anti-feminist Perspectives*, London: Tavistock.

Schorr, Juliet 1991, *The Overworked American: The Unexpected Decline of Leisure*, New York: Basic Books.

Seccombe, Wally 1973, 'The Housewife and Her Labor Under Capitalism', *New Left Review*, 83: 3–24.

Seccombe, Wally 1983, 'Marxism and Demography', *New Left Review*, 137 (January–February): 22–47.

Seeman, Melvin 1958, 'On the Meaning of Alienation', *American Sociological Review*, 24 (December): 783–91.

Shachar, Orly 2001, 'The Invisible Female Patient: The New Reproductive Technologies Discourse in the Medical Literature', *The Pantaneto Forum*, 2 (April), available from: http://www.Pantaneto.co.uk/issue2/front2.htm#top. Last retrieved in 2014.

Shanin, Teodor 1985, *Russia as a 'Developing Society'*, New Haven, CT: Yale University Press.

Sivard, Ruth Leger 1985, *Women ... A World Survey*, Washington, DC: World Priorities.

Skeggs, Beverley 1997, *Formations of Class and Gender*, London: Sage Publications.

Smart, Carol 1987, 'There is of course the Distinction Dictated by Nature: Law and the Problem of Paternity', in *Reproductive Technologies: Gender, Motherhood and Medicine*, edited by Michelle Stanworth, Minneapolis, MN: University of Minnesota Press.

Smith, Joan 1990, 'All Crises are not the Same: Households in the United States during Two Crises', in *Work without Wages: Comparative Studies of Domestic Labor and Self-Employment*, edited by Jane L. Collins and Martha E. Gimenez, New York: SUNY Press.

Smith, Joan, Immanuel Wallerstein and Hans-Dieter Evans 1984, *Households and the World Economy*, Beverly Hills, CA: Sage Publications.

Smith, Gavin 1990, 'Negotiating Neighbors: Livelihood and domestic Politics in Central Peru and the Pais Valenciano', in *Work Without Wages: Comparative Studies of Domestic Labor and Self-Employment*, edited by Jane L. Collins and Martha E. Gimenez, New York: SUNY Press.

Sochen June (ed.) 1971, *The New Feminism in Twentieth-Century America*, Lexington, MA: D.C. Heath & Co.

Sorenson, Corina and Phillipa Mladovsky, 'Assisted Reproduction Technologies in Europe: An Overview', Research Note, European Commission, Brussels.

Spallone, Patricia and D.L. Steinberg 1987, *Made to Order: The Myth of Reproductive and Genetic Progress*, Oxford: Pergamon Press.

Sparr, Pamela 1987, 'Re-Evaluating Feminist Economics: Feminization of Poverty Ignores Key Issues', *Dollars & Sense*, Special Issue on Women and Work, (September): 12–14.

Spengler, J.J. 1966, 'Values and Fertility Analysis', *Demography*, 3 (February): 109–30.

Sreenivas, Mytheli 2013, 'Introduction', *Frontiers: A Journal of Women Studies*, 34, 3: vii–xix.

Stallard, Karin et al. 1983, *Poverty in the American Dream: Women and Children First*, Boston: South End Press.

Stanworth, Michelle (ed.) 1987, *Reproductive Technologies: Gender, Motherhood and Medicine*, Minneapolis, MN: University of Minnesota Press.

Stein, R.L. 1972, 'The Economic Status of Families Headed by Women', in *Woman in a Man-Made World*, edited by Nona Glazer and H. Youngenson Waehrer, New York: Rand McNally.

Steinberg, Deborah L. 1990, 'The Depersonatisation of Women through the Administration of "in Vitro Fertilization"', in *The New Reproductive Technologies*, edited by M. McNeil, I. Varcoe and S. Yearley, New York: St. Martin's Press.

Stiglitz, Joseph E. 2002, *Globalisation and its Discontents*, New York: W.W. Norton & Co.

Stiglitz, Joseph E. 2013, 'Inequality is a Choice', *New York Times*, available from: http://opinionator.blogs.nytimes.com/2013/10/13/inequality-is-a-choice/

Strathern, Marilyn 1992, *Reproducing the Future: Anthropology, Kinship, and the New Reproductive Technologies*, London: Routledge.

Strathern, Marilyn 1995, 'Displacing Knowledge: Technology and the Consequences for Kinship', in *Conceiving the New World Order: The Global Politics of Reproduction*, edited by F.D. Ginsburg and R. Rapp, Berkeley, CA: University of California Press.

Tanner, Leslie B. (ed.) 1970, *Voices from Women's Liberation*, New York: Signet Books.

Therborn, Goran 1976, *Science, Class and Society: On the Formation of Sociology and Historical Materialism*, London: NLB.

Timpanaro, Sebastiano 1975, *On Materialism*, Atlantic Highlands, NJ: Humanities Press.

Twine, Frances Winddance 2011, *Outsourcing the Womb: Race, Class and Gestational Surrogacy in a Global Market*, London: Routledge.

US Bureau of the Census 1974, 'Supplementary Report on the Low Income Population: 1966–1972', Washington, DC: US Government Printing Office.

US Bureau of the Census 1974–87, 'Current Population Reports, Series P-60, Nos. 95–157, Characteristics of the Population Below the Poverty Level', Washington, DC: US Government Printing Office.

US Bureau of the Census 1985, 'Current Population Reports, Series P-60, No. 147, Characteristics of the Population Below the Poverty Level: 1983', Washington, DC: US Government Printing Office.

US Bureau of the Census 1986a, 'Current Population Reports, Series P-60, No. 152, Characteristics of the Population Below the Poverty Level: 1984', Washington, DC: US Government Printing Office.

US Bureau of the Census 1986b, 'Current Population Reports, Series P-60, No. 157, Money Income and Poverty Status of Families and Persons in the United States, 1985', Washington, DC: US Government Printing Office.

US Bureau of the Census 1986c, 'Statistical Abstracts of the United States 1987 (107th Edition)', Washington, DC: US Government Printing Office.

US Bureau of the Census 1987a, 'Current Population Reports, Series P-60, No. 157, Money Income and Poverty Status of Families and Persons in the United States, 1986', Washington, DC: US Government Printing Office.

US Bureau of the Census 1987b, 'Money Income and Poverty Status of Families and Persons in the United States: 1986 (Advanced Data from the March 1987 Current Population Survey)', *Current Population Reports*, Series P-60, No. 157, Washington, DC: US Government Printing Office.

US Bureau of the Census 1999, Historical Poverty Tables – Table 7, available from: www.census.gov/hhes/poverty/histpov7.html. Last retrieved in 2014.

US Bureau of the Census 2006, 'Poverty: 2006 Highlights', available from: http://www.census.govhhes/www/poverty/poverty06/povo6hi.html. Last retrieved in 2014.

US Bureau of the Census 2014, 'Income and Poverty in the United States: 2013', *Current Population Report* P60–249, Washington, DC: US Government Printing Office, available from: https://www.census.gov/content/dam/Census/library/publications/2014/demo/p60-249.pdf

US Department of Health, Education and Welfare 1973, *Work in America*, Cambridge, MA: The MIT Press.

Vogel, Lise 1979, 'Questions on the Woman Question', *Monthly Review*, 31 (June): 39–59.

Vogel, Lise 1981, 'Marxism and Feminism: Unhappy Marriage, Trial Separation, or Something Else?', in *Women and Revolution*, edited by Lydia Sargent, Boston, MA: South End Press.

Vogel, Lise 1995, *Woman Questions: Essays for a Materialist Feminism*, New York: Routledge.

Vogel, Lise 2014 [1983], *Marxism and the Oppression of Women: Toward a Unitary Theory*, Chicago, IL: Haymarket Press.

Wacquant, Loïc 2009, *Punishing the Poor: The Neoliberal Government of Social Insecurity*, Durham, NC: Duke University Press.

Waite, Linda 1981, 'US Women at Work', *Population Bulletin*, 36, 2 (May), Washington, DC: Population Reference Bureau.

Wallerstein, Immanuel 1974, *The Modern World System*, Waltham, MA: Academic Press.

Wallerstein, Immanuel 1983, *Historical Capitalism*, London: Verso.

Wallerstein, Immanuel 1985, 'The Construction of Peoplehood: Racism, Nationalism, Ethnicity', Mimeographed paper, Fernand Braudel Center for the Study of Economies, Historical Systems and Civilizations, New York: SUNY Binghamton.

Wallerstein, Immanuel 1995, *After Liberalism*, New York: New Press.

Wallis, Victor 2015, 'Intersectionality's Binding Agent', *New Political Science*, 37, 2: 604–19.

Wang, Wendy, Kim Parker and Paul Taylor 2013, 'Breadwinner Moms', available from: http://www.pewsocialtrends.org/2013/05/29/breadwinner-moms/

Watson, Debra 2011, 'The Dramatic Effects of Poverty on Death Rates in the US', available from: https://www.wsws.org/en/articles/2011/07/pove-j13.html

Weber, Max 1958, 'The Social Psychology of the World Religions', in *From Max Weber: Essays in Sociology*, edited by C.W. Mills and H. Gert, New York: Oxford University Press.

Weber, Max 1969, *Economia y Sociedad*, Mexico D.F.: Fondo de Cultura Economica.

Weber, Max 1982, 'Determination of Class situation by Market Situation', in *Class, Power and Conflict*, edited by A. Giddens and D. Held, Berkeley, CA: University of California Press.

Weiss-Altaner, Eric R. 1977, 'The Influence of Socio-Economic Conditions on the Fertility of Women in the Third World', in *International Union for the Scientific Study of Population (IUSSP)*, International Population conference, Mexico, Vol. 2, Liege, 65–75.

West, Candace and Sarah Fenstermaker 1997, 'Doing Difference', in *Women, Men and Gender*, edited by M. Roth Walsh, New Haven, CT: Yale University Press.

Wicke, Jennifer 1994, 'Celebrity Material: Materialist Feminism and the Culture of Celebrity', *South Atlantic Quarterly*, 93, 4: 751–78.

Wilson, William Julius 1978, *The Declining Significance of Race*, Chicago: University of Chicago Press.

Wood, Charles H. 1977, 'Infant Mortality Trends and Capitalist Development in Brazil: The Case of Sao Paulo and Belo Horizonte', *Latin American Perspectives*, 4, 4 (Fall): 56–65.

Wood, Ellen Meiksins 1986, *The Retreat from Class*, London: Verso.

Wood, Ellen Meiksins 1995, *Democracy Against Capitalism: Renewing Historical Materialism*, London: Cambridge University Press.

Wright, Erik O. 1976, 'Class Boundaries in Advanced Capitalist Societies', *New Left Review*, 98 (July–August): 3–41.

Wright, Erik O. 1978, *Class, Crisis and the State*, London: Verso.

Yuval-Davis, Nira 2011, 'Beyond the Recognition and Re-Distribution Dichotomy: Intersectionality and Stratification', in *Framing Intersectionality: Debates on a Multi-Faceted Concept in Gender Studies*, edited by Helma Lutz, Maria Teresa Herrera-Vivar and Linda Supik, Farnham: Ashgate.

Zaretski, Eli 1973, 'Capitalism, the Family and Personal Life', *Socialist Revolution*, 13–14: 69–125.

Zelditch Jr., Morris 1955, 'Role Differentiation in the Nuclear Family: A Comparative Study', in *Family, Socialization and Interaction Process*, edited by T. Parsons and R.F. Bales, New York: The Free Press.

Zipper, Juliette and Selma Sevenhuijsen 1987, 'Surrogacy: Feminist Notions of Motherhood Reconsidered', in *Reproductive Technologies: Gender, Motherhood and Medicine*, edited by Michelle Stanworth, Minneapolis, MN: University of Minnesota Press.

Index